THE CHANGING LAW OF THE EMPLOYMENT RELATIONSHIP

The Changing Law of the Employment Relationship
Comparative Analyses in the European Context

NICOLA COUNTOURIS
University of Reading, UK

LONDON AND NEW YORK

First published 2007 by Ashgate Publishing

Published 2016 by Routledge
2 Park Square, Milton Park, Abingdon, Oxon OX14 4RN
711 Third Avenue, New York, NY 10017, USA

Routledge is an imprint of the Taylor & Francis Group, an informa business

Copyright © 2007 Nicola Countouris

Nicola Countouris has asserted his moral right under the Copyright, Designs and Patents Act, 1988, to be identified as the author of this work.

All rights reserved. No part of this book may be reprinted or reproduced or utilised in any form or by any electronic, mechanical, or other means, now known or hereafter invented, including photocopying and recording, or in any information storage or retrieval system, without permission in writing from the publishers.

Notice:
Product or corporate names may be trademarks or registered trademarks, and are used only for identification and explanation without intent to infringe.

British Library Cataloguing in Publication Data
Countouris, Nicola, 1975-
  The changing law of the employment relationship:
  comparative analyses in the European context
  1. Labor laws and legislation - Europe
  I. Title
  344.4'01

Library of Congress Cataloging-in-Publication Data
Countouris, Nicola, 1975-
  The changing law of the employment relationship : comparative analyses in the European context / by Nicola Countouris.
      p. cm. -- (Studies in modern law and policy series)
  Includes bibliographical references and index.
  ISBN 978-0-7546-4800-0
  1. Labor laws and legislation--Europe. 2. Personnel management--Europe. I. Title.

  KJC2855.C68 2007
  344.401--dc22

2007009692

ISBN 9780754648000 (hbk)

Contents

Table of Cases	*vii*
Table of Legislation	*xi*
Preface	*xix*
List of Abbreviations	*xxi*

Introduction		**1**
	1. The aims of the book	1
	2. Scope and methodology	2
	3. Structure and summary of the book	12
1	**The Employment Relationship and the Contract of Employment in Industrialised Societies**	**15**
	1. Introduction	15
	2. The industrial revolution and the birth of the contract of employment	16
	3. The unitary notion of contract of employment	25
	4. The breakdown of the employment relationship	40
	5. The contractual dimensions of the employment relationship	53
	6. Conclusions	55
2	**Reshaping the Personal Scope of LabourLaw: An Analysis of Current Debates in Europe**	**57**
	1. Introduction	57
	2. Stretching the notion of 'employee'	58
	3. The debate over the 'grey zone' between employment and self-employment	71
	4. Re-targeting labour law	81
	5. Conclusions	83
3	**Atypical Employment Relationships: A Comparative Analysis of Fixed-term, Part-time and Temporary Agency Work in Europe**	**87**
	1. Introduction	87
	2. Early legislation and the status of atypical workers	89
	3. Regulation and unemployment: typical rights for atypical workers	105
	4. Flexibility and special rights for 'more and better' atypical jobs in the 1990s: from social stability to social acceptance and normalisation?	121
	5. Conclusions	141

vi   *The Changing Law of the Employment Relationship*

4   **The ILO Notion of the Worker and the Scope of the Employment Relationship**   **147**

1. Introduction   147
2. The personal scope of application of ILO instruments   147
3. The ILO regulatory instruments on atypical work   154
4. The ILO initiative on the scope of the employment relationship   161
5. Conclusions   168

5   **The Personal Scope of Application of EC Social Legislation**   **171**

1. Introduction
2. The personal scope of application of EC social and employment law   172
3. The directions of development of EC law   191
4. Conclusions: a theoretical structure for the personal scope of EC social and employment law   197

6   **EC Regulation of Atypical Forms of Work – Between Employment Law and Employment Policy**   **205**

1. Introduction
2. EC legislative measures on atypical work   207
3. The EU notions of 'flexibility', 'security' and 'flexicurity'   211
4. Looking at the national employment policies through the distorting mirror of National Action Plans and Employment Recommendations   220
5. Divergences between EES and EC employment law on atypical work and the European Court of Justice   227

Conclusions   **231**

Bibliography   *237*
Index   *247*

Table of Cases

European Court of Justice

Alphabetical list

Barber v *Guardian Royal Exchange* (Case C-262/88) [1990]
ECR I-1889 — 291

Bestuur van de Sociale Verzekeringsbank v *M. G. J. Kits van Heijningen*
(Case C-2/89) [1990] ECR I-1755 — 287

Bettray v. Staatssecretaris van Justitie (Case 344/87) [1989] ECR 1621
[1991] 1 CMLR — 280, 312

Bilka-Kaufhaus Gmbh v. *Weber von Hartz* (Case 170/84) [1986] ECR
1607 — 174, 290

C.P.M. Meeusen v. *Hoofddirectie van de Informatie Beheer Groep*
(Case C-337/97) [1999] ECR I-3289 [2000] 2 CMLR 667 — 278, 311, 313

Criminal Proceedings against Carra and others (Case C-258/98)
[2000] ECR I-4217 [2002] 4 CMLR 9 — 195

Debra Allonby v *Accrington & Rossendale College and others*
(Case C-256/01) (Judgement of 13 January 2004) — 91, 216, 217, 292-295, 315, 360

Defrenne v *Sabena* (Case 149/77) [1978] ECR 1365 315

Deutsche Post AG v *Elisabeth Sievers and Brunhilde Schrage*
(Joined cases C-270/97 and C-271/97) [2000] ECR I 929 — 315

E.C. Commission v. *Belgium (Re Access to Special Employment*
Programmes) (C-278/94) [1996] ECR I-4307 — 312

EJM de Jaeck v *Staatssecretaris van Financiën* (Case C-340/94)
[1997] ECR I-00461 — 287, 314

Foreningen af Arbejdsledere i Danmark v *A/S Danmols Inventar*
(Case 105/84) [1985] ECR 2639 — 303, 306, 318

Galinsky v *Insurance Office* (Case 99/80) [1981] ECR 941   287

Gerster v *Freistaat Bayern* (Case C-1/95) [1997] ECR I-5253 [1998]
1 CMLR 303 — 176

Hoekstra (née Unger) v *Bestuur der Bedrijfsvereniging voor*
Detailhandel en Ambachten (Case 75/63) [1964] ECR 177 — 277, 287, 314

Inge Nolte v *Landesversicherungsanstalt Hannover* (Case C-317/93)
[1995] ECR I-4625 — 155

Jenkins v *Kingsgate* (Case 96/80) [1981] ECR 911 — 290

Job Centre Coop arl (Case C-55/96) [1997] ECR I-7119 [1998]
4 CMLR 708. — 195

Jyri Lehtonen and Another v. FRBSB (Case C-176/96) [2000]
ECR I-2681 [2000] 3 CMLR 409 — 281

viii *The Changing Law of the Employment Relationship*

Klaus Höfner and Fritz Elser v *Macrotron GmbH* (Case C-41/90)
[1991] ECR I 1979 [1993] 4 CMLR 306   195
Kording v *Senator für Finanzen* (Case C-100/95) [1997]
ECR I-5289 [1998] 1 CMLR 395   173, 176
Kowalska v *Freie und Hansestadt Hamburg* (Case 33/89) [1990]
ECR I-2591   174, 290
Lawrie-Blum v. *Land Baden-Württemberg* (Case 66/85) [1986]
ECR 2121 [1987] 3 CMLR 414   278, 312
Levin v. *Secretary of State for Justice* (Case 53/81) [1982] ECR 1035
[1982] 2 CMLR 467   277, 278, 311, 312
Martínez Sala v. *Freistat Bayern* (Case C-85/96) [1998] ECR
I-2691   281, 312
Mary Carpenter v *Secretary of State for the Home Department*
(C-60/00) [2002] ECR I 6279   313
P. v *S. and Cornwall County Council* (Case C-13/94) [1996] ECR
I-2143   315
R v *Secretary for Trade and Industry ex parte Broadcasting,*
Entertainment, Cinematographic and Theatre Union (BECTU)
(Case C-173/99) [2001] ECR I- 4881   299, 300
R v *Secretary of State, ex p Seymour-Smith and Perez* (Case C-167/97)
[1999] ECR I-623 [1999] 2 CMLR 322   152, 189, 190, 290
Raulin v. *Minister van Onderwijs en Wetenschappen* (Case C-357/89)
[1992] ECR I-1027 [1994] 1 CMLR 227   279, 312, 295
Razzouk and Beydoun v *Commission* (Joined Cases 75/82 and 117/82)
[1984] ECR 1509   315
Reinhard Gebhard v *Consiglio dell'Ordine degli Avvocati e Procuratori*
di Milano (Case C-55/94) [1995] ECR I-4165   282, 283
Rinner-Kuhn (Case 171/88) [1989] ECR 2743   174, 290
Secretary of State for the Home Department v *Hacene Akrich*
(Case C-109/01) [2003] ECR 0   313
Shirley Preston and Others v *Wolverhampton Healthcare NHS Trust*
and Others (Case C-78/98) [2000] ECR I-3201   115, 116, 290-292, 315
Steymann v. *Staatssecrretaris van Justitie* (Case 196/87) [1988]
ECR 6159 [1989] 1 CMLR 449   280, 312
Union Royale Belge des Sociétés de Football Association (ASBL) v.
Bosman Case (C-415/93) [1995] ECR I-4921 [1996] 1 CMLR 645   281

United Kingdom

Alphabetical list

BBC v *Ioannou* [1975] ICR 267   151
BBC v *Kelly-Phillips* [1998] ICR 587 [1998] IRLR 294   151
Carmichael v *National Power plc* [1999] ICR 1226 83, 85, 105, 114, 116, 139, 295
Clarke v. *Powell and Eley (IMI) Kynoch Ltd* [1982] IRLR 131   180

Table of Cases

Cloroll Pension Trustees Ltd v *Russell* [1994] IRLR 586	180
Clymo v *Wandsworth Borough Council* [1989] IRLR 241	179
Construction Industry Training Board v *Labour Force Ltd* (1970) 3 All ER 220	66, 168
Dacas v *Brooks Street Bureau (UK) Ltd* [2003] IRLR 190	166, 167
Debra Allonby v *Accrington & Rossendale College* [2001] IRLR 354	217
Devonald v *Rosser & Sons Ltd* [1906] 2 KB 728	46
Emmens v *Eldertonn* (1853) 13 CB 495	36
England v *The Governing Body of Turnford School* [2003] WL 21047416	207
Franks v *Reuters Ltd* [2003] IRLR 423	167, 168
Hall v *Lorimer* [1994] ICR 218	103
Hanley v *Pease & Partners* [1915] 1 KB 698	46
Hewlett Packard v. *O'Murphy* [2002] IRLR 4	168
Home Office v *Holmes* [1984] IRLR 299	179, 180
Ironmonger v. *Movefield Ltd t/a Deerings Appointments* [1988] IRLR 461 (EAT)	90, 162, 168
Kidd v. *DRG (UK) Ltd* [1985] IRLR 190	180
Lancaster v *Greaves* (1829) 9 B & C 627.	36
Lane v *Shire Roofing Company (Oxford) Ltd* [1995] IRLR 493 (CA)	102
Market Investigations Ltd v *Minister of Social Security* [1969] 2 QB 173	57
McMeechan v *Secretary of State for Employment* [1995] ICR 444 [1995] IRLR 461	66, 162, 165
Montgomery v *Johnson Underwood Ltd* [2001] ICR 819 IRLR 269	90, 162, 165, 166, 170
Montreal v *Monteral Locomotive Works* [1947] 1 DLR 161	57, 102, 103
Morren v *Swinton and Pedelebury Borough Council* [1965] 1 WLR 576	55
Motorola Ltd v *Davidson* [2001] IRLR. 4	165
O'Kelly v *Trusthouse Forte Plc* [1983] ICR 728 [1984] QB 90	83, 103, 105, 114, 116, 132, 139, 295
O'Sullivan v *Thompson-Coon* (1972) 14 KIR 108	66, 164
Preston v *Wolverhampton Healthcare* NHS Trust [2001] UKHL 5 (2001), [2001] ICR. 217	115, 116
R v *Secretary of State, ex p Seymour-Smith and Perez.* [1994] IRLR 448 [1995] IRLR 464, CA [1997] IRLR 315 HL	152, 189, 190
Ready Mixed Concrete (South East) Ltd v *Minister of Pensions and National Insurance* [1968] 2 QB 497	55, 103
Simmons v *Heath Laundry Co* [1910] 1 KB 543	45
Simpson v. *Ebbw Vale Steel, Iron & Coal Co.* [1905] 1 KB 453	40
Staffordshire County Council v *Black* [1995] IRLR 234	180
Stevenson, Jordan & Harrison v *MacDonald & Evans* [1952] 1 TLR 101	56
Underwood v *Perry* [1932] W.C. & I. Rep. 63	45
Wickens v *Champion Employment* [1984] ICR 365	162, 165
Yewens v *Noakes* (1880) 6 QBD 530	54

x   *The Changing Law of the Employment Relationship*

France

Chronological order

Civ 6 juillet 1931 (arrêt *Bartdou*) *DP* 1931. 1. 121	55
Cass Ass Plén 18 juin 1976 *Dalloz* 1977 J 173	100
Cass Soc 29 juin 1977 *Dalloz* 1977 IR 359.	64
Cass Soc 7 décembre 1983 *Bull Civ* V n 592	101
Cass Soc 6 juin 1991 *RJS* 7/91 n 817	224
Cass Soc 7 juillet 1998 *RJS* 10/98 n 1311	215
Cass 14 mai 1999 *Bull Civ* V n 174	107
Cass Soc 19 décembre 2000 *Dalloz* 2001 IR 355	56, 138
Cass. 4 décembre 2001 *Dalloz* 2002 JC 1934	138

Italy

Chronological order

C. Cost. 20 Maggio 1976 n 117 *Rep Corte Cost* 1976 1646	61
Cass. 14 Giugno 1979 n 3353 *Giustizia Civile* 1979 1462	113
Cass. 7 Aprile 1992 n 4220 *Giustizia Civile* 1992 559	113
Cass. 1 Ottobre 1997 n 9606 *Giustizia Civile* 1997 1835	113
Cass. 6 Maggio 1999 n 4558 *Giustizia Civile* 1999 1030	113
Cass. 22 Novembre 1999 n 12926 *Giustizia Civile* 2000 2319	117
Cass. 23 Febbraio 2000 n 2039 *Giustizia Civile* 2000 2319	117
Cass. 18 Novembre 2000 n 1924 *Giustizia Civile* 2000 416	117
Cass. 06 Luglio 2001 n 9167 *RIDL* 2002 II 272.	105
Cass. 27 Novembre 2002 n 16805 *Giustizia Civile* 2002 16805	105
Cass. 27 Febbraio 2003 n. 3020 *Giustizia Civile* 2003 410	169
Cass. 9 Marzo 2004 n. 4797 *Giustizia Civile* 2004 3	63
Cass. 18 Marzo 2004 n. 5508 *Giustizia Civile* 2004 3	63

Germany

Chronological order

BAG 1976, AP, n 2 *sub* sec. 62 *BAT*	174
BAG 1982, AP, n 1 *sub* sec. 1 *BetrAVG*	174
LAG Niedersachsen 6 Sept 1989 LAGE § 611 BGB Arbeitnehmerbegriff Nr 24	110
LAG Köln 30 June 1995 LAGE § 611 BGB Arbeitnehmerbegriff Nr 27 110	

Table of Legislation

Treaty Provisions

Article 2	316
Article 3	316
Article 13	316
Article 43	281
Article 49	281,282
Article 138	308
Article 141 (ex Article 119)	288,290,291,292,294,315 (155, 189, 288, 289, 315)

Council legislation

Regulations

Regulation 3/58 [1958] JO 561	285
Regulation 4/58 [1958] JO 597	285
Regulation 1612/68 [1968] OJ Spec. Ed. L257/2	281
Regulation 1408/71[1971] OJ L149/2	286
Regulation 1390/81 [1981] OJ L143/1	286

Directives

Directive 75/117/EEC [1975] OJ L45/19	289
Directive 75/129/EEC [1975] OJ L48/29	318
Directive 76/207/ EEC [1976 OJ L39/40	289
Directive 77/187/EEC [1977] OJ L61/26	79, 301, 304, 306
Directive 77/576/EEC [1977] OJ L229/12	317
Directive 80/987/EEC [1980] OJ L283/23	318
Directive 86/613/EEC [1986] OJ L 359/56	289, 296
Directive 90/365/EEC [1990] OJ L180/26	313
Directive 91/383/EEC [1991] OJ L206/19	164, 298, 305, 327, 328
Directive 91/533/EEC [1991] OJ L288/32	300, 320
Directive 93/104/EEC [1993] OJ L307/18	299
Directive 96/71/EEC [1997] OJ L18/1	284
Directive 97/81/EC as amended by Dir 98/23/EC [1998] OJ L131/10 consolidated [1998] OJ L131/13	202, 210, 302, 324, 325, 329, 330, 342
Directive 98/50/EEC [1998] OJ L201/98	301, 304, 321

Directive 99/70 [1999] OJ L175/43   146, 182, 185, 188, 190, 217, 217, 302, 324, 325, 329, 330, 339
Directive 2000/43/EC [2000] OJ L 180/22   296, 316
Directive 2000/78/EC [2000] OJ L 303/16   296, 316

Decisions and Resolutions

Council Resolution of 15 December 1997 on the 1998
Employment Guidelines [1998] OJ C 30/1   335, 336
Council Resolution of 22 February 1999 on the 1999 Employment
Guidelines [1999] OJ C 69/2   316, 339
Council Decision of 19 January 2001on Guidelines for Member States'
employment policies for the year 2001 [2001] OJ L 22/18   337
Council Decision of 18 February 2002 on Guidelines for Member States'
employment policies for the year 2002 [2002] OJ L 60/67   337
Council Decision of 22 July 2003 on Guidelines for the employment
policies of the Member States [2003] OJ L 197/17   337, 338

Recommendations and Declaration

Declaration of Council accompanying Directive 68/360 [1968] OJ
Spec. Ed. L257/13 Council   281
Recommendation of 19 January 2001 on the implementation of
Member States' employment policies [2001] OJ L 22/33   337, 344
Council Recommendation of 18 February 2002 on the implementation
of Member States' employment policies [2002] OJ L 60/70   345, 346
Council Recommendation of 22 July 2003 on the implementation
of Member States' employment policies [2003] OJ L 197/26   349

COMMISSION (various)

Communication from the Commission Concerning its Action
Programme relating to the Implementation of the Community
Charter of Basic Social Rights for Workers COM(89) 568 final   326-328
Commission Proposal for a Council Directive on certain employment
relationships with regard to working conditions COM(90) 228 final
[1990] OJ C 224/04   298, 327
Commission Proposal for a Council Directive on the Approximation
of Laws of the Member States Relating to Certain Employment
Relationships with Regard to Distortions of Competition COM(90)
228 final [1990] OJ C 224/06   298, 327
EC Commission *Green paper – Partnership for a new organisation
of work* COM (97) 128 final 16.4.1997   333, 334, 337
EC Commission Communication *Modernising the Organisation of*

Table of Legislation   xiii

work – A positive approach to change COM(98) 592 final 12.10.1998   334, 336
Commission Proposal for a Directive of the European Parliament
and the Council on working conditions for temporary workers
COM (2002) 0149 final [2002] OJ C 203/1   226, 324, 331, 332
Amended proposal for a Directive of the European Parliament
and the Council on working conditions for temporary workers COM (2002)
701final 28.11.02.   324, 331, 332

ECOSOC (opinions)

Opinion of the Economic and Social Committee on the 'Proposal
for a Directive of the European Parliament and the Council on
working conditions for temporary workers' [2003] OJ C 61/124, 126   340

International Labour Organization

Conventions

ILO Convention C1: Hours of Work (Industry) Convention   243
ILO Convention C2: Unemployment Convention   244
ILO Convention C3: Maternity Protection Convention   244
ILO Convention C4: Night Work (Women) Convention   244
ILO Convention C26: Minimum Wage-fixing Machinery Convention   244, 245
ILO Convention C30: Hours of Work (Commerce and Offices) Convention   245
ILO Convention C87: Freedom of Association and Protection of
the Right to Organize Convention   245, 246
ILO Convention C95: Protection of Wages Convention   246
ILO Convention C97: Migration for Employment Convention   247
ILO Convention C98: Right to Organize and Collective Bargaining
Convention   245
ILO Convention C102: Social Security (Minimum Standards)
Convention   248, 247, 273
ILO Convention C103: Maternity Protection Convention   245
ILO Convention C111: Discrimination (Employment and Occupation)
Convention   257
ILO Convention C132: Holidays with Pay Convention   246
ILO Convention C153: Hours of Work and Rest Periods
(Road Transport) Convention   248
ILO Convention C154: Collective Bargaining Convention   249
ILO Convention C155: Occupational Safety and Health Convention   249
ILO Convention C156: Workers with Family Responsibilities Convention   249
ILO Convention C158: Termination of Employment Convention   249, 250
ILO Convention C172: Working Conditions (Hotels and Restaurants)
Convention   250

ILO Convention C175: Part-Time Work Convention   254
ILO Convention C177: Home Work Convention   251, 258
ILO Convention C181: Private Employment Agencies Convention   89, 161, 258,
                                                      259, 260, 264, 272,
ILO Convention C183: Maternity Protection Convention   252, 256

National Legislation

United Kingdom

Combination Act 1824	34
Conduct of Employment Agencies and Employment Businesses Regulations1976	162
Conspiracy and Protection of Property Act 1875	36
Contracts of Employment Act 1963	50
Control of Employment Act 1939	65
Defence of the Realm Act 1915	65
Disability Discrimination Act 1995	130
Employer's Liability Act 1880	40
Employers and Workmen Act 1875	36, 46
Employment Agencies Act 1973 (as amended by the Employment Protection Act 1975 and the Deregulation and Contracting Out Act 1994)	161
Employment Equality (Religion or Belief) Regulations 2003	130
Employment Equality (Sexual Orientation) Regulations 2003	130
Employment Protection Act (EPA)1975	161, 178
Employment Relations Act (ERA) 1999	169
Equal Pay Act (EqPA)1970	130, 291
Fixed-term Employees (Prevention of Less Favourable Treatment) Regulations 2002	220-221, 225
Health and Safety at Work Act 1974	129, 164
Master and Servant Act of 1867	35
Master and Servant Acts 1747	35
Master and Servant Acts 1766	35
Master and Servant Acts 1823	35
Maternity and Parental Leave etc Regulation 1999	152
National Insurance Act 1946	48
National Minimum Wage Act (NMWA) 1998	13, 131, 169, 263
Part-time Work (Prevention of Less Favourable Treatment) Regulations 2000	204-208, 210-212
Race Relations Act 1976	130
Sex Discrimination Act (SDA) 1975	130, 179
Statute of Artificers 1563	31, 35
Statute of Labourers 1349	31, 35
Statute of Labourers 1351	31, 35
Trade Dispute Act 1906	46

Table of Legislation

Trade Union and Labour Relations (Consolidation) Act (TULR(C)A) 1992   130
Trade Union Reform and Employment Rights Act (TURERA) 1993   151
Working Time Regulations (WTR) 1998   131, 169, 299
Workmen's Compensation Act 1897   40
Workmen's Compensation Act 1906   44, 45

France

Code du Travail
  Art L
para. 121.5   151
para. 122.1. al.1   183
para. 122.1.1   181, 220
para. 122.1.2   181, 183, 184, 223
para. 122.1.3   181
para. 122.2   159, 181, 192, 221
para. 122.2.1   183
para. 122.3   182
para. 122.3.1   181
para. 122.3.2   181
para. 122.3.3   184
para. 122.3.4   181, 225, 184
para. 122.3.8   225
para. 122.3.11 al. 2   183
para. 122.3.11 al. 3   183
para. 122.3.11.   183, 223
para. 122.3.13   184
para. 122.3.17.1   221, 224
para. 122.4.3 al. 2   173
para. 122.4.3 al. 3   173
para. 122.4.4   194
para. 124.2.2, al. 2   192
para. 124.2.2, al. 3   192
para. 124.4.2   191, 193
para. 124.4.3   193
para. 125.1   50, 65
para. 125.3   65
para. 212.4   202, 208
para. 212.4.2   172, 203
para. 212.4.2, al. 5.   172
para. 212.4.3   154, 172, 214, 215
para. 212.4.3 al. 6.   216
para. 212.4.4   215
para. 212.4.5   202
para. 212.4.5 al. 7.   173

para. 212.4.6	215
para. 212.4.7	209
para. 212.4.9	209
para. 351.1	184, 226
para. 721.1	106
para. 721.6	106
para. 751.1	106, 137
para. 761.2	107, 137
para. 762.1	107, 137
para. 763.1	107, 137
para. 773.1	106
para. 781.1	106, 137
para. 782.1	106
para. 931.8.2	213
para. 931.12	225

Code Civil Art 1780	38
Code Civil Art 1781	38

Loi 2-17 mars 1791 (décret d'Allarde)	33, 37
Loi du 9 avril 1889	40
Loi du 9 avril 1908	47
Loi du 5 avril 1910	47
Loi n 72-1 du 3 janvier 1972	159, 191, 192
Loi n 73-680 du 13 juillet 1973	50
Loi n 79-11 du 3 janvier 1979	73, 150, 153
Loi n 81-64 du 28 janvier 1981	171-173
Ordonnance n 82-130 du 5 février 1982	151, 159, 173
Ordonnance n 82-272 du 26 mars 1982(Auroux reforms)	74, 153, 173
décret du 3 avril 1985 n 85-399	181
Loi n 85-772 du 25 juillet 1985	181, 191
Ordonnance n 86-948 du 11 août 1986	181, 191, 192
Loi n 90-613 du 12 juillet 1990	182
Loi n 92-1446 du 31 décembre 1992	202
Loi quinquennale n 93-1313 du 20 décembre 1993	154, 202
Loi n 98-461 du 13 juin 1998 (Aubry)	153, 203, 214
Loi n 2000-37 du 19 janvier 2000 (Aubry II)	153, 203, 214, 215
Loi n 2002-73 du 17 janvier 2002	221

Italy

Civil Code of 1865 Articolo 1627 n1	39
Civil Code of 1865 Articolo 1628	38

Codice Civile Articolo 2094	120

Codice Civile Articolo 2224	120
Codice di Procedura Civile Article 409(3)	119, 125
Legge 5 giugno 1893 n 215	42
Regio Decreto Legge n 1825 del 1924	60
Legge 13 marzo 1958 n 264	57, 81
Legge 23 ottobre 1960 n 1369	50, 65, 67, 230
Legge 18 aprile 1962 n 230	148, 185
Legge 20 maggio del 1970 n 300 (Statuto dei Lavoratori)	50, 178
Legge 11 agosto 1973 n 533	119
Legge 18 dicembre 1973 n 877	57, 81
Legge 19 dicembre 1984 n 863	156, 171, 176
Legge 28 febbraio 1987 n 56	186
Legge 8 agosto 1995 n 335	129
Legge 24 giugno 1997 n 196	160, 197-199
Decreto Legislativo 25 febbraio 2000 n 61.	208, 208, 214
Decreto Legislativo 6 settembre 2001 n 368	185, 219, 220, 222, 225
Decreto legge 30 settembre 2003 n 269	129
Decreto Legislativo 10 settembre 2003 n 276	108, 124-128, 230-234

Germany

Weimar Constitution Article 157	60
Gesetz zu Korrekturen in der Sozialversicherung und zur Sicherung der Arbeitnehmerrechte' (BGBI. I S. 3843, v art 3, modifying § 7 of book IV of the Social Security Code)	107
Sozialgesetzbuch Sections 7 *Sozialgesetzbuch-SGB*, § 7	108, 119
1924 White-Collar Workers' Social Insurance Act	60
1963 *Bundesurlaubsgesetz*	119
1985 *Beschäftigungsförderungsgesetz* (The 1985 Law on Improvement of Employment Opportunities)	73, 155,
1972 *Arbeitnehmeruberlassungsgesetz*	50, 158
1974 *Tarifsvertragsgesetz* (law on collective agreements)	118
1994 *Arbeitsgerichtsgesetz*	118
1999 *Gesetz zur Förderung der Selbständigkeit* (Law on the promotion of self-employed work)	108, 129
2001 *Teilzeit – und Befristungsgesetz (TzBfG)*	202, 208-210, 213, 221, 225
Law 23 December 2002	108
2002 Law on 'Modern services on the labour market'	195, 228-230

Preface

This book presents a comparative analysis of the changing legal notions of the employment relationship in four European countries – the UK, Germany, France and Italy. It analyses the ways in which, during the past few decades, industrialised countries have witnessed a progressive crisis of the regulatory framework sustaining the binary model of the employment relationship based on the subordinate employment/autonomous self-employment dichotomy. New atypical and hybrid working arrangements have emerged, challenging the traditional notions of, and divisions between, autonomy and subordination. This in turn has strained labour law systems across industrialised countries that were previously based on the notion of dependent and subordinate employment to cast their personal scope of application triggering a de-regulatory dynamic that some Italian scholars have described as *la fuga dal diritto del lavoro*. Legal systems, at a national and supranational level, are constantly trying to catch up with these changes, and the core of the present work closely scrutinises the extent of their successes or failures.

The book is written at a time where no single solution to the problems being analysed has emerged, and in that respect it is very much a product of its time. It presents the various re-regulatory approaches currently being developed and argues that a new dynamic equilibrium can be achieved by using a mix of regulatory techniques and approaches aiming at expanding the legal notion of the employment relationship and at providing ad hoc regulation for a number of atypical forms of work. One of the major challenges in completing the present work has been to keep abreast of the constantly evolving legal framework at a national and supranational level. For a number of obvious and less obvious reasons, I have often had to take the difficult decision of leaving outside the scope of this book a number of legal developments that, according to my perhaps unwise judgment, were not strictly necessary to the substance and structure of the book. The work seeks to state the law as it stood on 31 November 2006, although one or two subsequent legal developments have been included at proof stage.

One of the first seminars on research method I attended whilst a young doctoral student at St Edmund Hall, Oxford, provided me with the rather daunting warning that 'research is essentially a solitary vocation'. It is with great relief that, a few years down the line, I can happily assert that this is perhaps the only foundational lesson I have been imparted during my DPhil years that I have found not to be entirely true. Surely enough the present work is the product of numerous hours spent researching and studying in the Bodleian Law Library and organising, shaping and re-shaping arguments, ideas and draft chapters, constantly tormented by the thought of modifying them again and again. But nowhere during this thrilling journey have I felt the slightest sign of intellectual or existential solitude.

I have no doubt whatsoever that the greatest credit for that must go to Professor Mark R. Freedland, who as a supervisor first and, more recently, as a senior colleague, has constantly inspired me with an unparalleled wealth of mind-blowing suggestions, comments and ideas. I am particularly grateful to him for introducing me to this constantly changing and challenging area of employment law and for making me realise the importance, and the limits, of comparative analysis in approaching the study of the employment relationship. I am also very grateful to Dr Anne Davies, Professor Simon Deakin and Professor Sandy Fredman for their precious comments and feedback on earlier drafts of this work. I have also benefited greatly from discussion, general and particular, with Dr Alexandra Braun, Professor Damian Chalmers, Professor Chris Hilson, Miss Rachel Horton, Dr Catherine Jacqueson, Dr Grace James, Miss Isobel Renzulli, and Professor Derrick Wyatt and I thank them for their genuine and generous support. I am in no doubt that both the process and, hopefully, the outcome of the present work have also greatly benefited from the possibility of sharing some of its central ideas during conferences and workshops with other distinguished colleagues inside and outside the United Kingdom. In this respect my gratitude goes to Dr Giuseppe Casale, Professors Hugh Collins, Professors Judy Fudge and Mario Giovanni Garofalo, Dr Claire Kilpatrick, and Professors Alan Neal, Silvana Sciarra and Aurora Vimercati. I am aware that I owe a great debt of gratefulness to a number of institutions that, in different ways, have supported me whilst working on this book, and in particular to St Edmund Hall and St John's College, the University of Oxford, the Arts and Humanities Research Board and the University of Reading. And I am also conscious that the work as such would have probably never appeared had it not been for the support and comfort offered by good friends and relatives, and in particular by Ida Liuni, Antonios Kountouris, Teresa d'Aloya, Giacomo Tortora, Laura Bradley, Philip Barfred, Yonatan Witztum, Harrys Papadopoulos, Alexandros Tsadiras and, *dulcis in fundo*, by my partner Isobel Renzulli. Last but not least, my gratitude goes to those who have interacted, in various capacities, with the extremely efficient editorial machinery of Ashgate Publishing. I am particularly grateful to the two earnest and perceptive anonymous referees, to the series editor Professor Ralph Rogowski and to the ever so kind, helpful and painstakingly meticulous Mrs Alison Kirk and Emily Gibson.

It goes without saying that while all the aforementioned colleagues, friends and institutions deserve credit for disproving the dictum that 'research is essentially a solitary vocation' none of them bears any responsibility whatsoever for the – no doubt several – shortcomings of this work.

Nicola Countouris
Oxford, 10 April 2007

Abbreviations

AG	Advocate General
All ER	All England Law Reports
BAG	Bundesarbeitsgericht
BCLR	Bulletin of Comparative Labour Relations
C Cost	Corte Costituzionale
CA	Court of Appeal
Cas Soc	Cour de Cassation Chambre Sociale
Cass	Corte di Cassazione
CB	Common Bench Reports
CBR	Centre for Business Performance
CEEP	Centre Européen d'entreprise publique
CGIL	Confederazione Generale Italiana del Lavoro
CISL	Confedereazione Italiana Sindacati Liberi
CLLJ	Comparative Labor Law Journal
CML Rev	Common Market Law Review
CMLR	Common Market Law Reports
CSDLE	Centro Studi di Diritto del Lavoro Europeo
DG	Directorate General (of the European Commission)
DS	Droit Social
DTI	Department of Trade and Industry
EAT	Employment Appeal Tribunal
EC	European Community
ECJ	European Court of Justice
ECOSOC	European Economic and Social Committee
ECR	European Court Reports
ECT	European Community Treaty
EEC	European Economic Community
EES	European Employment Strategy
EIRO	European Industrial Relations Observatory
EIRR	European Industrial Relations Review
EPA	Employment Protection Act
EqPA	Equal Pay Act
ESCR	Economics and Social Research Council
ESF	European Social Fund
ETUC	European Trade Union Congress
EU	European Union
GB	Governing Body (of the ILO)
GDLRI	Giornale di Diritto del Lavoro e Relazioni Industriali
GU	Gazzetta Ufficiale della Repubblica Italiana

HL	House of Lords
H&S	Health and Safety
ICR	Industrial Court Reports (1972-74) Industrial Cases Reports (1975-)
IJCLLIR	International Journal of Comparative Labour Law and Industrial Relations
ILJ	Industrial Law Journal
ILO	International Labour Organisation
ILR	International Labour Review
IR	Information Rapides
IRES	Istituto di Ricerche Economiche e Sociali
IRLR	Industrial Relations Law Reports
ITR	Industrial Tribunal Reports
JCMS	Journal of Common Market Studies
JER	Joint Employment Report
KB	King's Bench
KIR	Knight's Industrial Reports
LAG	Landes-Arbeitsgericht
LQR	Law Quarterly Review
MLR	Modern Law Review
NAP	National Action Plan
NIDIL	Nuove Identitá di lavoro
OJ	Official Journal
OUP	Oxford University Press
QB	Queen's Bench
RGL	Rivista Giuridica del Lavoro e della Previdenza Sociale
RIDL	Rivista Italiana di Diritto del Lavoro
RRA	Race Relations Act
SDA	Sex Discrimination Act
TULR(C)A	Trade Union and Labour Relations (Consolidation) Act
TURERA	Trade Union Reform and Employment Rights Act
UIL	Unione Italiana del Lavoro
UK	United Kingdom of Great Britain and Northern Ireland
UNICE	Union of Industrial and Employers' Confederations of Europe
WLR	Weekly Law Reports

Introduction

1. The aims of the book

The individual employment relationship is increasingly under the scrutiny of labour lawyers, judiciaries, law and policy makers. The relevance of this kind of scrutiny is obvious to any legally minded observer. Since 20th century employment protection systems have developed by using the notion of 'standard employment relationship' as a cast to shape their personal scope of application, any changes affecting the employment relationship inevitably reverberate throughout the realm of labour law. Indeed, British legal scholarship has been at the forefront of the many debates linked to the study of the individual employment relationship, first and foremost those related to the individual scope of application of labour law.[1] But this type of analysis is hardly alien to the Continental legal debate[2] since in the rest of Europe, just as in the UK, access to employment rights largely depends on the type of employment relationship under which a person is engaged.

A number of changes have taken place in the last thirty years or so that have modified the traditional notions of the employment relationship. The present book seeks to define the terms of these changes and the ways in which they are affecting the scope of application of labour legislation. It also explores the ways in which the various legal systems at a national and supranational level are trying to come to terms with these changes and what, if anything, is to be learned from the various regulatory approaches. More precisely, it seeks to provide an analysis of the changes of the *scope* and *taxonomy* of employment relationships in four European Union (EU) Member States (MSs): the United Kingdom, Germany, France and Italy.

The following introduction lays out the research plan of our investigation. But before doing this it is important to define and circumscribe the domain, that is to say the scope, and the method of our enquiry while defining some important terms and key concepts of the present work.

---

1   M. Freedland, *The Personal Employment Contract* (OUP, Oxford, 2003); S. Deakin and F. Wilkinson, *The Law of the Labour Market – Industrialization, Employment and Legal Evolution* (OUP, Oxford, 2005).

2   A. Supiot (ed.), *Au delà de l'emploi. Transformations du travail et devenir du droit du travail en Europe* (Flammarion, Paris, 1999); U. Carabelli and B. Veneziani (eds), *Du travail salarié au travail indépendant: permanences et mutations* (Cacucci, Bari, 2003).

2. Scope and methodology

The legal dimension of the employment relationship

The nature and notion of the employment relationship have been subject to the close scrutiny of several distinct disciplines, ranging from law and economics to industrial relations, social psychology and morals and philosophy.[3] There is little doubt that all these disciplines offer between them a unique prism through which the nature of the employment relationship can be observed and evaluated. Each discipline uses different analytical tools and typically focuses on different aspects of the relationships linking employers and workers. Some disciplines, for instance economics and human resource management, predominantly focus on what it is perhaps possible to define as the *factual* dimension of the employment relationship, that is to say on decisions and dynamics relating to the ways enterprises formulate their specifications for acquiring and using labour resources and on the reciprocal choices made by individuals offering their skills and labour to an employer for a price, a salary. This dimension has to do with business choices defining the quantities of labour energies to be purchased, the different types of labour energies that need to be acquired (in terms of human capital and skills), the use that businesses make of the labour energies acquired and the temporal patterns of acquisition and use of these labour energies. And of course it also pertains to the factors shaping the choices of individual workers in establishing an employment relationship.

The current work will focus centrally upon the *legal* dimension of the relationship between workers and employers. By *legal* dimension it is meant the legal arrangements into which the aforementioned factual arrangements relating to the purchase, sell, use and management of labour energies are translated. These legal arrangements are subject to specific regulatory regimes and our enquiry will exclusively focus on these regimes. Block, Berg and Belman offer a rather illuminating description of the distinction between the economic base and the legal structure of the employment relationship.

> Whereas economic theory provides a tool to understand the employment relationship, the extent to which societies allow market forces to determine or dominate the nature of the employment relationship is a public policy decision reflected in the laws that govern employment and labor relations.[4]

It is precisely on these public policy decisions and, ultimately, on these laws that the current work seeks to focus its analysis.

There is a lot to say and to research on how the economic system influences the factual notions of the employment relationship and about the ways the factual notions concur in shaping the *legal* notions of the employment relationship. Some

---

3 For a recent and comprehensive overview of some of the disciplines that have embarked in the analysis of the employment relationship see J.A.-M. Coyle Shapiro, L.M. Shore, M.S. Taylor, and L.E. Tetrick (eds), *The Employment Relationship – Examining Psychological and Contextual Perspectives* (OUP, Oxford, 2004).

4 R.N. Block, P. Berg and D. Belman in Coyle Shapiro et al., p. 94.

Introduction 3

recent studies in that direction are particularly valuable and they will be duly referred to from time to time. On the other hand it is arguably increasingly evident that the analysis of the legal notion of the employment relationship has been and, to some extent, is still being unduly influenced by some misconceptions about its economic and factual base. For a very long time an implicit or explicit assumption in legal and social scholarship has been that the legal notions of the employment relationship reflected and regulated, as best as they could, a number of commonly displayed factual arrangements and market dynamics. It appeared that labour law identified and circumscribed a number of these factual arrangements, translated them into legal categories and notions, and placed some of them within the protective scope of its provisions. During the 20th century, access to employment rights was built on the premise of a legal notion of employment relationship that the legal analyses had construed as essentially *binary*. Under this kind of legal construction most working people were employed either as *dependent employees* or as *independent self-employed*. The former category of workers, as opposed to the latter, was entitled to enjoy a number of rights provided by labour legislation.

To some extent it seemed plausible that the established dominant system of production – that some would define as industrial mass production – determined the emergence of an essentially binary factual notion of employment relationship that, in turn, fostered the creation of an essentially binary legal model. This type of argument, which if overstated, can easily degenerate into excessively deterministic reasoning, can to some extent be justified in the light of a number of phenomena such as the steady decline of intermediate forms of labour subcontracting in most industrial sectors during the early years of the 20th century. There is certainly some truth in the institutionalist claim that the emergence of the firm as a business actor has fostered the growth of a subordinate and more or less continuous notion of the employment relationship.[5] On the other hand, it is increasingly clear that both the legal and the pre-legal political discourses played an active role in fostering the perceived emergence of a binary *factual* notion of the employment relationship. In recent years, several authors[6] have started considering the possibility that the essentially binary model of employment relationship has, at least in part, been the product of political, social and ultimately *legal* pressures favouring its establishment. By the same token, a number of authors have also started arguing that the changes that have started affecting and, essentially, altering the binary model of the employment relationship, are not just the consequence of some deeper transformations affecting the (global) economic base of capitalist societies, but also the result of a number of changes taking place in the realm of law or, to be more specific, in the realm of the 'politics of law'. In commenting upon the regulation of the tri-lateral work relationship in

---

5   R.H. Coase, 'The Nature of the Firm', *Economica* (1937): 386. On the limits of this analysis, S. Deakin, 'The Many Futures of the Contract of Employment' (Working Paper No. 191, ESRC Centre for Business Research, University of Cambridge, December 2000).

6   Just to name a few, S. Deakin, 'The Contract of Employment: a Study in Legal Evolution' (Working Paper No. 203, ESRC Centre for Business Research, University of Cambridge, June 2001), M.R. Freedland, *The Personal Employment Contract* (OUP, Oxford, 2003), A. Lyon-Caen, 'Actualité du contrat de travail', *DS* (1988): 541.

4 *The Changing Law of the Employment Relationship*

France, Professors Pélissier, Supiot and Jeammaud cast the relationship between human resource management preferences and employment law in a rather crude but equally perceptive way:

> *Le rêve de nombreux employeurs est de pouvoir disposer d'une main-d'oeuvre sans avoir de salaries. Ce n'est pas un rêve irréalisable. ... la loi pose une interdiction de principe à la fourniture de main-d'oeuvre à but lucrative, en apportant cependant une exception importante à cette interdiction (autorisation du «travail temporaire»).*[7]

The present work seeks to develop a type of analytical discourse that tries to unveil the ways in which factual and legal arrangements mutually concur to shape each other, and to do that in a comparative legal context. Chapter 1 in particular endeavours to test this type of analysis against a historical reconstruction of the 'rise and fall' of the binary notion of the employment relationship in a number of European countries.

Regulatory strategies in dealing with the changing notion of the employment relationship: scope and taxonomy

It is crucial to highlight a major analytical caveat. There is a risk that, by overemphasising the relevance of legal categories, one might disregard or ignore several phenomena suggesting that the present legal framework is becoming inadequate to regulate societal and economic dynamics. It can be argued that some analyses of the employment relationship have fallen into the trap of legal determinism. Indeed the emerging inadequacy of the protective scope of labour law can be partly attributed to a refusal, by judiciaries and lawmakers alike, to fully acknowledge the consequences deriving from a number of deeper changes affecting the *legal* notion of the employment relationship in industrialised societies, as the following chapters endeavour to prove.

These changes, taking place in the last thirty years or so, have occurred at two levels. At a first level, employers have modified and varied the *legal* terms of the arrangements under which they have sought to acquire the labour energies necessary to their businesses. At a second level, these new arrangements have modified the *legal* composition of the workforce, introducing new legal categories such as casual workers, intermittent workers, quasi-dependent or para-subordinated workers, 'bogus-self-employed' workers and other that escape some or all of the protective devices created by labour law systems during the second half of the 20th century. Several attempts have been and are being made at a national and, increasingly, supranational level to address these changes and their derivate problems. The present work will try to provide a comparative, at times critical, description of these efforts and try to highlight some patterns of the various reform approaches.

---

7 J. Pélissier, A. Supiot and A. Jeammaud, *Droit du Travail* (Dalloz, Paris, 2006), p. 389. 'The dream of numerous employers is to be able to avail themselves of a workforce without also having salaried workers. This is not a dream that cannot materialise ... the law poses a prohibition of principle to the supply of work for profit, by introducing, though, a significant exception to this prohibition (authorisation of "temporary work").' (Own translation)

Introduction 5

Over the last few years, two distinct regulatory strategies have progressively emerged at a national and supranational level that try to tackle the problematic issues deriving from the changing notion of the employment relationship. A first re-regulatory strategy has attempted to redefine the *scope* of application of existing labour legislation to cover new forms of work. The implicit idea behind this type of approach is that some new atypical and hybrid working arrangements are progressively emerging in what can be defined as a grey zone between self-employment and subordinate work, a zone where the notions of autonomy and subordination are no longer as clear-cut as in the past. This redefinition has aimed at attracting as many as possible of these new working arrangements within the scope of subordinated employment and labour law. A second re-regulatory approach has attempted to *typify* – that is, to identify and treat as a distinct type – some specific forms of atypical employment and to introduce specific, ad hoc, legislation aimed at regulating and protecting them. In this case the assumption has been that some patterns of dependent work that did not display all the features of the traditional legal notion of subordinate employment relationship (for instance, continuity, full-time working hours, bilaterality) also deserved some kind of protection. It could be said that this second type of discourse focuses its attention on the *taxonomy* of the employment relationship rather than on its scope, but it is important to further clarify the various ways in which law has dealt with the emergence of new types of legal arrangements and forms of work that were not consistent with the traditional notion of subordinate employment.

It is the central systematic and organizing idea of this book, which is reflected in its chapter structure, to describe the interplay of these two regulatory strategies. However, there are also other reform strategies and proposals, progressively emerging in recent years, that appear to depart from the employee/self-employed dichotomy. An important example of these new proposals is contained in the so-called Supiot reform project that will be discussed in the final sections of Chapter 2.

Regulatory approaches in dealing with atypical employment relationships: prohibition, conversion, encouragement and normalisation with or without parity

The comparative analysis carried out in the main part of the present work suggests that there are at least five ways in which *law* has interplayed with the employee/self-employed binary model of employment relationship while addressing what has been described as the taxonomy of the employment relationship. These five regulatory approaches can be referred to as the *prohibition* model, the *conversion* model, the *encouragement* model, the *normalisation without parity* model and the *normalisation with parity* model. The first two models have been mostly used to maintain and support the binary model of the employment relationship, while the remaining ones are arguably less clear-cut concepts.

Firstly, for a considerable part of the 20th century, law has sought to *prohibit* a number of factual patterns of employment that did not fit within the binary model or that emerged outside the scope of the standard employment relationship. A typical example of this type of approach is the prohibition of some forms of labour

6 *The Changing Law of the Employment Relationship*

intermediation and labour sub-contracting in Continental Europe.[8] To some extent the legally imposed or, more often, collectively negotiated continental thresholds for the number of part-time or fixed term contracts in a given workplace – discussed in the second and third sections of Chapter 3 – can also be seen as a vestige of this regulatory approach. The aforementioned fragment from the work of Professors Pélissier, Supiot and Jeammaud precisely reminds us that some types of atypical work arrangements were always 'dreamt of' by employers, but – until recently– some of them were systematically thwarted by an openly unsympathetic legal framework. Secondly, law has often automatically *converted* atypical employment relationships into contracts of subordinate employment. This has been the typical approach of a number of Continental systems in regulating successive renewals of fixed-term contracts of employment and traces of this approach are still present in national and EC legislation.[9] Thirdly, law has arguably attempted to *discourage* workers from entering in employment relationships that did not fit within the binary model. An example of this kind of approach can be found in the fewer legal protections and rights that workers engaged in atypical work relationships receive. But arguably this model can be seen both from the employer and the employee perspective. By and large it could be argued that regulation that attributes to atypical workers fewer rights than those enjoyed by comparable typical employees discourages workers from entering into these under-protected employment relationships. But at the same time it may well encourage employers to modify their contractual arrangements in purchasing the necessary labour resources under the guise of these under-protected and usually cheaper forms of labour.

It appears that the effectiveness of this type of discouragement is greatly affected by employment and unemployment rates and by the regulatory framework of a given labour market, which may often force workers into undesirable and under-protected employment relationships. When this has been the case, it is possible to say that the regulatory framework produced a *normalisation* of atypical work *without parity*, that is to say without seeking to grant to atypical workers the same rights enjoyed by standard subordinate employees. The result has often been, as in the case of the UK, a proliferation of atypical working arrangements outside the scope of dependent work and labour legislation. A similar trend has emerged in more recent times in France, culminating with the hotly contested project of introducing the *contrat première embauche* (CPE) in 2006. This contractual form exemplifies a string of 'special contracts' that have proliferated in France over the past few years from which essential aspects of the *statut salarial* – such as the protection from unfair dismissal during the first two years of employment – have been effectively excluded.

Finally it seems to us that a further regulatory strategy interfacing with the taxonomy of the employment relationship is represented by what could aptly be defined as the 'normalisation with parity' model. Recognising the lack of protection for atypical dependent workers, national and supranational legal systems have progressively introduced ad hoc legislation aimed at affording rights to part-time and fixed-term employees on an equal-treatment basis with comparable standard

---

8   See further the second section of Chapter 3.

9   See further the second sections of Chapter 3 and Chapter 6.

employees. Many European countries have produced similar legislation for agency workers too. This model can be supported by a rather sophisticated rationale: making atypical work *normal*, that is to say socially acceptable, with the aim of attracting more and better qualified workers into part-time and fixed-term and, more generally, flexible contractual arrangements. In recent times normalisation with parity has more or less completely marginalised the idea of prohibiting atypical work and can be seen as fulfilling the same protective concerns that in the 1970s and 1980s were addressed by converting atypical contracts into standard ones. This model, whether implicitly or explicitly, creates ad hoc normative regimes for the regulation of atypical forms of work, or at least for the most practically significant ones. The effect of the *parity* elements is such as to drag these types of working arrangements within the scope of application of most of the labour rights traditionally afforded to standard workers. On the other hand it will be pointed out that this model is hardly a panacea to the protective lacunae affecting the legal position of some atypical workers, and that atypical workers may well be in need of ad hoc atypical protections that go beyond those afforded to comparable standard employees.

The crisis of the binary model and alternative constructions of the employment relationship: third types, and normalisation without parity

In studying the changing notion of the employment relationship there is the risk of falling into economically deterministic discourses. It is increasingly claimed that deep structural transformations occurring in the economic structure of industrialized societies are producing some irresistible pressures and changes in economic relations to which law in general, and labour law in particular, should conform. This deterministic orthodoxy argues that the introduction of new technologies, new flexible systems of production, the expansion of the service sector and several other phenomena should justify a progressive retraction of labour legislation if not a demise of some important institutions such as the notion of subordinate labour. It is undeniably the case that the continuous emergence of new patterns of employment is putting under serious strain the notions of contract of employment and subordination and the labour law systems that use these notions as a central organising idea. The third sections of Chapter 2 and Chapter 5 will highlight that several systems are progressively approaching the strategies of solving the coverage issue of labour legislation either by simply *expanding its personal scope* or by attempting to normalise some forms of atypical work in order to bring these forms of work within the realm of labour law protection ('normalisation with parity'). As a consequence of these trends, recent years have registered the progressive growth of atypical work *outside* the scope of dependent work.

However, any economic determinism should be resisted. For example, in the UK, where atypical work has traditionally developed outside the employee category and only in relatively recent times has a link been established between some forms of atypical work and employee status, the impact of economic changes on this development is hardly a novelty. The flourishing of quasi-subordinate and formally autonomous, albeit in most of the cases economically dependent, forms of work has prompted a further regulatory strategy aimed at introducing some intermediate

8 *The Changing Law of the Employment Relationship*

legal categories of work and labour protection. In some countries, such as the UK, legislators have re-elaborated the scope of application of *some* specific legislation to make it applicable to independent contractors or quasi-dependent *workers*. A typical example is UK legislation granting protection against discrimination to working persons or rules relating to the National Minimum Wage in respect of workers.[10] Similarly, some Continental legal systems have bestowed some rights (mainly linked to the labour dispute process and health and safety) to quasi-subordinate workers loosely defined.

This strategy, as it will be argued in the third and fifth sections of Chapter 2, appears to have undergone an evolutionary process in countries such as Italy that have been attracted by the idea of regulating in a systematic way atypical quasi-subordinate activities and thus depart from a strictly binary model of employment relationship. The so-called 'Biagi law'[11] provided a clear, albeit problematic, example of this tendency. The law introduced a narrow and quite precise definition of *project-workers*, that at a theoretical level filled the space that was previously occupied by the *Collaborazioni Coordinate e Continuative* (*co.co.co.*) quasi-subordinated category. The problem is that what in theory should have been a departure from the binary notion of the employment relationship appears to be an attempt to typify an atypical form of work, resembling what in the past has been done for part-time and fixed-term work, but embodying a clear preference for the normalisation without parity model. Paradoxically, the more one tries to define a *tertium genus* of work, the more there is the risk of merely creating a further category of atypical, and under protected, employment. It is tempting to consider that these actions typifying quasi-subordinate forms of work will replicate the steps that lead to the normalisation with parity of atypical forms of work such as part-time and fixed-term work. But so far there seems to be a noticeable difference between these types of actions and the ones that had previously concerned part-time and fixed-term work. While in the case of part-time and fixed-term work the key word progressively became *equal treatment* (*normalisation with parity*), here we seem to be heading towards a *normalisation without parity*.

This is arguably a conscious regulatory choice of the political and legal system that is often presented as an economic necessity with which law should comply by merely providing a legal structure. The author of the present work acknowledges the need for law to evolve and address social change, but believes that some of the arguments put forward are greatly misconceived. On a first level it is arguable that economic change influences legal (and political) change just as the latter can influence the former. But on a less philosophical level, the perceived current inadequacy of labour law systems has more to do with the legal conceptualisations shaping the perception of the economic structure than with this structure itself. And it is precisely these kinds of conceptualisations and the debates surrounding their reform that will form the object of the analysis of the present book. It seems plausible, and worthwhile exploring at a comparative level, that there are good

---

10 See the third section of Chapter 2.

11 See the third section of Chapter 2.

Introduction 9

reasons to believe, as suggested by a number of authors,[12] that the binary concept of the employment relationship has not exclusively appeared and emerged as the natural product of a given economic system, and that law has had a great deal of influence in determining its structure. Similarly, legal arrangements can have a strong influence on its evolution and changes. Paraphrasing Heisenberg's 'uncertainty principle'[13] we could say that, as far as the relationship between law and economics in shaping the notion of the employment relationship, the *factual* object of the observation has been greatly affected by the *legal* observer and that, to some extent, it has been the observer, just as much as the observed, that has shaped reality.

The purposes and consolidated principles of comparative legal analysis

Before we progress to the various stages of our analysis, it is important to clarify what the relevant methodological scope of the research is. The study will be conducted following a comparative methodology, and the comparison will involve a number of European Member States. This methodological choice is not a random one but, on the contrary, provides a major analytical advantage. Indeed it is perceived as the best way to unveil the deep incoherence of some national discourses tainted by economic or legal determinism. As for economic determinism, a purposeful use of comparative methodology can help to highlight the substantial diversities existing between different 'varieties'[14] of regulatory systems shaping capitalist societies. In practice, comparative methodology can show us, if not also help us understand, how similar evolutions of the economic structure in different countries are addressed in different ways by their legal superstructures and how similar legal measures can be adopted by countries with different 'varieties' of economic capitalist structures. As for the risks deriving from legal determinism, a comparative analysis of different regulatory experiences can prove the futility of trying to approach socio-economic and legal changes through obsolete and inadequate legal frameworks.

A few years ago, Zweigert and Kötz commented in relation to 'comparative law' in general, that 'so recent a discipline could not be expected to have an established set of methodological principles. Even today the right method must largely be discovered by gradual trial and error.'[15] If this is true for comparative law in general, it could be seen as an article of faith for comparative employment law in particular.[16] But this should not become an easy scapegoat for avoiding confrontation with some well-reasoned yardsticks of legal method whose lucidity is so evident that they may

---

12   See above footnote (4).

13   G. Gembillo (ed.), *W Heisenberg – Indeterminazione e realtà* (Guida, Napoli, 1991), pp. 37–67.

14   P.A. Hall and D. Soskice, *Varieties of Capitalism – The Institutional Foundations of Comparative Advantage* (OUP, Oxford, 2001).

15   K. Zweigert and H. Kötz, *An Introduction to Comparative Law* (Clarendon, Oxford, 1987), p. 41.

16   Compare A.C. Neal, 'Comparative Labour Law and Industrial Relations: "Major Discipline?" – Who Cares?', in C. Engels and M. Weiss (eds), *Labour Law and Industrial Relations at the Turn of the Century – Liber Amicorum in Honour of Prof. Dr. Roger Blanpain* (Kluwer, The Hague, 1998), p. 55.

well be tantamount to methodological canons. Of course there are certainly going to be some specific research necessities that may well justify an ad hoc adaptation of these analytical tools. Nevertheless even in these cases the principles will have to pass at least the tests of functionality, analytical rigour and descriptive accuracy satisfied by the more well-established principles.

Otto Kahn-Freund, when elucidating the taxonomy of the purposes of comparative law, introduced a threefold distinction. 'Foreign legal systems may be considered first, with the object of preparing the international unification of the law, secondly, with the object of giving adequate legal effect to a social change shared by the foreign country with one's own country, and thirdly, with the object of promoting at home a social change which foreign law is designed either to express or to produce'.[17] That author had already realised the boost that the first of these three comparative *teloi* would have received from the process of European integration. But he also highlighted that the areas of law subject to these processes might resist unification, each time unifying legislation was confronted with 'economic, cultural or political' obstacles.

As far as labour legislation was concerned, Otto Kahn-Freund introduced a further distinction between the 'area of individual labour relations where ... transplantation is comparatively easy, especially between countries which have reached similar stages of economic development',[18] and rules 'concerned with collective relations between unions and other groups of workers and management' such as those on 'collective bargaining, on the closed shop, on trade unions, on strikes',[19] where transplantation was seen as virtually impossible. These aspects of labour law were seen as too 'closely linked with the structure and organisation of political and social power in their own environment' to allow a smooth and easy transplantation eventually leading to a supranational unification. That very environment, Professor Kahn-Freund finally suggested, had to be thoroughly studied and understood, as 'to use a pattern of law outside the environment of its origin continues to entail the risk of rejection'. The concluding remark was that the use of comparative method 'requires a knowledge not only of the foreign law, but also of its social, and above all its political, context' and it 'becomes an abuse ... when it is informed by a legalistic spirit which ignores this context of the law'.[20]

More recently other authors have elaborated in some detail the elements of which the aforementioned context appears to be composed.

Any approach to comparative labour law must, at the very least, ... in its *historical component* recognise the explosive forces which nineteenth century *laissez faire* liberal capitalism unleashed on workers within a developing factory system. It must appreciate, as part of its *political component*, the social pressures to which this gave rise, and the threat which these were perceived to offer to the established order. More specifically, when dealing with its *legalistic component*, it must account for the impetus to adapt the traditional instrument of law as means for limiting collective power or for preventing mass

---

17 O. Kahn-Freund, 'Uses and Misuses of Comparative Law', *MLR* 37 (1974): 1–2.
18 Ibid., p. 22.
19 Ibid., p. 20.
20 Ibid., p. 27.

Introduction 11

social reactions to what is widely perceived as the inherent imbalance of bargaining power in the work relationship. Furthermore, in addressing the *economic and social components*, it must trace the transition of the *laissez faire* economic order – through two World Wars, by way of a 'Cold War', and on into the 'post Communist' era, with its accompanying rise to prominence of so-called 'free market' doctrines – into systems of Labour law built upon detailed regulation of contractual relationships, against a safety-valve created by a social security 'floor of rights' introduced and regulated by statute. On top of this, that approach to comparative labour law must also, in relation to its inherent *international component*, take into consideration the impact of newly evolved legal systems (such as the developing legal order of the European Community), as well as crucial aspects of international law embodied in instruments of the kind created through global institutions such as the United Nations, or formulated under the auspices of regional bodies as the Council of Europe.[21]

It is certainly useful to consider Lord Wedderburn's reminder 'if you wish to understand a country's labour law, first examine its labour movement and industrial history' though it would be 'certainly wrong to exclude other factors'.[22] In this way it is possible to explain the rationale of different legislative choices in different countries sharing similar economic structures. The following chapters will stress the fact that in labour law, both individual and collective, nothing, or almost nothing, is casual, while everything, or almost everything, is causally linked to deeper socio-economic and political equilibria that need to be thoroughly studied and understood. The task of exploring the relationship between labour law and industrial relations is both facilitated and rendered more difficult by the comparative approach. It is facilitated because, as Dunlop put it, the 'comparative method leads to questions regarding the reasons for the observed comparisons and contrasts'.[23] But it is also rendered more difficult by the fact that comparison requires the capacity to grasp some deeper political, economic and socio-cultural nuances that might not be evident at a first sight. 'Goethe, of course, does not describe or analyse German labour relations, but without a knowledge of Goethe's writings a non-German cannot expect to fully grasp what is behind "co-determination"'.[24]

The comparative study of industrial relations can therefore prevent labour lawyers from falling in the methodological and substantive errors highlighted by Otto Kahn-Freund. And it can be a useful tool for the understanding of the *nexus* existing between economic-industrial changes and the legal regulation of work and, in the context of the present research, of the employment relationship in its factual and legal dimensions. The present work incorporates methodological suggestions that have accompanied the discipline of comparative labour law and industrial relations for the last three decades while taking historical and comparative account of the pressure that produced the emergence and, subsequently, the transformation of the legal notion of the employment relationship from the industrial revolution to

---

21 Neal, pp. 59–60.

22 K.W. Wedderburn, 'The Right to Strike: Is There a European Standard?' in K.W. Wedderburn, *Employment Rights in Britain and Europe: Selected Papers* (Lawrence & Wishart, London, 1991), pp. 289–290.

23 J. Schregle, 'Comparative Industrial Relations', *ILR* (1981): 27.

24 Ibid., p. 29.

12   *The Changing Law of the Employment Relationship*

our days. Chapter I in particular emphasises and highlights the relevance of some key changing elements of the employment relationship that, although described and observed from a legal perspective, are deeply embedded in the social and political fabric of the legal systems under examination.

3. Structure and summary of the book

The book comprises eight chapters including this Introduction and the Conclusions. Chapter 1 provides an introduction to the legal history of the theme of the monograph and describes the emergence of the traditional binary model of the employment relationship while providing a summary of the pressures it has been subject to in recent years. Chapters 2 and 3 give a comparative account of the various national regulatory approaches aimed at tackling the problems deriving from the changing notion of the employment relationship. Chapters 4, 5 and 6 seek to provide a similar analysis for the actions taken at a supranational level by the ILO and the EC. But different chapters are also linked by the approach they adopt to analyse the changes affecting the employment relationship. For instance Chapter 2, sections of Chapter 4 and Chapter 5 analyse the actions taken to *define* or *re-define* the *scope* of application of labour law at a national and supranational level. Chapter 3, the central part of Chapter 5 and Chapter 6 explore the various approaches aimed at *typifying* atypical employment relationships and the many and sometimes conflicting rationales underpinning these approaches.

More specifically, Chapter 1 will provide a historical reconstruction of the legal notions of the employment relationship from the early industrial developments of Western societies until the present. It will attempt to indicate, through comparative analysis, how diverse social, political and legal traditions interfered with this development and determined the establishment of different variations of the notion of employment relationship throughout Europe. It will also point out how, in spite of these differences, the notion of the employment relationship that emerged in the 20th century appeared to have a number of universal and common legal features (personal subordination, continuity, full and rigid working time and bilaterality). But it will also stress that, in the last three decades or so, some new legal features of the employment relationship have emerged, such as enhanced autonomy, intermittence or discontinuity, and multilaterality. In conclusion it will be pointed out that these changes have placed under strain the traditional legal notion of employment relationship, exposing several weaknesses and lacunae in the traditional regulatory framework largely developed during the mass-industrialisation period. The following chapters will discuss and critically analyse the various legal approaches to the re-regulation of this complex area of employment legislation.

Having identified the nature of the changes affecting the employment relationship and the emerging lacunae of labour law in the previous chapter, Chapter 2 will go through the debate, taking place in the European countries under examination, over the future of labour law. Most of these debates seek to explore ways of expanding the coverage of labour legislation by redefining and reconceptualising the *scope* of the legal notion of the employment relationship. This chapter will highlight both

Introduction 13

what the grand designs for the future of labour law are, and how specific problems related to the notion of employment contract, the employment relationship and the individual scope of labour law are being tackled in different ways by different systems of industrial relations and by the legal doctrines. Currently there are three main ways in which the various European legal doctrines are attempting to address the problems at stake. The first one stretches as far as possible the notion of employee status to introduce within its protective range as many workers as possible. The second one implicitly departs from the binary model of employment relationship and seeks to define a *third type* of worker, located in the 'twilight zone' between the traditional employee and the self-employed, and to afford them a series of rights traditionally linked to employment status. The third main doctrinal path has the universalistic ambition of exploring the feasibility of a *ius commune* covering all types of workers, and eventually grants a different range of specific rights to certain categories. These debates all have different strengths and weaknesses and their applications often overlap in reality. For each of them the potential advantages and disadvantages will be presented and discussed. The analysis will highlight the national specificities, but it will also try to expose the fact that the heated problems they are addressing are much more common to the various systems than the legal debate might lead one to suppose.

Chapter 3 will provide a comparative analysis of the regulation of the most relevant and common atypical employment relationships in the four MSs selected for the purposes of the present work. It will be argued that the regulation of atypical work can be understood as a process of adaptation of the legal system to a new, and increasingly fragmented, taxonomy of the legal notion of the employment relationship. Specific attention will be devoted to the ways part-time, fixed-term and temporary work are regulated and their underlying employment relationships disciplined. The analysis will span across the last three decades of often-contradictory reform discourses and regulatory approaches.

The three subsequent chapters seek to provide a supranational perspective to the study of the changing notion of employment relationship and to the transformations that labour law is undergoing to adapt itself to these changes. Chapter 4 will describe and analyse the most salient features of the scope of application of the ILO instruments, while also giving an account of the substantive protection afforded by ILO instruments to workers engaged in atypical work relationships, including the problematic initiatives on contract labour and economically dependent workers that eventually led in June 2006 to the successful adoption of an ad hoc Recommendation on scope of the employment relationship. In practice Chapter 4 will describe the rather fragmented ILO attempts to reconceptualise both the *scope* and the *taxonomy* of the employment relationship, and will assess the efforts made by the Organization in 'clarifying' the employment relationship through the 1996 Recommendation on the Employment Relationship.[25]

Chapter 5 will critically describe the various notions of 'worker' adopted by EC law through an exploration of the individual scope of application of EC social and

---

25   ILO Recommendation R 198: Recommendation Concerning the Employment Relationship (95th Conference Session, Geneva, 15 June 2006).

employment legislation. The concluding section of the chapter will also try to make sense of these various different notions by purporting an explanatory analysis of the various regulatory rationales underpinning each major area of EC social law. Chapter 6 will give a more focussed insight into the EC notions of flexibility and security in the intertwined areas of EC employment *law* and EC employment *policy*, highlighting some apparent inconsistencies progressively emerging in the evolution of the two regulatory discourses. The analysis will unveil how these two discourses have affected EC legislation regulating atypical work and also how they have influenced the relationship between EC and national labour legislation on part-time and fixed-term work. The Conclusions to the book will provide a synoptic account of some of the salient analytical points brought to light in the previous chapters, and argue that the complexity of the problem requires a joined analytical and regulatory effort at both the national and supranational level along some common lines that seem to have emerged in the last few years across different legal orders. The normative core of the concluding chapter amounts to a simple, albeit not necessarily uncontroversial, suggestion. It is suggested that national, and supranational, reform discourses should embrace two coordinated regulatory strategies. The first one should seek to expand the *scope* of the notion of *personal employment contracts*. Valuable and purposeful examples of this strategy are discussed in Chapters 2, 4 and, to a more limited extent, in Chapter 5 of the present work. The second regulatory strategy should seek to 'typify' atypical forms of work. That is to say to isolate, highlight and define the salient aspects of emerging atypical personal work relationships and provide ad hoc regulatory frameworks with an intention of 'normalising' these atypical work relationships by reference to the standard notion of the subordinate employment relationship. This book – particularly in Chapters 3 and 6 – suggests that this is an approach that has been largely and successfully adopted in respect of atypical forms of employment such as part-time and fixed-term work, and that more should be done to apply the same rationale to trilateral employment relationship such as temporary agency work.

Chapter 1

The Employment Relationship and the Contract of Employment in Industrialised Societies

1. Introduction

This chapter provides a historical reconstruction of the evolution of the legal notion(s) of the employment relationship from the early industrial developments of Western societies until the present day. The first main section describes the legal and economic environment and the social and political context that, during the 18th and 19th centuries, produced the progressive collapse of the pre-modern legal notions of employment relationship. The analysis highlights how, in this period, a number of reforms and social changes produced a progressive and steady decline of the notion of *status* as the pivotal element of the employment relationship. This decline was accompanied by a gradual spread of the notion of contract as the fulcrum of the employment relationship and of economic relations at large. This spread was by no means a simple and uncontroversial phenomenon, and comparative analysis points out how different legal systems addressed the progressive contractualisation of the employment relationship in different ways and, partly, in different periods. In particular, it highlights how the contractual notion, whilst emerging and establishing itself as the central organising idea of the employment relationship, has also managed to coexist with other more relational elements that many have, perhaps rightly, perceived as being at odds with a strictly contractual framework.

The subsequent, third, section roughly spans the early decades and the second half of the 20th century, where the contractualisation of the employment relationship was consolidated and its binary nature was crystallised in labour and social legislation, case law, collective bargaining and legal analysis. All these regulatory and normative pressures fostered, through a process of legal and social engineering, the emergence of an inherently unitary notion of contract of employment that embraced a multifarious range of working relationships and numerous categories of workers. This notion of the contract of employment tended towards the socially and politically desirable standardisation and decasualisation of the employment relationship. In this period, the contract of employment emerged as an inherently *unitary* contract characterised by the elements of (i) *personal* (albeit only *functional*) *subordination* in the performance of work, (ii) *continuity* and *full* and *fixed working time* and (iii) *bilaterality*. Comparative analysis teases out both the similarities and the different fine tunings that each of the three aforementioned elements was subjected to in the four countries under study. The importance of this unitary notion of the contract of employment in shaping the scope of application of labour legislation is also stressed.

The fourth section unveils how, in more recent times, the social and legal engineering discussed in the third section (which was aimed at fostering the concept of the unitary contract of employment and the binary model of the employment relationship) entered into a period of profound crisis. In the last few decades a number of changes – of which only the legal ones will be isolated and analysed – produced a progressive fragmentation of the previous unitary notion of the contract of employment. Both the traditional taxonomy and scope of the employment relationship were deeply affected. New legal categorisations of working people were progressively coined from the economic and legal environment alike. In a period of increasing legal deregulation, enterprises started modifying the legal terms under which they were willing to purchase and manage labour energies and human resources. The changing notions of the employment relationship were confronted by different and at times incongruent regulatory approaches. The work also presents a number of emerging features of the changing notion of the employment relationship (*formal autonomy, intermittence* and *multilaterality*) that have progressively distanced it from the previous conceptualisations discussed in the previous section. To some extent, these emerging features are both the result of changes in the legal terms under which enterprises engage and manage workers *and* the product of the legal and judicial discourse attempting to formulate a first response, albeit not necessarily a satisfactory one, to these phenomena.

It is hoped that a historical reconstruction of the many evolutionary phases of the employment relationship will provide a picture of the reasons and nature of the changes affecting the legal notion of the employment relationship. The chapter concludes with the argument that the legal notion of the employment relationship has effectively cast itself in contractual terms, and that modern contract theories ought to be able to accommodate the concerns of those that think that some strong elements of status and statutory regulation still pervade the employment relationship. Moreover, the resilience of this contractual framework over the past century or so would seem to suggest that the future of the employment relationship will still be deeply embedded in the contractual discourse. It is hoped that this assessment will pave the way for a deeper comparative analysis of the legal changes affecting the scope and the taxonomy of the employment relationship that will be carried out in the remaining chapters.

2. The industrial revolution and the birth of the contract of employment

Here, we introduce the notions of 'employment relationship' and 'contract of employment' by describing the conception of these notions in Western capitalist liberal democracies in the aftermath of the industrial revolution. It will be argued that the modern notion of the employment relationship sprang from the interplay of two social phenomena emerging in Europe between the 18th and 19th centuries, namely the *industrial revolution* and the rise of *liberal ideas*, which led to a completely novel rearrangement of the division of labour and of economic relationships in society, clustered around the liberal notion of *freedom of contract*, and the progressive abandonment of pre-modern notions of *status*. But, as perceptively pointed out by Deakin and Wilkinson,[1] whilst the industrial revolution and the rise of liberal ideas were two necessary preconditions for the development of the modern binary notion of the employment relationship, they were by no means sufficient ones. In fact a more complete 'contractualisation' of the employment relationship took place only in the late 19th and early 20th centuries, with the development of collective bargaining, social legislation and the emergence of the welfare state.

The gradual transition from status to contract took place in the industrialised societies under consideration in this work, with the progressive establishment of the notion of the *contract of service*, or the Continental analogous notions of *locatio operarum* or *louage de services*, all concepts that constitute the evolutionary link between the pre-modern idea of *status* and the modern contract of employment. It will be shown however that these *contractualisation* dynamics were also steered by country-specific political, and often ideological, dynamics that had an important role in determining the pace, intensity and, at times, direction, of these developments in different Western European states. Max Weber pointed out that, in some ways, '"capitalism" and "capitalist" undertakings ... have existed in all civilised countries of the world for as far back as our economic documents can take us. They have existed in China, India, Babylon, Egypt, the ancient Mediterranean and the Middle Ages. But ... in the modern West, there exists a completely different form of capitalism, which has developed nowhere else in the world: the rational capitalist organisation of (formally) *free labour*'.[2] Weber also stressed that 'the modern rational organisation of the capitalist enterprise would have not been possible without ... the *separation of the household from the place of work*'.[3]

In mature 20th century capitalism, the rational organisation of *free* labour outside the household has typically been implemented through the notion of the employment relationship legally embedded in the contract of employment. But some first changes in this direction were already taking place between the 18th and 19th centuries, a period that saw the progressive decline of the guild system, which was based on a rigid state control over the labour market, on an inflexible and closed mercantile economy, and on a 'guild organisation of professions and trades based on the principle of jealous protection of its own interests by each trade'.[4] The guild system had produced a web of rules regulating the working relationship based on an apprentice/servant-master dualism whereby strict control over the numbers in each trade or profession was maintained through rules governing entry, acquisition of skills, methods of work and salary. The rules were established by each guild and the

---

1   S. Deakin and F. Wilkinson, *The Law of the Labour Market – Industrialization, Employment and Legal Evolutions* (Oxford, 2005), pp. 41–109.

2   M. Weber, 'The Origins of Industrial Capitalism in Europe', in W.G. Runciman (ed.), *Weber Selections in Translations* (CUP, Cambridge, 1978), pp. 335–336. Emphasis original.

3   Ibid., p. 336. With *rational book keeping* being the third element of the Weberian reconstruction of modern capitalism. Emphasis original.

4   B. Veneziani, 'The Evolution of the Contract of Employment', in B. Hepple (ed.), *The Making of Labour Law in Europe: A Comparative Study of Nine Countries up to 1945* (Mansell, London, 1986), p. 35.

18   *The Changing Law of the Employment Relationship*

statutes containing them, often tailored to the needs of the wealthiest masters, were administered and backed by the political authorities to control the labour market and ensure *social peace* by directing workers towards those sectors where there was a low concentration of labour. Typical English examples of guild legislation were the Ordinance and Statute of Labourers of 1349 and 1351 and the Statute of Artificers of 1563, with their criminal law restrictions on labour mobility, breach of contract and right to combine.

It would be inexact to claim that contractual working relationships were completely unknown to this monopolistic and closed regime. In a sense apprentices were accepted on the basis of a written contract that was drawn up and deposited in the guild archives. On the one hand the master was obliged to provide professional skills, and even protection, to his apprentice, and on the other the apprentice had to obey and even pay a fee. But unsurprisingly the *doctrine* stressed that this kind of contract could not be classified as a hiring of services, and even less as a form of subordinate employment. French *compagnons* (journeymen or workers) saw their wages fixed by public order and risked imprisonment for breach of contract if they broke terms which had not yet expired, and this 'arrangement' was not uncommon in the rest of Western Europe. This was 'closer to the relationship of family subordination based on the status found in the predominantly feudal type of cottage industries .... When the economic structure began to change, so did the structure of the relationship'.[5]

The economic system changed drastically between the 18th and 19th centuries. Marx's description of the manufacturing process in the mid-19th century shows clearly this transition from one mode of production to the other:[6]

> A carriage ... was formerly the product of the labour of a great number of independent artificers, such as wheelwrights, harness-makers, tailors, locksmiths, upholsterers, turners, fringe-makers, glaziers, painters, polishers, gilders, etc. In the manufacture of carriages, however, all these different artificers are assembled in one building where they work into one another's hands.

But these changes did not by themselves trigger a transformation in the modes by which the economic system acquired and organised labour resources within the productive process. Some authors have argued that it was only the rise of the liberal ideas of *equality* and *freedom*, that in countries such as France emerged in a dramatic way through revolutionary processes,[7] that determined the start of a *de jure* passage from *status* to contract.[8] Indeed, while before the emergence of liberal idea(l)s the power relations existing inside society at large and, in particular, inside the factory could be easily 'crystallised' through the concept of *status*, a similar simple operation was no longer possible after the establishment of the new societal order established

---

5   Ibid., p. 38.

6   K. Marx, *Capital – A Critical Analysis of Capitalist Production Volume 1* (Lawrence & Wishart, London, 1974), pp. 318–319.

7   On the contractual emphasis placed by the codes inspired by the 1789 French revolutionary ideas see A. Supiot, *Critique du Droit du Travail* (PUF, Paris, 2002), p. 14.

8   M.G. Garofalo, 'Un Profilo Ideologico del Diritto del Lavoro', *GDLRI*, 81 (1999): 9.

with them. These political changes and the rejection of the corporative, illiberal system they brought with them,[9] laid the legal foundations of modern capitalism.

But now a new challenge was arising: how to bestow legitimacy to the power position enjoyed by the capitalist entrepreneur *vis á vis* the reciprocal subordinate position of the employee or worker, in a society – and a legal order – recognising subjects as free and equal, and only admitting social relations on the grounds of their voluntary – contractual – nature. The solution to this dilemma today seems obvious: if all subjects are free and equal, no power relation between them can ever be conceived, and their societal connection can only be ensured via a *commodity exchange*. The worker, from an economic point of view, happens to own a particular type of commodity that she might wish to exchange in the market: her labour resources. Thus, if labour resources are separated from the worker, the employer will not exercise any more any control over the person, but, on the contrary, he will always control the commodity that he can obtain in the market through a voluntary exchange for another commodity, the salary. The contract thus bestows legitimacy upon the factory system. Since the employer buys labour resources (and the contract also controls the amount of resources he needs to buy) he has to be considered, both in economic and legal terms, as the original owner of the products of the factory system.

For Continental systems, largely based on the Roman law tradition, this evolution from status to contract occurred through the shift from the *locatio servi* to the *locatio operarum* model. The old Roman model of *locatio conductio* was disaggregated and a distinction was drawn between the *locatio* of goods as opposed to services, with the worker appearing as hiring his labour energies.[10] In Britain, and the common law countries where Roman law conceptions had a limited influence and the rhetoric of the French Revolution had only a distant echo, freedom of contract and the formal equality of contracting parties were achieved through a different route, worked out mainly by the courts along traditional common law lines. Veneziani argues that this also explains the relative delay with which the evolutionary processes analysed so far took place in Britain. 'The social figures of pre-industrial society inhabited the judicial mind until long after the Industrial Revolution'.[11] But things were due to change in the country that had invented the industrial revolution, albeit with a considerable 'legal time lag'.[12]

Deakin points out that, in Britain, 19th century law on employment did not recognise the modern distinction between dependant employment and self-employment; 'nor did it consistently see the obligations of the parties to the employment relationship as "contractual". Most industrial workers were still subject to a model based on

---

9   Cf. for instance the French *décret d'Allarde (Loi 2-17 mars 1791)* eliminating controls and limitations over labour mobility.

10   Cf. Pothier's *Traité du Contract de Louage* analysed in O. Kahn-Freund, 'Blackstone's Neglected Child: The Contract of Employment', *LQR* (1977): 514–515.

11   Veneziani, 'The Evolution of the Contract of Employment', pp. 60–61.

12   O. Kahn-Freund, 'Blackstone's Neglected Child: The Contract of Employment', p. 524.

master and servant relations'.[13] The important operation that British courts and statutory legislation achieved in the 19th century was precisely the transformation of these service relations into a fundamentally new and specific legal concept of service embodied in the *contract of service*. But again this was a slow process and one that initially only affected higher status non-manual workers, whereas for a very long period the employer-workman relationship was identified along the lines of the master-servant relationship.

For centuries the Statutes of Labourers of 1349 and 1351 and the Statute of Artificers of 1563 had managed to strike a widely accepted social balance in British society. Even the Master and Servant Acts of 1747, 1766 and 1823, to a certain extent 'grew out of the system of wage regulation and discipline contained in the pre-modern Statute of Artificers'.[14] The Master and Servant Acts gave local magistrates the traditional power to fine and imprison workers for offences such as refusing to enter into an agreed hiring and quitting before the end of the agreed term.[15] But Kahn-Freund stresses that a first substantial glimpse of change already appeared on the scene with the repeal of the Combination Acts in 1824 as 'the freedom of workmen to combine in order to improve their ... conditions of employment implicitly presupposed that these conditions were based on contract and not on status'.[16] Public control powers now could not apply to independent contractors and higher status workers and in the Master and Servant Act of 1867 it was stated that the magistrates' jurisdiction covered only the classes of 'servant' and 'labourer'. These groups were identified by the test known as 'exclusive service', already created by the courts.[17] A new legal notion of employment relationship based on the 'contract to serve' was progressively emerging, embracing most industrial and agricultural workers. At the same time, for the excluded categories of professional,[18] managerial and clerical workers 'a more clearly contractual model began to develop: the "employee" had the right to sue for damages for wrongful dismissal and for the failure of the employer to provide work as agreed'.[19] In practice, it was not so much the type of contract that differentiated the two categories, but rather the *nature* of the person's work: 'There may indeed be a service, not for any specific time or wages, but to be within the contract there must be a contract for service by the party exclusively'.[20]

---

13   S. Deakin, 'The Evolution of the Contract of Employment, 1900–1950' in N. Whiteside and R. Salais, *Governance, Industry and Labour Markets in Britain and France – The Modernising State in the Mid-twentieth Century* (Routledge, London, 1998), p. 213. See also the fuller account provided in S. Deakin and F. Wilkinson, *The Law of the Labour Market – Industrialization, Employment and Legal Evolutions* (OUP, Oxford, 2005).

14   Ibid., p. 214.

15   S. Deakin, *The Contract of Employment: A Study in Legal Evolution* (ESCR Working Paper No. 203, June 2001), p. 19.

16   Kahn-Freund, 'Blackstone's Neglected Child', p. 525.

17   *Lancaster* v *Greaves* (1829) 9 B & C 627.

18   Cf. *Emmens* v *Elderton* (1853) 13 CB 495, where a company solicitor was recognised a having a contractual action for wrongful dismissal.

19   Deakin, 'The Evolution of the Contract of Employment', p. 214.

20   *Lancaster* v *Greaves* (1829) 9 B & C 627, 631–32 (Parke J).

The employees' and labourers' contractual rights were only substantially harmonised in 1875 when the Disraeli Government, partly in an attempt to attract the support of the newly enfranchised urban (male) working class,[21] dismantled the aforementioned criminal law apparatus applying in respect of breach of contract.[22] Local magistrates still maintained under the provisions of the Employer and Workmen Act 1875 some powers over the contracts of agricultural and industrial workers which exceeded those of the ordinary civil courts and which continued to shape the service relationship (for example, the power to supervise the terms of the contract and, under section 3(3) to grant specific performance). Later (this will be explored in the subsequent section of this chapter), the criterion of 'exclusive service' was substituted by the one of 'control' that was once more used to introduce a distinction between manual and non-manual employees as the legal basis of the contract of service. As pointed out by Deakin and Morris, 'it is only in decisions of the early twentieth century that the courts can first be seen applying the contractual model, which they had developed for the middle classes, to industrial workers'.[23] In the meantime, a further and crucial differentiation between the two contractual relationships, was that

> notice periods varied according to the status of the worker or employee in question. Higher status workers such as clerical and managerial employees benefited from long notice period .... By contrast, most industrial workers during the period after 1875 were employed on contracts with short notice periods, possibly of no more than a day or even an hour.[24]

But it would be erroneous to assume that while England was experiencing these slow evolutionary processes, the Continental systems were adopting uninterrupted changes leading to a complete and uncontroversial contractualisation of the employment relationship. Certainly, these changes were more drastic and evident in countries that had experienced radical regime changes, with the hegemonic establishment of new ruling classes. In France for instance, the so-called *décret d'Allarde (Loi 2-17 mars 1791)* eliminated controls and limitations over labour mobility and established the principle of *liberté du travail* whereby *'les raports de travail sont abandonnés à la liberté contractuelle'*.[25] The *Code Civil* recognised the notion of *louage de services*, that is to say *'louage des gens de travail qui s'engagent au service de quelqu'un'*, and by which *'domestiques et ouvriers'* exchange their labour resources for a wage, but this notion was *not* regulated in its contents and form. All elements were, on the contrary, left to the will of the parties, though in practice this often meant that all the workers could do was to accept a pre-determined contract laid down by the employer. The latter could, in practice, recruit and dismiss whoever and whenever he wanted, given that even contracts without a

---

21 Representation of the People Act 1867.

22 Conspiracy and Protection of Property Act 1875.

23 S. Deakin and G.S. Morris, *Labour Law* (Butterworths, London, 2001), p. 28.

24 Deakin, *The Contract of Employment: A Study in Legal Evolution*, p. 27.

25 'Employment relationships are left to *contractual freedom*', see J. Pélissier, A. Supiot and A. Jeammaud, *Droit du Travail* (Dalloz, Paris, 2000), p. 8.

22 The Changing Law of the Employment Relationship

pre-determined duration could be unilaterally terminated since, to prevent lifelong hiring, too similar to the illiberal notion of *servage*, '*on ne peut engager ses services qu'à temps ou pour une entreprise déterminé*'.[26] More recently legal historians have further highlighted the instrumental use that the French revolutionary legislator made of the earlier Roman law categorisations that inspired the creation of the *louage de services* and *louage d'ouvrage* categories. Deakin warns us that in many respects the two versions of the *locatio conductio* contained in Article 1780 of the *Code Civil* – that is to say the *louage d'ouvrage* and the *louage de services* – were only 'loosely' based on the Roman law notions of, respectively *locatio conductio operarum* and *locatio conductio operis*. In each case, the link to Roman law concepts was more tenuous than it might seem at first sight. The concepts used in the *Code Civil* were adaptations – they were 'the same as the old *locatio conductio* in name only'.[27]

Just as in England, in France Napoleonic law did not ensure a complete contractualisation of the employment relationship and contractual equality between the parties. According to Article 1781 of the *Code Civil*, repealed in 1868 almost one century after the Revolution, in case of dispute over the amount and payment of the wages, the employer's word had to be taken for good. Furthermore, as early as in 1803 the *livret ouvrier* was introduced, formally a logbook with the employment history of the worker but one that the employer could withhold when dismissing the worker if there was any outstanding claim against wages, thus limiting his possibilities of finding a new job. This document was only abolished in 1890. Workbooks and penal sanctions were common to most Continental systems and they were only repealed in the later 19th century. In Germany the workbook was only abrogated in 1869, though it has to be said that the Prussian industrial revolution had been considerably delayed. Only the Netherlands saw an early and definitive repeal of the workbook legislation in 1815.

By the mid-second half of the 19th century most Western European countries were progressively aligning their respective notions of the employment relationship to contractual schemes. Criminal sanctions for breach of contract were replaced by a system of compensation or damages leading to a further 'contractualisation' of the employment relationship. The Italian *Codice Civile* 1865 notion of *persone* (Article 1627, n.1) was considerably wider in scope than the French category of *gens de travail*, as the Italian *locator operarum* could also be the skilled manual or clerical worker even when '*produttor(e) di opere della «mente»*'.[28] This was a relatively broad and unitary notion, certainly as compared to the French or British one.

Nineteenth-century Germany was at the crossroads of numerous internal and external legal influences and the elaborations of the employment relationship are an excellent indicator of these pressures. Germany had to deal with its legal traditions,

---

26 Article 1780, *Code Civil*. Similarly see Article 1628 of the Italian Civil Code of 1865.

27 S. Deakin, *The Comparative Evolution of the Employment Relationship* (Working Paper No 317, ESRC Centre for Business Research, University of Cambridge, December 2005), p. 9.

28 B. Veneziani, 'Contratto di lavoro, potere di controllo e subordinazione nell'opera di Ludovico Barassi', *GDLRI* (2002): 56.

The Employment Relationship and the Contract of Employment   23

the inevitable influences deriving from Napoleonic law and its own internal doctrinal and jurisprudential debates, overwhelmingly opposing an individualistic conception of the employment relationship in favour of a communitarian one. Supiot, again, unveils how the old, pre-industrial, Germanic notion of *Treudienstvertrag* was inevitably eclipsed by the emerging contractual notion of *Dienstvertrag* not too dissimilar from the French concept of *louage de services*, although in practice influential authors, such as Otto von Gierke, resisted the individualistic aspects apparently deriving from the French contractual analyses claiming that 'the ultimate source of any right is the common conscience (*Gemeinsbewusstsein*)'.[29] These communitarian ideologies would later inspire early 20th century elaborations of the contract of employment, as will become clearer in the following sections. Also, in spite of the literal correspondence of the two terms, there were a number of substantive differences between the *louage de services* and the *Dienstvertrag*.

> ... there is no clear reference in the *BGB* to the binary divide between employees and the self-employed: 'at the time the *BGB* was drafted ... the distinction between employment and services had not been established, so the term *Dienstvertrag* ... covered both types of agreement. This means that in the context of Art. 611 [*BGB*], *Dienstvertrag* refers both to the contract for service ... and the contract of employment'. The modern notion of the employment relationship or *Arbeitsverhältnis* came later, as in France, with the adoption of protective legislation and the legal accommodation of collective bargaining.[30]

Progressively, during the 19th century, French law developed a number of '*lois sociales*' whose effects on the *contract d'ouvrages*, as the legal standard of the employment relationship, were very similar to the ones produced in Italy by the *legislazione sociale* reforms and in England by social legislation. To many extents these dynamics were common to all European rapidly industrialising countries and probably attained a historical acme with the social reforms introduced by Bismarck in 1889. A primary object explicitly set by the most relevant stream of social legislation of this period was the provision of compensation for work-related personal injuries. In the United Kingdom, the exact definition of the personal scope of application of legislative acts such as the Employer's Liability Act 1880 and the Workmen's Compensation Act 1897, very soon became a delicate issue significantly affected by the restrictive interpretations of British courts. The Workmen's Compensation Act 1897 applied to 'any person who is engaged in an employment to which this Act applies [that is, railways, mining and quarrying, factory work and laundry work], whether by ways of manual labour or otherwise'.[31] But, for instance, the judiciary quickly eroded this definition by excluding high-ranking employees.[32] In other European experiences, it was soon clarified that the scope of application of similar legislative initiatives had to prevent these risks. That was the case, for instance, in France, where the important *Loi du 9 avril 1889* obliged the employer to indemnify the *manual worker* or *employee* injured in a work-related accident. The

---

29   A. Supiot, *Critique du Droit du Travail* (PUF, Paris, 2002), pp. 16–17.
30   Deakin, *The Comparative Evolution of the Employment Relationship*, p. 10.
31   Workmen's Compensation Act 1897, s. 7.
32   See for instance *Simpson* v *Ebbw Vale Steel, Iron & Coal Co.* [1905] 1 KB 453.

next section of this chapter will analyse more deeply the effects that 20th century welfare state structures had deployed on the notion of employment relationship, but it is already evident that this kind of legislation was progressively pushing towards a homogenisation and unification of the notion of subordinate employment relationship springing from a contractual basis.

To sum up, the 18th and 19th centuries saw a steady decline of the artisanal world in favour of new modes of production based on an enhanced division of labour, coordinated by a single employer within an enterprise. This process interfaced with the liberal ideas developing under the pressure of the emergence of the new ruling capitalist class, and precipitated the reorganisation of economic relations under new liberal and, at least nominally, more egalitarian legal arrangements. The notion of status was reformulated in new and socially acceptable terms, and progressively replaced with the one of *contract*. This contractualising dynamic was more evident in those legal systems that were more explicitly influenced by French liberal ideals, but were clearly not at all alien to other traditions such as the British and German ones.[33]

On the other hand these developments were not free from inherent contradictions, and for a considerable period 'old and new cohabitate[d]'[34] and mutually affected each other. At first it was assumed that for a contract to be established between two *equal* subjects, those subjects needed to participate in the formation of its contents as *individuals*. Therefore all European countries saw collective activities and actions of the labour force addressed in punitive terms. The resulting imbalance of power within the employment relationship was often formalised in legal terms, with employers enjoying the power unilaterally to determine the duration of the employment relationship and the terms of the economic exchange. It soon became evident that a floor of rights was needed for this system to achieve a minimum social and political stability. Social legislation was gradually introduced and, towards the second half of the eighteenth century, coalitions of workers were granted progressive recognition in all European industrialising countries. Both elements would contribute to the shaping of the modern employment relationship based on the contract of employment as it is now understood.

In practice, as Deakin stresses, 'the nineteenth-century law on employment did not recognise the modern distinction between dependent employment and self-employment; nor did it consistently see the obligations of the parties to the employment relationship as "contractual"'[35]. But inevitably the notion of contract had been brought to life with liberal revolutions, and by the end of the 19th century, working arrangements based on a contract of employment were spreading more and more, both within the factory system – particularly on the Continent[36] – and

---

33 See the considerations of Supiot, *Critique du Droit du Travail*, pp. 15–17.

34 Veneziani, 'Contratto di lavoro, potere di controllo e subordinazione', p. 53.

35 Deakin, 'The Evolution of the Contract of Employment', p. 213.

36 See the Italian L. 5 giugno 1893, n. 215 affording to the Probiviri tribunals the competence over controversies arising from contracts of employment between 'industrials' and manual workers, including apprentices.

The Employment Relationship and the Contract of Employment   25

in managerial and professional positions.[37] Whilst the rise of liberal ideology and the industrial revolution were not *per se* sufficient elements to establish a unitary notion of contract of employment, there is little doubt that they were instrumental and essential in the emergence and contractualisation process of the modern notion of employment relationship, which was further consolidated and developed in the early decades of the 20th century. In this period European legal systems, and most evidently the Continental ones, experienced a further transition from the contract of service (or *locatio operarum*, or *louage de services*) model to the notion of contract of employment. This was a transition that was probably not as straightforward and natural as the contemporary legal scholarship wanted it to be, and was perhaps 'done to lend the appearance of continuity to the law at a time when the concept of the *contrat de travail* was still relatively new'.[38] Legal history tells us that 'by the early twentieth century, Continental countries had witnessed the establishment of the contract of employment as an autonomous legal category distinct from other types of contract, such as sub-contracting, self-employment and mandate'.[39] And this is precisely the period that the forthcoming section seeks to explore.

3. The unitary notion of contract of employment

The first decades of the 20th century were a period of rising *industrialisation* for most western societies. The growth of secondary industry was to some extent a factor contributing to the stabilisation of the employment relationship, with industrial enterprises progressively learning to exploit internal labour markets and retain workers and their human capital for longer periods in order to recover training costs. But most importantly it created a number of social and political pre-conditions (for instance the expansion of the blue-collar working 'class' and trade unionism, a stable and increasing global demand and economic growth, the construction of welfare states) that determined the progressive introduction of legislation favouring the widespread use of a *contractual, dependent, stable* and *bilateral* notion of the employment relationship based on the contract of employment. These phenomena eventually led to the emergence of the sociological ideal-type of *male subordinated worker employed under an indefinite duration full-time contract of employment* around which labour legislation developed through the 20th century.

But again a number of caveats against this reasoning need to be stressed. First of all, just as there was a 'legal time lag' between the 18th century industrial and liberal revolutions and the legal conceptualisation of the emerging working patterns into new economically and socially acceptable models, so there was a considerable time lag between the establishment of mass production as the dominant system of industrial production and the conscious adoption of the aforementioned paradigm of

---

37   Some pre-industrial remnants were still enduring though, for instance in the case of domestic servants, agricultural workers – particularly in southern Europe – and in some categories of public servants.

38   Deakin, *The Comparative Evolution of the Employment Relationship*, p. 10.

39   Veneziani, 'Contratto di lavoro, potere di controllo e subordinazione', p. 67.

26   *The Changing Law of the Employment Relationship*

the full-time worker employed under a contract of employment for the purposes of labour legislation.

Second, although it is impossible to overstate the importance of mass industrialisation in the emergence of homogeneous dependant working patterns and the corresponding rise of the 'unitary' concept of contract of employment, it is also fair to say that this emergence was not as spontaneous or automatic as one might think. It is true that the new production arrangements caused a decline in 'intermediate forms of labour sub-contracting',[40] but legislation and to some extent judge-made legal principles, as we shall soon highlight, had an important role in further curbing the use of some of these pre-industrial employment practices, often by explicitly outlawing some of them. In a way it could be argued that there was a 'forced' unity of the contract of employment, or as Freedland says in relation to the British experience, a 'false' one.[41] The following paragraphs of this section seek to analyse the legal phenomena that contributed to consolidating the contractual nature of the employment relationship. Subsequently, the legal measures that fostered the emergence of the other constitutive elements of the traditional notion of employment relationship – that is to say dependence, continuity and bilaterality – will be presented and discussed.

In the case of Britain, legal history suggests that a more complete 'contractualisation' of the employment relationship was very largely the result of the socialising influence of welfare state legislation.[42] Some first pieces of social legislation adopted in the late 19th century had already paved the way for a progressive homogeneous treatment of subordinate working relationships based on the contract of employment. The British Workmen's Compensation Act 1906 established a personal scope of application that deeply marked UK labour law. A workman was defined as 'any person who has entered into or works under a contract of service or apprenticeship with an employer, whether by way of manual labour, clerical work or otherwise, and whether the contract is expressed or implied, in oral or in writing'.[43]

But even these legislative attempts were subverted by the British courts still resistant to the idea of creating a single unitary contractual category for all dependant employment relationships. The judicial introduction of a particularly narrow 'control test'[44] served this purpose and the idea of keeping middle-class employees outside the service relationship 'because they were perceived as enjoying a high degree of autonomy and discretion in the way they carried out their work, autonomy which was not compatible with the status of servant or workman'.[45] Another obstacle was the

---

40   S. Deakin, *The Many Futures of the Contract of Employment* (CBR Working Paper No. 191, December 2001), p. 2.

41   M.R. Freedland, *The Personal Employment Contract* (OUP, Oxford, 2003), pp. 16–17.

42   Deakin, 'The Evolution of the Contract of Employment', p. 213. And see the extremely comprehensive reconstruction of this process in S. Deakin and F. Wilkinson, *The Law of the Labour Market* (OUP, Oxford, 2005).

43   Workmen's Compensation Act 1906, s. 13.

44   With cases such as *Simmons* v *Heath Laundry Co* [1910] 1 KB 543 and *Underwood* v *Perry* [1932] WC & I Rep 63.

45   Deakin, 'The Evolution of the Contract of Employment', pp. 219–220.

The Employment Relationship and the Contract of Employment   27

legislative exclusion of casual workers employed 'otherwise than for the purposes of their employer's trade or business' and of outworkers and family workers.[46] Though rising industrialism and the adoption of increasingly integrated and hierarchical models of industrial production reduced the risk of workforce dispersion outside the factory, several industries, for instance the construction, mining and ship-building industries, were inevitably affected by this exclusion, whose effects were exacerbated by a strict application of the 'control test'. Against this background of judicial reaction to a unitary notion of contract of employment, legislation was leading a fierce and systematic struggle. Indeed British statutory intervention kept focusing on a unitary category for all employment relationships, and the Trade Dispute Act (TDA) 1906 referred to 'workmen' as including 'all persons employed in trade or industry'[47] and this was interpreted so as to include virtually all forms of activity, including occupations in local government.

Progressively, some judicial decisions started applying to manual workers the same contractual model they had developed for the middle classes. In *Hanley* v *Pease & Partners*[48] it was held that an employer had no implied right to suspend the contract of a mine worker without pay for disobedience in the absence of an express *contractual term* providing for suspension and that the employee had the right to bring a claim for damages for breach of contract. A spill-over effect of the TDA 1906 immunities was an increase in collective bargaining, another important factor in the decline of the service model. It led to a reduction of the notice period for most industrial workers, and introduced collective arbitration arrangements for labour disputes, thus de facto nullifying the last remnants of disciplinary powers enjoyed by magistrates and county courts under the Employers and Workmen Act 1875. At the same time of these legislative changes, collective agreements started using individual contracts to spread their normative effects throughout the workforce, greatly contributing to their adoption in corporations eager to rationalise and simplify the relationships with their workforces.

The first two decades of the 20th century also signalled a growth of industrial work. Just as the service model was declining in favour of the contract of employment, the notion of *control* typical of the service model was progressively evolving towards a concept of subordination tailored around the need of industry for continuous control over the employment relationship. Initially subordination was treated as a characteristic of the relationship of domestic servants to their masters and was seen as not applying to the contract of *locatio*. But soon the notion changed because of the expansion of large-scale Fordist industry. Managerial control over the provision of labour energies for a relatively long period of time was a sociological characteristic of industrial work that soon permeated the contractual definitions too, further homogenising all workers within the factory system, whether blue or white collar. Just as contemporary British legislation had done, French and Italian laws of 9 April 1908 and 1904 on industrial accidents and the French law of 5 April 1910 on

---

46   Workmen's Compensation Act 1906, see Deakin and Wilkinson, *The Law of the Labour Market*, p. 89.

47   TDA 1906 s. 5.

48   [1915] 1 KB 698. Cf. also *Devonald v Rosser & Sons Ltd* [1906] 2 KB 728.

28 *The Changing Law of the Employment Relationship*

pensions defined the contract of employment in terms of dependency and control. Italian legislation in 1902 stressed the fact that subordination meant control in the sense of subjection to 'directions', while Germany started developing the concepts of 'social dependence', further refined in the Weimar period. The Italian *Probiviri* soon stressed that the criterion of subordination consisted 'in the commitment to work for a relatively long period of time, thus presuming a certain stability in the contractual relationship' and 'included the worker's obligation to follow out instructions and the employer's power to see that they were carried out'.[49] The notion of subordination received a much stronger and more patronising re-elaboration under the Fascist dictatorships of the first half of the previous century.

In any case, between the end of the 19th century and World War II all Continental systems completed the transition process establishing the contract of employment as the pivotal element of the typical employment relationship. The universalistic and egalitarian pressures of post–World War II *welfare states* and the period of economic growth and full employment experienced throughout Western Europe during the 1950s and 1960s, would have consolidated these trends in all systems, including Britain. Here the establishment of a modern 'Beveridge-style' welfare state was undoubtedly *the* element contributing to the final shaping of a unitary notion of employment relationship based on the contract of employment and extending to all categories of wage-earners. A 'major aspect of the Beveridge Report was the abolition of distinctions between different categories of employees ... regardless of their annual income or of their professional status'.[50] The National Insurance Act of 1948 accordingly established two main classes of contributors: 'employed earners', defined as 'any persons gainfully occupied in employment ... being employed under a contract of service', and those employed on their own account. This was the gravestone of the traditional distinction between manual and non-manual workers with the notions of contract of service and contract of employment merging and becoming synonyms.

As for collective bargaining, increasingly flourishing in the 1950s and 1960s, it certainly had the effect of marginalising individual bargaining. But it would be erroneous to assume that it also reduced the importance of the personal contract of employment as the pivotal element around which the employment relationship and the personal scope of application of employment law revolved. The continuing centrality of the contract of employment as the normative framework for employment protection helped to ensure, both in terms of positive law and of the theoretical discourse, that it would remain the obvious way of defining the personal scope of labour law. After World War II Britain was characterised by the marginal presence of statutory legislation, with collective bargaining being the predominant model of regulation. In this '*collective laissez-faire*' environment, collective bargaining soon emerged as the most effective way to redress the weak protection that a strict application of common law contractual principles afforded to workers.[51] In

---

49　Veneziani, 'Contratto di lavoro, potere di controllo e subordinazione', p. 65.

50　Deakin, 'The Evolution of the Contract of Employment', p. 221.

51　P.L. Davies and M. Freedland, *Labour Legislation and Public Policy: A Contemporary History* (OUP, Oxford, 1993), p. 25.

The Employment Relationship and the Contract of Employment 29

Italy, collective bargaining provided the first substantial protections against unfair dismissal.[52] Rules contained in collective contracts would override any contrary provision laid down into individual contracts whose principal role was to provide a means by which to articulate and convey the normative and regulatory effects of a collective contract upon the rights and obligations of individual parties. The somewhat paradoxical effect was that the individual contract of employment, albeit being often marginalised or even overridden by collectively agreed provisions, was consolidated in its position of fulcrum of the employment relationship.

A further step towards the contractualisation of the employment relationship and the fostering of the unitary model of contract of employment derived eventually from the introduction of statutory labour legislation during the 1960s and the early to mid-1970s, a phenomenon common to most European countries and often building on and consolidating the early regulatory achievements of the now progressively declining[53] collective bargaining systems.[54] As Chapter 3 will point out in greater detail, numerous pieces of legislation explicitly *prohibited* a number of patterns of employment that did not fit within the binary model. A typical example of this type of approach was the prohibition of some forms of labour intermediation and labour sub-contracting in Continental Europe.[55] Additionally, employment law often sought to *convert* a number of atypical employment relationships into contracts of subordinate employment. This has been the typical approach of a number of Continental systems in regulating excessive or abusive renewals of fixed-term contracts of employment.[56] Finally, labour legislation and jurisprudence alike would implicitly *discourage* workers from entering in employment relationships that did not fit within the ideal-type of full-time work of undetermined duration. An example of this kind of approach could be found in the fewer legal protections and rights that workers engaged in atypical work relationships received.[57]

One should not forget the importance of labour legislation on job security. Deakin and Morris rightly assert that this stream of legislation 'gave the contract of employment a new lease of life'.[58] Indeed by reducing employers' ability to terminate the relationship at will, it further consolidated the contract of employment as the fulcrum of the employment relationship. This was also the case in those Continental experiences where extra-contractual interventions concerning terms and conditions

---

52 The first *accordo interconfederale* of 7 August 1947 followed by a number of subsequent agreements in the early 1950s introduced the idea of just cause or justified reason for dismissal.

53 Davies and Freedland, *Labour Legislation and Public Policy*, p. 36.

54 Some of these achievements were the Contracts of Employment Act 1963, the Italian *Statuto dei Lavoratori* of 1970 and the 1973 French legislation on termination of employment.

55 Cf. the German prohibitions introduced, but later scaled down, the 1972 *Arbeitnehmeruberlassungsgesetz*; the Italian ones contained in the L. n. 1369 of 1960 and the French provisions contained in Article L. 125.1 of the *Code du Travail*. See, further, the second, third and fourth sections of Chapter 4.

56 Cf. Chapter 3, second and third sections.

57 Cf. Chapter 3, second section.

58 Deakin and Morris, (2001), p. 26.

30 *The Changing Law of the Employment Relationship*

of employment were of such importance as to push the doctrine and the jurisprudence to envisage the autonomous existence of an *arbeitsverhältnis* existing even in the presence of an invalidly entered contract of employment[59] or a *relation de travail* '*née du seul fait de l'appartenance à l'entreprise*'.[60] And this is probably a difference that is worthwhile highlighting. While the *contract of subordinate employment* was the key to access the heaven of protection provided by labour law in all countries considered in this work, it is fair to say that the UK was placing a stronger emphasis on the aspect of contractuality and, crucially, of common law on contracts, whereas other European systems where more keen to underplay the 'contractual' aspects of the relationship whenever it was clearly a 'dependent employment' one. As emphasised by Ewing, 'in some other European systems, ... the role of contractual concepts has been a more marginal one'.[61] The next chapters, and particularly the second section of Chapter 2, highlight how these differences concretely affected the position of workers in relation to their ability to access statutory protection, particularly with respect to intermittent and atypical working patterns.

To sum up, it could be said that a number of phenomena, such as changes in the structure of industrial production, the emergence of a more self-conscious *class* of industrial workers, the influence of collective bargaining, the rise of the welfare state and social legislation, contributed to the establishment of the contract of employment as the central organising idea both for positive law and in the theoretical discourse. By the second half of the 20th century, that 'binary divide'[62] between employees and the self-employed, to which modern labour lawyers have been accustomed, was firmly emerging in legislation and legal reasoning. To use Deakin's words, 'the contract of employment was the result of these parallel processes, in the political and economic spheres, which at this time tended towards the standardization and stabilisation of the employment relationship'.[63] This chapter now returns to explore in greater detail the elements that came to shape the notion of the *standardised* dependent and contractual employment relationship; that is to say, the elements of *personal subordination* in the performance of work, *continuity* and *full* and *rigid working time* and *bilaterality*.

Personal (functional) subordination in the performance of work

Subordination is *the* distinguishing feature of the 20th century contract of employment, expressing both the sociological and the legal aspects of dependent labour. At a conceptual level it emerged alongside the transition from *status* to contract to make sure that the use of labour energies within the factory system was still subject to

---

59   M. Weiss, *European Employment and Industrial Relations Glossary: Germany* (London, 1992) pp. 50, 144.

60   J. Pélissier, A. Supiot and A. Jeammaud, *Droit du Travail*, p. 142.

61   K.D. Ewing, *Working Life – A New Perspective on Labour Law* (Lawrence & Wishart, London, 1996), p. 44.

62   M. Freedland, 'The Role of the Contract of Employment in Modern Labour Law', in L. Betten (ed.), *The Employment Contract in Transforming Labour Relations* (Kluwer, Deventer, 1995), p. 17.

63   Deakin, *The Contract of Employment: A Study in Legal Evolution*, p. 2.

considerable managerial control.[64] In fact the notions of contract of employment and subordination are almost inextricably linked to each other. 'The main impetus for [the] adoption [of the notion of *contrat du travail*] was an argument by employers in larger enterprises that the general duty of obedience should be read into all industrial hirings'.[65] Throughout the 20th century the concept of subordination went through a number of mutations elaborated by courts and doctrine and aimed at including an increasing number of categories of workers other than the manual worker of the early years of industrialisation. Subordination could also easily describe the employment relationship outside secondary industry, particularly in all bureaucratic structures such as those of public administration and public services characterised by high levels of vertical, hierarchical control and internal labour markets. This process of progressively embracing new categories of workers other than the typical manual worker also occurred through a constant rethinking and reworking of the constitutive elements of subordination carried out mainly by courts in the form of judicial tests for distinguishing dependent employment relationships from self-employment.

Unsurprisingly, the first tests used to determine dependant employment have the hallmarks of a master-servant type of employment relationship that, similar to the ones that later emerged within the factory system, was characterised by particularly high degrees of personal subordination. Hence the British *control* test as first developed in *Yewens* v *Noakes* is a paradigmatic example of a legal test coined in a work context with high levels of functional but also personal subordination. In this case the 'servant' was described as 'a person who is subject to the command of his master as to the manner in which he shall do his work'.[66] And it is not a coincidence that in the UK, as seen in the previous section, the 'servant' category of the late 19th century was much narrower than the modern notions of the 'employee' or wage-earner (as opposed to the self-employed) and that, in the case in question, it was concluded that a salaried clerk 'is not in the position of a servant' any more than 'the manager of a bank, a foreman with high wages, persons almost in the position of a gentlemen'.[67]

The first elaborations of the notion of subordination made by the Italian *probiviri* also display a similarly *strong* notion of direct and personal control. Subordination was 'understood as subjection' of the worker 'to the direction or control' of the employer and this 'situation of dependency was, from the jurisprudence itself, linked not so much to the existence of the factory organization understood as a datum external to the contract of employment, but actually to the availability' of the labour resources of the worker.[68] These first versions of the 'control test' still bear some traces of the notion of status, albeit being obviously developed in an industrialised, or at least rapidly industrialising, context. The idea of constant and permanent control seems, consciously or not, tailored to the relationship between the master and the domestic or household servant.

---

64 A. Fox, *Beyond Contract: Work, Power and Trust Relations* (Faber, London, 1974).

65 S. Deakin, *The Comparative Evolution of the Employment Relationship*, p. 10.

66 *Yewens* v *Noakes* (1880) 6 QBD 530, 532, 533.

67 Ibid., 538.

68 E. Ghera, *Diritto del Lavoro* (Cacucci, Bari, 2002), p. 57.

32 *The Changing Law of the Employment Relationship*

Supiot acutely stigmatises the fact that the earlier German approaches to the notion of subordination were equally concerned with the insertion of novel forms of status into the employment contract.

> Thus in the definition itself of the contract of employment, the personal element of the employment relationship finds itself integrated, by means of the notion of personal subordination (*persönliche Abhängigkeit*) that thus distinguishes itself from the French notion of juridical subordination. To this idea of personal subordination are attached notions such as that of the duty of fidelity (*Treuepflicht*) of the salaried worker, and that, which is reciprocal, of the duty of assistance (*Fürsorgepflicht*) that burdens the employer.[69]

It is possible to hear in these words the not so distant echo of the communitarian doctrinal approaches typical of the earlier German legal scholarship, echoes that were quick to spread to Italy in the early decades of the 20th century.[70]

But despite these similarities, the Italian doctrine (and Civil Code) had no doubts about the unitary and contractual nature of both manual and clerical work. Ludovico Barassi could clearly see by 1901 a series of crucial similarities between '*l'operaio [e] il direttore di banca*'. 'The one and the other do not aim to a determined result, but merely to a supply of their labour resources for those ends to which, *the control and surveillance* of the factory proprietor or the board of directors of the bank intends to direct them'.[71] As Kahn-Freund[72] acutely pointed out, the British version of control postulated a 'combination of managerial and technical functions in the person of the employer', which was clearly not in tune with the organisational paradigms being developed by the emerging vertically integrated Fordist enterprises. A far more realistic picture was that of control as the employer's 'right to supervise, direct and chose the *means of work*'[73] rather than the work itself, with the worker performing his work '*sous la direction, la surveillance et l'autorité*'[74] of the employer, something that would later be described as control 'over the work' and embodied in a sort of second-generation control test best expressed as 'the power of deciding the thing to be done, the means to be employed in doing it, the time when and the place where it shall be done'.[75]

It was progressively becoming clear that in the modern factory system control could be exercised either directly by the employer–factory proprietor or, more realistically, indirectly through the organisation and institutional arrangements set up by the latter and in which the worker and her labour were integrated. These considerations, coupled with the progressive numerical increase and diversification

---

69 Supiot, *Critique du Droit du Travail*, p. 29.

70 Ibid., pp. 18–19.

71 L. Barassi, *Il contratto di lavoro nel diritto positivo Italiano* (Società Editrice Libraia, Milano, 1901), p. 29. My translation, emphasis original.

72 O Kahn-Freund 'Servants and Independent Contractors', *MLR* (1951): 505. And also Lord Parker CJ in *Morren* v *Swinton and Pedelebury Borough Council* [1965] 1 WLR 576, 582.

73 Barassi, *Il contratto di lavoro*, p. 34. Emphasis added.

74 Arrêt *Bartdou*, Civ., 6 juil. 1931, *D.P.* 1931. 1. 121.

75 *Ready Mixed Concrete (South East) LTD* v *Minister for Pensions and National Insurance* [1968] 2 QB 497, 515.

The Employment Relationship and the Contract of Employment 33

of the working class, triggered a number of expansive constructions of the notion of dependency and subordination that in some quarters, close to the Weimar Republic, went as far as to develop concepts such as 'economic dependency'.[76] While declining this option, the French Court de Cassation declared that the 'duties applying to a doctor as a consequence of the contract linking him to the owner of a sanatorium …, made the dependency of the former towards the latter apparent, even if he maintained "a full professional independence in the exercise of his art"'.[77] This reasoning would have later been labelled as the test of '*intégration de l'intéresseé dans la structure d'un service ou d'une entreprise*',[78] or 'integration test'[79] in the UK. Doctors employed by hospitals, journalists working for newspapers, managers and professional workers employed in companies and corporations throughout Europe, owe their employee status to this test developed all over Europe in the first decades of the 20th century.

The integration test had been introduced to stress the relevance of business organisation as a system for the rational combination of factors of production. And just as owning and organising, directly or indirectly, the factors of production within a business was seen as peculiar to the employer's position, so it is typical of the worker to own, control and provide exclusively, or predominantly, his labour. '*Par là s'affirme la dépendance du travailleur en économie capitaliste vis-à-vis d'un chef d'entreprise détenteur des moyens de production*'.[80] This was already clear by the end of the 19th century, at least for authors such as Philip Lotmar and Lodovico Barassi,[81] and it became one of the pivotal distinguishing elements for the British test of 'economic reality'.[82] The latter test also aimed at highlighting which party was taking the ultimate risk of loss or chance of profit and deciding from that upon the status of the worker,[83] as highlighted by Otto Kahn-Freund.[84]

Another index soon to emerge from the same discourse would be the 'personal performance of work', that is to say whether the employee had to perform the

---

76 This idea is commonly associated to Weimarian doctrine and Sinzheimer, though it was probably a concept already present in Lotmar's work. Cf. L. Gaeta, 'Ludovico Barassi, Philip Lotmar e la Cultura Giuridica Tedesca', *GDLRI* (2001): 180. In France the idea was supported for some time by authors such as Cuche, Savatier and Rouast. See A. Jeammaud, 'L'avenir sauvegardé de la qualification de contrat de travail. A' propos de l'arrêt *Labanne*', *DS* (2001): 232.

77 Jeammaud, 'L'avenir sauvegardé', 232. Civ., 25 juil. 1938, *D.H.* 1938 350.

78 G.H. Camerlynck, *Le Contrat de Travail* (Dalloz, Paris, 1982), p. 76.

79 *Stevenson, Jordan & Harrison* v *MacDonald & Evans* [1952] 1 TLR 101, 11 (Denning LJ).

80 Camerlynck, *Le Contrat de Travail*, p. 72.

81 L Gaeta 'Lodovico Barassi, Philipp Lotmar e la cultura giuridica tedesca' *GDLRI* (2001) 90 GDLRI 176.

82 Deakin and Morris, p. 160. *Montreal* v *Montreal Locomotive Works Ltd* [1947] 1 DLR 161, 169 (Wright LJ).

83 *Market Investigations Ltd* v *Minister of Social Security* [1969] 2 QB 173.

84 O. Kahn-Freund, 'A Note on Status and Contract in Modern Labour Law', *MLR* (1967): 635–644.

34 *The Changing Law of the Employment Relationship*

work assigned personally or whether he could 'hire his own helpers',[85] an element of subordination of such importance as to become the preferred yardstick of Italian legislation and jurisprudence on home-workers.[86] Similarly in the United Kingdom 'personal performance' became a salient defining element of the contract of employment. In fact the existence of an element of discretion on the part of a working person to provide work or service through a substitute has been seen as incompatible with the notion of contract of employment,[87] and even with the status of 'worker',[88] and an index of self-employment.

Continuity, full and rigid working time

The *legal* notion of standard employment relationship emerging by the early 20th century was soon characterised by the elements of continuity and full and fixed working time. As this section points out, these elements of stability were to some extent a legal construction but at least in part they were also determined by some underlying changes in the *factual* notion of employment relationship within the factory system. Coase highlighted the advantages for the entrepreneur in hiring his workforce under a stable, in the sense of long-term, employment relationship. In his famous article *The Nature of the Firm*[89] he argued that it 'may be desired to make a long-term contract for the supply of some article or service. This may be due to the fact that if one contract is made for a longer period, instead of several shorter ones, then certain costs of making each contract will be avoided'.[90] Another clear advantage of the long-term employment relationship was that 'the service which is being provided is expressed in general terms, the exact details being left until a later date. All that is stated in the contract is that the *limits* to what the person supply the commodity or service is expected to do'.[91] The link between the firm and the long term employment contract was so obvious to the author that he claimed that 'a firm is likely ... to emerge in those cases where a very short term contract would be unsatisfactory. It is obviously of more importance in the case of services – labour – than it is in the case of the buying of commodities'.[92] As stressed by Marsden, the 'other side of the coin [was] that workers [would] contract to supply labour services of a certain kind in the future, and thereby gain continuity of employment'.[93] Admittedly a long-term employment relationship also carried a number of risks for

---

85   *Market Investigations Ltd* v *Minister of Social Security* [1969] 2 QB 173, 185 (Cooke J).

86   See both L. 13 marzo 1958 n. 264 and L. 18 dicembre 1973 n 877 Art. 1.

87   *Express & Echo Publications Ltd* v *Tanton* [1999] IRLR 367; *Staffordshire Snetinel Newspaper Ltd* v *Potter* [2004] IRLR 752; *Lanksford* v *Business Post Ltd* [2004] EWCA Civ. 1448.

88   See the use of *Tanton* made in *Commissioners of Inland Revenue* v *Post Office Ltd* [2003] IRLR 199.

89   R.H. Coase 'The Nature of the Firm', *Economica* (1937): 386.

90   Ibid., 391.

91   Ibid., 392. Emphasis added.

92   Ibid., 392.

93   D. Mardsen, *A Theory of Employment Systems* (OUP, Oxford, 1999), p. 27.

The Employment Relationship and the Contract of Employment   35

employees potentially subject to their bosses' opportunistic behaviour,[94] but certainly the 'frequent interruptions in earnings'[95] so typical of labour subcontracting, were progressively becoming a reminiscence of the past.

Having stressed the relevance of the industrial firm in decasualising working patterns, it is also important to acknowledge that continuity in employment first emerged as a distinct aspect of the salaried employees' employment relationship in the early years of the 20th century, and that only later did it also became a common trait of manual work and dependent work in general. As seen in the previous paragraphs, 19th century Continental debates, by stressing the similarities in the mode of provision of labour (that is, subordination), could already argue in favour of the *contractual* nature of both manual and clerical employment relationships.[96] But at the same time, the legal regulation of the two working categories was inevitably sliding towards differentiated protection. Late 19th century Italian legislators, and the same could be said for the contemporary German ones, had a clear political goal in their minds: affording more rights to salaried employees, as opposed to manual workers, in an attempt to introduce some social distinctions within the working class itself.[97] Even the Weimarian promise of a 'unified labour law'[98] would have been flouted by conservative opposition[99] backing this political goal. The Italian legislator of 1924 formally introduced the category of *impiegato* (white-collar employee) among the dependent workers of the enterprise system.[100] The *impiegato* definition excluded workers whose activity consisted solely of manual work.[101] In the same period a similar process took place in Germany with the 1924 White-Collar Workers' Social Insurance Act introducing the *angestellter* category[102] and 'the distinction between the legal rights and obligations of manual workers, salaried employees and civil servants was carried over from Imperial Germany into the Weimar system'.[103]

The typical feature of the *impiegato* employment relationship was cooperation (*collaborazione*), rather than control, and it is arguably accurate to say that it is precisely in relation to salaried employees or, in French, *collaborateurs*[104] – rather

---

94   On this important qualification of institutionalist theories, cf. Marsden, *A Theory of Employment Systems*.

95   Mardsen, *A Theory of Employment Systems*, p. 26.

96   As early as 1898 French legislation on work accidents of '*ouvriers et employés*' made protection exclusively affordable to '*salariés lies par un contrat de travail caractérisé par un lien de subordination*'. P. Pigassou, 'L'évolution du lien de subordination en droit du travail et de la Sécurité sociale', *DS* (1982): 578.

97   A. Garilli, 'Il contratto di lavoro e il rapporto di impiego privato nella teoria di Lodovico Barassi', *RGL* (2001): 385.

98   Article 157 of the Weimar Constitution.

99   R. Lewis and J. Clark, *Labour Law and Politics in the Weimar Republic – Otto Kahn-Freund* (Blackwell, Oxford, 1981), pp. 33–34.

100 R.D.L. n. 1825.

101 Ibid., Article 1.

102 M. Weiss and M. Schmidt, *Labour Law and Industrial Relations in Germany* (Kluwer, The Hague, 2000), pp. 47–48.

103 Lewis and Clark, *Labour Law and Politics in the Weimar Republic*, p. 33.

104 Pélissier, Supiot and Jeammaud, *Droit du Travail*, pp. 208–209.

36 *The Changing Law of the Employment Relationship*

than manual workers – that some typical elements of the so called *standard* employment relationship – such as *continuity* and *long-term employment* – were first given a legal basis, both in Germany[105] and Italy.[106] From a doctrinal point of view it had long been argued that an employee is he 'who commits his work in a continuous and permanent manner'. [107]

> The nature of the ideologies desired by the ruling powers is shown clearly by the special legal norms established to cover the contract of employment of salaried employees; continued payment of salary in case of illness, and long, excessively long notice of dismissal, embodied the principle that the salaried employee does not receive payment for his work, but a kind of claim to a livelihood in return for subordinating his labour power.[108]

But on the other hand one can identify the origin of continuity partly in industrial employment, even if in relation to clerical staff rather than blue collars; it is clear that the German and Italian legislators of the 1920s, when stressing the element of collaboration, had in the back of their minds precisely the employee of an industrial enterprise because the 'selective function [of collaboration] operates only in manufacturing where the division between organizational labour and production labour is clear-cut',[109] far more obviously than in the employment relationship in services and commercial businesses. Most importantly, after World War II the different treatment of white-collar and blue-collar workers underwent a steady and uninterrupted convergence process where most of the typical features of salaried clerical work (security, continuity, monthly payment) progressively extended to all categories of workers. In that sense, the Italian Republican Constitution, and the jurisprudence of the Constitutional Court,[110] had the same unifying effects as those of the of British post-war welfare state, and a further unification was achieved through the activities of trade unions, collective bargaining[111] and legislation,[112] with 'job-security' statutes addressing workers and employees independently of their manual rather than intellectual job descriptions.

With the introduction of this type of labour statutes, continuity and stability in employment became a common feature in most kind of jobs. In this respect the interplay between the underlying dynamics of the system of production, such as the relevance of internal labour markets and legal arrangements, established a new

---

105 Lewis and Clark, *Labour Law and Politics in the Weimar Republic*, p. 166.

106 Garilli, 'Il contratto di lavoro e il rapporto di impiego privato', pp. 375, 384.

107 Barassi in Garilli, 'Il contratto di lavoro e il rapporto di impiego privato', p. 384.

108 Lewis and Clark, *Labour Law and Politics in the Weimar Republic*, p. 166.

109 Garilli, 'Il contratto di lavoro e il rapporto di impiego privato', p. 386.

110The principle that 'a [discriminatory] discipline with regard to situations and needs common to workers of both categories' is not allowed was introduced. See C. cost. 20 maggio 1976 n. 117 in *Mass. Giur. Lav.*, 1976, p. 672.

111 Ghera, *Diritto del Lavoro*, p. 187.

112 Cf. M. Rodriguez-Pinero and B. Ferrer, *Individual Dismissal in the Member States of the European Community: The Advantages and Difficulty of Community Action* (Report for the Commission of the EC, DGV V/5767/93 EN). Also B. Hepple, 'European Rules on Dismissal Law' *CLLJ* (1997): 204.

paradigm. Statute and collective bargaining stabilised the dependent working patterns achieving what Otto Kahn-Freund defined 'decasualisation'.[113] Decasualisation was a legislative practice in Continental European systems too, where 'the protective intervention of the legislator has traditionally pursued the objective of protecting the worker's interest in continuity and stability of employment, by dictating a discipline aimed at restricting the contractual freedom of parties in the formation and execution of the contract'.[114]

In Germany this legal process of decasualisation went through two different phases. As Weiss and Schmidt recall[115] initially, during the Weimar era, courts 'continuously developed limitations upon a contract for a definite period. The reason for court intervention was the development of protective Acts against dismissals', but as the 'courts prohibited contracts for a definite duration if they were concluded to circumvent the rules against fair dismissal' and as 'the focus was on the employer's intention' in practice, given the difficulty to prove the intention of the employer, these contracts were 'in general still legal and only exceptionally illegal'. In a second phase, 'this relationship between rule and exception' was reversed. The German labour courts

> no longer focused on the employer's intention, instead searching for objective criteria to control the danger of circumvention of dismissal protection more easily .... A contract for a definite period is lawful only on condition that there is a reason justifying the time limit. During the 1970s and the 1980s the Federal Labour Court, by raising the conditions for a 'justifying reason', tended to limit this exception more and more.[116]

Typically the employer's concerns about the economic future of his business were not accepted as justifying reasons and in practice the only reason that was consistently accepted was the employee's wish to limit the duration of the contract. Just as in Germany, other European countries – as will be shown in the following section of this chapter and in Chapter 3 – witnessed the adoption in the 1950s, 1960s and early 1970s of some extremely tight legislation and jurisprudence restricting the use of 'atypical' work relationships such as part-time, fixed-term and temporary agency work, generally perceived as excessively detrimental to the interest in job-security of workers, if not also assumed to be implicitly fraudulent. Under these circumstances, a very specific and, in a way, narrow notion of continuity and regularity – continuity as non-casual and regular work – became so closely associated to subordinate work as to '*présumer la subordination*',[117] that is to say, to create a presumption of subordination, thus becoming a benchmark of dependent labour.

---

113 O. Kahn-Freund, 'Status and Contract in Labour Law' *MLR* (1967): 642.

114 Ghera, *Diritto del Lavoro*, p. 609.

115 Weiss and Schmidt, *Labour Law and Industrial Relations in Germany*, p. 51.

116 Ibid.

117 Soc. 29 juin 1977, D. 1977, I.R. 359. Pélissier, Supiot and Jeammaud, *Droit du Travail*, p. 155.

Bilaterality

Prima facie, bilaterality could appear as a natural element of any employment relationship as, from an economic point of view, employment involves the synallagmatic exchange between labour and salary for the mutual satisfaction of a worker and her employer. But in a more profound sense even this apparent simplicity emerges as one of the many abstractions of the legal mind manifested in 20th century labour law. As the present section is about to argue, the element of bilaterality was at least in part instigated by the legal systems of workers' protection, to make sure that at any given time a worker engaged in a dependent employment relationship could always identify the subject against which she could exercise the legal rights deriving from labour protection legislation and collective bargaining.

This goal was achieved in several ways and undoubtedly the highly integrated system of production, exemplified by what is widely known as the mass production system, played a major role. Most European systems of labour law introduced a number of restrictions upon the practice of *intermediation* in the employment contract, that is to say to the presence of another party between the person who profits from the work activity and the worker. Italy adopted a very principled stance in this regard, introducing in 1960 public law restrictions[118] (so called *legislazione antifraudolenta*) on the parties' contractual freedom to establish the types of non-typical employment relationship and establishing a general 'prohibition of intermediation and interposition in the supply of work'.[119] Other Continental systems followed more or less along the same lines[120] laying down a number of general prohibitions on intermediation and the hiring out of labour 'considered to be incompatible with the [public] monopoly in the area of labour exchange'.[121] These prohibitions constituted the dogmatic background against which successive 'deregulatory' legislation was to carve out, from the 1970s onwards, areas of specific exceptions from the general rule mainly linked to what in Chapter 3 is described as 'temporary agency work'.

In striking contrast with the Continental experience, in Britain the hiring out of workers for profit was never prohibited, in line with an absence of anything such as a state monopoly in the recruitment of labour.[122] Furthermore whilst, from the 1970s onwards, Continental legislation progressively allowed agencies to hire out temporary workers, British private employment services have traditionally handled both recruitment of temporary workers and permanent recruitment of full-time or part-time staff. Moreover, the British legislative vacuum stimulated a large number of typologies of triangular working relationships, often to the detriment of the worker who, as will be seen in Chapter 3, was unable to identify either his employment

---

118 With L. 23 ottobre 1960, n. 1369.

119 Gazz. Uff. 25 novembre 1960 n. 289.

120 Cf. Article L. 125.1 and 125.3 of the French Labour Code.

121 M. Weiss, in R. Blanpain (ed.), 'Private Employment Agencies', *Bulletin of Comparative Labour Relations* (1999): 255.

122 Other than in war-time. Cf. Regulation 8(B) of the Defence of the Realm Act 1915 in World War I and Control of Employment Act 1939 during World War II. See D. Brodie, *A History of British Labour Law* (Hart, Oxford, 2003), pp. 127, 223.

status or his employer or both. Indeed, while normally an agency worker would have a 'contract of some kind with the agency'[123] or intermediary, sometimes that contract would have not been a contract of service.[124] In 1970 the Queen's Bench Division of the High Court said that 'where A contracts with B to render services exclusively to C, the contract is not a contract for services (or of service) but a contract *sui generis*, a different type of contract from either of the familiar two'.[125] Whatever that *sui generis* contract was, it would not allow the worker to be considered an employee and either of the two other parties his employer, in practice disentitling the worker from statutory labour law protection. The fact that agency workers, depending on the totality of the terms upon which they make themselves available for work, can sometimes be considered as employees of the agency[126] merely proves that, in the area of trilateral relationships, legal certainty can often be at risk.

In practice it could be said that *bilaterality* was indeed a feature of the standard model of employment relationship, although that implied different things in Britain and in the rest of Europe. While in the Continental experience bilaterality was a natural, albeit legal, constitutive element of the employment relationship, with legislation prohibiting trilateral relationships with an intermediary between worker and employer, in the UK bilaterality became an implicit *requirement* for workers to be able to obtain a clear and uncontested 'employee' status, in practice restricting entitlement to statutory employment rights. This represented a striking difference with the position of, say, an Italian worker involved in an illicit trilateral relationship, who would have seen his relationship with the intermediary annulled and his relationship with the user automatically converted into a standard subordinated employment relationship.[127] On the other hand, industrialisation and mass production were in a way compressing the quantitative relevance, if not the qualitative heterogeneity, of the trilateral work relationship, and this was arguably the case both in the UK and in the rest of Europe. But by the same token, as the next section will try to highlight, the issue was soon to attain a new and unprecedented relevance with the progressive change of the political, social and regulatory climate that had hitherto supported the unitary notion of contract of employment.

4. The breakdown of the employment relationship

The previous sections explored the changes that led to the birth and emergence of the modern binary legal concept of the employment relationship and the unitary notion of the contract of employment. The analysis highlighted how its birth was deeply intertwined with the economic and political phenomena taking place in the period of the so-called industrial revolution and the nexus existing between these changes and the emergence of a contractual approach. But it was also shown how, in its

---

123 Deakin and Morris, *Labour Law*, p. 176.

124 *O'Sullivan* v *Thompson-Coon* (1972) 14 KIR 108.

125 *Construction Industry Training Board* v *Labour Force Ltd* (1970) 3 All ER 220, 225.

126 *McMeechan* v *Secretary of State for Employment* [1995] ICR 444.

127 Article 1, co. 5, L. n. 1369 of 1960.

40 *The Changing Law of the Employment Relationship*

earlier stages of development, the employment relationship struggled to detach itself from the concept of *status*, and how this evolution took place at a different pace in each European country under examination. A more evident convergence towards the (ideal) typical binary model of employment relationship based on the unitary notion of contract of employment only took place towards the mid-20th century partly as the result of the egalitarian pressures of modern social legislation and partly as a consequence of the pervasiveness of highly integrated industrial mass-production. But even if this notion of employment relationship was consistently characterised by the elements of *personal subordination, continuity* and fixed working time and *bilaterality*, a number of significant differences were unequivocally maintained in each national system.

In recent years the doctrine has correctly pointed out that, to a great extent, this ideal-typical notion of dependent employment relationship was – just like the unitary concept of contract of employment – by and large an artificial effect produced by implicit or explicit political choices necessitated by and reflected in labour legislation and collective bargaining, certainly until the 1970s.

> There is a temptation to question, in retrospect, the soundness of this position … and to suggest that this unitary concept of the law of the contract of employment represented a false unity by that stage, perhaps even from the outset. That suggestion would amount to the view that the postulated evolution of a single standard pattern for the dependent employment relationship was never fully realised, so that the expounding of the law of the contract of employment on that assumption amounted to papering over the cracks between different types of dependent employment relationship.[128]

As Lyon-Caen put it, '*quoiqu'on dise, il y a jamais eu de modèle juridique unique. Mais la diversité ne recevait pas d'encouragement public et elle rencontrait des bornes, notamment dans celles que les juges puisaient dans des règles générales*'.[129]

The previous sections of the chapter highlighted how these 'unifying' goals were pursued through legislative and judicial activity. In the last thirty years or so, western industrialised economies started undergoing a number of deep, some may say structural,[130] changes in their arrangements for production and industrial organisation, in the modes of acquisition of the labour resources necessary to the economic system and in the attitude of organised interests and the state towards the management and regulation of industrial relations. These evolutions have taken place along with other fundamental transformations such as changes in the household and the growing access of women to employment, technical changes and the development of information technology, the abandonment of Keynesian macroeconomic policies exemplified by the demise of the Bretton-Woods institutional arrangements, the establishment of

---

128 M. Freedland, *The Personal Employment Contract* (Oxford, 2003), p. 17.

129 A. Lyon-Caen, 'Actualité du contrat de travail', *DS* (1988): 541. Translation: 'Whatever one says there has never been a single legal model. But diversity did not receive public encouragement and it encountered some limits, notably in what judges enshrined in general rules'.

130 M. Piore and C. Sabel, *The Second Industrial Divide: Possibilities for Prosperity* (Basic Books, New York, 1984), p. 4.

The Employment Relationship and the Contract of Employment 41

neo-liberal macroeconomic and financial policies constraining public expenditure, cyclical periods of economic recession and the rise in unemployment.

Undeniably, by the mid-1970s, the traditional legal shape of the employment relationship was increasingly being placed under strain by a number of changes in the political, economic and social environment. It is argued by some that the progressive deindustrialisation[131] of western economies and the growth of the service sector caused, among the other things, a slow but steady contraction of the number and political influence of blue-collar workers and a parallel expansion of sectors where casual employment had *always* been common.[132] Employers also started exploring and adopting new and less integrated models of flexible industrial organisation and human resource management.[133] According to Atkinson,[134] the processes of industrial transformation linked to the appearance of the flexible firm produced the emergence of a two-tier workforce. 'Numerical flexibility' and 'distancing', both catering for the need to increase and reduce labour in such a way as to match demand fluctuations in the market, created an expanded 'peripheral' workforce, characterised by employment insecurity and external contracting, whilst 'functional flexibility', the firm's ability to reorganise jobs through a secure pool of skills that can quickly adapt to technological changes, was sought from a permanently employed 'core' workforce. The validity of these theories has sometimes been questioned, and it is often argued that the rising new 'varieties' of more flexible industrial organisation have not replaced mass production as such,[135] while some authors even cast doubts on the 'utility of the mass production/flexible specialisation dichotomy itself'[136] fearing that it could be 'premised on technical determinism ... because its promoters have invested particular combinations of labour and capital [and] particular production or technological systems with a completeness or totality which does not mirror the ongoing production diversity within capitalism as a whole'.[137]

In any case, the present work does not seek to explore the validity of these theories nor the extent of the impact of these phenomena on working arrangements. Even without going through some inevitably complex factual and economic investigations, it seems sufficiently evident that – for whatever reason – employers have in the past few decades progressively started to modify and diversify the legal terms under which they acquire their labour resources. These legal terms were not necessarily those representing the traditional notion of the employment relationship based on the

---

131 R. Rowthorn and R. Ramaswamy, *Deindustrialization – Its Causes and Implications* (IMF Publications Services, Washington, 1997).

132 T. Walsh, 'Flexible Employment in the Retail and Hotel Trades' in A. Pollert, *Farewell to Flexibility?* (Blackwell, Oxford, 1991), p. 104. J. Atkinson, 'Flexibility or Fragmentation? The UK Labour Market in the Eighties', *Labour and Society* (1987): 87

133 See A. Amin, *Post-Fordism: a Reader* (Blackwell, Oxford, 1994).

134 J. Atkinson, 'Flexibility or Fragmentation?', p. 87.

135 B. Coriat, 'Technical Flexibility and Mass Production', in G. Benk and M. Dunford (eds), *Industrial Change and Regional Development* (Belhaven, London, 1991), p. 150.

136 J. Tomaney, 'New Work Organization and Technology', in A. Amin (ed.), *Post-Fordism: A Reader* (Blackwell, Oxford, 1994), p. 164.

137 C. Smith, 'From Automation to Flexible Specialization', in A. Pollert, *Farewell to Flexibility?* (Blackwell, Oxford, 1991), p. 155.

contract of employment. It also seems evident that more and more workers – again, for whatever reason – have been willing to accept these new terms under which they had to provide their labour. Having said that, what this book seeks to analyse and understand, from a legal perspective, is the stance of labour legislation towards these changes in the legal terms shaping the demand and supply of labour, the effect of these changes on the traditional scope of the employment relationship and of labour legislation, and the measures adopted at a national and supranational level to tackle the problems deriving from these changes.

Therefore the next few paragraphs will only cursorily refer to some of these phenomena, as reported by literature, while discussing and analysing the transformations that the *legal* notion of employment relationship has sustained over the last few decades, with the caveat that a fuller discussion of the factual changes of the employment relationship would go beyond the scope and means of the present work. What is within the scope of this book is, firstly, the discussion of the various approaches that law could have taken in regulating the tensions deriving from the progressive diversification of the modes by which employers acquire and manage their labour resources and, secondly, the effect of the concrete regulatory options on the scope and taxonomy of the employment relationship.

Regulatory and deregulatory approaches

Whether actual or merely perceived, the economic, social and technological transformations discussed above were clearly creating an ideal environment for justifying regulatory intervention aimed at relaxing the statutory and judicial arrangements supporting the existence of a unitary or standard notion of the contract of employment. Furthermore, economic pressures and rising neo-liberal political ideologies were colluding to promote and accelerate the decline of the traditional employment relationship. Davies and Freedland have disentangled and clarified the exact role of rising Monetarism in restructuring the British labour economy.[138] But if Britain was undeniably the European country where the epitaph of the labour legislation and industrial relations of the industrial mass-production era was first spelled out, other countries were no less affected by the precursors of the very same dynamics. At a national level, by the late 1970s and early 1980s, unemployment was hitting hard all over Europe. This was aggravating social conflict and unrest while at the same time weakening the bargaining position of trade-union movements. In Italy the so called 'Forty thousand' Fiat white-collar workers' rally[139] became the symbol of the decline of the labour movement and, in a way, of the hostility of middle classes towards a system of labour law largely perceived, rightly or not, as *droit ouvrier*. If in Britain the Thatcher Governments were abolishing Fair Wage Standards[140] and curbing the power of unions, in Italy workers were seeing the

---

138 Davies and Freedland, *Labour Legislation and Public Policy*, mainly Chapters 9 and 10.

139 Taking place on 14 October 1980 and *de facto* ending a long struggle of blue-collar workers against a number of planned redundancies.

140 Davis and Freedland, *Labour Legislation and Public Policy*, p. 539.

scala-mobile being abolished and, roughly at the same time, some important labour reforms being introduced providing for a deregulation of the labour market under what was to become known as the '*diritto del lavoro della crisi*'.[141]

Even in Germany, a bastion of job security, in the mid-1980s the 'Federal Government initiated an Act whose underlying idea [was] that employment for a definite period is still preferable to unemployment'[142] and on 1 May 1985 the *Beschäftigungsförderungsgesetz* (Act for the Improvement of Employment Opportunities) was adopted. In France, after a first deregulatory phase in the late 1970s,[143] even the 1981 election of a socialist government and the 'euphoric'[144] adoption of the *Auroux* reforms in 1982 could not prevent the progressive 'flexibilisation' of French employment law and labour market. By the late 1980s, Antoine Lyon-Caen could comment that

> *on a vue se multiplier les formes juridiques de mise au travail, hors du contrat de travail, depuis les premiers stages en entreprise jusqu'aux stages d'initiation à la vie professionnelle, en passant par les travaux d'utilité collective ... Parallèlement à ce développement des formes de mise au travail, hors du contrat de travail, la typologies des contrats de travail s'enrichit: contrat a durée déterminée, contrat a temps partiel, contrat de travail intermittent sans oublier les contrats de travail particuliers dont la diversité s'est accrues. Dans ce mouvement, où se trouve la nouveauté? Elle ne se trouve pas dans la diversité. Quoiqu'on dise, il n'y a jamais eu de modèle juridique unique. Mais la diversité ne recevait pas d'encouragements public et elle rencontrait des bornes, notamment dans celles que les juges puisaient dans des règles générales. La nouveauté provient ainsi de la promotion de la diversité.*[145]

These words could have easily applied to all European labour law reforms during the 1980s and 1990s. As the third section of Chapter 3 will discuss in greater detail, legislators and governments alike progressively abandoned the idea of limiting the fragmentation of working patterns by marginalizing or even prohibiting specific forms of atypical work. Statutory intervention was now principally aimed at promoting an increasing diversity that had always existed – despite being 'pushed aside both by labour law ... and by social attitudes'[146] – and which, after developing in the *interstitia* of the economic system, was now emerging in managerial and political decision-making, often presented in the guise of a overriding need of the new production arrangements.

---

141 Ghera, *Diritto del Lavoro*, p. 23.

142 Weiss and Schmidt, *Labour Law and Industrial Relations in Germany*, p. 51.

143 Law on fixed-term contract of 3 January 1979, cf. special number of *DS* September–October 1980.

144 A. Mazeaud, *Droit du travail* (LGDJ Montchrestien, Paris, 2002), p. 24.

145 A. Lyon-Caen, 'Actualité du contrat de travail, brefs propos', *DS* (1988): 541.

146 Y. Kravaritou-Manitakis (ed.), *New Forms of Work – Labour Law and Social Security Aspects in the European Community* (European Foundation for the Improvement and Working Conditions, Dublin, 1988), p. 13.

Deakin and Reed[147] have clarified the fact that the term 'flexibility' has several concurring and sometimes conflicting meanings. Similarly, it could be argued that all regulatory approaches adopted in the field of atypical work have reflected the very same tensions. Legislatures were facing at least three alternative options as far as regulation of the 'atypical' phenomenon was concerned. A first option was regulatory action aimed at introducing rules upholding and enforcing the 'typical' employment relationship. A second one was, more simply, abstaining from any form of regulation, thus leaving market forces to tackle the adjustment processes of the economic base. A third more articulated option was to regulate these new forms of work in an attempt to strike a (new) balance between economic needs, social goals and the protection of some fundamental rights *or/and* to *promote*, as Lyon-Caen says, their spreading. All these approaches had a number of advantages and disadvantages and all of them, as the next two chapters will highlight, have manifested themselves in most European systems. Regulating new forms of work meant, even when the underlying intention was genuinely a protective one, legitimating them; and, in any case it seemed a Sisyphean process as 'every time law manage(d) to regulate an employment relationship, another atypical employment relationship (would come) immediately into being, frustrating the restraints envisaged by the regulations'.[148]

As for the promotional element, it often derived from the very same regulatory apparatus that in the past had been used to discourage workers from entering into atypical work relationships. As briefly shown in the previous section, this goal was often pursued through labour and social security regulation aimed at formalizing *de jure* the less favourable working conditions and legal attributions of atypical or self-employed workers *vis-à-vis* typical and subordinate ones, for instance by allowing different and less advantageous treatment in the area of pay, dismissal and social security benefits. Paradoxically, the other side of the coin of such legislation was that, in periods of rising unemployment and rapid social change, workers – often female workers – were still willing to accept fewer rights and legal protections than those afforded to employees engaged under a typical contract of employment, and employers were certainly willing to hire a cheaper or more 'numerically flexible' workforce.

The second approach, the 'abstentionist' one, was typically favoured by countries like the UK where neo-liberal and de-regulatory ideas were rapidly proliferating amid the havoc present in the labour movement. As Chapter 3 will point out, some traits of that stance are still visible today, for instance, in the very lightly regulated area of temporary agency work. But a partial or total absence of regulation was often the result of the constant mutations of atypical forms of work, with novel working patterns and legal arrangements frequently emerging outside the scope of application of pre-existing legislation. The result, in both cases, was that all forms of work that could not fit under any 'typical' description, inevitably fell into a grey

---

147 S. Deakin and H. Reed, 'The Contested Meaning of Labour Market Flexibility: Economic Theory and the Discourse of European Integration', in J. Shaw (ed.), *Social Law and Policy in an Evolving European Union* (Hart, Oxford, 2000).

148 Kravaritou-Manitakis, *New Forms of Work*, p. 23.

zone of the labour market associated either with casual and unprotected work or with self-employment.

As for the first approach, one should say that it had few followers amongst governments and managers of enterprises, at all points along the political spectrum there was a conviction that these new forms of work were a sort of inevitable result of some deeper structural economic changes. Even trade unions, whose power of resistance was anyway curbed by high levels of unemployment, were in a way conceiving their role as constrained by the fact that they had no control over the organisation of the economic base and accepting that their activity was to be confined to shaping the legal superstructure for the provision and use of labour. In any case, assuming that the underlying economic changes were a structural element of capitalism, such strategies would have only sprung into atypical forms of work proliferating outside the official labour market. As Gino Giugni put it 'one must observe that the [informal economy] reaches the highest levels in countries having fragile public structures of control but at the same time having, in the area of employment relationships, particularly intensive and expensive restrictive regulations'.[149]

The emerging legal features of the changing notion of the employment relationship

Enhanced autonomy   The most important and overarching effect of these changes taking place in human resource management strategies and the production systems with regard to all forms of the employment relationship, typical and atypical, was to render the descriptive and prescriptive function of traditional tests of *subordinate* employment less and less meaningful. The effectiveness of the 'control test', for instance, has been at best diluted and at worst destroyed. As far as traditionally subordinate employees are concerned, control appears now extremely watered down by the constant upskilling of workers, often resulting in a visible enhancement of their decision-making prerogatives, and by the many faces of 'outsourcing'. Outsourcing, in most European countries during the early 1980s, came about in two different waves. Initially outsourcing involved the disaggregation of branches of non-core activities (such as cleaning, production of semi-assembled parts, maintenance, catering and so on) sometimes in the form of transfers of parts of businesses. In this phase, collective bargaining and legislation on acquired rights and transfer of undertakings, which by the mid-1970s was already solidly established in most European countries, provided workers with some comfort in helping them to maintain their previously acquired working and economic treatment.[150]

---

149 G. Giugni, 'Aspects Juridiques de l'Économie Informelle' in *Les transformations du droit du travail – Études offertes à Gérard Lyon-Caen* (Dalloz, Paris, 1989), p. 259.

150 Cf. C. Barnard, *EC Employment Law* (Oxford, 2000), p. 456. P. Davies, 'Transfer of Undertakings' in S. Sciarra, *Labour Law in the Courts: National Judges and the European Court of Justice* (Oxford, 2001), p. 130. P. Davies, *The Relationship Between the European Court of Justice and the British Courts over the Interpretation of Directive 77/187/EC* (Working Paper No. 2, European University Institute, 1997).

46   *The Changing Law of the Employment Relationship*

The most complex problems occur when the activity is outsourced to an independent contractor and the employer is transformed into a client of the latter. Here we have what J. Atkinson described as 'distancing', a practice that 'represents the displacement of employment contracts by commercial contracts'.[151] In these cases the 'control test', in any of its traditional configurations, has no grip upon the contractual relationship of the worker. Nevertheless, under modern technological and managerial arrangements, the performance and *modus* of delivering labour resources (as opposed to the delivery of an end-product, for instance) by independent contractors can be subject to other forms of 'control' that are no less restrictive and compelling than the traditional ones. The 'client' for instance can implicitly delegate supervisory powers to third parties whose legal position is well outside the contractual relationship linking the contractor to the 'client', but who can nonetheless scrutinise the work and the services delivered and give crucial feedback to the organisation coordinating or using the activities provided.

An extreme example of such practices is the so called 'Well-Driven?' Scheme[152] whereby road users are encouraged by a flashy logo applied on the back of vans and lorries to contact a phone number and communicate their complaints and impressions over the driving abilities of the lorry driver. Later the same call-centre will take care of contacting the 'transport operator', that is, the road-haulage business owning, or as is often the case in this sector of road transport hiring, that specific lorry and its driver; and it is self-evident what the repercussion of this kind of 'control' over the 'business' relationship involving the driver and his 'client' can be. In other cases the general public may be asked if the cleaning standards of a particular airport toilet are kept at a satisfactory level by the sub-contracted cleaning company. Sometimes it will be up to consumers to assess the performance of a specific business activity, by filling in a questionnaire or ticking some boxes on a leaflet.

More frequently, control over the activity of a contractor will be exercised through electronic means of surveillance in the workplace or, more simply, by imbuing the provision of the service or work with a number of detailed guidelines that might meet some, but not all, facets of the 'control test' such as the specification of working time, or the compliance with a number of pre-set guidelines. Post-modernity, as sociologists know, is particularly inventive when it comes about conceiving systems of control and modern working activities, whether dependant or not, have a central place in this 'panopticon' structure. There are reasons to believe that, under some circumstances, these new post-modern elements of control, should also be taken into account by courts deciding on the status of a given worker, particularly when other elements such as the size of his business and the number of clients can highlight a situation of dependency from that particular client. Freedland has aptly highlighted the difficulties of some of these persons with a 'semi-dependent worker's contact' can face when caught in a vicious circle of not having a business of their own, but

---

151 J. Atkinson, 'Flexibility or Fragmentation? The UK Labour Market in the Eighties', *Labour and Society* (1987): 87.

152 http://www.fta.co.uk/services/welldriven/index.htm (15 January 2006).

The Employment Relationship and the Contract of Employment 47

not being in a position of legal subordination to, or dependence upon, another person so as to become employees, as in cases such as *Hall* v *Lorimer*.[153]

Similarly the 'integration test' has been placed under strain. Homeworking and teleworking are two other problematic facets of outsourcing and decentralisation of production as they have severed the spatial – and more visible – dimension of the 'integration test'. The traditional concept of 'integration into the business' has progressively become 'less effective in explaining the position of outworkers or workers employed by a sub-contractor of the ultimate user of labour: their work may frequently be "integral" to their business, without them necessarily being its employees'.[154] This of course is more common in countries such as Britain where there has never been a prohibition upon labour-only sub-contracting.

Though the 'personality test' seems by and large still a rather effective one, the increase of sub-contracting and outsourcing practices have also increased the chance that some degree of substitution might have to take place in the course of a given work relationship. This is particularly the case in home working practices and one of the systems imposing this requirement most stringently is Italy, where the element of substitution constitutes the dividing line between dependent and independent home workers.[155] As for the United Kingdom, the personality element has reached such levels of prescriptiveness that employers can be tempted to avoid the application of statute by inserting so called 'substitution clauses' which are conceived and designed precisely to exclude the obligation to provide personal services, and therefore any *mutuality* element, even where *de facto*, as in *Tanton*,[156] the worker never availed himself of such possibility. Not only can substitution clauses deprive a person of the employee status, but they have also been used to deprive working persons of the status of 'workers'.[157]

Intermittence and discontinuity　As seen in the previous section of this chapter, in European jurisprudence and doctrine, the temporal elements of the employment relationship – continuity of employment and the respect of a given working time – have emerged with remarkable consistency as symptomatic elements of subordination and employee status. It goes without saying that most of the new, atypical, forms of work developing in industrialised countries from the early 1970s onwards could not systematically meet these requirements being inherently temporary, intermittent and discontinuous just as were the peaks in demand that they were meant to satisfy. On the other hand it needs to be said that most systems, including the British one, did have the instruments necessary to discern between the essential and the secondary temporal aspects of the employment relationship. As Chapter 3 will point out, working time, at least in the sense of *full working* time, was one of the first temporal

---

153 [1994] ICR 218 (CA). See M. Freedland, *The Personal Employment Contact* (OUP, Oxford, 2003), pp. 29, 30–33.

154 Deakin and Morris, *Labour Law*, p. 159.

155 Cf. L. 13 marzo 1958 n. 264 and L. 18 dicembre 1973 n. 877 Article 1.

156 *Express and Echo Publications Ltd* v *Tanton* [1999] IRLR 367.

157 See the use of the *Tanton* line of reasoning made in *Commissioners of Inland Revenue* v *Post Office Ltd* [2003] IRLR 199.

aspects to be considered as not strictly essential to the attribution of statutory and collective labour rights to workers engaged in part-time employment relationships. Moreover the aspect that has posed the biggest hurdle for such attribution, has been the requirement of *continuity.*

Continuity in the UK is essential both to meet some qualifying periods for statutory protection and to establish a (contractual) employment relationship *tout court.* The latter aspect is, to some degree, also present in the Continental doctrinal and jurisprudential discourses. Before British courts and tribunals, doubts about contractual continuity have almost paradigmatically resulted in casual workers being denied employee status.[158] Here, we stress that there are two distinct notions of continuity that are relevant for the establishment of a dependent (and contractual) employment relationship, and these two notions have often been so closely juxtaposed, if not also confused, by courts and doctrines to create an overwhelming hurdle for casual intermittent workers seeking to have their employee status recognised.

It is here suggested that, on the one hand, a work relationship may be regarded as being continuous in the sense of not being casual when, as Deakin and Morris say in relation to the statutory concept of continuity, it is sufficiently *long* and *regular.*[159] In this sense continuity can be defined as a protraction and extension over time of a given labour activity, and admittedly more often than not it will be a symptomatic indication of a dependent labour relationship. But a protracted labour activity may equally well denote either a dependent employment relationship or a series of distinct contracts for services (or, for that matter, a sequence of separate contracts of service). Admittedly, in most factual situations, and for a number of reasons that will soon be explored, this type of factual continuity will be a clear indication of the presence of a dependent employment relationship, and this consideration was particularly true in the historical period that was examined in the previous section of this chapter. But, when translated into legal terms, that conception of continuity should be seen as a merely descriptive, rather than prescriptive, index of subordination and nothing more.

Continuity can also be seen as requiring (i) the availability for a specified, or unspecified, amount of time of the labour resources provided by a worker *combined with* (ii) the worker's explicit or implicit availability and *commitment* to provide these labour resources in compliance with the directions received from the employer and, *functionally* to serve the needs and aims of the enterprise, (iii) these being such as to generate a reasonable *expectation* on the employer's side that the employer can trust and rely upon the worker's future supply of labour rather than having to re-organise the system of production because of a sudden interruption in that supply. It needs to be stressed that already by the mid 1970s, the British doctrine had developed a strong legal reasoning leaning in part towards such a notion of continuity, at least in respect of typical work.

---

158 *O'Kelly* v *Trusthouse Forte* [1983] ICR 728 or *Carmichael* v *National Power plc* [1999] ICR 1226.

159 Deakin and Morris, *Labour Law,* p. 188.

The Employment Relationship and the Contract of Employment 49

In the case of the contract of employment, the exchange is of service against remuneration; but there is more to the contract than this simple exchange, because the employee undertakes an obligation to make himself available to render service, while the employer undertakes to enable the employee to earn his remuneration. ... Hence the contract has a two-tiered structure. At the first level there is an exchange of work and remuneration. At the second level there is an exchange of mutual obligations for future performance. The second level – the promises to employ and be employed – provides the arrangement with its stability and its continuity as a contract. The promises to employ and to be employed may be of short duration, or may be terminable at short notice; but they still form an integral and most important part of the structure of the contract. They are the mutual undertakings to *maintain* the employment relationship in being which are inherent in any contract of employment properly so called.[160]

This 'second level' made of 'mutual undertakings to maintain the employment relationship in being' is, arguably, very similar to the second notion of continuity discussed above. In a way, it is argued here, British courts did have the necessary material, as far as legal elaboration of logical frameworks, to adapt the concept of continuity to atypical, intermittent employment. Nonetheless[161] UK courts, with their very narrow version of 'mutuality of obligation test',[162] have consistently used this 'second level' to deny the status of dependent employee, to casual workers in intermittent relationships, focusing predominantly on the concrete, temporal elements of duration and length, as opposed to the psychological, less tangible elements of commitment and expectations.[163]

Interestingly, the same author, to whom the paternity of this version of 'mutuality' justifying the contrast between continuous contract of employment and intermittent employment relationships has been implicitly attributed, has recently stressed that

such a contrast, implied though not strongly intended in the original work, would seem to be misconceived. The two-level analysis should be regarded as applying to personal employment contracts generally and not just to contracts of employment strictly so called. Contracts of employment are rightly seen as having a relational dimension even if they are of very short duration. Semi-dependent workers' contracts are more likely to be of very short duration, but that is no reason to deny them a relational dimension.[164]

Similarly, under the notion of continuity presented in this section of the chapter *length* loses much of its decisive importance in favour of a *teleological duration* of the relationship (that is, one aimed at satisfying the productive aims of the organisation). For instance it might well be that the employer follows a practice of inserting regular gaps between one provision of labour input and the next. It might

---

160 M. Freedland, *The Contract of Employment* (OUP, Oxford, 1976), p. 20. Emphasis added.

161 Cf. Chapter 2, second section.

162 Cf. Deakin and Morris, *Labour Law*, p. 161, footnote 15.

163 Cf. *Carmichael* v *National Power Plc* [1999] ICR 1226. Also second section of Chapter 2.

164 M.R. Freedland, *The Personal Employment Contract* (OUP, Oxford, 2003), pp. 91–92.

well be that he does this for reasons genuinely inherent to his business arrangements rather than for opportunism. But the mere fact that the employer knows that he will not have to modify his business arrangements because he will always be able to count on future provisions of labour resources, provided in accordance with his business arrangements and needs, from that specific worker, should be sufficient to indicate that there is *continuity* in the employment relationship, and from there to argue that the relationship is of dependent labour rather than a sequence of contract for services.

This reasoning argues both for a 'prospective' and a 'retrospective' notion of commitment and teleological continuity. From a 'prospective' point of view, it is believed that, in many concrete situations and for a number of circumstances, 'the worker takes the risk that there will not be any job to perform', but the employer does *not* appear to take the supposedly associated risk 'of the unavailability of a worker by not offering any form of permanent employment'.[165] From this viewpoint, continuity does not depend on any length or typified notion of regularity. The acquisition of labour resources, however casual or sporadic it might appear, takes place under a spirit of trust, often enforced by labour market pressures entangled with contractual ones, whereby the employer knows that he will not have to modify, slow down or alter his system of production because he can rely on the future performance of the labour resources of the worker in an orderly manner and in functional accordance with his preset arrangements. An atypical employment relationship where this element of teleological and functional availability – completely disconnected from a continuous provision of labour resources – is particularly evident is casual on-call work. Here, even more evidently than in the examples referred above, there is between each separate 'call' a clearly discernible pressure for continuous engagement (in the form of availability fostered by contractual clauses prescribing, for instance, the deletion of the unresponsive worker from the on-call list[166]) connecting intermittent specific engagement for employment (the 'calls').

As for the 'retrospective' notion of continuity, it appears that courts should be able to consider the working person as a continuously employed employee or a continuously employed worker for the purpose of qualifying for specified statutory employment rights, where there is a clearly discernible *pattern* or *expectation* of continuous engagement that connects intermittent specific engagement for employment. As can be seen in section two of Chapter 5, in some judicial quarters – namely the European Court of Justice – a similar notion of continuous employment relationship is beginning to emerge.

Multilaterality Another aspect of these post-industrial production arrangements is what could be labelled as multilateralism, or trilateralism, in the acquisition and provision of labour resources. By these expressions we mean that, more and more often, employers in search of labour provision have recourse to private intermediaries, organised in the form of employment 'agencies', specialising in the

---

165 H. Collins, 'Employment Rights of Casual Workers', *ILJ* (2000): 73.

166 As Collins puts it, 'the real sanction is that the employer will simply not ask the worker again, which is a far more coercive sanction'. Collins, 'Employment Rights of Casual Workers', p. 77.

supply of workers to third parties. But the way these agencies operate across Europe differs substantially from country to country. Trilaterality is a *factual* but not also necessarily a *legal* feature of all new forms of work involving the presence of an employment agency. It will be argued that, of the four systems under review in this work, those of Italy, France and Germany – as opposed to the UK – have put in place a normative framework by which each type of lawful trilateral activity results in a *bilateral* employment relationship whereby it is always clear which entity is the ultimate employer of the worker involved.

Under the ILO definition these agencies can provide three distinct, but often concurrent, services:

a. services for matching offers of and applications for employment, without the private employment agency becoming a party to the employment relationships which may arise therefrom;

b. services consisting of employing workers with a view to making them available to a third party, who may be a natural or legal person (referred to below as a 'user enterprise') which assigns their tasks and supervises the execution of these tasks;

c. other services relating to jobseeking, determined by the competent authority after consulting the most representative employers and workers organizations, such as the provision of information, that do not set out to match specific offers of and applications for employment.[167]

These three rather distinct typologies of 'trilateral' relationships are characterised by the fact that the intermediary, whatever its role, is acting as a profit-seeking business.

In practice these three typologies of services are not as discernible in all systems as the wording of Convention 181 might lead the reader to assume. In systems where the practices of intermediation in the employment relationship have traditionally been regulated in a rather restrictive way, their activities are subject to extremely detailed legal parameters and administrative authorisations. In countries such as Italy and France, for instance, it is clear that any employment relationship seeing an agency involved under (a) will ultimately see the worker directly engaged by the user enterprise that will undertake all the duties competing to the employer. In Germany, to take another example, employment relationships of type (b) have traditionally seen the worker as employed under a contract of indefinite duration, whereas a fixed-term engagement is the norm in France and Italy. In any case in all Continental systems, the activities of an intermediary leave untouched the employment relationship that remains essentially bilateral so far as statutory regulation is concerned.

But in countries such as the UK where, as the second section of Chapter 3 highlights, statutory regulation of employment agencies is minimal, situations such as (b) will be rarely discernible and often confusingly coinciding with arrangements under (a) or (c). In the absence of any clear normative guidance, courts have used their traditional

---

167 ILO Convention C181, Private Employment Agencies Convention (Convention Concerning Private Employment Agencies), Geneva, 1997, Article 1.

52　　　　The Changing Law of the Employment Relationship

'tests' to establish a contract of employment between the worker and the agency *or* the user enterprise, but these tests have often provided them with contradictory and incompatible results. The consequence is that very often the worker will find herself in a contractual *limbo* whereby she will not satisfy all the tests necessary to be considered an employee of the agency, normally paying her remuneration, nor all the requirements necessary to establish a contract of employment with the user enterprise, into whose business she is visibly integrated.[168]

In part, but only in part, this confusing situation seems to be due to a sclerotised application by British courts of what in the previous section of this chapter we have called 'bilaterality'.[169] In a sense, what used to be a natural component of the mass-industrial production model of the employment relationship, has been transformed into a judicial requirement for the construction of an employment contract, and this in a new economic context where more and more working persons are in an employment relationship such that the functions of the employer are distributed between two or more persons or enterprises. Paradoxically, in the few cases where English courts have distanced themselves from enforcing this bilaterality requirement, the result has been the creation of a *sui generis* relationship not qualifying the working person either as an employee or even as a worker.[170] Continental systems, as stressed in the second section of Chapter 3, have found a way out of this problem through statutory intervention prohibiting, on the one hand, a number of intermediation activities and spelling out exactly, on the other hand, what the nature of the respective contractual relationships between the subjects engaged in a lawful trilateral arrangement is supposed to be. In Britain, in the absence of anything comparable to this kind of legislation, it now appears that 'the legal arrangements instituted as a result of these developments may also be used to evade the consequences of employment protection legislation or … legislation which seeks to give effect to fundamental legal principles in regard to the employment market'.[171]

5. The contractual dimensions of the employment relationship

The changes discussed in the previous section have undoubtedly introduced a new series of challenges to the contract of employment and to its claim of remaining the central organizing idea in the regulation of employment relationships. Fortunately, Simon Deakin reassures us that the contract of employment has already survived numerous 'conceptual crises'.[172] In fact, through its history, the contract of employment has maintained its descriptive and prescriptive relevance and has

---

168 *Montgomery* v *Johnson Underwood Ltd* [2001] IRLR 269 (CA).

169 Freedland, *The Personal Employment Contract*, pp. 40–41.

170 Cf. *Ironmonger* v *Movefield Ltd t/a Deerings Appointments* [1988] IRLR 461 (EAT).

171 Opinion of A.G. Geelhoed in Case C-256/01, *Debra Allonby* v *Accrington & Rossendale College* [2004] ECR I-00873, [45].

172 S. Deakin, *The Comparative Evolution of the Employment Relationship* (Working Paper No. 317, ESRC Centre for Business Research, University of Cambridge, December 2005), p. 1.

remained the fulcrum of the employment relationship in spite of the rise and fall of collectivism and in spite of the progressive 'juridification' of the employment relationship through statutory intervention. On the other hand the more recent changes affecting the notion of the employment relationship seem to raise different and more structural issues that, as already perceptively pointed out by Bob Hepple in the mid-1980s, may well require a progressive departure from the contractual scheme in favour of more relational approaches.[173]

The comparative analysis conducted in the following chapters will highlight the fact that the contract framework is likely to retain its conceptual relevance for some years to come.[174] What this sections points out is that there are two main types of reasons why this is likely to be the case. The first reason, and the one that will be fully developed in the course of this book, is that reforms of the present structural elements of the contract of employment are certainly *necessary* for it to remain the fulcrum of the employment relationship. The necessity of reforms would only bring into question the relevance of the contractual framework of the employment relationship if this framework did not prove itself malleable enough to absorb the necessary changes. But, as the following paragraphs argue, the contractual framework appears to have all that it takes to successfully survive the reforms it needs to survive.

Mark Roheling has convincingly argued that 'the claim that a contractual framework is no longer appropriate ... reflects a particular, classical view of what constitutes a contract. ... One's assessment of the suitability of the contractual framework for the employment relationship may depend on the theory of contract that is adopted'.[175] This author resorted to post-modern 'relational contracting theory' to explain the persisting relevance of the contract of employment model in the face of a growing juridification of the employment relationship. Similarly, Hugh Collins has made a very compelling case for the ability of the contract of employment to adapt to the changing implicit expectations produced by the changes in human resource management and the increasing demands for functional flexibility.[176] Here the author recurs to the 'symbiotic contract theory' to argue his case.

What these approaches have in common is the belief that the contractual framework can still cope with the pressures placed on it by the changing notion of the employment relationship. This is true, of course, as long as one accepts a reading of the contract that goes beyond the strict principal-agent model of classical

---

173 B.A. Hepple, 'Restructuring Employment Rights', *ILJ* (1986): 69.

174 It brings some comfort to see that the majority of the academic world appears to share this view. See P. Davies and M. Freedland, 'Changing Perspectives Upon the Employment Relationship in British Labour Law', in C. Barnard, S. Deakin and G. Morris, *The Future of Labour Law – Liber Amicorum Sir Bob Hepple* (Hart, Oxford, 2004), p. 129; S. Deakin, *The Comparative Evolution of the Employment Relationship* (Working Paper No 317, ESRC Centre for Business Research, University of Cambridge, December 2005).

175 M.V. Roheling ,'Legal Theory: Contemporary Contract Law Perspectives and Insights for Employment Relationship Theory' in J.A.-M. Coyle Shapiro, L.M. Shore, M.S. Taylor and L.E. Tetrick (eds), *The Employment Relationship – Examining Psychological and Contextual Perspectives* (OUP, Oxford, 2004), p. 76.

176 H. Collins, 'Flexibility and Stability of Expectations in the Contract of Employment', *Socio-Economic Review* (2006): 139.

contract theory, or the marginally re-qualified notion introduced by neo-classical contract theory. Indeed, one should instead accept that that a contractual relationship between two parties can be shaped by obligations that are not necessarily *internal* to the contract, but that that can be either *exogenous* (such as constraints imposed by employment legislation, obligations that the parties may have contracted with other parties that are not directly participating to the main contract, social norms and expectations, the balance between work and life, habits) or *endogenous* to the contractual relationship itself (changes in the psychological contract, emerging pressures deriving from functional flexibility requirements) and that may come to affect to a considerable extent the elements of personal subordination, continuity and bilaterality as discussed in the previous sections. This sort of reading of the contractual relationship would allow the notion in question to embrace a situation as diverse as the worker employed under a standard contract of employment, the freelance journalist working for more than one paper, the full-time worker who decides to shift to a part-time or casual work relationship because of family or other personal responsibilities or the worker employed through a private or public employment agency.

On the other hand, Freedland has recently suggested that accepting such an ever-increasing level of diversity in work relationships may well require a departure from an individual employment relations system strictly centred upon the contract of employment towards a system where the central organising concept is what he describes as a 'Personal Work Contract' (a wider family of contract of which the contract of employment is only one – albeit possibly preponderant – member) coupled to what he calls the 'Personal Work Nexus' (a surrounding web of legal relationships, not necessarily contractual in nature, between the working persons and the employing entities).[177] It seems that, at least in the near future, the contractual dimension, and within it the contract of employment, will still play the major roles as central organising concepts of the individual employment relations system. Having said that, there is little question that this contractual framework, and in particular the notion of contract of employment, are in need of – and are indeed subject to – considerable reform. The following chapters will focus precisely on the reforms discourses currently undertaken in four major European legal systems and, at a supranational level, by the EC and the ILO.

6. Conclusions

The second and third sections of this chapter presented and analysed the historical and legal background that paved the way for the birth and emergence of the typical and binary model of the employment relationship based on the unitary notion of contract of employment. The third section also discussed some of the distinguishing legal characteristics of the typical employment relationship. The next section sketched out some of the more recent political, economic and social phenomena against

---

177 M. Freedland, 'From the Contract of Employment to the Personal Work Nexus', *ILJ* (2005): 1.

which the traditional notion of employment relationship, discussed and described in the earlier sections, has progressively undergone a number of radical changes that eventually deprived it of its near-monopoly of the contractual construction by which labour resources can be purchased by the economic actors in work relations. It has been argued that although in many respects the binary notion of employment relationship had always been a chimera, the approach taken by modern legislation has somewhat promoted the legal diversity of the contractual arrangements by which labour resources are purchased on the labour market. Although the standard employment relationship still provides for the legal structure of the vast majority of work relationships, an increasingly relevant number of new forms of work simply cannot fit into its rigid traditional construction.

The fourth section also explored the distinguishing features of these new forms of work and some of the challenges they pose to the personal scope of application of traditional labour law. More specifically it was seen how, in the evolution of the legal discourse, the traditional ideas of dependency, continuity and bilaterality are struggling to adjust to the needs of these new forms of work that are more and more independent, discontinuous and 'multilateral'. The fifth section argued that all these changes are indeed putting under considerable pressure the current contractual constructions of the employment relationships, but that all indications seem to suggest that in the near future the contractual framework, and with it the contract of employment, will still play a major role in the individual employment relations system.

The next two chapters will discuss in greater detail the efforts made by national legal orders to adjust their labour protection systems to the new challenges posed by the changes depicted in the previous paragraphs. It will be argued that these efforts have substantially taken two directions The first one, discussed in Chapter 2, may amount to what we could call a re-definition of the traditional notion of the employment relationship, often with the adoption of new *ad hoc* tests, in an attempt to expand its boundaries and attribute at least part of the labour protection prerogatives to workers previously excluded. The second one, discussed in Chapter 3, amounts to a sort of 'typificatory' activity with regard to atypical forms of work, whereby regulatory and judicial intervention have attempted, and are still trying, to isolate a number of new employment relationships deploying some common and homogeneous characteristics (the analysis will focus on part-time, fixed-term work and agency work) and create *ad hoc* legal structures aimed, again, at affording to the workers engaged therein some of the protection traditionally granted to typical employees. Though the two chapters touch upon contiguous legal themes it can be said that they present two distinct regulatory strategies that seem to be emerging in national and supranational legal systems. The first one, to be presented and discussed in Chapter 2, aims at remodelling the scope of the employment relationship and, indirectly, the scope of application of labour legislation, while the second one, analysed in Chapter 3, aims at producing a new taxonomy of the employment relationship(s) with atypical forms of work receiving *ad hoc* and specific regulation.

Chapter 2

Reshaping the Personal Scope of Labour Law: An Analysis of Current Debates in Europe

1. Introduction

A thin logical nexus, as clarified here, links the present and the next chapter. Both chapters deal with issues concerning the scope and coverage of employment legislation that have been haunting the legal theorists for the last few decades. Both chapters seek to describe and analyse the efforts made at a national level to tackle these crucial issues satisfactorily. But each chapter focuses on a fundamentally distinct approach adopted by national judiciaries and legislators to refocus and adapt the scope of employment legislation to the modern notions of the employment relationship. The present chapter looks into the attempts made by judiciaries and legislators to modify the scope of application of labour law through a re-elaboration of the scope of the subordinate employment relationship. Chapter 3, on the other hand, seeks to explore what appears to have emerged as a tangential mode of extending the coverage of labour legislation. This second strategy has typically consisted in isolating specific types of employment relationships and bestowing upon them a number of legal entitlements, whether derived from those typical of standard subordinate employees or specifically created to suit the special needs of these atypical and special employment relationships, with the ultimate aim of bringing these relationships as far as possible within the realm of labour law, granting them a treatment equal to that enjoyed by standard employees. To sum up, it could be said that the next chapter focuses on concepts pertaining to the *taxonomy* of the employment relation while the current one mainly analyses its *scope* as defined and elaborated in the four legal systems under examination.

The ways the categories of workers – to which the substantive provisions of labour law apply – have been traditionally identified, varies from country to country. National jurisdictions have made use of different definitions of the notion of the employment relationship, each being more or less inclusive or exclusive than the others. These notions have also varied over time, as within a single jurisdiction the scope of the employment relationship has often been reformulated to include or exclude specific kinds of work relations. While the primary actors in these dynamics have undoubtedly been the judiciaries and the legal theorists, any account of the individual scope of employment law must also consider the role of legislation and of collective bargaining.

The last few decades have exposed numerous lacunae in the traditional ways in which the issue of the individual scope of labour law has been tackled in Europe. As highlighted in Chapter 1, a number of authors have analysed both the structural reasons for their emergence and their impact on the traditional ways of defining and identifying the employment relationship. But the purpose of this chapter is not to review or discuss this kind of legal analysis. What the present chapter seeks to present is a comparative analysis of the many debates that, at present, are flourishing in the European legal doctrines over the future and possible reforms of labour law. It will exclusively focus on the debates and proposed reforms aimed at expanding the protective scope of application of labour law by redefining the boundaries of the scope of the dependant employment relationship.

There are three main ways in which the various European labour law systems, the legal doctrines, the judiciaries and, often, the legislators are attempting to address the problems at stake. The first stretches the notion of 'employee' so as to introduce within its protective range as many types of workers as possible. The second carves out and defines a *tertium genus* or 'third type' of worker, located in the 'twilight zone' existing between the traditional employee and the self-employed, and to afford her a series of rights traditionally linked to employment status. The third main doctrinal path has the universalistic ambition of exploring the feasibility of a *ius commune* covering all the types of workers, and eventually granting a differentiated range of specific rights to certain broad categories. All these debates have different strengths and weaknesses and their applications often overlap in reality even within the same jurisdiction. For each of them the potential advantages and disadvantages will be presented and discussed. The analysis will highlight the national specificities, but it will also try to expose the fact that the heated problems they are addressing are much more common to the various systems than the legal debate may let one suppose.

2. Stretching the notion of 'employee'

The traditional beneficiary of the protective rights that constitute the substance of any labour law system has been what in the English tradition is called the 'employee'. Employees are those workers who are linked to an employer through a *contract of employment*. The deep changes in the labour market and in the workforce that have occurred in the last decades have put under considerable strain the 'employee' and the other similar continental notions in all European jurisdictions. As pointed out in the previous chapter, new types of workers and working patterns have emerged, placing a considerable share of the workforce outside the protective scope of labour laws. These new types of workers and working patterns had in common a distinct feature: the *subordination* of the worker to the employer was watered down to such extent as to render apparently legitimate the disentitlement of the worker from the specific protection afforded by labour legislation.

The way this exclusionary process has developed differs from country to country, and even within any given jurisdiction it has taken several forms. This section explores two main forms of this process. The first is common to all the four states and, with a great degree of approximation, could be linked to the emergence of new patterns of work, in which the worker is seen as independent enough from his employer to be identified as self-employed. This form of exclusionary process will be defined as '*qualitative*' exclusion and is mainly due to an increasingly recurrent pattern in arranging the legal features of the employment relationship in ways that emphasise the notions of autonomy to the expense of the notions of dependence and subordination. A second way in which workers have been pushed outside the 'employee' status and the domain of labour law is typical in countries where such status is accorded only after a qualifying period. In these latter cases, the exclusion has often been selective, that is to say limited to one or more specific rights whose attribution and enjoyment require a specific qualifying period. This latter form of exclusion shall be called, for the purposes of the present work, '*quantitative*' exclusion, and it will be argued that it mainly depends on the perceived lack of sufficient continuity in an increasingly recurrent number of employment relationships. Arguably both forms of exclusion share a common rationale: for one reason or another the underlying assumption is that the *subordination* link between worker and employer is not firm enough, either from a qualitative point of view (for example, in performing her work, the worker is seen as outside the control of the employer) or from a quantitative one (in other words, the worker is not committing herself for a long and continuous enough period to deserve the status).

This work presents a comparative description of these two exclusionary dynamics and, most importantly, of the main steps taken in the various jurisdictions to overcome their consequences. What is already clear is the psychological framework and the possible shortcomings of the kind of discourse which is being described. The underlying assumption is that workers are divided into two categories, employees and self-employed, the former falling into the domain of labour law, and the latter within the domain of contract and commercial law. The effort made on both sides is to push the 'boundary' of one's own domain as far as possible in order to expand one's own legal empire at the expenses of the other domain. The most evident shortcoming of this kind of analysis is that it only contemplates the existence of a black and white labour market, without accepting and confronting the idea of any intermediate situation.

Qualitative exclusions from the employee status and debated reforms

Since the mid-1970s and 1980s, employers have deeply transformed the ways in which they acquire labour resources for the purpose of running their businesses. These transformations, whose socio-economic rationale is beyond the explanatory purposes of this chapter, have to some extent increased the distance between employer and workers. By distance it is meant here both the physical distance, for instance with the development of home-working and teleworking practices, and the managerial distance, with the entrepreneur and the worker managing their relations in a horizontal rather than vertical way, in which the authority structure typical of the traditional notion of the employment relationship is substantially watered down or masked. These changes have deeply affected the traditional tests used by the judiciaries to attribute to a labourer the status of employee, and have seriously hampered the effectiveness of the traditional scope-determination rules provided by

60 The Changing Law of the Employment Relationship

labour statutes. There have been two kinds of reactions to these changes. The first and most notable one has been put forward by the national judiciaries, the second one by the legislators.

Judicial intervention Supiot argues that the technique adopted by the judicial power is to make recourse to what he defines the *'faisceau d'indices'*,[1] what in English could be termed as a spectrum, or multiplicity, of tests. In France, for instance, judicial attempts to define the notion of *travail dependant* still focus on the quest for indications of a subordinate relationship between a worker and his employer. But in the last few decades, *'ce critère de la subordination s'est considérablement enrichi et complexifié'*.[2] This new complexity, aimed at 'enlarging the notion of contract of employment' by exploring whether the worker is exercising his freedom to work or his freedom to undertake, takes the shape of two new tests adopted by the French courts. The first one is that of 'integration into an organised service', in which the courts ask themselves whether the beneficiary of the service is actually directing and controlling the terms and conditions for the execution of the work, as opposed to the mere execution of the work.[3] The second test, called *'participation dans l'entreprise autrui'* is a negative one, in which the courts verify that the worker is neither employing other workers for the performance of the required service, nor that he has his own clientele, or that the he is the bearer of the enterprise risk.[4] It is worthwhile stressing that these criteria and tests are only a further qualification of, and not a substitute for, the traditional concept of subordination.

A similar trend is noticeable in Germany where the notion of *persönlicher Abhängigkeit* (personal dependency) is traditionally used for the purpose of distinguishing the employee (*Arbeitnehmer*) from the self-employed (*freier Dienstvertrag*). And once more, two tests, a positive one and a negative one, have been introduced as a qualification to the notion of subordination. The courts verify dependency by checking whether the worker is integrated into a productive organisation controlled by a third person and, from a negative point of view, by making sure that the worker is not working on her own behalf, that she is not participating in the profits and to the losses, that she does not own the means of production nor have a clientele of her own.

Italian courts have similarly developed a great number of tests for the detection of the type of employment relationship. The doctrine refers to them as 'subsidiary' criteria for the detection of *subordinazione*. With the judgment *Cass., Sez. Un., 30 giugno 1999, n. 379*, it became clear that the *faisceau d'indices* strategy is also adopted by the Italian judiciary. 'Where the element of the subjection of the worker to someone else's directives cannot be easily appreciated, one must refer to complementary and subsidiary criteria – such as collaboration, continuity of performance, observance of predetermined working time, payment at regular intervals of a predetermined remuneration, coordination of working activity to the

---

1   A. Supiot, 'Les nouveaux visages de la subordination', *DS* (2000) : 139.
2   Ibid., 140.
3   Jurisprudence Hebdo-prese: Cass. Ass. Plén. 18 juin 1976 D. 1977, J., 1973.
4   Soc. 7 déc. 1983, *Bull civ* V, n. 592 p. 423.

Reshaping the Personal Scope of Labour Law

organisational structure provided by the employer, absence of even the slightest entrepreneurial structure – that, though without any decisive power on their own, can be evaluated globally as indications providing evidence of subordination'.[5] This plurality of tests and indicatiors, builds on the firm basis provided by the other traditional tests of '*collaborazione*', '*continuità*', 'risk' and 'object of performance', the latter being identified with the provision of labour resources to the employer rather than with a specific 'result'.

Similar evolutions are also noticeable in the British jurisdiction. In the UK, decisions such as *Lane* v *Shire Roofing Company (Oxford) Ltd*[6] have shown a judicial concern on the part of the courts to go beyond the traditional strict interpretation of the 'control' and 'mutuality of obligations' tests and to explore instead which business is really benefiting from the work provided by the worker who is formally engaged on a contract for services by the intermediate company. 'According to Henry LJ, applying the test of economic reality, the business involved in the work was that of the defendant, not the claimant's'.[7] Such reasoning is very close to the French negative test of *participation à l'entreprise autrui*, under which judges have to consider, inter alia, that the worker '*ne cour pas les risques de l'entreprise*'.[8] In *ABC* v *Gizbert*, the EAT re-qualified the extent of a worker's freedom to accept or refuse proposed assignments and therefore found the existence of the 'mutuality' requirement, by pointing out that he 'could decide whether or not to accept assignments offered to him but was to do so in *good faith*. [He] did not have an unfettered right to refuse assignments; he was obliged to act in *good faith*.'[9] Even more noticeably, the idea of using a '*faisceau d'indices*' is not completely alien to the British courts. Lord Wright in *Montreal* v *Montreal Locomotive Works*, recognised that 'in many cases the question can only be settled by examining the whole of the various elements which constitute the relationship between the parties'.[10]

Nevertheless, as Supiot rightly stresses,[11] the British 'multiple test' has often been used with the purpose of retrenching the notion of employee rather than expanding it.[12] A more 'inclusionary' strategy of the UK courts could be derived, as some mainstream doctrinal analysis points out,[13] from the use of a renewed 'dependency' test, more linked to the economic aspects of the dependence between worker and employer, rather than to the formal and legal ones. Such renewed use of the test could

---

5   E. Ghera, *Diritto del Lavoro* (Cacucci, Bari, 2000), p. 70.

6   *Lane* v *Shire Roofing Company (Oxford) Ltd* [1995] IRLR 493 (CA). Here the claimant was a building worker who was hired by the defendant employer to carry out a re-roofing job for a client, and for which he would have been paid a fixed sum of £200.

7   S. Deakin and G. Morris, *Labour Law* (Butterworths, London, 2001), p. 161.

8   Supiot, 'Les nouveaux visages de la subordination', p. 140.

9   *ABC* v *Gizbert* [2006] WL 2469644. Emphasis added.

10   *Montreal* v *Montreal Locomotive Works* [1947] 1 DLR 161, 169; see also *Ready Mixed Concrete (South East) LTD* v *Minister for Pensions and National Insurance* [1968] 2 QB 497 and *Market Investigations Ltd* v *Minister of Social Security* [1969] 2 QB 173.

11   Supiot, 'Les nouveaux visages de la subordination', p. 141.

12   *Ready Mixed Concrete (South East) Ltd* v *Minister of Pensions and National Insurance* [1968] 2 QB 497 and *O'Kelly* v *Trusthouse Forte* [1983] ICR 728.

13   S. Deakin and G. Morris, *Labour Law* (Butterworths, London, 2001), p. 168.

62 *The Changing Law of the Employment Relationship*

well be inferred, however, from important cases such as *Lorimer*,[14] in which the considerable number of clients of Mr Lorimer was seen as a clear indication of the fact that he was not economically dependent upon any one of them. The reasonable conclusion from this line of reasoning should be that when a worker is *de facto* and consistently economically dependent upon a single client or business, he should be considered an employee. 'An emphasis on economic dependence, so defined, would arguably produce greater predictability than the open-ended multiple test, in which any one of a number of factors could turn out to be essential in tipping the balance on one side or the other'.[15]

It is worth highlighting that some continental theorists and, often, judges, have rather consistently rejected the adoption of a widened notion of economic dependence. '*La notion de subordination économique est, en effet, trop imprécise*',[16] as a great number of persons may depend economically on others albeit keeping their professional, independent, status; such are the suppliers integrated in a network of distribution or 'franchised' tradesmen, the *agriculteur sous contrat*, the artisan working for an industrial enterprise.[17] On the same line of reasoning, Ghera seems convinced that a situation of *dipendenza economica* may occur even outside subordinate employment. 'Even if one can admit that the position of economic inferiority of the worker conditions his contractual autonomy and characterizes his social position ... it cannot be confused with the subordination of the provider of work to the direction and organization of the enterprise'.[18] But it should be stressed, at this point, that as far as Italy is concerned, the objections to the adoption of a wider notion of dependency – socio-economic as opposed to a more formal/personal – can be partly explained by the fact that this system recognises the existence of a third, specific, category of workers in which to fit situations where there is great discretion over the manners of performance of the work but there is still a great reliance, or dependence, on an employer's wages for subsistence: the so-called *parasubordinati.*

If placing more emphasis on the notion of economic dependence does not appear a very attractive option to the Italian doctrine and jurisprudence, it cannot be denied that in recent years some judgments have attempted to introduce an *attenuated* notion of subordination showing an unusual and exceptional understanding of a number of changes that other judiciaries appear to ignore or purposely neglect. In Decision 9167 of 2001, the *Corte di Cassazione* pointed out that with 'the evolution of the systems of organisation of labour, increasingly characterised by the tendency to outsource or tertiarize whole sectors of the cycle of production or series of specific professional skills, subordination becomes less and less significant, because of the impossibility of exercising full and direct control over the different phases of the

---

14 *Hall* v *Lorimer* [1994] ICR 218.

15 S. Deakin and G. Morris, *Labour Law* (Butterworths, London, 2001), p. 168.

16 J. Pélissier, A. Supiot and A. Jeammaud, *Droit du travail* (Dalloz, Paris, 2000), p. 151.

17 Ibid., pp. 151–152.

18 Ghera, *Diritto del Lavoro* (Cacucci, Bari, 2000), p. 64.

activity performed'.[19] The *Corte di Cassazione*, in a subsequent decision, stressed that 'subordination is an essential element of dependent labour; nevertheless it can also be present in attenuated forms by reason of the specific organization of labour and of the type of provision (particularly in the case of simple provisions, of the same type or repetitive) and can be perceived, in these specific circumstances, as making available to the employer the labour resources of the worker with continuity, loyalty and diligence, according to the directions given by the other party'.[20] The doctrine suggests that in these cases, the elements of 'collaboration' that are present in the employment relationship are such as to justify a degree of subordination, albeit an 'attenuated' one, even just understood as 'simple availability of the worker to the directives of the enterprise'.[21]

It is evident that a black-or-white notion of work may be too rigid to encompass the changes that have occurred in the labour market, and exposes itself to the obvious criticisms of either doing too much (when giving employee status to senior managers of big companies '*qui jouissent des lors des avantages de l'indépendance sans en supporter les risques*'[22]), or too little, as in several UK leading cases such as *Carmichael* or *O'Kelly*.[23] But it also seems clear that some judiciaries have made more steps than others in understanding the extent and repercussions of the changes of the legal and probably also factual notions of the employment relationship.

Statutory intervention As a consequence of (or despite) these conceptual shortcomings, several European Member States have attempted to expand the 'subordinate employee' domain and mark with a higher degree of clarity the line between employee and self-employed thorough statutory intervention. It should be stressed that statutory intervention has also been used to expand the opposite notion of self-employed,[24] but these pieces of law are beyond the scope of this chapter. One of the legislative techniques adopted for this purpose has been the statutory assimilation of some types of workers, whose status was doubtful, to either the 'employee' or the self-employed category, by means of *legal presumptions*. The French Labour Code has introduced a number of professional categories, often referred to as *situations mixtes*,[25] in its livre VII. Article L. 751-1 introduces a statutory qualification of employment status for *voyageurs représentants placiers* ('VRP'; door-to-door sales persons), regardless of whether the VRP works for one

---

19   Cass. 06.07.2001, n. 9167, in (2002) II *RIDL* 272.

20   Cass. 27.11.2002, n. 16805, in (2003) 3 *MGL* 127. See also Cass. 10.03.2004, n. 5508; Cass. 9.4.2004, n. 4797; Cass. 9.4.2004, n. 6983.

21   E. Ghera, 'Subordinazione, statuto protettivo e qualificazione del rapporto di lavoro', in D. Garofalo and M. Ricci (eds), *Percorsi di Diritto del Lavoro* (Cacucci, Bari, 2006), p. 332.

22   Supiot, 'Les nouveaux visages', p. 141.

23   *Carmichael* v *National Power Plc* [1999] ICR 1226; *O'Kelly* v *Trusthouse Forte Plc* [1983] ICR 728, [1984] QB 90.

24   A well-known example is the 1994 *Loi Madelin*.

25   Pélissier, Supiot and Jeammaud, *Droit du travail*, p. 166.

or more employers.[26] Article L. 781-1 has introduced a general legal 'presumption of contract of employment' for all small tradesmen whose business exclusively depends on a provider that has the power to dictate the prices to which they are allowed to sell their products. Furthermore, the Code has introduced a series of '*statuts speciaux*' creating ad hoc presumptions for the '*représentants de commerce*', journalists,[27] artists[28] and models.[29]

On the other hand there are serious doubts about the compatibility of some of these national legal presumptions with Community law. In a case decided in June 2006,[30] the ECJ found, *inter alia*, that the French rule introducing a 'presumption of salaried status'[31] for performing artists employed through an agency was incompatible with Articles 43 and 49 EC to the extent that it also applied to agencies and artists established in another Member State and seeking to operate in France. The French government representative argued, to no avail, that this was a procedural requirement in that it only amounted to a reversal of the burden of proof that artists seeking to operate as self-employed could easily rebut simply by filling in a specific form. It also pointed out that, in any case it ought to be justified under the Articles 46(1) and 55 exceptions or under the public interest doctrine. The Court held that the French 'presumption' fell squarely under Article 43 and 49,[32] and that even if it was justifiable it was still disproportionate.[33] The most interesting part of the Court's reasoning, for the purposes of our present discourse, is contained in paragraphs 52–53 of the decision:

> 52. With regard, secondly, to the objective of combating concealed employment, the fact that performing artists are normally engaged on an intermittent basis and for short periods by different show organisers cannot, of itself, mean that a general assumption of concealed employment is well founded. That is particularly so in this case because the performing artists in question are recognised as service providers, established in their Member State of origin, where they usually provide similar services.

> 53. In those circumstances, as the Commission suggests, the establishment of a system of ex post facto control, together with deterrent penalties to prevent and identify individual instances of the use of bogus amateur or unpaid status, would suffice to combat concealed employment effectively.

It is possible to see an emergence, by the back door, of an expanded notion of 'economic dependence' for the purposes of the qualification of the employment relationship. It is worthwhile highlighting how this approach radically differs from the one adopted in Italy to regulate what is commonly known as

---

26 See, on a similar line, L. 782.1, L. 773.1, L. 721.1 and L. 721.6 of the French Labour Code.

27 C. trav. art. L. 761.2. v. Soc. 14 mai 1999, *Bull. Civ.* V, n. 174.

28 C. trav. art. L. 762.1.

29 C. trav. art. L. 763.1.

30 Case C-255/04, *Commission v France* [2006] ECR I-05251.

31 Article L. 762-1 of the *Code du travail*.

32 Case C-255/04, [38].

33 Ibid., [48].

parasubordinazione. In fact while the Italian *parasubordinati* are only awarded a minor share of the protective panoply conferred by labour law and remain solidly anchored within the domain of self-employment, the French workers assimilated into these '*statuts spéciaux*' have '*la certitude de bénéficier des droits du travailleur subordonné*'.[34]

The second legislative technique is the one adopted in Germany, albeit in the limited field of social security law, between 1998 and 2002.[35] With the adoption of Law N. 3843 of 28 December 1998 the German legislature introduced a catalogue of four criteria qualifying the employment relationship as one of dependent labour for the purposes of social security. The newly introduced section 4 of paragraph 7 of the *Sozialgezetsbuch* (SGB) stated:

> In case of persons, who are in paid work and who in connection with their activity do not employ any employee liable to insurance deductions with the exception of family members, who work regularly and basically only for one contractor, who perform services which are typical of employed people, who are in particular subject to instructions given by the employer and are integrated in the work organisation of the employer, or who do not engage in any business activity, it is assumed that they are employed for remuneration, when at least two of the above mentioned criteria are met. The first sentence does not apply to commercial agents, who organise their work substantially in freedom and who can decide upon their working hours.'

In 1999 this wording was partly modified, and a fifth criterion was added so that the section in question read as follows:

> In case of a person, who is in paid work, ... it is presumed that she/he is an employee when at least three of the following five criteria can be found:
> 1. when in connection with his/her activity the person does not regularly employ an employee liable to social insurance contributions, whose remuneration from this employment exceeds regularly 325 Euros per month;
> 2. the person works on a continuous basis and principally only for one employer;
> 3. his/her employer or any other comparable employer let perform corresponding activities regularly by employees employed by him;
> 4. her/his activity does not show features which are typical of an entrepreneurial activity;
> 5. her/his activity appears to correspond to the activity which she or he has performed before for the employer on the basis of a subordinate employment relationship.
> The first sentence does not apply to commercial agents, who organise their work substantially in freedom and who can decide upon their working hours. The presumption can be rebutted.[36]

---

34 Pélissier, Supiot and Jeammaud, *Droit du travail*, p. 166.

35 '*Gesetz zu Korrekturen in der Sozialversicherung und zur Sicherung der Arbeitnehmerrechte*' (BGBl. I S. 3843, v. art. 3, modifying §7 of book IV of the Social Security Code). Cf. W. Däubler, 'Working people in Germany', *Comp Labor Law & Pol'y Journal*, (1999): 78. On the changes of this definition, see the critical commentary in R. Wank, 'Germany', in 'Labour Law in Motion', *Bulletin of Comparative Labour Relations*, (2005): 19.

36 Law of 20 December 1999 (BGBl 2000, s. 2).

These laws were focusing their attention on a number of criteria that revolved around the notion of financial and economic dependency[37] and on the absence of any genuine entrepreneurial economic activity. Unsurprisingly, some commentators considered this an implicit weakness of the Act[38] and have opposed any temptation to extend the same reasoning beyond the social security domain. In fact, the definition preferred by the Bundesvereinigung der Deutschen Arbeitgeberverbände (BAG), the German Federal Labour Court, and the majority of scholars in the labour law domain is the very simple one, that an 'employee is one who is, on the basis of a contract in civil law, obliged to work in the service of somebody else'.[39] And in any case the 'three out of five' criterion was repealed with the adoption of the Law of 23 December 2002[40] and does not feature in the current wording of paragraph 7, section 4 of the SGB.

A third type of statutory intervention aims at creating some pre-judicial administrative procedures for clarifying the status of workers. Two distinct examples are the German institute of *Statusfestellungsverfahren*, introduced in December 1999 with the Law on the promotion of self-employed work,[41] and the recently introduced *certificazione del contratto di lavoro* adopted by the Italian legislator with Articles 75–81 of the *Decreto Legislativo* n. 276 of September 2003. The German procedure[42] can be activated by either or both the parties of the work relationship, and it can therefore serve both as a pre-emptive procedure aiming at anticipating and, eventually, avoiding judicial litigation and as a sort of alternative dispute resolution mechanism. The effects of the procedure are limited to the worker's position for the purposes of social security legislation and in most of the cases it deals with employment relationships already in operation for a certain amount of time. Contrastingly, the *certificazione del contratto di lavoro* exclusively provides for the introduction of a sort of *preventive certification* of employment contracts, though its effects are not limited to the social security implications of the worker's status. The Italian decree authorises the creation of ad hoc administrative bilateral bodies for the purpose of providing these certificates, while the local labour offices and even university academics, if registered for the purpose, may be authorised to perform this type of certificatory activity.[43]

The explicit aim of this new legal device is to 'reduce litigation in the area of [contractual] qualification'[44] though of course, as stressed by Article 80 of the decree,

---

37 Cf. A. Supiot, *Beyond Employment* (OUP, Oxford, 2001), p. 15.

38 Cf. H. Buchner in U. Müchenberger, R. Wank and H. Buchner, 'Ridefinire la nozione di subordinazione? Il dibattito in Germania', *GDLRI* (2000): 329, 344.

39 *Preis*, ErfK, s. 611 BGB, note 45. See R. Wank, 'Germany', in 'Labour Law in Motion', *Bulletin of Comparative Labour Relations*, (2005): 19.

40 BGBl, 2002 I s. 4621.

41 Gesetz zur Förderung der Selbständigkeit.

42 Section 7(a–c) of the Sozialgesetzbuch IV modified with the Law of 23 December 2002. Cf. L. Nogler, *La certificazione dei contratti di lavoro* (Working Paper No. 23, CSDLE Massimo d'Antona, 2003), p. 50.

43 Article 76.

44 Article 75.

the parties to the certified contract are always free to appeal to the competent judicial bodies. Therefore the decree does not establish an alternative dispute resolution system or an ex-post qualification of the contract along the lines of the German experiment, but it suggests the creation of a consensual, and pre-emptive, certification procedure based on the letter of the agreement between the parties. The legislator provides no guidance to the adjudicator, although Article 78(4) promises that the Ministry of Labour will produce a 'good practice code' that at least in part could serve that purpose. Some 'Guidelines' were indeed produced in 2004,[45] but their contents do little more than reiterate the criteria already defined by statute. In any case, as pointed out by some commentators,[46] a preventive, *ex ante*, qualification of an employment relationship makes little sense, given that, in theory, this qualification should be both a matter of law *and fact* and as such heavily depends on the concrete factual conduct of the parties to the relationship, something that by definition can only be appreciated *ex post*, that is to say once the relationship has been in place for a certain amount of time. More recently, most commentators seem to have agreed that an *ex post* qualification of the employment relationship should also be possible, although this appears to be a rather abstract question given the slight interest that this new system seems to have attracted among workers and employers alike.[47] Even putting these criticisms aside, it needs to be pointed out that the law, at least so far, is only addressing procedural issues that tell us little or nothing about the substance of our problem, that is to say which aspects of the employment relationship one should take into account when formulating the tests necessary to define the status of workers.[48]

It is probably too early to say whether the Italian *certificazione* will be as successful[49] as the German *Statusfeststellungsverfahren*. It is also difficult to forecast to what extent the German notion of economic and financial dependence, as used in the area of social security, could be also adopted for the purposes of labour law, in Germany or elsewhere. Part of the German *doctrine*[50]would certainly favour such

---

45 'Linee guida alla certificazione – Elementi utili alla certificazione di alcune tipologie contrattuali', attached to *Circolare N 48/2004*, Roma, 15 dicembre 2004.

46 G. Pera, 'Sulle prospettive di estensione delle tutele al lavoro parasubordinato', *RIDL* (1998): 371, 379. M.G. Garofalo, 'La legge delaga sul mercato del lavoro: prime osservazioni', *RGL* (2003): 359, 376–382. L. Nogler, 'Sulla inutilità delle presunzioni legali relative in tema di qualificazione dei rapporti di lavoro', *RIDL* (1997): 311. L. Nogler, *La certificazione dei contratti di lavoro* (Working Paper No. 23, CSDLE Massimo d'Antona, 2003), p. 59.

47 See V. Brino, 'La certificazione dei contratti di lavoro tra qualificazione del rapporto e volontà assistita', *LD* (2006): 383, 417.

48 And on this point see the critical analysis of M.G. Garofalo, 'Contratti di lavoro e certificazione', in P. Curzio (ed), *Lavoro e diritti a tre anni dalla legge 30/2003* (Cacucci, Bari, 2006), pp. 581, 596.

49 Cf. Nogler, *La certificazione dei contratti di lavoro*, p. 50.

50 R. Wank, in U. Müchenberger, R. Wank and H. Buchner, 'Ridefinire la nozione di subordinazione? Il dibattito in Germania', *GDLRI* (2000): 329–350.

an expansion,[51] and probably so would some labour courts.[52] But, as seen in the previous paragraph, the French and Italian *doctrines* would have some difficulties in accepting a formulation of a notion – economic dependence – considered '*trop imprécise*',[53] and there is little doubt that the majority of the German legal world appears to prefer a more formal and legal approach to the definition of dependency.[54] On the other hand, the French *doctrine* argues that the use of special statutes, such as the one contained in livre VII, is the '*meilleur example d'un mélange de règles propres au travail indépendent*'.[55] But this kind of discourse is too similar to other continental doctrinal analyses that have given a special 'para-subordinated' status to workers whose contractual relations are formally free of any legal subordination *vis à vis* a specific employer, but whose condition is nevertheless tainted by a strong degree of economic dependence.

Quantitative exclusion and reforms

By quantitative exclusion from the employee status it is meant all those rules, whether of statutory or jurisprudential origin, that subject the recognition of the status to a certain period of time spent in a specific occupation or engagement. In theory, there are two distinct ways by which the lack of *continuity*, that is to say the insufficient time spent in an occupation, can disentitle workers, whose subordinate condition is beyond doubt, from the enjoyment of labour rights connected to the status of employee. A first type of exclusion is linked to the notion of *qualifying period*. It should be noted that where these qualifying periods apply, the status of employee is not necessarily put in doubt. In many cases, the law may well assume that the worker is an employee, but in order to afford her some particular labour rights (for instance protection against unfair dismissal, right to redundancy compensation), it requires that a certain period of time be spent working in that position. A second, and more fundamental, way in which an exclusion from the status can occur is linked to *intermittent* work, where the focus is not so much upon the (insufficient) *length* of the relationship but, rather, on the (lack of) *regularity*. In these cases the intermittence of the working pattern can be seen as an indication of lack of 'mutuality of obligations', such that the worker is not even recognised the status of employee and, as a consequence, she cannot even qualify for those labour rights that, in a given jurisdiction, are afforded from day one of the employment relationship.

This subsection, which explores the ways by which the employee status is being expanded, focuses only on the second of the aforementioned issues, namely intermittence. This is due to two main factors. First, as said before, qualifying periods

---

51   But this would still be a minority. Cf. Müchenberger, 'Ridefinire la nozione di subordinazione?', p. 329.

52   See the decision of the regional court of Cologne LAG Köln June 30 1995, LAGE §611 BGB. Arbeitnehmerbegriff Nr 27 and also the previous LAG Niedersachsen v Sept 6 1989, LAGE §611 BGB Arbeitnehmerbegriff Nr 24.

53   Pélissier, Supiot and Jeammaud, *Droit du travail*, p. 151.

54   R. Wank, 'Germany', in 'Labour Law in Motion', *Bulletin of Comparative Labour Relations*, (2005): 19.

55   Pélissier, Supiot and Jeammaud, *Droit du travail*, p. 166.

Reshaping the Personal Scope of Labour Law 69

do not cast doubt on the existence of 'employee' status; indeed they usually assume that such status exists, albeit requiring it to 'persist' for a certain period of time. Therefore the issue is outside the specific scope of this part of the book. Second, this problem, of central relevance in the UK, is seen as a less pressing one in other European systems where many labour rights are of constitutional nature and are afforded from day one, and therefore scarcely merits a deeper comparative study. In the next chapter it will be noted that in the last few years the position of atypical workers, particularly and adversely affected by the presence of qualifying periods, has slightly improved, at least in comparison to those workers affected by the lack of regularity in their (intermittent) labour relationship, still relying on the goodwill of the judiciaries.

Intermittence is a major hurdle for any worker in her quest to prove that she is employed under a contract of employment, as most jurisdictions, when addressing the 'labelling' issue, place considerable importance upon what the British doctrine describes as the presence of 'mutual promises of future performance'.[56] The analysis of Sandra Fredman appears to be particularly significant in this context:

> Many non-standard workers undertake intermittent paid work because of their obligations at home. ... But because of the focus on paid work alone, such engagements are constructed as merely short term or transactional contracts. Contractual status will not be afforded to the ongoing relationship, since it includes unpaid work, constructed as 'free' or independent time.[57]

In Italy the notions of 'continuity' and 'availability over a period of time' are equally important and are seen, both by the doctrine and the jurisprudence, as an essential aspect of *collaborazione*, one of the duties of the employee towards his employer. On the other hand the Italian doctrine has developed continuity as *continuità ideale*,[58] a concept that 'deploys its effects on a teleological, rather than temporal level, and is therefore different from the continuous or periodical execution of the performance, that is to say from the mere distribution over time of the fulfilment to the obligation'; continuity in the context of subordinate employment 'has to be understood not in its *material* sense but in the theoretical (*ideale*) one, as dependence or *functional availability*' of the worker 'in someone else's enterprise'.[59] This stance is confirmed by the Italian jurisprudence[60] that sees the 'theoretical continuity' of the availability of labour energies, rendered to the employer in such a way as to allow their purposeful insertion in the overall organisation of the enterprise, as a constitutive element of the employee's duty to collaborate. These considerations and concerns over the notions of continuity, intermittence and future commitment apply to most European Member States, given that they have been triggered by a transformation in the labour market that is shared by all of them: the growth of casual workers. Though

---

56 M. Freedland, *The Contract of Employment* (Clarendon, Oxford, 1976), p. 21.

57 S. Fredman, 'Women at Work: The Broken Promise of Flexicurity', *ILJ* (2004): 305.

58 E. Ghera, *Diritto del Lavoro* (Cacucci, Bari, 2000), p. 67.

59 Ibid. Emphasis original.

60 Cass. 14 giugno 1979, n. 3353; Cass. 7 aprile 1992, n. 4220; and more recently Cass. 6 maggio 1999, n. 4558; Cass. 1 ottobre 1997 n. 9606.

the idea of 'mutuality of obligations' is, in itself, a neutral one, it is evident that the way it has been interpreted by British courts in the recent past[61] has attributed to it an exclusionary effect as 'the absence of mutuality will most likely defeat a claim of employee status, without in itself being a sufficient condition'[62] for the attribution of the latter.

The proof that the 'mutuality test' could be used in an inclusive way too, both in the UK as elsewhere, is given by a judgment of the European Court of Justice, *Shirley Preston and Others* v *Wolverhampton Healthcare NHS Trust and Others*.[63] Without entering into the specific facts of the case and the questions referred to the ECJ by the House of Lords, it is important and possible to grasp some salient points of particular relevance for the issue of intermittence. The ECJ, in order to reply to the national court, was forced to focus its attention precisely on 'a number of actions before the national court which are distinguished by the fact that the claimants work regularly, but periodically or intermittently, for the same employer, under successive legally separate contracts' (paragraph 65). The ECJ proved to be aware of the possibility that 'such successive contracts may sometimes be covered by a framework contract (known as an "umbrella" contract), under which the parties are required to renew their various contracts of employment, thereby establishing a continuous employment relationship' (paragraph 23). But it was also aware of the fact that no such continuity would occur 'in the absence of an umbrella contract' (paragraph 65). The Court decided that it was possible to infer from the conduct of the parties whether enough mutuality of obligation occurred. Indeed, in cases where there is 'a succession of short-term contracts concluded at *regular intervals* in respect of the *same employment*' it is possible to assume that 'there is a *stable* relationship'.[64]

Regularity of intermittence and same employment are thus seen as 'features that characterise a *stable employment relationship*' (paragraph 70, emphasis added). To sum up, the ECJ detects the presence of a 'stable employment relationship ... from a succession of short-term contracts concluded at regular intervals in respect of the same employment' (paragraph 72). Arguably, previous decisions of the British courts, such as *Carmichael* and *O'Kelly*, are inconsistent with this reasoning of the ECJ. When, on 8 February 2001, *Preston* was finally decided by the House of Lords,[65] their Lordships did not hesitate to admit that it is possible to have 'a stable employment relationship' whenever there is 'a succession of short-term contracts concluded at regular intervals in respect of the same employment' (paragraph 35). And this even in those problematic cases where the workers with intermittent contracts are not 'regularly employed over a long period' (in other words, where

---

61 *Carmichael* v *National Power plc* [1999] ICR 1226 and *O'Kelly* v *Trusthouse Forte* [1983] ICR 728.

62 S. Deakin and G. Morris, *Labour Law* (London, 2001), p. 162.

63 Case C-78/98, *Shirley Preston and Others* v *Wolverhampton Healthcare NHS Trust and Others* [2000] ECR I 3201, [2000] ICR 961, [2000] 2 CMLR 837.

64 Case C-78/98, para. [69]. Emphasis added.

65 *Preston* v *Wolverhampton Healthcare NHS Trust* [2001] UKHL 5 (2001), [2001] ICR 217.

there was intermittence but the duration of the contract was anyway long, 'e.g. teachers on a termly or academic year contract'[66]) and even if they are 'not regularly employed but ... employed from time to time [and without having] what has been called an "umbrella" contract' (paragraph 32). In that respect a more recent decision by the Court of Appeal, also seems to suggest that British courts may now be prepared to make a meaningful use of the gap-filling device provided by section 212 of ERA 1999, whenever the various individual contracts are contract of service with a sufficient degree of mutuality, and effectively imply the existence of an umbrella contract with overall mutuality.[67]

It seems to us that the focus of the ECJ, and increasingly of British courts, on the attitude of the parties goes to some extent in the direction of the changes advocated by Deakin when he points out that a central question 'is how far the law is prepared to go in upsetting, after the event, the contractual allocation of risks which the parties have made'.[68] On the other hand it also appears to be the case that the decisions in *Preston* and *Prater* are not tantamount to a complete departure from a contractual foundation of the employment relationship. They lay down the correct interpretative and analytical basis for making sure that contractual 'shams' are actively discouraged and contractual arrangements providing for a regular series of dependent work engagements are correctly seen as giving rise to a dependent and stable employment relationship.

Similar interpretative positions are not uncommon in other jurisdictions.[69] As the Italian *Corte di Cassazione* pointed out in its decision n. 12926 of 1999, when the contract for services is a sham, 'the hidden *contract* prevails over the simulated one' and the latter *contract* has to be exposed by the adjudicator who 'must not limit himself to the literary meaning of the words, but must also evaluate the behaviour of the parties' when implementing the contract.[70] This kind of decision, far from questioning or disregarding the contractual analysis of the individual employment relationship, highlights to what a considerable extent legal reasoning in Italy, just as in Britain, believes that 'employment law is deeply, perhaps even irrevocably, committed to a contractual analysis of the individual employment relationship, but that this analysis need not be and should not be confined to the contract of employment as such'.[71]

3. The debate over the 'grey zone' between employment and self-employment

As mentioned in the introduction, the second doctrinal debate on the possible reforms of labour law aimed at allowing it to cope with the changes in the labour market revolves around the notion of a *tertium genus* of workers. This debate is a real obsession for many continental systems (primarily for Italy) but, albeit on

---

66 *Preston*, Footnote 35 of para. 32.

67 *Cornwall CC* v *Prater* [2006] EWCA Civ 102.

68 S. Deakin, 'The Changing Concept of "Employer" in Labour Law', *ILJ* (2001): 75.

69 Cass. 23 Febbraio 2000, n. 2039; Cass. 18 Novembre 2000, n. 1924.

70 Cass. 22 Novembre 1999, n. 12926. Emphasis added.

71 M. Freedland, *The Personal Employment Contract* (OUP, Oxford, 2003), p. 6.

72   *The Changing Law of the Employment Relationship*

a different scale and with different nuances, it is also possible to discern it in the United Kingdom. As hinted in the previous paragraphs, this third typology of workers, located between the traditional concepts of employee on the one hand and of self-employed on the other, borrows some characteristics from both. Similarly to the self-employed, these workers retain a considerable discretion over the manner and timing of performance of their work, but they are also economically dependent on wages and salary for their subsistence just as any dependent employee and they are still subject to some form of entrepreneurial control or coordination of their activities for a certain amount of time.

The doctrinal, and statutory, definition of this third-category of 'quasi-subordinated' workers is by no means a novelty in countries such as Germany and Italy, and it actually dates back to the early to mid-1970s. The *arbeitnehmerähnliche Personen* were first 'typified' by section 12a of the 1974 law on collective agreements (*Tarifsvertragsgesetz*) and defined as '*Personen, die wirtschaftlicht abhängig und vergleichbar einem Arbeitnehmer sozial schutzbedürftig sind*', that is to say, 'persons who [in spite of their formal independence] are economically dependent and, like an employee, in need of social protection'. To fall into this category the worker has to work alone, and the major part of his work (for example, one-third of his total income for journalists and artists) must come from a single employer. Right from the start, 'quasi-employees' were afforded the same procedural labour rights recognised for 'dependent workers', with section 5 of the *Arbeitsgerichsgesetz* covering employees as well as 'other persons who, because of a lack of economic autonomy, are treated as dependent workers'. In 1994 protection against sexual harassment in the workplace was extended to the *arbeitnehmeränliche Personen* under section 1 of the *Beschaftigtenschutzgesetz*. Traditionally, German economically dependant workers have also enjoyed a statutory entitlement to holidays and leave, under section 2 of the *Bundesurlaubsgesetz* 1963, and to social security contributions and protection and health and safety regulations.[72]

A similar set of rights was bestowed to the Italian '*parasubordinati*' by a series of statutory interventions. Law 533/1973, modifying for this purpose Article 409 of the Italian Civil Procedure Code, prescribed that the labour dispute regime also apply to the 'relationship of agency, of commercial representation and other relations of collaboration materialising in a continuous and coordinated provision, predominantly personal even if not of entirely personal character'. To put it simply, the labour process rules will apply when the provision of the service presents itself 'as characterised, in practice, by a predominantly personal activity of continuous and coordinated collaboration in an enterprise'[73] (the so-called *co.co.co. – Collaborazioni Coordinate e Continuative* – which in practice is a loose category of *parasubordinati*). The focus in Italy is not on the economic need for social protection,[74] as in Germany,

---

72   *Sozialgesetzbuch-SGB*, §7, s IV, Book IV. See A. Hoeland, 'A Comparative Study of the Impact of Electronic Technology on Workplace Disputes: National Report on Germany', *Comp. Labor Law & Pol'y Journal* (2005): 152–153.

73   E. Ghera, *Diritto del Lavoro* (Cacucci, Bari, 2001), p. 74.

74   On the other hand this was the focus of a reform proposed in the late 1990s by Professors Tiziano Treu and Giuliano Amato, available on http://www.uil.it/uil_lombardia/

but instead on the expectation, and power, of the employer to *coordinate* the activities of the worker (in the limited sense that he can expect to see his interest in having a sequence of 'result performances' satisfied), despite the lack of subordination. The characterising elements of *parasubordinazione*, as inferred from Article 409(3), are *collaboration, coordination, continuity* and the *predominantly personal provision of labour*.

In the context of *parasubordinazione*, the element of *collaboration* differs from the one applying in the context of standard dependent work under Article 2094 of the Italian civil code and requires that a subordinated worker be one who commits himself to 'collaborate in the enterprise'. In para-subordinated work, the same applies but the worker is in this case *disconnected* from any formal hierarchical role within the organisation of the enterprise (or with an entrepreneur) which uses the worker's services. *Continuity* implies that the collaboration involved in quasi-subordinated working arrangements must be aimed at *soddisfare un interesse durevole*[75] of the enterprise. This means that in practice any kind of autonomous work contract or self-employed relationship can be brought into the sphere of *parasuborinazione* if protracted for a certain amount of time (and coordinated). *Coordination* is another element that diversifies quasi-subordination from self-employment. According to Italian legal theory and jurisprudence, one cannot really coordinate autonomous work. All that a contractor/customer can do under Article 2224 of the Italian civil code is to verify that the execution of the work is proceeding 'according to the conditions set in the contract …'. So coordination is *the* element that provides a form of link between the worker and the business organisation of the employer. But coordination must not interfere with the autonomous organisation of the worker's activity (something typical of the employer-employee relationship). So the employer might give some *instructions* but no specific orders or directions.

The *co.co.co.* worker does not promise his personal labour resources for the fulfilment of any given entrepreneurial object the employer might want to pursue, but promises instead only the labour activity necessary to achieve the programme which was pre-determined when the contract was concluded. Ferraro points out that, at the end of the day, *any personal and continuous provision of services is also bound to be coordinated in a way or another* (but this author belongs to a minority of authors that likes to highlight the commonalities of *parasubordinazione* with dependent work).[76] Thus, he says, while continuity indicates a new added element *vis à vis* the typical, autonomous, contract for services, coordination has more than anything else a descriptive value, just reiterating that the continuous collaboration is implicitly functional to the needs of the enterprise. On the other hand, the element of the *predominantly personal nature of work*, along with that of *continuity*, univocally contributes to the distinction between para-subordination and autonomous work contracts. The relevance of the worker's *personal labour resources* – rather than the use of means of production (capital) and/or third persons that the worker might

---

articolatoddl.htm (15 January 2004).

75   Literally a 'durable interest', a concept that excludes a one-off provision of a specific service.

76   G. Ferraro, 'Dal lavoro subordinato al lavoro autonomo', *GDLRI* (1998): p. 461.

74   *The Changing Law of the Employment Relationship*

be able to employ himself – is another element that distinguishes para-subordinated workers from the self-employed. A total absence of this element of personality would be rather pointing to the existence of a business undertaking carried on by the individual.

In recent years Italian trade unionism has attempted to engage with and address the needs of these atypical workers. Initially it seemed another attempt to stick labels on jelly, but more recently some hopes have been cultivated. Earlier data made available by Nidil, the biggest trade union of atypical workers,[77] suggested that some 65 collective agreements had been signed by 2001, of which around 40 at the company level and 12 at the national and/or sectoral level and that the number of *parasubordinati* directly covered amounts to circa 73 000. Usually these collective agreements involved new-economy enterprises (call centers, telemarketing) or the public sector, but the number of agreements signed in the non-profit sector is steadily growing, while traditional private employers in the service sector had signed only 5 such agreements.[78] From a substantial point of view all these agreements made due reference to health and safety legislation, while the second most common provision was the requirement that the contract be in written form and that a copy be given to the worker. As far as the minimum duration of the contract, the is usually placed at two months. Working time was never the object of specific regulation in these agreements, while the issue of pay was tackled in a variety of ways ranging from forfeit-payments to explicit references to analogous collective agreements signed by typical workers' unions, and most of the agreements provided for remuneration to be matched with that of typical workers on a monthly basis. A considerable number of these agreements dealt with issues such as maternity, illness and accidents by providing that the individual contractual relationship be suspended, though none of the agreements suggested that workers on leave be entitled to at least some part of their remuneration. Some texts even provided a detailed list of the reasons for ending a contractual relationship and the minimum period of notice required. Almost all the non-profit and public sector agreements recognised a right of *parasubordinati* to be hired under a contract of employment if and where the enterprise decided to hire new employees. As for trade union rights, normally these contracts only afford to the workers the right to attend trade union meetings and to access and share trade union materials, and only very rarely the right to appoint a representative in the RSU, the Italian work council. But numbers matter, and in view of the fact that, in Italy, the overall number of para-subordinated workers is thought to be close to 2.4 million,[79] the effective impact of these pioneering agreements was – and still is – very limited.

For this reason, both theorists and legislators in Italy have sought a legislative solution to the under-protection of quasi-subordinated workers. The notion of

---

77   Available in English on http://www.eiro.eurofound.ie/2003/08/feature/it0308304f.html (15 January 2006).

78   S. Leonardi, 'Parasubordinazione e Contrattazione Collettiva. Una Lettura Trasversale degli Accordi Siglati', Quaderni di Rassegna Sindacale (2001).

79   G. Altieri and C. Oteri, *Terzo rapporto sul lavoro atipico in Italia: verso la stabilizzazione del precariato?* (IRES-CGIL, 2003), p. 2.

parasubordinazione has long been the object of a rather vibrant debate, with Italian academics disagreeing even on whether the *parasubordinati* should be seen as a *tertium genus*[80] or, as argued by the majority of authors and judicial decisions, a species of the self-employed genus.[81] In that respect some recent legislative reforms, which will soon be discussed, appear to have taken a stance implicitly favouring the *tertium genus* hypothesis and, according to some,[82] lay a gravestone upon the traditional binary model of employment relationship in the Italian context.

The so-called 'Smuraglia' proposal, discussed during the centre-left governments in the late 1990s, was approved by the Italian Senate,[83] but not by the lower chamber of the Parliament and thus was never translated into law. It was built on the same, loose, definition of quasi-subordinated work introduced in 1973 and discussed above. On the other hand, it aimed at introducing a rather broad set of statutory rights and protections guaranteeing, at least, the application of the basic Constitutional principles concerning labour protection. The initial draft imposed a written form for all these contracts and required that reference had to be made to the economic treatment provided by the collective agreements applicable to the type of workers whose conditions were closest to those of the para-subordinated. A preference in hiring in favour of the quasi-subordinate worker was introduced in all cases in which the enterprise decided to hire new employees, and in the case of termination of the contract, the worker was to be recognised the *trattamento di fine rapporto*, an Italian ad hoc lump sum severance payment. The relationship was taken away from the private law domain of the law of contracts and it was stated that a '*giustificato motivo*' was needed for a contract to be interrupted by the 'employer'. Further, basic rules on equality, non-discrimination, health and safety and training were introduced. Other norms conferred some traditional trade union rights (but not the right to strike) and the sanction provided in case of judicial recognition of misuse of *co.co.co* contracts was an automatic conversion of the worker's contract into a full time, indefinite duration contract of employment. The major drawback of the whole draft was undoubtedly the three months' qualifying period required for the law to apply. Evidently such a threshold would have introduced the practice of fragmenting the employment relationship into several short-term contracts, a risk that the Italian system is arguably no better equipped to face than any other system.

While the Smuraglia proposal was never translated into law, an alternative regulatory approach was adopted with Legislative Decree n. 276, approved by the Berlusconi Government in September 2003. This law does not build upon the broad, albeit rather imprecise, notion of quasi-subordinated employment relationship

---

80   R. De Luca Tamajo, R. Flammia and M Persiani, 'La crisi della nozione di subordinazione e della sua idoneità selettiva dei trattamenti garantistici. Prime proposte per un nuovo approccio sistematico in una prospettiva di valorizzazione di un tertium genus: il lavoro coordinato' in AA.VV. *Nuove forme di lavoro tra subordinazione, coordinazione, autonomia* (Cacucci, Bari, 1997).

81   V. Ballestrero, 'L'ambigua nozione di lavoro parasubordinato', *Lavoro e Diritto*, (1987) 41.

82   R. De Luca Tamajo, *Dal lavoro parasubordinato al lavoro 'a progetto'* (Working Paper No. 25, CSDLE Massimo d'Antona, 2003), p. 2.

83   *Disegno di legge* No. 2049 approved, by the Senate only, on 4 February 1999.

76 *The Changing Law of the Employment Relationship*

contained in the *codice di procedura civile* and discussed in the previous paragraphs. Instead, it

> circumscribes in a rather excessively rigorous way [the legal notion of *tertium genus*], re-baptised as '*lavoro a progetto*', but envisages a weak protective regime and one that can be opted-out, where the objective of impeding that practices aimed at eluding the protection of subordinate work or distortions of competition ... prevails over the legal certainty concern of recognising protection and rights to the new [legal categorisation].[84]

The law requires that all *co.co.co.* relationships, as defined in Article 409(3) of the civil procedure code, must be linked to one or more 'specific projects or work programs or phases' determined by the contractor and managed autonomously by the collaborator (Article 61(1)). Article 61(2) excludes occasional relationships (lasting less than 30 days in a given year) from the scope of the *contratto a progetto*, unless the remuneration for these short service arrangements exceeds the sum of 5000 euros. Also, all *co.co.co.* relationships already in place at the time the law was adopted could continue until 23 October 2004. Other exclusions from the scope of the law concern *co.co.co.* relationships requiring a registration in a professional register of the liberal professions, those involving amateur sport clubs, those concluded with the public administration,[85] commercial agents and representatives, and para-subordinated workers who are already in receipt of a pension.

All *co.co.co.* relationships that are not linked to a project or phase or program are prohibited, and where they are purported to be made in spite of this prohibition they are automatically converted into a standard open-ended contract (Article 69(1)). This sanction also applies if the contractual arrangement was indeed defined as a *contratto a progetto*, but the subsequent conduct of the parties is such as to establish a standard employment relationship (Article 69(2)). But for all its barking, Article 69 contains a third section that can often prevent the sanction from biting. Section 3 prescribes that adjudicators, when assessing the existence of the project, program of work or phase, are not allowed to 'scrutinize the merits of technical, organizational or productive evaluations and choices that belong to the contractor'. If this is understood as limiting judicial scrutiny to the merely contractual, that is to say formalistic, existence of a program or project to which the work relationship is attached, then inevitably *contratti a progetto* are conveniently going to display a concise and embarrassingly repetitive formula, merely paying lip service to the 'project' requirement.

As for the substantive rights accorded to these workers by the *decreto legislativo* 276/2003, it must be pointed out that the protection bestowed seems quite meagre, particularly if compared with the earlier Smuraglia proposals. The contract must be in writing and must specify the duration of the relationship, the type of project, the amount of pay and the powers of the contractor in coordinating the activities of the collaborator (Article 62). Article 63 merely recognises a right to 'compensation proportional to the quantity and quality of work, which must take into account the compensation normally awarded for analogous performances of self-employed

---

84 De Luca Tamajo, *Dal lavoro parasubordinato al lavoro 'a progetto'*, p. 11.
85 Cf. Article 1(2) of the decree.

Reshaping the Personal Scope of Labour Law   77

(workers)'. The relationship is suspended in case the of illness, pregnancy or work-related accident involving the collaborator, but no payment is required for the period of absence from work and the contract is extended only in case of absence due to pregnancy (Article 66). Health and safety legislation of course applies (Article 66(4)). Under Article 67(2) the contract can be terminated for just cause or 'according to the various causes or modalities, including notice, established by the parties in the individual contract', a vague wording that could even result in clauses introducing termination at will.

There are several reasons to believe that the wording and substance of these new rules, and particularly of those defining the notion of the *co.co.pro.* (*collaboratore a progetto*) worker, are tainted by a number of flaws. First of all, the law does not really offer a definition of the concept of *progetto*. If the term is analysed abstractly and out of context, one might well say that any kind of employment relationship or engagement can be broken down and subsequently linked to a project, a phase of a work or a program. And even if the intention of the legislator was to limit the use of quasi-subordinate work to fixed-term engagements, the fact that new engagements with the same employer are allowed, provided they are linked to a new project, seems to frustrate this goal too. A further ambiguity in the definition of the personal scope of application of the new rules derives from the fact that, while the project must be 'managed autonomously by the collaborator in view of the result, while respecting the coordination and with the organisation of the contractor' (Article 61(1)), the written contract must indicate the 'forms of coordination of the project worker with the contractor regarding the execution, and the temporal aspects' (Article 62(1)(d)) of the provision of the services. This may well result in contracts laying down something similar to broadly defined working hours and other working time requirements that appear to frustrate the formal requirement of total absence of personal subordination that should characterise this new form of work.[86]

On a substantive level, one cannot ignore the fact that even basic and fundamental protections, such as non-discrimination and equality rights, do not appear in any of the provisions regulating this type of employment relationship. As it will soon become apparent, the British category of 'workers' enjoys far more rights than the '*lavoratori a progetto*'. Finally, from a theoretical point of view, the law, far from recognising a *tertium genus* of workers and thus breach with the binary model of employment relationship, seems to be introducing a *quartum genus* of employment relationship. Indeed the introduction of a long list of *co.co.co.* relationships to which the prohibition contained in Article 69(1) does not apply, in spite of the absence of any 'project', means that the *co.co.pro* category is merely destined to add itself to the other types of subordinate employment, self-employment and the residual – and numerous – quasi-subordinate work relationships listed in Article 61. This point will be fully clarified in the concluding paragraph of this chapter, but it is already possible to argue that the scope of these new provisions does not appear to do justice to the profound theoretical debate surrounding the issue for the past three decades, and is

---

86   For a deeper and equally critical analysis of these issues, see V. Pinto, ' La categoria giuridica delle collaborazioni coordinate e continuative e il lavoro a progetto', in P. Curzio (ed.), *Lavoro e diritti a tre anni dalla legge 30/2003* (Cacucci, Bari, 2006), p. 431.

leading to the progressive emergence of a new and ambiguously defined special type of (under-protected) atypical employment relationship rather than to a long awaited *tertium genus* of workers.

On the other hand, quasi-subordinate workers have received some protection in the sphere of social security. In Germany this occurred with the aforementioned Law of December 1999. In Italy, Law N. 335 of 1995 initially introduced a 10 per cent social security contribution providing for some basic social security rights. The *decreto legge* 269/03 connected to the 2004 Budget introduced two contributory bands, one of 17.39 per cent and a second of 18.39 per cent, that are bound to increase in the next few years, considerably reducing the non-wage labour costs differences existing between employees and quasi-subordinated workers. These reforms have triggered an upsurge in the number of workers appearing under the label of *parasubordinazione* for social security purposes. Paradoxically, the country in which the workers in the 'grey zone' might be closer to obtain a legislative, albeit minimal, protection is the one in which the legal and doctrinal analysis over the exact identification of any given *genus* other than the traditional employee and the self-employed has never been accompanied by 'any great fanfare',[87] that is to say, the United Kingdom.

In the UK, labour law is primarily aimed at 'those employed under a contract of employment'. This is a very narrow scope and one that, as seen above, leaves outside a great number of casual and atypical workers. Nevertheless, some provisions of British labour law have always addressed a wider audience than the mere 'employee'. Under section 3(1) of the Health and Safety at Work Act 1974, the employer was already asked to 'conduct his undertaking in such a way as to ensure, so far as is reasonably practicable, that persons not in his employment ... are not exposed to risks to health and safety'. Furthermore, section 4 requires the employer to take such action and measures, as it is reasonably practicable, to ensure the safety of the premises. Clearly the wording of these provisions would be wide enough to include all the para-subordinated categories which have been the subject of continental elaboration. In the UK this scope has been seen wide enough as to include even 'independent contractors and their employees, provided that the work of the contractor can be regarded as the main employer's method for the "conduct of the undertaking" (e.g. *R.* v *Associated Octel Ltd* [1996] 1 WLR 1543 (HL))'.[88] Moreover, the continental *tertium genus* would certainly still fit into the notion of 'employment' as defined by the Sex Discrimination Act 1975, whose section 82(1) describes it as 'employment under a contract of service or of apprenticeship or a contract *personally* to execute any work or labour'.[89] Indeed, most of the quasi-

---

87 P. Davies and M. Freedland, 'Employees, Workers, and the Autonomy of Labour Law', in H. Collins, P. Davies and R. Rideout (eds), *The Legal Regulation of the Employment Relation* (London, 2000), p. 275.

88 H. Collins, K. Ewing and A. McColgan, *Labour Law* (Hart, Oxford, 2001), p. 169.

89 Emphasis added. Similarly s. 78 of the Race Relations Act 1976, s. 1(6)(a) of the Equal Pay Act 1970, and the more recent s. 68(1) of Disability Discrimination Act 1995 and s. 2(3) of the Employment Equality (Sexual Orientation) Regulations 2003 and of the Employment Equality (Religion or Belief) Regulations 2003.

subordinated fall within this definition, wide enough to contain any *professional providing personal services* or, as required in the context of the new *co.co.pro* category, any 'predominantly personal collaboration'.[90] It has been noted though that, in practice, the scope of British anti-discrimination legislation might not be much wider that the notion of 'worker' simply because it does not seek to exclude those operating a business undertaking and contracting with a customer:

> the Courts have effectively applied such an exclusion by another route. They have not treated the personal provision of *any* services as being sufficient to engage the legislation, however insignificant that may be under the contract. Rather they have asked whether the "dominant purpose" of the contract is the provision of personal services or whether that is an ancillary or incidental feature. It is only if it is the dominant purpose that the definition is engaged.[91]

What would probably still cover most of the *parasubordinati* or most of the *arbeitnehmerähnliche Personen* is the individual scope of application of that stream of labour legislation inaugurated with the Wages Act 1986 and with TULR(C)A 1992[92] and – after a few years' gap – consistently applied in the late 1990s by the New Labour governments, notably in the National Minimum Wage Act (NMWA) 1998 and in the Working Time Regulations 1998. Section 54 of the NMWA 1998 introduces a twofold taxonomy of the categories of labourers to which its provisions apply. The first category to which it is addressed is, of course, the 'employees'. The second is the category of other 'workers'. Section 54(3) clarifies that 'workers' are both those individuals who work under a contract of employment, and those who work under 'any other contract, whether express or implied and (if it is express) whether oral or in writing, whereby the individual undertakes to do or perform personally any work or services for another party to the contract whose status is not by virtue of the contract that of a client or customer of any profession or business undertaking carried on by the individual'. In practice 'workers' are a category that includes the 'employee' notion, and whose definitional boundaries are delimited by the positive requirement of 'personal performance' (similarly to the equal treatment legislation) and by the negative requirement of not dealing, by virtue of the contract, with a client or a customer (which is not present in the legislation concerning employment discrimination).

It should be noticed that the British formulation of the notion of 'workers' does not make any explicit reference to concepts of 'economic dependence', although clearly the notion resurfaces at a jurisprudential and doctrinal level.[93] As recently opined by Elias, though, the British notion of dependence is still embedded in a contractual reading of the overall relationship:

---

90   See V. Pinto, ' La categoria giuridica delle collaborazioni coordinate e continuative e il lavoro a progetto', in P. Curzio (ed.), *Lavoro e diritti a tre anni dalla legge 30/2003* (Cacucci, Bari, 2006), p. 441.

91   *James* v *Redcats (Brands) Ltd* [2007] WL 504779 at para. 53 (Elias J).

92   K.D. Ewing, *Working Life: A New Perspective on Labour Law* (Lawrence & Wishart, London, 1996), pp. 47–48.

93   See G. Davidov. 'Who is a Worker?', *ILJ* (2005): 57.

80   *The Changing Law of the Employment Relationship*

the degree of dependence is in large part what one is seeking to identify ... but that must be assessed by a careful analysis of the contract itself. The fact that the individual may be in a subordinate position, both economically and substantively, is of itself of little assistance in defining the relevant boundary because a small business operation may be as economically dependent on the other contracting party, as is the self employed worker, particularly if it is a key or the only customer.[94]

But even from a purely definitional perspective there are considerable similarities with the continental discourses regarding quasi-subordinate workers. For instance the requirement of *personal* performance is common to the German, Italian and British doctrinal and legislative elaborations.

Nevertheless, the greatest similarity between the 'worker' notion and the continental concepts of *parasubordinati* and *arbeitnehmerähnliche Personen* is not so much a 'definitional' one but one that relates to the 'function' of the concepts. Their common purpose is to allow for some labour law provisions (whether substantial or procedural) to apply beyond their strict traditional range (whether defined by a contract of employment or by subordination) and to extend into the category of the self-employed. Of course it should be noted that the British notion of 'employee' has been shaped by the courts in a considerably narrower way than the continental notions of *lavoratore subordinato*, or *Arbeitnehmer*, or *travailleur subordonné*, and this might explain in part the 'leap' made by some recent British statutes.

On the other hand, it should also be highlighted that the UK notion of 'worker' does not extend as far as that of 'para-subordination'. The British 'quasi-dependent labourers' 'are *employed* – they do not have their own business – without necessarily being *subordinated*'.[95] As a consequence, even if the notion of 'workers' includes *O'Kelly* situations, nevertheless 'commercial agents' (explicitly considered by the German and Italian laws) are still excluded, although they 'may nevertheless be vulnerable to loss of income and employment if, for example, their services are terminated at short notice'.[96] Overall this may well be the price to be paid for affording to 'workers' more substantive statutory rights that both the *parasubordinati* and the *arbeitnehmerähnliche Personen* enjoy. As Davies and Freedland point out, 'a broad personal scope may suggest a relatively light regulatory structure; a more focussed personal scope may permit tougher regulation'.[97]

In conclusion, it can be said that there is a vibrant debate in Europe on whether some of the labour rights traditionally afforded to subordinate employees should also be selectively granted to some categories of workers whose activity presents many similarities with those performed by the self-employed. The obvious benefit of such reforms is that that the expanding 'grey zone' between subordination and autonomy would at last receive some guarantees and protection. The obvious criticisms are that, by doing this, one might provide and incentive to a wider use and further

---

94   *James* v *Redcats (Brands) Ltd* [2007] WL 504779.

95   S. Deakin and G. Morris, *Labour Law* (London, 2001), p. 168.

96   Idem 173. But British courts can often give generous interpretations too: see *Harrods* v *Remick* [1997] IRLR 9.

97   Davies and Freedland, 'Employees, Workers, and the Autonomy of Labour Law', p. 285.

Reshaping the Personal Scope of Labour Law 81

expansion of these 'grey-zone' workers and, even worse, that the result would be the formalisation of the existence of a dualised labour market and labour protection, leading to further social inequality. The real shortcoming of this kind of selective expansion is that employers might try to by-pass and elude the new regulations by reorganising their human resource management and contractual arrangements so as to further alienate and increase the distance between their business and the workforce they use. We have already referred to the possibility of avoiding the 'bite' of legislative proposals such as the old Smuraglia law simply by entering into contractual relationships with *parasubordinati* for fewer than three months at a time. This would render their working life even more precarious than it currently is. Under these circumstances, a number of legal academics have proposed a third approach to the reform of labour law in the attempt to adapt it to the transformation of the economy and labour market. The ambition of this third approach is to see labour law becoming a *ius comune* covering all types of work relationships.

4. Re-targeting labour law

This third debate on the present and future of labour law goes beyond the traditional doctrinal analyses on the notion of employee and self-employed. In a way, it could be argued, it breaks away quite radically from the binary model of the employment relationship and, implicitly, from the unitary concept of contract of employment. Its declared ambition, as described by Alain Supiot, consists in 're-institutionalizing the employment relationship'. This process would imply 'employee status, which makes security contingent upon subordination, [being] replaced by a new labour force membership status based on a comprehensive approach to work, capable of reconciling the need for freedom and the need for security'.[98] It should be highlighted that, according to Supiot, substituting *employment* for *work* as the target of labour law is preferable to the other alternative, substituting *employment* for the – arguably over-extensive and probably unworkable – notion of *activity*. 'Work is distinguished from activity in that it [still] results from an obligation, whether voluntarily undertaken or compulsorily imposed. This obligation may result from a contract (employed person, self-employed person) or from a legal condition (civil servant, minister of religion). It may be assumed in return for payment (employment) or without payment (voluntary work, traineeship). But work always falls within a legal relationship'.[99]

Supiot envisages the creation of a new two-tier labour law system.[100] The first limb is constituted by a number of universal social rights to be guaranteed to everyone irrespective of the type of work and whether salaried or non-salaried. The second limb is supposed to introduce, with the help of collective negotiation, a number of 'special rights' applying to each kind of employment relationship. The first limb should definitely include a right to social security, a right to continuing

---

98 A. Supiot, *Beyond Employment: Changes in Work and the Future of Labour Law in Europe* (OUP, Oxford, 2001), p. 52.

99 Ibid., p. 54

100 A. Supiot, 'Les nouveaux visages de la subordination', *DS* (2000): 144.

82 *The Changing Law of the Employment Relationship*

vocational training, a right to participate in the definition of the object of work and the conditions for its execution (working time, terms and conditions) and a right to stability of professional contracts. It should be noticed that these rights are supposed to be attached to the individual independent of his position in the market, and they are supposed to accompany him all through his working life, no matter how many interruptions from periods of unemployment and changes of occupation. Similar analyses had appeared in the Italian doctrinal debates during the mid-1990s under the label of '*lavoro sans phrase*'.[101] Just as in the Supiot debate, Alleva's and D'Antona's proposals directly addressed and questioned, albeit in different ways, the binary model of the employment relationship.

Some avant-garde proposals on the part of British theorists also seem to be heading in the direction of a more radical re-thinking of the individual employment relationship.[102] In *The Personal Employment Contract*, Mark Freedland advanced a series of profound reconceptualisations of the individual employment relationship. In fact, by introducing the concept of the 'personal employment contract' – including both employee and worker contracts – and the subcategories of 'the contract for continuous employment', 'the contract for intermittent employment' and 'the contract for occasional employment' he departed both from the increasingly obsolete binary employment relationship model as well as from the more modern employee/worker/self-employed classificatory approach. An even more radical departure from the traditional British approach of analysing the employment relationship is clearly visible in the current research project of the same author in his article 'From the Contract of Employment to the Personal Work Nexus'.[103]

It is evident that this third approach amounts to a deeper 're-foundation' of the reform of labour law. This is a challenge that is second to none. It questions the foundations of traditional labour law; foundations that, although shaken and probably damaged by the transformations of the economic base, have not sprung like Athena from the head of Zeus but, on the contrary, have been laid down through a long historical process of struggles, industrial actions and political pressures, and has had as its driving force precisely the subordinated workers employed under a contract of employment. A few years ago, in occasion of a debate on the 'fates of labour',[104] Pietro Ichino, an Italian academic, provocatively asked the auditorium 'Why are dependent labourers enjoying all these protections whereas the autonomous ones are not?'. The late Massimo D'Antona, another famous Italian scholar, replied by saying: 'Because subordinated workers earned those rights .... Autonomous workers did not'. It is at

---

101 P. Alleva, 'Ridefinizione della fattispecie di contratto dellavoro. Prima proposta di legge', in G. Ghezzi (ed.), *La disciplina del mercato del lavoro, proposte per un testo unico* (Ediesse, Roma, 1996), p. 195. M. D'Antona, 'Ridefinizione della fattispecie di contratto di lavoro. Seconda proposta di legge' in G. Ghezzi (ed.), *La disciplina del mercato del lavoro, proposte per un testo unico* (Ediesse, Roma, 1996), p. 95.

102 M. Freedland, *The Personal Employment Contract* (OUP, Oxford, 2003).

103 M. Freedland, 'From the Contract of Employment to the Personal Work Nexus', *ILJ* (2005): 1. See the brief discussion of his ideas in the penultimate section of Chapter 1 of the present book.

104 S. Leonardi, 'Il lavoro coordinato e continuativo: profili giuridici e aspetti normativi', *Rivista Giuridica del Lavoro* (1999).

least difficult to foresee the ways in which such a 're-foundation' of labour law could occur in the present socio-economic and political context. Although, paradoxically, there is little doubt that it is precisely that very same context that justifies a more profound re-organisation of individual employment relations.

5. Conclusions

This chapter has explored the main themes that, at present, are being discussed by the European legal doctrines, judiciaries and legislators over the future and possible reforms of labour law, with the purpose of expanding or anyway remodelling its protective scope of application. These conclusions will now attempt to summarise these debates and link them to part of the discussion carried out in Chapter 1, cross-examining to what extent the attempts to the notion of the dependent employment relationship and the scope of application of labour law have succeeded or failed in addressing the new emerging features of the modern notions of employment relationship. The analysis will also focus on the successes and failures of the first two re-regulatory and jurisprudential strategies (stretching the notion of employee and the *tertium genus* workers) discussed above, and which have already been concretely tested for a number of years.

The idea of expanding the notion of dependent employment through new tests and new definitions of the constitutive elements of the subordinate employment relationship undoubtedly has many virtues, but also contains some risks. When this expansion occurs through legislative measures introducing mandatory qualifications[105] of subordinate status, law engages directly with the issue at stake to make sure that these workers, in spite of any absence of formal and contractually determined dependence or continuity and stability in employment, are considered employees.

But more often legislation will delegate to the judiciary the role of expanding the scope of application of labour law either by laying down legal presumptions of subordinate employment status[106] or by encouraging courts to assimilate the treatment of workers to that of dependent employees, even without qualifying them as subordinate workers.[107] It would appear from the French experience that when legislation takes this stance, judiciaries can feel encouraged to engage with the important changes that have affected the labour market and may adopt some bold and expansive decisions. In 2001 the *Cour de Cassation* did not hesitate to extend the scope of labour law to a number of 'franchisees'.[108] In these cases the workers were engaged in the delivery and collection of parcels under a commercial contract

---

105 For instance Article L. 751.1 of the *Code du Travail* for French VRP (sales representatives).

106 Ibid., Articles L 761.2, L 762.1 and L 763.1 respectively for journalists, artist and models.

107 Ibid., Article L 781.1.

108 Rulings Nos. 50105034, 35 and 36 of 4 Decembre 2001, *Soc. France acheminement c./Sierra* and *Dalval c./Soc. France acheminement.* See A. Jeammaud, 'L'assimilation des franchisés aux salariés', *DS* (2002): 158, 162.

84   *The Changing Law of the Employment Relationship*

formally defined as a franchise agreement. The Supreme Court was adamant about the irrelevance of the absence of a '*lien de subordination*'. It stated that when the franchisees 'work for a single enterprise', as it is often the case, and 'exercise their profession in premises supplied or approved by such company and at the conditions and prices imposed by the latter company', then 'whatever the enunciations of the contract are, the dispositions of the Labour Code are applicable'.[109] The case of franchised workers is a paradigmatic example, as here elements of formal autonomy and trilaterality/multilaterality in the employment relationship can combine to disentitle franchisees from any sort of employment protection.

Courts may also adopt expansive stances in the absence of any explicit legislative encouragement. The Italian notion of *attenuated subordination*, discussed in the second section of this chapter, is an example of the potential of this discourse. Another example could be the French *arrêt Labanne*[110] of 2000 stating that a person who drove a taxi under an automatically renewable monthly contract labelled as 'contract for the lease of a vehicle equipped as a taxi' and paid a sum described in the contract as 'rent' had to be treated as an employee. Again, putting aside the details of the decision of the *Cour de Cassation*, what is striking is the willingness of the French judges to go beyond the contractual and formal absence of dependence and characterise the taxi-driver as an employee 'because the economy of the contractual relationship was leaving him no real freedom in his activity'.[111] It is, arguably, the same analysis that the British courts have failed to make in cases such as *O'Kelly* and *Carmichael* when they fell short from realising that behind the 'regular' casual workers and those working on a 'casual as required basis' there was an economy of the *contractual* relationship that left no room for anything else but dependence from the work offered by the employer under that legal arrangement. As new developments in human resource management strategies are likely to further water down the elements of formal dependence and formal continuity, with the labour force being increasingly obtainable on an as-required basis, it is important that judiciaries evolve their understanding of the changes affecting the employment relationship and expand their notions of dependence, control, continuity and subordination.

Of course the expansion of the legal notion of dependent employment relationship cannot be seen as a panacea. There will always be some ambiguous borderline contractual arrangements that will resist any obvious qualification process based on the binary model of the employment relationship. A number of legal systems are trying to address this problem by carving a new category of employment relationship out of the area of self-employment or at least a *tertium genus* of 'grey-zone' workers. In the light of the discussion carried out in the previous sections of this chapter, it is possible to draw some analytical and critical conclusions regarding this type of

---

109 Ibid., p. 163.

110 Ruling No. 5371 of 19 Decembre 2000. *M.M Labanne c/Soc. Bastille taxi et autre.* See A. Jeammaud, 'L'avenir sauvegardé de la qualification de contrat de travail. À propos de l' *arrêt Labanne*', *DS* (2001): 227.

111 F. Adine Flammand and M.-L. Morin, 'L'activité professionnelle indépendante: quelle protection juridique?', *Le Notes du Lirhe*, (2001): 6. Also available on http://www.univ-tlse1.fr/lirhe/publications/notes/346-01.pdf (15 January 2006).

discourse. It seems that, for all its advantages and theoretical appeal, this debate is characterised by an inherent contradiction that this work would like to highlight by building upon the analysis of Paul Davies and Mark Freedland on the scope of application of employment law.[112] When the legislatures define these *tertium genus* workers in a broad way then it is likely that the latter working people will only receive a low, or even negligible, level of protection as it seems to be the case with the Italian traditional category of *parasubordinati* workers. But when the legislators attempt to narrow down their definition in an attempt to increase their legal entitlements, there is a concrete risk of defining a new typology of underprivileged and under-protected atypical workers, who provide their services under a considerable level of dependence but still are unable to enjoy the protections afforded to the standard employee. This, it has been suggested, would appear to be one of the possible outcomes of the creation of the *lavoratori a progetto* category in Italy, and the recent attempts of the new centre-left government to circumscribe its use seem to suggest an increasing awareness of this risk.[113] Of course this is a risk but it is also a potential of the 'grey-zone' workers discourse because it may well be that in the future legislators could progressively extend statutory employment rights to such a degree as to establish a substantial equality of treatment between some of these 'workers' and standard employees.[114]

In conclusion, it is evident that there is a growing concern over the inability of the traditional formulation of labour law to cope with the changes in the economy and the labour market. Although the great majority of workers are still employed under a contract of employment, there is a noticeable anxiety over the living and working conditions of a growing class of workers on which the weaknesses and evils of both autonomy and subordination seem to converge. It is difficult, at least at the moment, to imagine that this category of workers will ever have the power to conquer autonomously what the standard workers managed to achieve in the last century. And for the same reasons it is hard to believe that, even if granted a floor or rights, they would be able to build consistently on it through collective bargaining. Last but not least, any common floor of right bears the risk of being too thin for the 'standard employee' whose present allegedly privileged position has been achieved through a lengthy process of struggle. Any similar discourse carries the risk of '*lâcher la proie pour l'ombre*'.[115]

---

112 Davies and Freedland, 'Employees, Workers, and the Autonomy of Labour Law', p. 285.

113 See Circolare n. 17/2006 of 14 June 2006 trying to limit the use of this contract in the call-centre industry to genuinely self-employed situations.

114 Cf. the consultation document of the DTI, *Discussion Document on Employment Status in Relation to Statutory Employment Rights* (July 2002), mainly page 26 and following. Available on http://www.dti.gov.uk/er/individual/statusdiscuss.pdf (15 January 2006).

115 R. Castel, 'Droit du travail: redéploiement ou refondation?', *DS* (1999): 441.

Chapter 3

Atypical Employment Relationships: A Comparative Analysis of Fixed-term, Part-time and Temporary Agency Work in Europe

1. Introduction

Just as the analysis in Chapter 2 concerned what was described as the *scope* of the employment relationship, this chapter will unveil some key theoretical aspects of the regulatory approach that address the *taxonomy* of the employment relation. But the present chapter should also be considered in conjunction with the third section of Chapter 4 and Chapter 6 respectively, dealing with the analysis of 'atypical' employment relationships in the ILO discourse and at the EC level. This comparative examination of different regulatory regimes unveils how the different aims of regulation of atypical work have been applied by different actors and the consequences of these dynamics on national legal systems.

The present chapter progresses through three main stages, all focusing exclusively on the regulation of fixed-term, part-time and temporary agency work. The second section assesses the extent to which national legislation has succeeded in clarifying the *status* of those employed in some of the most common atypical employment relationships. In particular this section highlights the extent to which the constituent elements of atypical forms of work (enhanced autonomy, discontinuity, and so on), briefly mentioned in Chapter 1, have managed to distance atypical workers from those standard employees protected by labour law, and what legal devices have been adopted in different jurisdictions to bridge this 'status' gap, or at least make sure that the differences between atypical workers and standard employees have as few repercussions as possible on the legal regulation of their working relationships. The third section defines the extent to which atypical workers, whatever their status, have been afforded some substantive rights comparable to those enjoyed by standard employees and, most crucially, to what extent they have not. It considers which of the rights enjoyed by standard workers also apply to atypical ones while stressing the main deviations from the protective legislation applying to standard working conditions. The fourth section points out that the position of atypical workers is affected not just by the amount of protective labour provision they share with standard workers, but also by some 'special' rights tailored ad hoc to the specific needs deriving from

88 *The Changing Law of the Employment Relationship*

their atypical employment relationships. These specific provisions are examined and evaluated and their concrete impact on the employment relationship are assessed.

This chapter highlights how this *ratione materiae* subdivision largely coincides with a different, *ratione temporis*, evolution of the regulation of atypical forms of work, at least in Continental experience. By and large it could be said that in the first phase, largely during the 1970s, the main concern for most Continental law makers and judiciaries was to strike a balance between recognising atypical forms of work, or at least the ones having the greatest social visibility and economic relevance (such as part-time, fixed-term and temporary agency work), and making sure that their recognition did not result in an exclusion from standard labour protection legislation. This was not the easiest task, as legislatures had to reconcile the then-seemingly conflicting goals of protecting atypical workers without 'normalising' and implicitly encouraging the spread of atypical working arrangements. As it will be shown, the political and legal aspiration was, where possible, to transform these atypical employment relationships – still viewed with some suspicion and as a *minus quam perfectum* – into a typical form of standard full-time job, with this transformation operating both as a target and a sanction of the system in the case of successive atypical contracts.

In the second phase, largely occurring during the 1980s and early 1990s and inevitably linked to the previous phase, an overarching job creation rationale pushed all labour systems towards a partial deregulation or, according to some, 're-regulation'[1] of previous legislation and existing case law. This re-regulation was aimed at facilitating the conclusion and, most crucially, the renewal of some such contracts but also at encouraging employers, where necessary, and the labour force to adhere to these forms of work. Part and parcel of the latter effort was the progressive introduction of the element of *choice*[2] to counterbalance the enhanced flexibility of these forms of work, and *equal treatment*, or non-discrimination, to overcome some sort of 'precarious and unprotected work' stigma associated with atypical work.

These elements, emerging during the 1980s, were massively developed and structured in detailed legal terms in the middle and late 1990s, and this could well correspond to a distinct third phase, when flexible working patters were seen not merely as a way to employ fringes of unemployed workers, but also as a factor that could contribute to the expansion of employment rates and to the overall efficiency of European economies. In this third phase atypical work became increasingly surrounded by rhetoric arguments, in part supported by the European Community, and by the ambition to render atypical work good for the market *and* good, qualitatively speaking, for the worker. In this period the normalisation of atypical work was being progressively consolidated in the social and legal consciousness of Europe, although undeniably this achievement was more fully accomplished in some cases, for instance in the case of part-time work, than in others, with for instance successive and indefinite renewals of fixed-term contracts still being largely perceived as an

---

1 G. Giugni, 'Giuridificazione e deregolazione nel diritto del lavoro italiano', *GDLRI* (1986): 331.

2 The French idea of part-time as '*temps choisi*', coined in the context of part-time work, probably deserves the credit for introducing this rhetoric.

'abuse'.[3] This evolutionary path has been everything but uncomplicated, with underlying tensions visibly existing between the selection and prioritisation of the different policy objectives selected from time to time.

Some new legislation, adopted in recent years in Germany, Italy, and – not without some resistance – France, might be paving the way for a further regulatory phase where different forms of atypical work are discussed and addressed without any taboo, although one of the results of this stream of legislation appears to be the creation of sub-categories of workers formally excluded from labour protection and social security, as the result of a regulatory model of normalisation without parity regulatory.

2. Early legislation and the status of atypical workers

At a first glance, comparative analysis of the status of atypical workers could lead to the conclusion that the issue is at most a problem only for some systems – first and foremost the UK – or that it is largely a non-issue since, as seen in the previous chapter, most of the workers involved in forms of work such as part-time or fixed-term work, which account for the biggest part of the 'atypical' workforce, are more or less undisputedly seen as dependent workers. This section of the chapter will argue that these assumptions would be somewhat over-optimistic. It will begin by pointing out that, to some extent, it is true that all systems in ways and times peculiar to their own political and legal traditions and vicissitudes have indeed admitted a considerable number of 'atypical' workers into the realm of the dependent employee status, though it will be stressed that some exclusionary problems are still persisting. It appears indeed – and this will be highlighted later in this chapter – that a sort of divide has emerged between, on the one hand, a number of well-established and clearly defined atypical forms of work that are now more or less fully integrated within the scope of labour law and, on the other hand, other types of atypical activity, for example that of some types of agents or franchisees and workers involved in 'minor jobs', which although displaying some common features with atypical dependent work, are for a number of reasons still governed by civil or even commercial law or in any case excluded from labour law protection. This chapter will describe the emergence of the first group of 'typified-atypical' forms of work. It will point out how, right from the outset the intention of most European legislators has been to make sure that these jobs were as much as possible anchored to standard labour protection.

Fixed-term work

Arguably, of all atypical forms of work, the first to attract substantial regulatory attention by parliaments and judiciaries across European jurisdictions was fixed-term work; and this process begun with a rather impressive consistency well before the mid-1970s. Indeed, just as standard employment was receiving more and more the

---

3   Council Directive 99/70 of 28 June 1999 concerning the Framework Agreement on Fixed-term Work concluded by UNICE, CEEP and the ETUC [1999] OJ L175/43, clause 5(1).

90 *The Changing Law of the Employment Relationship*

protective attentions of labour law, a number of concerns were growing around the unrestrained freedom to apply a fixed term to the duration of a typical contract, often seen as a way to by-pass national legislation governing termination of employment. Already by 1962 Italy was introducing the first comprehensive law which did more than simply declare the exceptionality of fixed-term contracts, and laid down five rather narrowly defined sets of circumstances in which these contracts were lawful.[4] The aspiration of this legislation was also to steer the employment relationship towards the norm, that is to say, the contract of indefinite duration, in those cases where the contract was renewed more than once or it was *de facto* continued after the expiry of the term.[5]

In the same years in Germany, where during the Weimar era fixed-term work, albeit seen with considerable suspicion, was 'in general legal and only exceptionally illegal', the federal labour courts progressively built up a similar framework and reversed the rule/exception equation so that fixed-term contracts became 'generally illegal, and only in exceptional cases ... lawful ... on condition that there [was] a reason justifying the time limit'.[6] During the 1970s and early 1980s, the courts narrowed down the concepts of 'justification' or 'objective reason'[7] even more, with the result that, other than in the case where the employee chose it, fixed-term employment was in practice only legal in a limited number of cases such as 'auxiliary employment, situations where an employee temporarily replaces someone, occupations where the work is seasonal, or in cases where employment is entirely related to a limited specific project'.[8] There was no 'objective good cause' when the employer merely aimed at 'keeping flexible the management of his personnel' or where it was not 'possible to determine what the duration of a given activity [was] going to be'.[9] The burden was generally on the employer, and in the case of recurring contracts the justifying reason was even more difficult to prove.

In France the initial steps in relation to fixed-term contracts followed an opposite path:

> As the guarantees enjoyed by the contract of undetermined duration increase, they, by a phenomenon of contamination typical of the progressive character of employment law, tend to be adopted by and extended to fixed term contracts, by the jurisprudence and a number of collective agreements dealing with ... unlawful termination and severance pay.[10]

In practice the application and coverage of this 'contamination' was quite limited in scope to high-ranking professionals and, more often, to situations where 'the nature

---

4 L. 18 aprile 1962, n. 230, Article 1(a)–(f).

5 Article 2.

6 M. Weiss and M. Schmidt, *Labour Law and Industrial Relations in Germany* (Kluwer, The Hague, 2000), p. 51.

7 BAG AP n. 16, §620 BGB.

8 Ibid.

9 W. Däubler and M. Le Friant, 'Un récent exemple de flexibilisation législative: la loi allemande pour la promotion de l'emploi du 26 avril 1985', *DS* (1985) : 717.

10 G.H. Camerlynck and G. Lyon-Caen, *Droit du travail* (Dalloz, Paris, 1976), p. 112.

of the job itself implie(d) a certain duration (seasons in the hotel industry, the theatre or agriculture, specific task or temporary replacement)'.[11] Until 1979, when some first statutory regulation was enacted, the activity of French courts 'had had as an effect a perceptible limitation of the category of fixed-term contracts and the doctrine displayed ... on the one hand an "allergy to the civil law notion of *dies incertus*" and, on the other, a refusal to allow the retention of the fixed term nature of the contract in the case of its renewal'.[12] Gérard Lyon-Caen argued that this judge-made extension of rights to fixed-term workers had had the effect of discouraging the spread of this form of atypical work. '*La protection accordée au salarié recruté dans le cadre d'un tel contrat ... était devenue telle qu'il ne présentait plus d'avantages réels par rapport à celui à durée indéterminée*'.[13] In fact, the use of successive fixed-term contracts was practically impossible, since the French legislator believed that 'this formula [was] the only that could afford to the worker a real guarantee of the duration of his contractual relationship with the employer'[14] and then, even after the introduction of the neo-liberal and much criticised 1979 reform, Article L. 121-1 (2) would allow for only one renewal or two provided the fixed term relationship would not last, overall, for more than 12 months. Furthermore, any further fraudulent extension resulted in the 'contract resuming its true character as a contract of undetermined duration'.[15] With the *ordonnance* of 5 February 1982, French fixed-term contracts became *des contrats d'exception*, parties not being allowed to conclude them at will, even within specific time limits, but only in specific circumstances. The norm had to be that '*le contrat de travail est conclu sans détermination de durée*'.[16]

The UK also, as briefly explored in the previous chapter, affords – in principle – to fixed-term workers the status of employees. Traditionally, the expiry without renewal or extension of a fixed-term contract has been seen as tantamount to dismissal. But as opposed to their Continental counterparts, British fixed-term workers have effectively been deprived of unfair dismissal protection,[17] by the traditionally long qualifying periods provided by national legislation (two years from 1972, then six months between 1974 and 1979, then one year until 1985, then again two years and finally one since 1999) and by the possibility of waiving the right altogether when signing the contact. To make things worse, while in the past the waiver did not affect subsequently renewed contracts,[18] in more recent years, short-term renewals have been seen as an extension of all contractual terms.[19] Further, as opposed to

---

11 Ibid., p. 111.

12 G. Poulain, 'La loi du 3 janvier 1979 relative au contrat de travail à durée déterminée', *DS* (1979) : 68–69.

13 G. Lyon-Caen, 'Plasticité du capital et nouvelles formes d'emploi', Special issue Sept–Oct *DS* (1983) : 10.

14 Poulain, 'La loi du 3 janvier 1979', 72.

15 Ibid.

16 Article L.121.5 of the French Labour Code.

17 Though following Directive 92/85 implemented in TURERA 1993, the qualifying period of two years for claims for unfair dismissal on the grounds of pregnancy was abolished.

18 *BBC* v *Ioannou* [1975] ICR 267, 272 (Denning LJ).

19 *BBC* v *Kelly-Phillips* [1998] ICR 587, [1998] IRLR 294.

92   *The Changing Law of the Employment Relationship*

other systems, there has never been an issue of transforming the relationship into a standard one after a number of renewals, nor of limiting this kind of contracts to a specific range of occupations or to some substantive reasons. And, as will be seen, important rights such as maternity leave are still affected despite the recent, EC backed, Maternity and Parental Leave Regulations of 1999.[20] Most crucially British fixed-term 'workers' may still suffer considerable discrimination *vis-à-vis* standard 'employees' in the area of social security.[21]

Part-time work

Until recently, UK part-time workers have experienced a similar situation whereby they were more or less consistently considered as employees but a significant proportion of them were *de facto* excluded from a many of the rights typically accorded to standard employees. As seen in the previous chapter, statutory thresholds and their exclusionary effects on part-time workers were successfully challenged before the ECJ and national courts, whereas a similar result was not achieved in respect of fixed-term workers.[22] As discussed further in Chapter 5 and 6, the ECJ and EC law keep providing a number of stimuli for British legislation and case law to reduce and bridge the differences in treatment between these atypical workers and standard employees. As for Continental experience, the kind of discontinuity and working time contraction typical of fixed-term and part-time employment has never really had any exclusionary effect on the workers involved and, quite on the contrary, it has served as an incentive, at least in the early years of legislation, for a more interventionist and protective regulation of these forms of work. Overall one could argue that part-time work has been regarded with less suspicion than fixed-term work even if, in France in the last few years for instance, employment law has 'intervened to put an end to some abuses of part-time work'.[23] There has never been an issue about the status of part-time workers although, having said that, the regulation of their employment relationship has gone through a variety of phases, each supported by different rationales and justifications, and each resulting in higher or lower levels of protection. Sylvaine Laulom describes in very clear way the ways in which law and economic needs interplay with each other in France. The author reveals that the increase of part-time workers in France

> has not been regular. At the beginning of the 80s, and until 1986, one can observe, under the impulse of the first interventions on part-time work, a considerable increase. The

---

20   For instance, one year's continuity is still required to exercise the right to return to work within 29 weeks of childbirth after taking 'additional maternity leave'. The Maternity and Parental Leave etc Regulation 1999, 1999/3312, reg. 5.

21   See further in this chapter the analysis regarding the Fixed-term Employees (Prevention of Less Favourable Treatment) Regulations 2002.

22   *R* v *Secretary of State, ex p Seymour-Smith and Perez* [1994] IRLR 448; Case C-167/97 [1999] IRLR 253; 2000 IRLR 263. Cf. M. Freedland, 'Equal Treatment, Judicial Review and Delegated Legislation', *ILJ* (1994): 255.

23   J. Pélissier, A. Supiot and A. Jeammaud, *Droit du Travail* (Dalloz, Paris, 2000), p. 331 referring to the Aubry laws.

percentage of workers employed part-time then remained stable between 1987 and 1991, later increasing again when specific measures in favour of this form of employment were introduced. Since 1998, the rate of part-time workers in the active population seems to have remained unchanged.[24]

While equal treatment between full-time and part-time workers, at least *vis-à-vis* the enjoyment of statutory (as opposed to collectively agreed) rights has never been an issue,[25] the French definition of part-time worker, and therefore the scope of the related legislation, has gone through a number of distinct changes. Between the *ordonnance* of 26 March 1982, establishing a full equal treatment principle, and *Loi Aubry* of 2000, implementing, *inter alia*, the EC directive on part-time work, a worker was regarded as part-time when her working hours were less than four-fifths of the legal working time (then 39 hours) or the working time defined by collective agreements. Since 1993 the reference period could also be the year, and part-time workers were also defined as including those who alternated periods of work with periods of unemployment if their annual working time was at least one-fifth shorter than the yearly working time, as defined by legislation or collective agreements. In practice this definition introduced a sort of 'grey area' covering those working between 32 and 39 hours (often intermittent workers working those hours over the period of a year[26]), who were defined as '*travailleurs avec un horaire de travail incomplet*' and who could clearly not benefit from rights specifically attributed to part-timers.[27] Now, in line with EC law requirements, each worker working less than the legal or collectively agreed working time is considered a part-timer. Moreover, French law right from the outset did not miss the opportunity to stress that the tight regulation of part-time work was an implicit expression of preference for standard employment. Take the substantial formal requirement for having the contract of employment in writing contained in Article L. 212-4-3 of the Labour Code, in the absence of which the contract, far from being invalid or null, is considered as concluded for full-time work, thus placing the burden on the employer to prove the contrary.[28]

The French EC-inspired definition seen above nowadays applies, by and large, to Italian and German[29] part-timers too. In Germany, however, a number of thresholds have traditionally been in force excluding the so-called *geringfügig Beschäftigte* (minor part-time workers falling below 'the requirement of a minimum working time (15 hours) per week'[30] and whose income does not exceed one-seventh of the monthly reference wage or, where pay is higher, one-sixth of the total income) from social security areas such as unemployment insurance, health insurance and statutory pension schemes. This also applies to individuals whose earnings remain within these limits and whose occasional employment within a given year amounts

---

24 S. Laulom, 'Francia', *GDLRI* (2000): 559.

25 Being explicitly introduced already in the Law of 27 December 1973.

26 Cf. F. Favennec-Héry, 'Le travail á temps partiel', *DS* (1994) : 165, 169.

27 For a critical analysis over that state of affairs: F. Favennec-Héry, 'Le travail á temps partiel: changement de cap', *DS* (1999): 1005.

28 Soc. 14 mai 1987.

29 See Article 2(2) of the 1985 *Beschäftigungsförderungsgesetz*.

30 Weiss and Schmidt, *Labour Law and Industrial Relations in Germany*, p. 109.

94   *The Changing Law of the Employment Relationship*

to less than two months or 50 working days. Collective agreements might provide for lower thresholds (for example, the 1989 banking sector framework agreement requiring 13 hours a week) but this is not the rule. Although the implicit intention was that of discouraging minimal forms of part-time work, the result was the creation of a marginal and unprotected section of the atypical workforce. In any case, the causes and the effects of these exclusions, considered compatible with Article 119 of the EC Treaty,[31] have been partially reviewed and altered by the Law of 1999 obliging employers to contribute 10 per cent of the salary towards health insurance and a 12 per cent to pensions contributions. Furthermore the same law allows these *geringfügig Beschäftigte* workers to opt into the pension schemes available, and commit themselves to paying a special contribution of 19.3 per cent (with the employer again obliged to underwrite a 12 per cent contribution).[32] As for standard part-timers, national legislation only applies to enterprises with more than 15 employees and to workers with at least six months' seniority, in line with the general dismissal protection legislation.

Italian legislation first explicitly approached part-time work with a strongly regulatory stance, laying down a number of formal and substantial safeguards for those employed under these contracts. This stance, only developed in the mid-1980s, was nevertheless quite an improvement on the previous one actively discouraging the conclusion of part-time contracts, at least on the supply side.[33] A feature of Italian legislation in this area is the considerable regulatory latitude allowed to collective bargaining. Ghera reminds us that traditionally the latter 'had intervened to regulate the use of part-time work, often prescribing, as well as a maximum limit [*ndr. of working hours*], a lower limit to the duration of the employment'[34] and has also had the task of providing for the maximum proportion of part-time contracts lawfully employable in a given business or sector.[35] It is important to stress that this type of collective bargaining, being explicitly delegated by statutory legislation, has been viewed as having *erga omnes* effects, that is to say extending to all workers and enterprises in the sector concerned.

Temporary agency work

Where the differences between European countries become crucially significant is in the regulation of temporary workers. In this area, as already mentioned in Chapter 2, there is a real divide in the treatment of these workers, more or less coinciding with the traditional national stance towards intermediation in employment and with the historical role of the state in placement services. And actually a distinctive

---

31   See, for instance, Case C-317/93 *Inge Nolte* v *Landesversicherungsanstalt Hannover* [1995] ECR I-4625.

32   M. Fuchs, 'Germania', *GDLRI* (2000): 593–594.

33   Cf. P. Ichino, *Il tempo della prestazione nel rapporto di lavoro* (Giuffré, Milano, 1985), Vol. II *Estensione temporale della prestazione lavorativa subordinata e relative forme speciali di organizzazione*, pp. 395–397.

34   E. Ghera, *Diritto del lavoro* (Cacucci, Bari, 1998), p. 440.

35   Article 5(3) of Law 863 of 1984.

feature of agency work – at least by Continental standards – is precisely the ad hoc treatment it has received to distance it from the activity of 'an illicit placement office, since far from disappearing after having supplied the required worker to the client, the enterprise remains the permanent employer and responsible for all obligations *vis-à-vis* the [worker] concerned and the State'.[36] In a way it could be argued that Continental regulation of temporary agency work, far from attempting to sever the employment relationship existing between the worker and the agency, has traditionally done its best to stress that relationship and to ensure that the end-user enterprise was only linked to that relationship through a commercial contract, thus making the *'rêve de nombreaux employeurs ... de pouvoir disposer d'une main d'oeuvre sans avoir des salariés'* [37] come true.

In Continental Europe these 'three-way relationships' between a user-enterprise, an *employee* and an agency are structured around two distinct, albeit interconnected, contractual limbs. The first one[38] is set up between the agency and the worker, establishing what, by English terms, one would define an employment relationship based on a contract of employment, more often than not a fixed-term one. The second contractual limb,[39] existing between the agency and the user enterprise, is equally crucial for the regulation of the overall trilateral relationship, as its establishment and contents are regulated, quite strictly, to make sure that the employment of the agency worker reflects some genuinely *temporary* needs of the user-enterprise. Of course, these simple principles emerging from the Continental experiences have to be understood in their regulatory context, a context in which practices such as labour only sub-contracting and the provision of personal work through service companies were tightly regulated if not also prohibited.[40] As will be seen, often, British legislation in the area, far from discouraging any of these practices, makes the dream of both the intermediaries and the user enterprises of *pouvoir disposer d'une main d'oeuvre sans avoir des salariés* come true, with the agency worker often being unable to establish any employment contract with either business involved.

In Germany 'temps' were conceived of as more 'permanent' than their colleagues elsewhere in Europe. The 'hiring out' of workers 'was considered to be incompatible with the Federal Employment Office's monopoly in the area of labour exchange' until 1967, when the Federal Court asserted that 'temporary work ha(d) nothing to do with labour exchange if an indefinite employment relationship between

---

36 Pélissier, Supiot and Jeammaud, *Droit du travail*, p. 348.

37 G. Lyon-Caen, J. Pélissier and A. Supiot, *Droit du travail* (Dalloz, Paris, 1996), p. 262.

38 Known in France as *contrat de mission* and in Italy as *contratto per prestazioni di lavoro temporaneo.*

39 *Contrat de mise a disposition* in France and *contratto di fornitura di lavoro temporaneo* in Italy.

40 In Italy, for instance, the *appalto di manodopera* was effectively prohibited by law 1360/60 till the approval of D. Lgs 276/03, as discussed in Cass. 24/2/2004 n. 7762. In the UK these practices were never restricted, although since the adoption of s. 60 of the Finance Act 1999 the provision of personal work through services companies has been subject to the, according to some 'indirectly deterring', presumption of Schedule E taxation. See *Usetech Ltd* v *Young (Inspector of Taxes)* [2004] WL 2355783.

96 The Changing Law of the Employment Relationship

temporary employee and the hiring out enterprise is established'.[41] With the adoption of the *Arbeitnehmeruberlassungsgesetz*[42] in 1972 this orientation of the German constitutional jurisprudence was embodied in statutory legislation. The considerable amount of regulation contained therein[43] was further reinforced in 1982 by a strict ban on temporary manual workers in the construction industry. In any case, right from the outset, there was no doubt about the status of temporary agency workers, who have always benefited from the protection afforded by labour law.

In France the Law of 1972[44] did not require the *contrat de mission* to be of indefinite duration and, actually, the *ordonnance* of 5 February 1982 – brought forward by the newly elected socialist majority – insisted that this precarious employment relationship must be the subject of a *contrat à durée determinée*.[45] Successive legislation relaxed this requirement, and a number of limitations on the motives and objective reasons needed to set up a *contrat de mise à disposition* were introduced to limit, at least in theory, the inherent abuses of this form of work. Eventually 'the cases where recourse to temporary work is authorised [became] exactly those that allow the conclusion of a fixed-term contract, with the sole exception of the sets of circumstances contemplated under article L. 122-2 of the Labour code which relate only to fixed-term contracts'.[46]

Italy's regulation of this form of work was to some extent inspired by the French system. But a specific feature of Legge 24 Giugno 1997, n. 196, now partly abrogated by D. Lgs. n. 276 of 2003,[47] was the considerable latitude granted to the social partners in regulating a number of issues through collective bargaining, at a national and sectoral level.[48] The first two paragraphs of Article 3 of the Law summarised the points clarified here, that is to say that the agency is the *sole employer* of the worker (paragraph 1), that the agency worker can be hired through a fixed-term contract (paragraph 1(a)) or a contract of indefinite duration (paragraph 1(b)) and that the worker, during his assignment, shall provide his labour resources under the *direction and control of the user enterprise* (paragraph 2). Sanctions were once more aimed at transforming the atypical form of work into a standard one, for instance when the user enterprise kept availing itself of the worker's labour resources for more than ten days from the expiry of the labour supply contract (Article 10 (3)). By contrast with German law, and with the Italian law on fixed-term contracts, L. 196/97 did not introduce a list of temporal limitations for the use of temporary work, but

---

41 M. Weiss, 'Germany' in 'Private Employment Agencies', *Bulletin of Comparative Labour Relations*, (1999): 255.

42 Act on Temporary Employment Business.

43 Cf. Weiss, 'Germany', p. 255, and for a comparative analysis, U. Carabelli, 'Flessibilizzazione o Destrutturazione del Mercato del Lavoro? Il Lavoro Interninale in Italia ed in Europa', in *Scritti in Onore di Giugni* (Cacucci, Bari, 1999), p. 185.

44 Loi du 3 janvier 1972. Cf. B. Alibert, 'Le contrat de travail temporaire', *DS* (1984): 10.

45 Pélissier, Supiot and Jeammaud, *Droit du travail*, p. 356.

46 Ibid., p. 352; Article 122.2 relates to fixed-term work as job creation tool. See section below relating to fixed-term work in France.

47 See the third section of this chapter.

48 Published in *G.U.* n. 154 del 4 luglio 1997 – s.o. n. 136.

merely referred to the presence of 'needs of temporary character'. On the contrary the law, in Article 1, specified a number of objective reasons for the conclusion of these contracts[49] and a number of sets of circumstances where temporary work was prejudicially forbidden.[50] Interestingly, other than the routine references to workers absent as a consequence of industrial action, temporary contracts could not be concluded for filling positions previously occupied by workers made collectively redundant in the previous 12 months.[51]

In the UK, where the hiring out of workers for profit and labour-only subcontracting are permitted, temporary employment is far less regulated than in the rest of Europe and the range of contractual relationships dealt with by British employment agencies far more articulated and heterogeneous. Hepple stresses that

> unlike most other EU countries, the private employment services in the UK handle both permanent recruitment of full-time and part-time workers, and also the recruitment of temporary workers. A distinctive feature of UK regulation is that it is not limited to those supplying workers for a limited period, nor are there any restrictions on the period of assignment or renewal. .... In contrast with many other EU States, the UK agency or business may deal, without restriction, with 'temporary' or 'permanent' workers who may or may not be employed by the agency or business.[52]

In fact, the concept of employment as defined by the Employment Agencies Act 1973 (as amended by the Employment Protection Act 1975 and the Deregulation and Contracting Out Act 1994), is quite broadly phrased, including (a) employment by way of a professional engagement or otherwise under a contract for services and, (b) the reception in a private household under an arrangement whereby that person is to assist in the domestic work of the household in consideration of receiving hospitality and pocket money or hospitality only (section 13(2)).

Furthermore, the Employment Agencies Act 1973 (as amended by the Employment Protection Act 1975 and the Deregulation and Contracting Out Act 1994) and the Conduct of Employment Agencies and Employment Businesses Regulations 2003 apply to both 'employment agencies' and 'employment businesses'. The former type of agency is defined as one which provides services for the purpose of finding workers employment with employers or of supplying employers with workers for employment by them, and corresponds to the ILO definition of 'private employment *agency*' as formulated by Article 1(1)(a) of Convention 181[53]. The 'employment *business*' notion instead, corresponds to the ILO notion of 'private employment agency' defined in Article 1(1)(b) of the aforementioned Convention and would

---

49 Temporary use of labour skills normally not available within the user company, substitution of absent workers, other hypotheses laid down through national and sector-wide collective agreements.

50 Article 1(4).

51 Paragraph 4(c).

52 B. Hepple, 'United Kingdom' in 'Private Employment Agencies', *Bulletin of Comparative Labour Relations*, (1999): 380.

53 ILO Convention C181: Private Employment Agencies Convention (Convention Concerning Private Employment Agencies) (85th Conference Session, Geneva, 19 June 1997).

98   *The Changing Law of the Employment Relationship*

therefore be pertinent to the present discourse on temporary agencies. In spite of the fact that most businesses operating in the sector can act both as employment agencies and as employment businesses, and can therefore set up a vast and heterogeneous number of work relationship with their workforce, the 1976 regulations merely ask these intermediaries to issue to temporary workers a written statement of terms and conditions, indicating whether the agency considers[54] them as its employees or as self-employed. But, as argued below, this statement does not necessarily determine their status in law and can be often overridden by judicial decisions.[55]

Even the proverbial efficiency of the British civil service has struggled to cope with this heterogeneity:

> With regard to the number of temps, the leading industry organisation, REC produces figures that are often cited, but these are not considered very reliable as they are extrapolated from a survey with a very low response rate (about 7 per cent). Their figure of 1,130,000 temps working in a given week (in November 1999) almost certainly exaggerates the size of this sector of the industry. On the other hand figures from the main official source of labour market statistics, the Labour Force Survey (LFS), almost certainly underestimate the number of people supplied by the private recruitment industry. It has a measure of 'agency temps' (which is taken to include all temporary staff hire whether on an employment agency or an employment businesses basis) of about 290,000 in Great Britain in Winter 2001. *Some of the shortfall may be explained by the use of different definitions – with some workers supplied by temporary staff hire suppliers being classed in the LFS as 'fixed term' workers or 'self employed'. The LFS may also miss those temps supplied by agencies but paid by hirers.* In order to get more reliable figures, the DTI commissioned a survey, carried out by Bostock Marketing Group (BMG) during 1999. Estimates based on the BMG survey suggest that the number of people working in temporary jobs through agencies and employment businesses is about 700,000.[56]

And if the civil service is struggling to cope with this situation it is not surprising that workers are rather confused as well.

> The BMG survey suggests that 14 per cent of agency temps are *self-employed*. However, many respondents in the LFS survey might not consider themselves agency workers. ... Some workers use agencies to find a *second job*. While the LFS asks workers whether they have a second job, fewer questions are asked regarding the nature of the second job .... In general, more detailed information is given regarding the main job and one can assume that a respondent's working as a temp for an agency is generally regarded as a *second job*, and not the main job. ... The final group are workers on *fixed term contracts*. As in the case of the self-employed, workers on a fixed term contract may not consider themselves to be agency temps but rather as professionals, e.g. teachers or as employees

---

54   SI 1976/715, reg. 9(6)a.

55   *Wickens* v *Champion Employment* [1984] ICR 365; *Ironmonger* v *Movefield* [1988] IRLR 416; *McMeechan* v *Secretary of State for Employment* [1997] ICR 549; *Montgomery* v *Johnson Underwood Ltd* [2001] ICR 819, IRLR 269.

56   DTI, *Revision of the Regulations Covering the Private Recruitment Industry – Regulatory Impact Assessment* (June 2002), paragraph 25. Emphasis added. The same concerns are also voiced in page 7 of the revised, third, *Regulatory Impact Assessment* study published by DTI early in 2003.

of their workplace. These include approximately 6,000 teachers at all levels. Again, many of these are supplied by agencies. Although it is not possible to put exact figures to these three elements, it is considered that, taken together, the results from the BMG survey are a plausible estimate.[57]

Last but not least, British courts and tribunal have also rather inconsistent approach with respect to the status of British agency workers. The British judiciary has sought to apply its traditional 'tests', as seen in the previous chapter, but these have often proved ineffective in clarifying the status of workers involved in trilateral or multilateral relationships. As Deakin points out, even if these tests 'can be seen as identifying the enterprise in legal terms' they have their effectiveness shattered when the issue at stake goes 'beyond an analysis which focuses on the familiar issue of whether the applicant or claimant is an employee'.[58]

A quick review of English case law on 'triangular' work relationships involving, right from the outset of the establishment of the relationships,[59] an agency, a user-enterprise and a worker, can confirm the lack of legal certainty produced by the use of legal tests that were conceived in a strictly bilateral context and emerge as incapable of clarifying the 'allocation or assignment of the main functions which are comprised in the notion of employing workers or acting as an employer' in trilateral relationship.[60] Often, when the intermediary subject in a trilateral employment relationship is, *right from its inception*, an agency, courts have found the worker having a relationship 'of some kind',[61] and not necessarily a contract of employment, with the agency rather than with the user. That was the case in *O'Sullivan*[62] where the Divisional Court held that as the agency had performed the selection of the worker without the user having any control over the selection, and as the agency fixed the worker's remuneration and the terms on which she worked at the user's premises, and as the worker paid for her own stamps as a self-employed person for National Insurance purposes, she could not be defined as a worker falling within the usual 'person employed under a contract of service or apprenticeship' definition. But in other cases, courts dealing with this kind of trilateral relationships have instead pointed their finger on the user-enterprise as the entity employing the worker. In *Motorola*[63] the EAT dismissed the user company's argument that '*reality of control*

---

57 U. Hotopp, *Recruitment Agencies in the UK* (DTI, 2001), pp. 6–7. Available on the DTI website on http://www.dti.gov.uk/er/emar/recruitment.pdf.

58 S. Deakin, 'The Changing Concept of "Employer" in Labour Law', *ILJ* (2001): 72.

59 This clarification is important because, given the fluidity of the British legal framework, the intermediary can often be a labour-only sub-contractor not corresponding to the definition of agency or business *and*, to make things more complicated, the sharing of the employer functions can be 'redistributed in the course of [the] employment relationship'. See M. Freedland, *The Personal Employment Contract* (OUP, Oxford, 2003), p. 41.

60 Freedland, *The Personal Employment Contract*, p. 40.

61 S. Deakin and G. Morris, *Labour Law* (Butterworths, London, 2001), p. 176.

62 *O' Sullivan* v *Thompson-Coon* (1972) 14 KIR 108. The decision, ultimately discharging the claims of the worker for compensation after getting injured because of ill maintained machinery belonging to the user company, was taken prior the adoption of the Health and Safety at Work Act 1974 and of Directive 91/383, on which see Chapter 5.

63 *Motorola Ltd* v *Davidson* [2001] IRLR 4.

100   *The Changing Law of the Employment Relationship*

or its exercise' were not relevant to consider the worker – who had been employed through a contract for services by the intermediary agency – as its employee, and that instead the tribunal should have looked at the 'legal right or power to control' the worker, which laid with the agency that could at any stage have removed him and assign him elsewhere.

British courts have made clear that, even when confronted with a written statement where the agency itself recognises to the worker a contract of employment, they are free to decide otherwise since where a contract is wholly contained in a document, the question whether it is a contract of employment is a question of law to be determined upon the true construction of the document in its 'factual matrix'.[64] And indeed in *Wickens* the EAT stated that temporary workers on an employment agency's book were not employees since their contracts did not create a relationship that had the elements of *continuity* and *care* associated with a contract of employment.[65] Similarly, in *Montgomery* v *Johnson Underwood*, an employment agency appealed against a decision of the Employment Appeal Tribunal upholding a decision that Ms Montgomery, who was registered with it, was one of its employees. The agency had previously placed the worker in a company for over two years. The agency paid directly into Ms Montgomery's bank account the amount for the hours she had worked and terminated her assignment when asked to do so by the user company. Despite all these elements, all the judicial bodies involved in the case, that is to say the Employment Tribunal, the Employment Appeal Tribunal and, last, the Court of Appeal held that there was 'little or no control' of the applicant by the agency, something that the latter court, as opposed to the former two, considered as an 'irreducible minimum' in the absence of which any other factual inquiry was unfounded.[66] Moreover, as pointed out by Freedland, as a consequence of *Montgomery* v *Johnson Underwood* 'there seems to have been a full reversion to the view that there is no contract of employment either between the agency and the worker or between the end-user and the worker'.[67]

Apparently the legal uncertainty surrounding agency workers is set to continue, in spite of the positive conclusion of the *Dacas*[68] saga, that finally seems to achieve some degree of coherence with other recent decisions such as *Franks* v *Reuters*.[69] In *Dacas*,[70] the EAT was confronted with a claim by the worker that 'she was either an employee of the agency,... which placed her in the job she carried out at the West Drive Mental Health Hostel as a cleaner, or that she was employed by the ... Wandsworth Borough Council'.[71] Ms Dacas had been assigned by the agency to work exclusively as a cleaner at the hostel in question for six years. In the first

---

64 *McMeechan* v *Secretary of State for Employment* [1995] IRLR 461.

65 *Wickens* v *Champion Employment* [1984] ICR 365.

66 *Montgomery* v *Johnson Underwood Ltd* [2001] ICR 819 (CA).

67 Freedland, *The Personal Employment Contract*, pp. 44–45.

68 *Dacas* v *Brook Street Bureau* [2004] IRLR 358.

69 *Frank* v *Reuters Ltd* [2003] IRLR 423. More recently the same approach was taken in *Cable & Wireless* v *Muscat* [2006] IRLR 354. See A. Davies, 'Casual Workers and Continuity of Employment', *ILJ* (2006): 196.

70 *Dacas* v *Brooks Street Bureau (UK) Ltd* [2003] IRLR 190.

71 Ibid., p. 191.

Atypical Employment Relationships

instance, the Employment Tribunal had found that she had not been employed by either. With regard to the employment agency, the tribunal found that although the agency exercised considerable control over her, both generally and in terms of discipline, and that there was mutuality of obligation as between her and the agency, 'the intention of the parties when they first entered into the relationship was that Ms Dacas would not be an employee of the agency, and there was nothing in her assignment at the hostel which marked it out as different from any other'.[72] The EAT here stressed the same point as had been made by the Court of Appeal in *Johnson Underwood*:

> Having found that the agency exercised considerable control over the applicant and that there was mutuality of obligation as between the applicant and the agency, it was not open to the tribunal to treat the fact that the parties had not originally intended the relationship to be that of employer and employee.[73]

The EAT remitted the case to the Employment Tribunal for a finding of unfair dismissal to be considered, after stating that the temporary worker was an employee of the agency. However the Court of Appeal held by a majority that the tribunal had made an error of law by neglecting to consider adequately the possibility that there was a implied contract of employment between Ms Dacas and the end-user of her services, while Mummery and Sedley LJJ suggested that a triangular employment relationship, with the agency and the user being co-employers, might well have been an adequate way to address the relations affecting Ms Dacas.[74]

The Court of Appeal decision resembles in many respects the decision in *Franks v Reuters*,[75] where the Court did remit the question but only after heavily hinting that the temporary worker had an (implied) contract of employment with the user company, Reuters, thus reversing the ET and EAT decision that Mr Franks 'was not an employee of either respondent (and) had no claim for anything against either of them'. 'The available documentation relates almost entirely to the regulation of the relations between (a) Mr Franks and First Resort and (b) First Resort and Reuters. The crucial relationship is that between Mr Franks and Reuters. It is the third limb of the tripartite work arrangements. It is hardly documented at all.'[76] But this 'very lack of documentation of the work relations between Mr Franks and Reuters highlights the importance of considering all the evidence relevant to the possible formation of an *oral or implied contract of service*',[77] the Court said. It added that 'dealings between parties over a period of years, as distinct from the weeks or months typical of temporary or casual work, are *capable* of generating an implied contractual

---

72   Ibid., p. 190.

73   Ibid.

74   Unfortunately by the time the Court of Appeal reached its conclusion the user company had ceased to be a party in the litigation, so it will remain unknown if it could have been fixed with liability.

75   *Franks* v *Reuters Ltd* [2003] IRLR 423.

76   Ibid., [21].

77   Ibid. Emphasis added.

relationship'.[78] But this aspect, of crucial importance in the Continental regulation of temporary work, had never really impressed British judges before.[79]

In this rather confusing panorama it is hardly surprising that an Employment Appeal Tribunal decision of December 2006 re-opened the debate over the recently introduced notion of 'implied contractual relationships' between the temporary worker and the user enterprise by pointing out that

> When the arrangements are genuine and when implemented accurately represented the actual relationship between the parties – as is likely to be the case where there was no pre-existing contract between worker and end user – then we suspect that it will be a rare case where there will be evidence entitling the Tribunal to imply a contract between the worker and the end user .... Typically the mere passage of time does not justify any such implication to be made as a matter of necessity, and we respectfully disagree with Sedley LJ's analysis in *Dacas* on this point.[80]

This position was effectively endorsed by Bean J in the recent decision of *Craigie* v *London Borough of Haringey*.[81] But what is interesting is that these two cases do not part altogether with the notion of 'implied contract'. As put by Elias J:

> It will, we suspect, be more readily open to a tribunal to infer a contact in a case like *Muscat* where the agency arrangements were super-imposed on an existing contractual relationship. It may be appropriate, depending on the circumstances, to conclude that arrangements were a sham and that the worker and end user have simply remained in the same contractual relationship with one another, or that even if the intention was to alter the relationship that has not in fact been achieved.[82]

Effectively, the decisions in *James* and *Craigie* narrow down the possibility of implying a contract between the workers and the user to cases where, as in *Muscat*, a multi-party arrangement is *superimposed on a pre-existing* bilateral relationship merely to 'disguise' it and escape the application of employment protection legislation. While this is definitely a possible reading of what may constitute a 'sham' and a 'disguised employment relationship', it is arguably not the only one, and it is perhaps the most restrictive and least valuable of all possible interpretations. In many respects, similar types of superimpositions involving an intermediary agency will be already covered by TUPE legislation, as made clear in *Manpower UK Ltd* v *Mulford*.[83] As for alternative and more generous readings of the notion of 'sham' contract, it is enough to consider, for instance, the 2006 Commission Green Paper 'Modernising Labour Law to Meet the Challenges of the 21st Century', pointing out

---

78   Ibid., [29].

79   Cf. *Hewlett Packard* v *O'Murphy* [2002] IRLR 4, where an individual who had hired himself out through an agency to work for a company for *six* years was held not to be an employee as there was no contract and no mutuality of obligation with the company.

80   *James* v *Greenwich Council* [2007] IRLR 168, paragraph 60 of the decision.

81   Of 12 January 2007, Appeal No. UKEAT/0556/06/JOJ, not yet reported at the time of writing.

82   *James* v *Greenwich Council* [2007] IRLR 168, paragraph 60 of the decision.

83   *Manpower UK Ltd* v *Mulf*ord [2003] WL 23508894.

Atypical Employment Relationships

that 'disguised employment occurs when a person who is an employee is classified as other than an employee so as to hide her true legal status and to avoid costs that may include taxes and social security contributions'.[84] Nowhere does it suggest that for a personal work relationship to be a disguised one, it must have been superimposed on a pre-existing relationship covered by labour law.

The ET can hardly be blamed for taking the stance it did, and there is no doubt that its position is fully consistent with other previous decisions taking a narrow view on implied contracts, and requiring a strict test of 'necessity', 'necessary that is to say in order to give business reality to a transaction and to create enforceable obligations between parties who are dealing with one another in circumstances in which one would expect that business reality and those enforceable obligations to exist'.[85] But, as put by both Elias, and in words echoing the flexicurity debate,

> There are obvious benefits in flexibility for employers in hiring agency staff, and many employees, particularly those with specialist skills, may also benefit from the flexibility as well as giving tax and fiscal advantages. A careful analysis of both the problems and the solutions, with legislative protection where necessary, is urgently required.[86]

The three possible outcomes explored so far – employee of the agency, self-employed, employee of the user company – are further enriched by a fourth one as British courts, in an effort to square the circle, have given the impression of inventing 'new categories of employment status at will'.[87] Indeed *Construction Industry Training Board* v *Labour Force Ltd* introduced the possibility that 'where A contracts with B to render services exclusively to C, the contract is not a contract for services, but a contract *sui generis*, a different contract from either of the familiar two'.[88] The concept was repeated in *Ironmonger* v *Movefield Ltd t/a Deerings Appointments*.[89] In this extremely confusing panorama, and in the absence of a clear and consistent definition of the functions and legal standing of the subjects involved in these trilateral relationships, it is therefore possible that the agency worker is wholly deprived even of the, second best we may say, status of semi-dependent 'worker'. To reduce, if not eliminate, this risk more recent legislation has specifically stated that 'agency workers who are not otherwise workers' should be accorded a number of statutory minimum rights;[90] but it has been pointed out that 'it is deeply

---

84   COM(2006) 708 final, at 9. In respect of taxes see the recent decision of *Hudson Contract Services Limited* v *Her Majesty's Revenue & Customs* [2007] EWHC 73, where a similar unwillingness to imply a contract in multi-lateral employment relationships is displayed.

85   *The Aramis* [1989] 1 Lloyd's Rep 213. Interestingly no such requirement exists in cases of 'temporary deemed employer' status for the purposes of employer's liability. See *Hawley* v *Luminar Leisure Ltd* [2006] IRLR 817.

86   *James* v *Greenwich Council* [2007] IRLR 168, paragraph 61. See also Bean J at paragraph 17 of *Craigie* v *London Borough of Haringey*.

87   S. Deakin and G. Morris, *Labour Law* (Butterworths, London, 2001), p. 178.

88   [1970] 3 All ER 225 (QBD).

89   [1988] IRLR 461 (EAT).

90   NMWA 1998, s. 34; WTR 1998, reg. 36; ERA 1999, s. 13. See further in the next section of this chapter.

104 *The Changing Law of the Employment Relationship*

unsatisfactory that statutory variants of such complexity have to be constructed because of the lack of clarity of the approach of the law of personal employment contracts to the question of triangular or multilateral employment relationships'.[91] Interestingly, some of the larger temporary work agencies have sought to clarify the regulatory framework in which they operate by providing, either unilaterally or by means of agreements signed with representative unions, that the personnel they employ and place in temporary assignments is to be accorded full employee status, albeit on a temporary, 'pay as you work' or 'zero-hour contract' basis.[92]

To sum up, one has to conclude that the British legal system is struggling to make sense of trilateral employment relationships, at least in the area of labour law.[93] It needs to be stressed that, in that respect, Continental jurisprudence has achieved a more perceptive picture of what Freedland perceptively describes as 'the organization of employment between employing entities',[94] though it is all too clear that it has relied on a sound statutory apparatus in order to do so. Recently the *Corte di Cassazione*,[95] for instance, stressed once more that *lavoro interinale* is

> ... an employment relationship characterized by the scission between the *normative management* and the *technical-productive management* of the worker, completely different from the typical one that, instead, postulates an identity between the subject managing the normative phase and the one managing the technical-productive phase.

> In [the agency work regulatory framework] there is a clear distinction of roles as a consequence of which the supplying agency takes the one of the employer, albeit being deprived of the managerial power in respect of the labour resources provided by the worker which are, instead, to be used by a different employer who, nevertheless and other than [exceptionally] as a guarantor, bears none of the wage or social security liabilities which are imposed on the supplying agency.

> The role of the user enterprise is therefore that of mere management that, according to its needs, makes use of the worker made available by the supplying enterprise: as a consequence, the regulation of the employment relationship, in which its duration is the essential element, resides exclusively in the temporary work contract [*contratto di prestazione di lavoro temporaneo*].

---

91 Freedland, *The Personal Employment Contract*, p. 56.

92 See for instance the Agreement signed between the Communication Workers Union and Manpower UK, as reported in TUC, *The Hidden One-in-Five – Winning a Fair Deal for Britain's Vulnerable Workers* (2006), p. 12. Manpower has a consolidated track record of directly employing the staff it seconds to its clients under a contract of employment. See *Manpower UK Ltd* v *Mulford* [2003] WL 23508894 and *Manpower UK Ltd* v *Vjestica* [2005] WL 3027210.

93 Indeed not so much 'when fiscal considerations arise'; see S. Deakin, 'The Changing Concept of 'Employer' in Labour Law', *ILJ* (2001): 75–76.

94 Freedland, *The Personal Employment Contract*, p. 40.

95 Cass. 27 febbraio 2003, n. 3020. My translation.

All this would suggest that in the UK, as the judges have frequently reminded,[96] statutory intervention is crucially needed to solve this intricate matter and draw temporary workers out of their limbo.

3. Regulation and unemployment: typical rights for atypical workers

As discussed, the initial regulatory experience of atypical employment relationships coincided, at least on the Continent, with a deeply sceptical, if not ostensibly restrictive, stance. The approaches taken by the various legislators varied considerably. By and large legal systems did their best to bridge the gap between atypical and standard workers. In the previous section it was seen how one of the strategies adopted to bridge the gap was, ultimately, to seize a number of opportunities occurring in the course of the legal regulation of the employment relationship to re-qualify it into a typical one. But it was also shown how another approach has been that of discouraging or explicitly limiting some forms of atypical work; for instance, in Italy, by explicitly introducing trade union–backed quotas to limit the spread of part-time work. On the same lines one should mention that the initial stance of Italian labour law towards part-time work was clearly that of either discouraging workers from entering into this kind of employment relationship or the introduction, in France but also in Italy, of a number of substantial formal requirements whose breach often resulted in the conversion of the atypical employment relationship into a typical one. But by the early to mid-1980s a number of concerns related to unemployment rapidly pushed European governments towards a new approach to atypical, flexible, work, seen by many as one of the ways to revive an increasingly stagnant labour market. Many, though not yet all,[97] of the discouraging approaches seen above were progressively abandoned and a more positive, at times explicitly encouraging, stream of legislation soon began to flow.

Part-time work

The French reforms of the early 1980s exemplify this transformative phase. The 1981 laws were conditioned by a general perception that with regard to part-time work '[*les*] *inconvénients ... soient suffisamment réduits pour ne pas créer des obstacles d'ordre pratique ou psychologique a son utilisation*'.[98] Part-time work had clearly been subject both to legal obstacles and social stigma. The 1981 Law on part-time work was not aimed at limiting the spread of these contracts and any notions of quotas and thresholds were quickly dismissed.[99] Furthermore the agreement of trade unions and workers' representatives would no longer be needed, with consultation

---

96 *Montgomery* v *Johnson Underwood Ltd* [2001] IRLR 269 [42], [43] (Buckley J), [48] (LJ Brooke).

97 And this is particularly true for Italy, see below the comments on L. 863 of 1984.

98 B. Teyssié, 'La loi du 28 janvier 1981 sur le travail à temps partiel', *DS* (1981): 520.

99 See French Senate debates in JO, séance du 5 novembre 1980, p. 4413, 2 col., and p. 4405.

106　　　　　*The Changing Law of the Employment Relationship*

becoming sufficient.[100] But if one had to point to the one single aspect that caused the 1981 reforms to be associated with the idea of deregulation and flexibility, that would probably have to be the regulation of the *heures complémentaires*, that is to say the extra hours that the employer could ask part-timers to work, without the overall working time reaching the then 40 hours per week as a legal maximum. The setting of these additional working hours was left for individual contracts or, where possible, collective agreements to determine, and the absence of a statutory ceiling was rightly perceived as potentially leading to abuses. On the other hand, under the new article L. 212-4-3, in the absence of a contractual agreement on the *heures complémentaires*, the worker could refuse to comply with a request of the employer to work those hours, without this refusal being a reason for justified dismissal.

And although deregulatory as that legislation has been judged by many,[101] it no doubt represented a step forward in the concrete implementation of the equal treatment[102] and *pro-rata temporis* principles, and this was equally true in the areas of '*formation professionelle, rémunération, congés, avantages sociaux, etc.*',[103] including redundancy payments and retirement.[104] Seniority rights and career progression were taken into account on a strict equality basis and, by contrast with the situation in, for instance, Germany, without the application of the pro-rata principle.[105] The fundamental approach of the 1981 law, in other words, normalising part-time work and making it as 'neutral' as possible, was not radically modified by subsequent legislation, including the socialist government *ordonnances* of 1982. Admittedly, the latter granted to works councils a number of information rights over the hiring and use of part-time workers,[106] and introduced the significant limitation to the 'complementary hours' that they could not amount to more than one-third of the weekly or monthly working time specified in the contract,[107] with a continuance of these hours eventually leading to the revision of the whole working time regime for the employment relationship in question.[108] Undeniably they 'made possible the affirmation of new rights for the [part-time] workers'.[109] But the overall objective was still that of brokering the social and legal normalisation of part-time work in the consciousness of French workers and, crucially, employers as the '*avantages qu[e*

---

100 F. Favennec-Héry, 'Le travail á temps partiel', *DS* (1994): 166.

101 See P. Saint-Jevin, 'Existe-t-il un droit commun du contrat de travail?', *DS* (1981): 517, regretting the impact that the massive access of part-time workers would have on trade union and employee representation in the workplace.

102 Article L. 212.4.2.

103 Teyssié, 'La loi du 28 janvier 1981 sur le travail à temps partiel', p. 527.

104 Article L. 212.4.2, al. 5. Women enjoyed a two-year '*bonification*' for each child.

105 The ECJ has stressed in numerous occasions that a pro-rata system can lead to indirect discrimination. See Case C-100/95 *Kording* v *Senator für Finanzen* [1998] 1 CMLR 395.

106 Article L. 212.4.5, al. 7.

107 Article L. 122.4.3, al. 2.

108 If the employee does not object to the change, and only after 12 consecutive weeks. L. 122.4.3, al. 3.

109 A. Lyon-Caen, 'Le recours au travail à durée limitée', *DS* (1983): 18.

les nouvelles mesures] présentent pour les employeurs compensant les charges que les droits des travailleurs sont susceptibles d'entraîner'.[110]

Part-time work became, during the 1980s, the *enfant gâtée* of most European legal systems. This was due both to its job creation credentials and to its Janus-like ability of being able to strike an apparently fair balance between costs and benefits for both parties to the employment relationship, reconciling the time-flexibility needs of the employee – particularly the female employee – with some of the time flexibility requisites of the enterprise. In Germany the *Beschäftigungsförderungsgesetz* of 1 May 1985 aimed at part-time work 'being rendered more attractive by the fact that it takes a "more socially acceptable" form'.[111] The law enshrined the equal treatment principle[112] already developed by the German courts[113] although, as the ECJ would soon realise,[114] it neglected to address directly gender equality issues with respect to the 'objective justification' clauses contained in the Act and the leeway granted to collective bargaining by Article 6(1) allowing *in pejus* alterations to the statutory regime.[115]

With the 1985 Act the Federal Republic first laid down some detailed regulation in respect of *Kapovaz*,[116] considered the 'very example of flexible work'.[117] It consists in a special form of variable working hours under which the workers' labour resources are used only as and when the employer's demand for labour so dictates. In regulating this form of part-time work the German law paradigmatically pursued the two interlinked objectives of workers' protection and social and legal acceptance. Article 4 of the law specified that the contracting parties are required to specify in advance the amount of working time due over a given period, and that in the absence of such a specification a ten hours per week ceiling was presumed to apply. Further it was specified that the worker could refuse to provide her services unless the employer had communicated to her with four days of notice the exact distribution of her working time. This was to ensure a minimum degree of reconciliation between *Kapovaz* working commitments and private life, or a second job.[118] It was also provided that the performance of work must not be demanded at

---

110 Ibid.

111 W. Däubler and M. Le Friant, 'Un récent exemple de flexibilisation législative: la loi allemande pour la promotion d l'emploi', *DS* (1986): 715.

112 Article 2(1).

113 Cf. the initial stance taken in 1976 by the Federal Labour Court in *BAG, AP*, n. 2, *sub* sec. 62, *BAT* modified in 1982 favour of an equal treatment principle with *BAG, AP*, n. 1, *sub* sec. 1, *BetrAVG*.

114 The *Bilka* decision coming soon afterwards. *Bilka-Kaufhaus GmbH* v *Weber von Hartz* [1986] ECR 1607 and being followed by a stream of decisions (C-170/84, C-171/88, C-33/89, C-360/90, C-457/93, C-399/92).

115 But the German Federal Court soon stepped into the matter with *BAG, AP*, n. 18, *sub* sec. 1, *BetrAVG Gleichbehandlung* imposing the equal treatment in collective contracts too.

116 Acronym for '*kapazitätsorientierte variable Arbeitszeit*', in other words, capacity-related variable working time.

117 Däubler and Le Friant, 'Un récent exemple de flexibilisation législative: la loi allemande pour la promotion d l'emploi', p. 718.

118 M. Fuchs, 'Germania', *GDLRI* (2000): 589.

108 *The Changing Law of the Employment Relationship*

unreasonable times and that, unless the parties decide otherwise, the employer must employ the employee for at least three consecutive hours on each occasion, and in any case pay the corresponding remuneration. Works councils, where present, were also given co-determination rights in respect of the timing of *Kapovaz*.

As for job security and seniority, German part-time workers were already treated on a non-discriminatory and pro-rata basis with full-timers. A peculiarity here was that the employer seeking to make redundant a part-time worker and hire a full-time worker instead had first to offer to the part-timer the possibility of modifying the employment relationship and only a refusal of that offer would have made the redundancy fair. As for the threshold necessary of five workers to trigger unfair dismissal protection, part-timers normally working less than 10 hours a week would count at the rate of 25 per cent (in other words, 20 of these part-timers would have to be employed for the statute to apply), with an additional 25 per cent added for every ten weekly extra hours. Furthermore, other than for those involved into 'minor jobs',[119] social security benefits were applied to all part-timers on a pro-rata basis. Notoriously the pro-ratisating of career progression or seniority has sometimes clashed with the EC concept of indirect discrimination.[120]

This legislation also contained provisions aimed at bestowing official legitimacy upon *job-sharing* arrangements, although here it seems that job flexibility rationales had the upper hand over job protection concerns. The statute addressed two main issues: first, it made clear that, when one of the two workers is absent due to illness, the other worker could not be forced to replace him unless a specific agreement had been previously made. A general 'replacement clause' could only exist in respect of 'urgent needs' of the undertaking, but it is clear that in practice both exceptions could be imposed on job-sharers. Fortunately the law stressed that job-shares could not be treated as 'Siamese twins' and that when one of the two was fired or resigned the other could not be automatically sacked to hire a new pair of workers. Italy, as already mentioned above, decided to maintain a rather firmer grip on the diffusion of part-time work, and collectively negotiated quotas played a major role in the overall regulatory framework of L. 19 dicembre 1984, n. 863. A number of requirements for the validity of the part-time work contract were introduced in respect of its form and contents. Furthermore, supplementary working hours were strictly regulated and actually prohibited unless specifically authorised by collective agreements and justified by specific organisational needs.[121]

But this tight control on the proliferation and flexible use of part-time work was matched by a more flexible approach regarding the temporal aspects of the relationship. The law defined and formally introduced the distinction between *vertical* and *horizontal* part-time and, more controversially, it paved the way for the introduction of the so-called 'elastic clauses' (*clausole elastiche*); that is to say, some

---

119 But as seen in the second section of this chapter, the situation of these workers (working less than fifteen hours per week and with incomes not exceeding one-seventh of the monthly reference pay) has been changed by the 1999 reform.

120 See Case C-100/95 *Kording* v *Senator für Finanzen* [1998] 1 CMLR 395, [16]–[19], and Case C-1/95 *Gerster* v *Freistaat Bayern* [1998] 1 CMLR 303, [30]–[35].

121 Article 5(4).

specific agreements allowing the employer to benefit from a variable distribution of the working time. These clauses, initially backed by the *Corte di Cassazione*, became very popular in working practice; this resulted in part-time work becoming on-call part-time work. But by the early 1990s, the Italian higher courts modified their stance, and made clear it that it was still too early for Italy's legal consciousness to consider these flexible part-time arrangements as normal. The Italian Constitutional Court[122] deemed the *clausole elastiche* to be unconstitutional, and declared that their presence would systematically convert the relationship into a full-time one. The Court considered that these clauses not only affected the work/life balance of part-timers, but also did not allow the worker to plan and schedule her working life so as to be able to take on extra employment and make a decent living out of her two part-time jobs. This was a completely different story from *Kapovaz*'s regulation and acceptance in Germany.

Furthermore Italy was not yet ready to introduce the words *equal treatment* in its vocabulary for the regulation of part-time work, something that only occurred, as it will be seen in the next section, with the law implementing the Part-time Work Directive. On the other hand it made sure that the presence of part-time workers in an undertaking was taken into account, pro rata, to reach the thresholds necessary for the business to apply for financial benefits. Later the same principle was adopted in respect of the unfair dismissal protection contained in Article 18 of the *Statuto dei Lavoratori*. But altogether Italian legislation and judicial bodies had only made a comparatively small step forward in the crusade to render part-time work socially acceptable and palatable for workers and businesses.

That was not the case in the UK, where a rather low level of regulation provided employers with strong incentives to hire part-timers and a considerable leeway in determining their working conditions, while the long-working hours culture sustaining (male bread-winners') full-time work[123] pushed a number of, mostly female, workers towards part-time arrangements. This overwhelmingly female composition of the part-time workforce was the factor ultimately allowing, from 1994 onwards, the radical changes in the qualifying thresholds policy introduced, *inter alia*, by the EPA 1975. In practice, between 1975 and 1995, British legislation had been requiring part-timers working between eight and sixteen hours per week to be continuously employed for five years to access rights related to unfair dismissal, redundancy payments, pregnancy and maternity protection and, in general, all the panoply of labour law protection afforded to standard employees, with the exception of race and sex discrimination legislation and dismissal for trade union membership reasons (for some of period, even those working more than sixteen hours per week needed at least two years of continuity in employment to qualify for some basic labour rights). Furthermore, National Insurance contributions and benefits have traditionally been linked to a minimum income currently represented by the Lower Earnings Limit and excluding about one-tenth of British employees.

---

122 Sentenza 4 maggio 1992, n. 210.

123 See the Memorandum of S. Walby to the House of Commons Select Committee on Education and Employment in *Part-Time Working* (volume 2, 2nd report, 1998–1999), paras 1.2–1.3.4.

110 *The Changing Law of the Employment Relationship*

Self-evidently, British labour law provided different kinds of incentives at least to employers, for widespread part-time work. On the other side of the relationship, female workers were pushed into this form of work by a number of social pressures linked more to their 'reproductive' and caring roles than to their productive aspirations. And again it was the predominantly female composition of the part-time workforce that resulted in the provision of some rights and some equal-treatment relief for part-time workers. It has to be said that British courts did their best to facilitate the extension of these dynamics and allow an easy transition of women from full-time to part-time work as *Holmes* and similar decisions can testify.[124] In *Holmes* the Home Office had rejected Ms Holmes' request to return to her job on a part-time basis after giving birth to a second child. It was held that the employer's obligation to work full-time was a 'requirement' or 'condition' within the SDA 1975, section 1(1)(b) and that it was to Ms Holmes's detriment within section 6(2)(b) because she could not comply with it. As the Home Office had failed to show that the requirement was justifiable, Ms Holmes had been unlawfully and indirectly discriminated against.

But the fact that these rights and protections derived from anti-discrimination statutes meant that a number of inconsistencies emerged in the case law addressing part-time workers. For instance, the reasoning applied in *Clarke*,[125] whereby it was found discriminatory that collective redundancies targeted predominantly female part-time workers as opposed to male full-time colleagues, could not apply to the all-female workplace in the *Kidd* case.[126] Similar problems can occur in relation to the issue of occupational pension schemes where it is often impossible to demonstrate sex discrimination where the scheme in question is a female-only one, whether employed part time[127] or full time.[128] In practice in the UK, as in the case of Italy, pro-ratisating of entitlements and equal treatment only emerged as leading concepts in the late 1990s and in conjunction with EC legislative initiatives. The next section of this chapter assesses the relevant legislation, but it should be anticipated that the introduction of these principles in British statutes clashed, particularly in some economic sectors, with the results of many years of de-regulation, often resulting in what Freedland and Kilpatrick have called '*part-time workplaces*'[129] where, by definition, finding a full-time comparator poses an insuperable obstacle.

Fixed-term work

As for fixed-term contracts, the 1980s were also the period where the traditional distrust of this form of work were balanced against job-creation anxieties. A brief

---

124 *Home Office* v *Holmes* [1984] IRLR 299; *Clymo* v *Wandsworth Borough Council* [1989] IRLR 241.

125 *Clarke* v *Powell and Eley (IMI) Kynoch Ltd* [1982] IRLR 131.

126 *Kidd* v *DRG (UK) Ltd* [1985] IRLR 190.

127 *Cloroll Pension Trustees Ltd* v *Russell* [1994] IRLR 586, para. 104.

128 *Staffordshire County Council* v *Black* [1995] IRLR 234.

129 C. Kilpatrick and M. Freedland, 'The United Kingdom: How is EU Governance Transformative?' in S. Sciarra, P. Davies and M. Freedland (eds), *Employment Policy and the Regulation of Part-time Work in the European Union. A Comparative Analysis* (CUP, Cambridge, 2004) 317.

excursus upon French legislation in that decade will prove the point and show the complexity of this balancing act. The previous paragraph explored how the decree of 5 February 1982 narrowed down the cases where a fixed-term contract could be concluded.[130] These provisions were coupled with an equal treatment principle contained in Article 122.3.4 of the Labour Code. Subsequently, though, the law of 25 July 1985 admitted some new justifications for fixed-term work mainly inspired by a job creation rationale, and a decree of 3 April 1985 authorised the conclusion of these contracts for whatever reason when the job-seeker had been registered as unemployed for the previous 12 months. The new neo-liberal parliamentary majority backed in August 1986 a reform removing the limitation upon cases in which a fixed-term or temporary contract could be concluded. Instead it introduced the – very vague – principle whereby the conclusion of such contracts was in principle prohibited when their object was to provide permanently a job linked to the normal activity of the business.[131] Subsequently, under the newly elected Mitterand presidency, the previous system was reintroduced by a national intersectoral agreement, with a further expansion of the list of cases where the conclusion of a fixed-term contract was possible. The framework provided by the agreement was later embodied in Law 12 July 1990 which, by and large, is still in force and deemed to be substantially in line with the requirements of Directive 99/70 on Fixed-term Work.

As it stands, the French Labour Code only permits the conclusion of fixed-term contracts to replace absent workers, to cope with a temporary peak in demand, in the case of seasonal work, or with the aim of offering a job to registered unemployed.[132] According to Article L. 122.1.2, the overall duration of a fixed-term contract cannot extend beyond 18 months, unless the work is performed abroad in which case a term of 24 months applies. In practice the overall framework is not much different from the one laid down in 1982, although now a web of collective agreements, administrative regulations and government decrees have considerably expanded the scope of the job-creation category.[133] A number of prohibitions explicitly support these provisions. Under Article L. 122.3, a fixed-term worker cannot be substituted for a worker whose contract has been suspended in consequence of an industrial dispute.[134] Further, under the same provision, fixed-term contracts cannot be concluded in a number of hazardous occupations contained in a list drafted by *arrêté ministerial*. Apart from that, an employer cannot immediately conclude a new contract to fill a post left by a worker whose fixed term contract has just expired. Article L. 122.3.11 provides that such a new contract can be only concluded after a specific period amounting to

---

130 Article L. 122.1.1, temporary replacement of an absent worker; Article L. 122.1.2, occurring of an exceptional and temporary increase of the activity; Article L. 122.1.3; Article L. 122.3.1; Article L. 122.3.2; respectively occasional, seasonal, professional task; Article L. 122.2, cases where the hiring is under specific public programs against unemployment.

131 Pélissier, Supiot and Jeammaud, *Droit du travail*, p. 315.

132 Article L. 122.1.1 of the French Labour Code as modified by *Ordonnance n° 2004-602 du 24 juin 2004 art. 7.*

133 Pélissier, Supiot and Jeammaud *Droit du travail*, p. 317.

134 It is not too clear if that includes solidarity strikes. Cf. Pélissier, Supiot and Jeammaud, *Droit du travail*, p. 318.

one-third of the duration of the first contract has expired.[135] This prohibition will not apply if the first posting was interrupted by the worker before the expiry of its term, or if the worker refused to renew it once it expired.[136] Furthermore Article L. 122.2.1 prohibits the conclusion of a fixed-term contract within the six months following a redundancy unless the contract is less than three months long or it is linked to an unforeseen peak of exports.

Finally, on a more general basis, Article 122.1, al.1, spells out that '*les contrats de travail á durée déterminée, quel que soit son motif, ne peuvent avoir ni pour objet ni pour effet de pourvoir durablement des emplois liés á l'activité normale et permanente de l'entreprise*'. To make sure that this rule is not ignored in practice, the labour code requires that a term be specifically mentioned in the written fixed-term contract. The term can exceptionally be 'imprecise', for example when the fixed-term worker is replacing a temporarily absent worker, but then a minimal duration will have to be specified. When the term falls in the open category of 'precise term' then it shall not be longer than eight months.[137] The equal treatment principle, first introduced by the 1979 law,[138] is clearly still a pivotal element of the French regulation of fixed term work and is contained in Article L. 122.3.3. The principle applies to all aspects of the employment relationship (remuneration, working conditions, social security, job security during the relationship, unemployment benefits[139]). But fixed-term work contains an inherent flaw severely interfering with this principle and consisting in the fact that a great many rights and benefits, whether of statutory or collective nature, are linked to seniority which by definition is disrupted and often unachievable in the context of fixed-term work. To compensate for this flaw, French law says that when the expiry of the contract is not followed by an indefinite duration job offer, the worker is entitled to special compensation.[140]

The legislation is rather stringent both as far as sanctions are concerned and with regard to renewals of fixed-term contracts. Typically any substantial violation of a great many of the provisions considered above will result in the contract being 'requalified' into one of indefinite duration.[141] As for renewals, Article L. 122.1.2 only authorises a single renewal for a maximum period of 18 months, though now it is no longer required that a specific clause authorising such renewal was agreed and inserted in the original contract. Further or unlawful renewals trigger the 'conversion' sanction contained in Article L. 122.3.13.

The second section highlighted that the Italian legislator's initial stance towards fixed-term work was at least as sceptical and restrictive as the one taken, over the years, by the French lawmaker. Just as in the case of French law, Italian statutory

---

135 Half the length where the first contract was shorter than two weeks.

136 Article L. 122.3.11, al. 2.

137 Article L. 122.1.2. Twenty-four if the job is to be done abroad, and nine when there are health and safety issues or while waiting for a worker already hired through a standard contract.

138 Article L. 122.3.4. See J. Pelissier, 'Travail á durée limitée et droits des salariés', *DS* (1983): 18.

139 For the latter, see Article L. 351.1.

140 Article L. 122.3.4.

141 Article L. 122.3.13, containing a list of the cases where such sanction is applicable.

Atypical Employment Relationships   113

regulation has traditionally been pivoted around some rather narrowly defined sets of conditions in which these contracts were lawful[142] and could be lawfully renewed,[143] the principles of equal treatment and pro rata[144] applying to pay and working conditions, and the idea that the best sanction in case of unlawfully concluded contracts[145] is the creation of an open-ended employment relationship.[146] The same principles, as discussed in the next section of this chapter, have in part inspired D. Lgs n. 368 of 2001, implementing Directive 99/70/EC, although a far more deregulatory approach in the application of these principles is now noticeable. For instance, as far as extensions and renewals are concerned, Article 4(1) of the law provides that the contract can be consensually extended only when the initial term was shorter than three years, and that the extension can only take place once and when 'it is demanded by objective reasons and refers to the same working activity'. It is then stated that there is a maximum limit of three years upon the overall duration of the extended fixed-term work relationship. The sanction is still the usual one but is now applied more gradually. Article 5(1) says that a continuation of the working relationship beyond the limits set by the initial or extended contract will lead to a 20 per cent increase of the workers remuneration in the first 10 days, which goes up to 40 per cent for each extra day and up to a limit of 20 or 30 days (depending on whether the initial contract was shorter or longer than six months). After this *periodo di tolleranza* the contract is converted *ex nunc* into a standard one.

Having said that, one must stress a substantial feature characterising the Italian regulation of fixed-term work during the 1980s and 1990s and, it can confidently be predicted, in the near future too. This feature consists in what authors have termed as *liberalizzazione controllata*, that is the liberalisation of the controlling regime through collective bargaining.[147] Law 28 February 1987, n. 56, allowed collective agreements, concluded by the 'most representative trade unions' at a national or local level, to lay down further cases where fixed-term contracts were to be considered lawful, when necessary imposing quotas. The application of this law led, for instance, to the conclusion of the *accordo interconfederale* of 18 December 1988 which, with a declared aim of helping the job opportunities of those registered as unemployed, substantially liberalised[148] the conclusion of fixed-term contracts provided they lasted longer than four months and less than twelve. This national agreement was followed

---

142 L. 18 aprile 1962, n. 230, Article 1(a)–(f).

143 Just as in France only one renewal was deemed lawful, by the now-repealed Article 2 of Law 230/62 and for a term equivalent or short to the one of the first contract.

144 L. 18 aprile 1962, n. 230, Article 5.

145 A new contact would have deemed to be an unlawful renewal when less than 15 or 30 days (for initial contracts lasting more than six months) had elapsed from the conclusion of the second contract. These terms have now been reduced to 10 and 20 days respectively.

146 Article 2 of L. 230/62. Though here it is worthwhile anticipating that D. Lgs 368/2001, implementing Directive 99/70/EC has rendered the sanction more gradual as now Article 4(1) of the law provides

147 E. Ghera, *Diritto del Lavoro* (Cacucci, Bari, 1998), p. 433.

148 The only limits being that it would normally apply to those above the age of 29 (although this limit was qualified by a number of substantial exceptions; for instance it did not apply in the Mezzoggiorno, and for low skill jobs) and a 10 per cent quota.

by a series of renewals and by a stream of similar agreements concluded at a national or local level that, along the same lines, expanded the scope of fixed-term work well beyond the statutory constraints. Furthermore, this kind of collective activity had the result of inspiring the legislator to provide, for instance, with Article 8(2) of Law 23 July 1991, n. 223, that all workers affected by redundancies and registered in the *lista speciale di mobilitá* could be hired on one-year fixed-term contacts. On top of that, it should not be forgotten that contacts such as the *contatto di formazione lavoro* were, in spite of their vocational content and rationale, fixed-term contracts as well. What is clear though is that the European Court of Justice is determined to stand firm on the protective provisions contained in Directive 99/70 and that it will not accept unquestioningly every derogations from what it increasingly sees as a European floor of rights. Thus in Case C-53/04 it imposed a series of strict conditions on national rules limiting the conversion of successive fixed term contracts to the private sector, albeit conceding that the Italian legislation under scrutiny was, prima facie, consistent with the requirements consistent with the requirements of Directive 99/70.[149] In conclusion, it might well be that during the 1980s fixed-term work in Italy and France did not fully succeed in winning the hearts and minds of workers and society at large and that, as opposed for instance to part-time work, it still carried a considerable stigma associating it with precarious and low-quality employment. But it is a fact that while the 1985 French and Italian proportions of fixed-term workers as a share of the working population were, respectively, a meagre 4.7 and 4.8 per cent, a decade or so later, the 1997 figures had leaped to an impressive 13.1 per cent for France and to 8.2 for Italy.[150] In Germany the situation was rather different. By the 'mid-1980s, restrictions on the labour contract for a definite period as developed by the Federal Labour Court were questioned in view of increasing unemployment'.[151] The 1985 Law on the Improvement of Employment Opportunities suspended to a great extent the application of the case –law, described in the previous section of this chapter, which regulated fixed-term work.[152] Article 1 of the law abolished the 'objective justification' requirement for the conclusion of the first fixed-term contract, merely requiring a maximum duration of 18 months.[153] A fixed-term contract was not deemed to be the first one where 'it has a close and material connection with a previous contract for a definite or undefined period concerning the same worker'; and such a connection was assumed each time that the period between the two contracts was shorter than four months. If the contract was not a new one or if the employer wanted to conclude it for more than two years, in practice the old judge-made principles on 'objective reason' would apply, which

---

149 C-53/04, *Marrosu and Sardino* v *Azienda Ospedaliera San Martino* (not yet reported at the time of writing). On a similar tone, but in respect of the Greek implementation provisions, see C-212/04, *Kostantinos Adeneler and others* v *Elog* [2006] ECR I-06057.

150 EC Commission, *Employment in Europe 1999* (Luxembourg, 1999), pp. 133–135.

151 Weiss and Schmidt, *Labour Law and Industrial Relations in Germany* (Kluwer, The Hague, 2000), p. 52.

152 Däubler and Le Friant, 'Une recent exemple de flexibilisation', p. 717. Initially the suspension was limited until 1990, but that deadline was then postponed a number of times till, in 2001, a new law on part-time and fixed-term work came into force.

153 Later, in 1996, changed into two years.

meant that on some, though not many, occasions a fixed term relationship could last more than 18 or, after the 1996 reform, 24 months.

Emphasising the job creation aims of fixed-term work, a legislative amendment of 1 October 1996 allowed up to three renewals without a justifying reason provided that the overall duration of the relationship did not go beyond the two-year maximum, while if the worker was 60 years old or more even that maximum would not apply.[154] A termination of the contract before the end of its term was only possible in the form of a summary dismissal for an important reason, or a reason contractually provided for.[155] It is also worthwhile noticing that in Germany an explicit prohibition of discrimination against fixed-term workers only came into force in 2001 with the law implementing EC Directive 99/70, and that will be analysed in the next section. At the end of the day it appears that German legislation had liberalised to a very great extent the conclusion of fixed-term contracts with the declared aim of reducing unemployment.[156] But as Weiss and Schmidt have stressed,[157] it is uncertain whether the policy was a successful one. Eurostat data show that in 1985, on the year the *Beschäftigungsförderungsgesetz* was enacted, some 10 per cent of the 26 489 000 West German workers were employed under a fixed-term contract. Almost a decade later, in 1996, the now reunified Federal Republic could count on some 11.1 per cent, of the overall 34 423 000 workforce, working under a fixed-term contract.[158] This was not a big change and actually, considering that fixed-term work became more popular in the ex-DDR territories[159] one might be inclined to conclude that the 1985 Act had not really been very successful.

In the United Kingdom, fixed-term work, like part-time work, has been a relatively unregulated area of labour law. A further similarity is that, traditionally, fixed-term workers – and for that matter temporary workers in general – have been adversely affected by the presence of qualifying periods and continuity requirements just as their part-time colleagues have. But as opposed to part-timers, British fixed-term workers were less successful in challenging their 'qualifying period' hurdles. In *R v Secretary of State, ex p Seymour-Smith and Perez*[160] it was claimed that the two-year qualifying period for unfair dismissal introduced by the Unfair Dismissal (Variation of Qualifying Period) Order 1985 was indirectly discriminatory against women and therefore incompatible with the Equal Treatment Directive and, later in the Court of Appeal hearing, what was then Article 119 of the EC Treaty. Seymour-Smith had been dismissed by her employer before reaching the two-year qualifying period needed to bring a claim for unfair dismissal. Evidence brought before the courts showed that between 1985 and 1991, between 72 per cent and 77.4 per cent of male employees working 16 hours or more per week had reached the required

---

154 Weiss and Schmidt, *Labour Law and Industrial Relations in Germany*, p. 52

155 ILO, *Termination of Employment Digest* (Geneva, 2000), p. 153.

156 Däubler and Le Friant, 'Une recent exemple de flexibilisation', p. 717

157 Weiss and Schmidt, *Labour Law and Industrial Relations in Germany*, p. 53.

158 EC Commission, *Employment in Europe 1999* (Luxembourg, 1999), p. 130.

159 Weiss and Schmidt, *Labour Law and Industrial Relations in Germany*, p. 53.

160 [1994] IRLR 448 (DC), [1995] IRLR 464 (CA); [1997] IRLR 315 (HL); Case C-167/97 [1999] IRLR 253; [2000] IRLR 263 (HL).

116 *The Changing Law of the Employment Relationship*

qualifying service, compared to a 63.8 to 68.9 per cent figure for women. In practice, in the seven-year period under consideration, for every ten men who were qualified to pursue unfair dismissal claims against their employers, only nine women were eligible.

The ECJ in its judgement stated that the statistics brought forward did 'not appear, on the face of it, to show that a considerably smaller percentage of women than men is able to fulfil the requirement imposed by the disputed rule'.[161] But the House of Lords concluded instead that, though a case of adverse impact had been successfully made out, the qualifying period was objectively justified. Indeed, it was argued, the 'object of the 1985 Order was to encourage recruitment by employers. This was a legitimate aim of the Government's social and economic policy, and this aim was unrelated to any sex discrimination'.[162] In practice the qualifying period could be used on the grounds that it fell within 'the broad margin of discretion afforded to governments when adopting measures of this type'.[163] Once more, in Britain as elsewhere, when the choice was between job protection and job creation, the latter principle appeared to strike more chords than the former. In 1999 a reduced qualifying period of one year's continuous employment was introduced with regard to unfair dismissal protection, but the two-year qualifying period for redundancy compensation was not modified. And it wasn't until EC Directive 99/70 was implemented that pay and pensions discrimination against fixed-term workers was prohibited. And given the overall absence of any specific regulation on temporary agency workers, something already stressed in the previous section of this chapter, the overall lack of specific protection affected a significant proportion of British workers.

Temporary agency workers

The situation was different for French *intérimaires*, who had been able to count on well-structured ad hoc statutory protections since 1972. In 1982 French law on temporary workers further narrowed down the cases in which the use of fixed-term workers was permitted and first introduced an embryonic form of an equal treatment principle by specifying that 'temporary workers are entitled to an amount of remuneration equal to that that would be received, in the user company, after a *période d'essai*, by an employee with comparable qualifications occupying the same employment'.[164] Soon, however, job creation concerns started pushing towards a progressive relaxation of the regulatory framework, and in 1985 the very same socialist majority took a step back with the *Loi du 25 juillet 1985*, by which new conditions for agency work were introduced and longer postings were authorised. The *ordonnance* of 11 August 1986 completely dismantled the system of predefined and limited conditions for the lawful conclusion of temporary contracts introduced in 1972, providing instead

---

161 Case C-167/97 *R* v *Secretary of State, ex p Seymour-Smith and Perez* [1999] ECR I-623, [1999] 2 CMLR 322 [64].

162 [2000] IRLR 270 (Lord Nicholls).

163 [2000] IRLR 271.

164 Then Article L. 124.4.2 of the Labour Code. At that time research showed that there was a 20–25 per cent pay gap between temps and employees of the user company.

that end-users could rely on agency workers '*pour l'exécution d'une tâche précise et temporaire*' called '*contrat de mission*'. As discussed, the 1986 *ordonnance* also considerably facilitated the recourse to fixed-term work, with the regulation of the two types of contract being substantially harmonised. And similarly, in 1990 the pre-existing system was essentially reintroduced with 'temporary work appearing as one of the forms of fixed-term work when one considers the relationship between the temporary employment business and the temporary workers'.[165]

In fact, as seen above, there is in French law a substantial identity of the cases where recourse to temporary work and fixed-term contracts is allowed. The *contrat de mission* has to be in writing and its total duration, coinciding with that provided for fixed-term contracts, cannot extend beyond 18 months.[166] The maximum duration of a *contrat de mission* is reduced to nine months when a worker recruited on an open-ended contract is waiting to take up the post or where the object of the contract is urgent work required for safety reasons, but it is extended to 24 months if the work is performed abroad, if a worker is leaving prior to abolition of his post, or if the enterprise, or a subcontractor, receives an exceptional export order.[167] Only contracts with a precise term can be extended and only one extension is permitted. The overall duration of the relationship shall not go beyond the *maxima* set for that specific type of *mission*.

The equal treatment principle applies, as seen in relation to fixed-term work, to pay.[168] Furthermore, French temporary agency workers are entitle to paid holidays and, at the expiry of their placement, to an *indemnité de congés payés* that cannot amount to less than one-tenth of the total remuneration due to the comparable employee.[169] Last but not least they are normally entitled to an *indemnité de précarité de situation*,[170] a unique feature of French labour law. As mentioned in the previous section, the other limb of the relationship, tying together the agency and the user-enterprise, is no less regulated. The *contrat de mise à disposition* has to be in writing and it can be concluded only to carry out a non-permanent task. As with fixed-term work, the *contrat de mise à disposition* may be used to replace a worker who is absent on leave, or due to illness, maternity, occupational accident or national service, or who has left because her post is to be abolished, or who has been recruited on an open-ended contract and is waiting to take up the post. Other justifications are temporary increases in the company's activities, seasonal work, or the fact that the company operates in specific sectors defined by legislation and collective agreements, mainly in the hotel and catering industry, entertainment, cultural activities, or the performing arts. The prohibitions upon concluding this type of contracts are also in line with those provided for fixed-term work. In the user

---

165 Pélissier, Supiot and Jeammaud, *Droit du travail*, p. 350.

166 Article L. 124.2.2, al. 2.

167 In this case, the duration may be no less than six months.

168 Article L. 124.4.2.

169 Article L. 124.4.3.

170 '*Cette indemnité est égale à 10 % de la rémunération totale brute due au salarié*'. Article 122.4.4 defines the situations where it is not due, as provided by *Loi n° 2005-841 du 26 juillet 2005, art. 23*.

118 *The Changing Law of the Employment Relationship*

enterprise, temporary workers are subject to the same rules as permanent employees in terms of work schedule, working hours, rest periods, health and safety, employment of women and minors.[171] The breach of most of these substantial requirements will trigger the typical sanction provided by the French law on atypical workers, namely the transformation of the atypical contract into a typical one.

In Germany the strong protection[172] that was assumed to derive a contract of indefinite duration between the worker and the agency was matched by a rather less austere stance with respect to the other limb of the trilateral relationship involving the agency and the user company. Indeed a user company did not have to comply with any substantial limitation of the kind present in France or in Italy. Traditionally German law provided only for a number of procedural hurdles, such as consultation with the work council, or temporal limits to the duration of the posting that have progressively increased from the original three months to the current twelve. The steady relaxation of these limits has coincided with the dramatic evolutions forced upon German law on job placement by the ECJ.[173] Before 1997, a breach of the time limit implied a breach of the tenuous and narrow justification introduced by the Federal Court to shelter temporary contracts from the law regulating employment intermediation and the associated public monopoly in job placement. Therefore, the breach of these time limits resulted in a standard employment relationship automatically being construed between the worker and the user company. With the end of the state monopoly in job placement, this sanction was transformed into an administrative fine[174] and, most notably, the 'indefinite duration contract' requirement was brought to an end, with the agencies now being able to hire workers on fixed-term contract as well, although now the 'repetitive conclusion of such [contracts] in principle is … forbidden [unless] a specific justification can be given'.[175] However, this requirement 'does not apply if the renewed fixed-term temporary employment contract follows immediately upon another fixed-term temporary employment contract with the same hirer-out'.[176] In practice the result is that Germany's temporary workers have been, paradoxically, less protected than their fellow workers directly employed by a company on a standard fixed-term contract and which was subject to a maximum time limit.

It is also worth noticing that, until recent legislation was introduced,[177] German fixed-term workers could not rely on an explicit 'equal treatment' provision. A form

---

171 Pélissier, Supiot and Jeammaud, *Droit du travail*, p. 354.

172 Though in practice temps were very frequently 'waiving' this right and accepting short, fixed-term contracts: U. Carabelli, 'Flessibilizzazione o Destrutturazione del Mercato del Lavoro? Il Lavoro Interninale in Italia ed in Europa' in *Scritti in Onore di Giugni* (Cacucci Bari, 1999), p. 227.

173 Case C-41/90 *Klaus Höfner and Fritz Elser* v *Macrotron GmbH* [1991] ECR I 1979, [1993] 4 CMLR 306. Cf. also Case C-55/96 *Job Centre Coop arl* [1998] 4 CMLR 708 and Case C-258/98 *Criminal Proceedings against Carra and others* [2002] 4 CMLR 9.

174 Carabelli, 'Flessibilizzazione o Destrutturazione del Mercato del Lavoro?', p. 222.

175 Weiss, 'Germany', in 'Private Employment Agencies', *BCLR* (1999), p. 256.

176 Weiss and Schmidt, *Labour Law and Industrial Relations in Germany*, p. 58.

177 A package of legislation inspired by the Hartz Commission proposals was passed on 15 November 2002 and will be discussed in the following section.

of control at that level was nevertheless exerted by the works council (*Betriebsrat*) of the user-company, and this despite the absence of an employment relationship directly linking the temporary worker to the user company. The works council's co-determination rights in this area granted to it 'the right to monitor whether unjustified discrimination of temporary employees' occurred.[178] Although temporary agency workers are members of the agency's *Betriebsrat*, they have the right to attend the meetings of the user-company's works council, which has the right to be informed and consulted before every temporary worker is assigned. Co-determination, in theory, gives full power to the employees' representative body to deny consent to the hiring of a temporary agency worker if, due to the temporary worker's employment, 'there is a likelihood that employees of the respective establishments will be dismissed or will suffer other disadvantages'.[179] However, it has to be mentioned that in actual practice the proof of such a link is very difficult. In theory, and given the proverbial centralisation of the German systems of industrial relations and collective bargaining, some substantial 'equal treatment' relief could derive from sectoral collective agreements. But Weiss informs us that the hostility of trade unions towards this form of work, coupled with the very low level of unionisation among temporary workers, has traditionally precluded the conclusion of any such contract at a national level.[180] A first national cross-sector agreement was signed in February 2003 after new regulations on agency work were introduced. Before that, a number of *sui generis* agreements had been concluded in some industries, such as mining for instance, whereby the users agreed to apply the rules of the respective collective agreement covering their employees also to their temporary staff. But this did not apply to areas such as pay for which agencies were solely responsible.

In Italy, the regulation of temporary agency work has relied heavily on the activity of the social partners. Some authors have gone to the extent of seeing temporary agency work as 'an experiment under the control of the social partners',[181] and this judgment probably still applies after the introduction of the new notions of '*somministrazione a tempo determinato*' and '*a tempo indeterminato*' that, with the coming into force of the Biagi Law, D. Lgs n. 276 of 2003, was substituted for the old type of *lavoro interinale*. When listing the restrictions upon the conclusion of temporary contracts, Article 1(4)(a) of Law 196/97 included 'jobs indicated by the national collective agreements of the category to which the user company belongs made with most representative trade unions, with special precaution with regard to the tasks the performance of which can present a particular danger for the safety, of the worker or of third parties'. National collective agreements have also been given the function of setting the quotas of temporary contracts as a percentage of the standard employees working for the user company.[182] The 2002 *Contratto Collettivo*

---

178 Weiss, 'Germany', in 'Private Employment Agencies', *BCLR* (1999), p. 258.
179 Ibid.
180 Ibid.
181 M. Biagi, 'Italy', in 'Private Employment Agencies', *BCLR* (1999): 274.
182 Article 1(8).

Nazionale per la categoria delle imprese fornitrici di lavoro temporaneo[183] provided for detailed regulation of the temporary agency employment relationship. It both reaffirmed principles already contained in statutory legislation and filled a number of gaps left by Law 196/97. For instance, it reiterated in Article 18 the equal treatment principle already articulated in Article 4(2) of Law 196/97. Article 28 of the CCNL specified that renewals and extensions of the initial contract can occur for a maximum of four times and 24 months. Even after the adoption of the legislative decree 276/2003, the 2002 national collective contract was extended to the new *imprese di somministrazione di lavoro a tempo determinato.*[184] Sector-wide national agreements provide for the fine-tuning of the regime setting out, for instance, the maximum number of temporary workers that each business can lawfully employ.

The role left to Law 196/97 was therefore that of specifying the formal and substantial requirements necessary for the valid operation of the two contractual relationship, the *contratto di fornitura* and the *contratto per prestazioni di lavoro temporaneo*, and the basic rights and sanctions attaching to them. Both contracts had to be in writing and a number of administrative (communication to the public authorities and to the parties involved, record keeping, and so on) and substantive requirements, mainly relating to their content, were attached to them. The latter, as said before, could either be a fixed-term contract or a standard one, and in the – actually not very numerous – cases of indefinite duration employment the agency was responsible for the payment of an *indennitá mensile di disponibilitá* directly paid by the agency for the periods in which the worker did not have an assignment but was available for work.[185] Though remuneration and social security contributions had to be paid by the agency, the user enterprise was required to act as a guarantor in case of non-compliance by the direct employer of the worker.[186] Last but not least the typical protection a worker could rely on in the case of substantial breach of the duration of his posting was, ultimately, the re-qualification of his relationship and the creation of a new contract permanently linking him to the agency or user company depending on who breached the relevant requirement or rule.[187] In case of a prolonged relationship, going beyond the limits set by the contract or by statue, the typical sanction of re-qualification was similar to that afforded since 2001 in the case of fixed-term work, involving a *periodo di tolleranza*, lasting only ten days as opposed to twenty or thirty, where the remuneration is increased of 20 per cent for every extra day of work after the expiry of the term. After the tenth day the worker was to become an employee of the user company.[188]

The 1980s and early 1990s were a period in which growing unemployment pushed governments into *flirting* with atypical forms of work. In some cases

---

183 CCNL, Signed on 23 September 2002 by *Confinterim* (*Associazione Italiana Imprese Fornitrici di Lavoro Temporaneo*) and the three major confederations (Cgil, Cisl, Uil) and their respective atypical workers' unions Cgil-NidiL, Alai-Cisl, Cpo-Uil.

184 Accordo of 2003. See last section.

185 Article 4(3) of Law 196/97.

186 Article 6 (3) of Law 196/97.

187 Article 10.

188 Article 10(1), (2), (3) of Law 196/97.

reforms were bluntly deregulatory, as in the case of Germany with the 1985 reforms or the mid-1980s French reforms, later superseded in the early 1990s. Otherwise, as in the case of France and Italy, the conclusion of atypical work contracts was progressively made easier, the relationships were substantially structured and their regulation attempted to make these forms of work more appealing to business and workers alike. Initially part-time work attracted most of the regulatory interest and attention, but subsequently a great deal of regulation was also specifically devoted to fixed-term work and temporary work, whose regulation has tended to converge significantly. As we are about to see, and will fuller discuss in Chapter 6, by the mid- to late 1990s the situation was mature enough to attract considerable interest from the European Community, eager to increase the employment rate and economic performance of the European Union. The adoption of hard and soft EC regulation triggered a number of national reforms. The British panorama does not seem to fit into this evolution though, and it appears to have developed along different lines peculiar to the legal, social and gender dynamics of the UK, where market forces seemed only to be contained by basic anti-discrimination principles.

4. Flexibility and special rights for 'more and better' atypical jobs in the 1990s: from social stability to social acceptance and normalisation?

If the underlying aim of legislation produced by Continental systems of labour law in the 1970s, and to some extent in the 1980s, had been that of providing *occupational stability* for atypical workers by reducing as far as possible the regulatory gap existing between some mainstream forms of atypical work and standard employment, the implicit goal of more recent legislation has been that of associating, or mixing, occupational stability with a new notion of *social stability*. It was seen how, arguably, one of the many goals of statutory legislation produced in the 1980s had been that of increasing the *social acceptance* of atypical employment by vesting those engaged under these kinds of contracts with a number of rights that would reduce as far as possible a certain stigma of precariousness attached to these forms of work. It was also pointed out how this first layer of 'social acceptance' measures was strongly intertwined with the hope of fighting unemployment through atypical jobs.

Part-time work

This section highlights how governments, and the EU, have attempted to boost the social acceptance of atypical work by introducing a corollary of *special rights* and prerogatives, spanning the area from vocational training to measures aimed at easing the transition from standard work to atypical work (and vice versa). It will be argued that these special or *atypical* rights have been – and are being – introduced while a new wave of 're-regulation' is in effect removing the last vestiges of pre-existing regulation aimed at limiting the recourse to atypical work. This new re-regulatory approach sidelines the policy aim of reducing unemployment while at the same time increasing employment rates, an aim requiring a difficult balancing act between deregulation of limits upon the establishment of atypical employment relations and

122   *The Changing Law of the Employment Relationship*

new regulation aimed at affording new rights that will lure inactive potential workers into atypical jobs.

The Part-time Work Directive[189] forced, or encouraged, most European Member States (MSs)to modify their existing legislation in order to comply with EC law requirements and principles. Other than France, all other countries surveyed in the present work on considered that new and specific legislation[190] was necessary to place their national regulation on part-time work in line with the EC Directive's requirements. As seen in the previous sections, French legislation had already introduced in the Labour Code a number of pivotal elements of the EC Directive such as the equal treatment and *pro-rata temporis*[191] principles. In December 1992 and December 1993 two laws had promoted the conclusion of part-time contracts by granting considerable financial aid to companies adopting them and by introducing job-sharing schemes while also introducing the concept of *annualisation* of part-time work.[192] In 1995 a national interprofessional collective agreement provided a framework for sectoral collective bargaining and introduced 'equal treatment regarding collectively agreed rights, and individual and collective procedures to ensure the transition from part-time to full-time work'.[193] Finally, in the late 1990s the socialist Jospin Government promoted a thorough re-elaboration of part-time work in the context of working time reduction. Two main legislative acts were adopted on 13 June 1998 and on 19 January 2000 which, with the aim of '*moraliser le temps partiel*'[194] (placing part-time work on an ethical basis) and reducing a number of perceived abuses, introduced limitations to the interruption of the working day, new rules on complementary hours, and suppressed annualised part-time work and the financial incentives that had been introduced in the early 1990s.

---

189 Council Directive 97/81/EC of 15 December 1997 concerning the Framework Agreement on part-time work concluded by UNICE, CEEP and the ETUC OJ L 104 20/1/1998/ 9–14. For a review of its implementing legislation in EU MSs see EC Commission, *Report by the Commission's Services on the Implementation of Council Directive 97/81/EC of 17 December 1997 Concerning the Framework Agreement on Part-time Work Concluded by UNICE, CEEP and the ETUC* (Brussels, 2003).

190 Germany adopted the *Teilzeit – und Befristungsgesetz* (TzBfG), in force since 1 January 2001 and repealing the 1985 *Beschäftigungsförderungsgesetz*; the UK, the Part-time Work (Prevention of Less Favourable Treatment) Regulations 2000, in force since 1 July 2000, and Italy the Legislative Decree of 25 February 2000. Subsequent amendments have partially modified these first implementing measures. Only Austria, and to some extents the Netherlands, Sweden and Norway, followed the French example and considered their existing legislation in line with EC requirements, although more recent legislation has provided some minor amendments. Cf. S. Clauwaert, *Survey on the Implementation of the Part-time Work Directive/Agreement in the EU Member States and Selected Applicant Countries – Report 73* (ETUI, Brussels, 2002), pp. 15–21.

191 Article L. 212.4.5.

192 Pélissier, Supiot and Jeammaud, *Droit du travail*, p. 331.

193 Clauwaert, *Survey on the Implementation of the Part-time Work Directive/Agreement*, p. 17.

194 Ibid.

The second *Loi Aubry* of 19 January 2000 introduced the new definition of part-time work.[195] The Italian *decreto legislativo* n. 61 of 2000 provides for a similar definition,[196] where part-time work is abstractly defined in relation to full-time, normal work.

It is worthwhile recalling that the EC Directive provides for a less general definition whereby the term 'part-time worker' is defined in relation to a '*comparable full-time worker*'.[197] In the EC definition, as opposed to the ones contained in French and Italian legislation, the notion of what a comparable worker is becomes crucially important to the scope of application of the regulation and of the Directive, which it is supposed to implement.[198] German legislation, for instance, defines a part-time worker as 'any worker whose usual weekly hours of work are shorter than those of a *comparable* full-time worker',[199] the latter being a worker engaged under the same employment relationship in the same or similar activity, while if there is no comparable worker in the same establishment, comparison is made by reference to the applicable sectoral collective agreement.

The British implementing legislation, however, introduces a more elaborate definition[200] that is novel both with respect to the European panorama and to definitions traditionally used in previous UK legislation.

2. A worker is a part-time worker for the purpose of these Regulations if he is paid wholly or in part by reference to the time he works and, having regard to the custom and practice of the employer in relation to workers employed by the worker's employer under the same type of contract, is not identifiable as

---

195 Article L. 212.4.2. '*Sont considérés comme salariés a temps partiel, les salariés dont la durée du travail est inférieure ... à la durée légale ou lorsque ces durées sont inférieures à la durée légale, à la durée du travail fixée conventionnellement pour la branche ou l'entreprise ou aux durées du travail applicables dans l'établissement.*' The current version of the article, as last modified by *Loi n° 2004-626 du 30 juin 2004, art. 2*, also includes a definition by reference to the monthly and yearly normal working time.

196 Article 1(2)(b), as modified by D. Lgs. n. 100 of 2001 and by Article 46 of D. Lgs. n. 276.

197 Clause 3(1). Emphasis added. A comparable worker is, according to clause 3(2), 'a full-time worker in the same establishment having the same type of employment contract or relationship, who is engaged in the same or a similar work/occupation, due regard being given to other considerations which may include seniority and qualification/skills. Where there is no comparable full-time worker in the same establishment, the comparison shall be made by reference to the applicable collective agreement or, where there is no applicable collective agreement, in accordance with national law, collective agreements or practice'.

198 Whereas in France and Italy it is only relevant in relation to the application of the equal treatment principle.

199 A definition covering minor workers irrespective of their social security entitlements. See Clauwaert, p. 31.

200 Reg. 2(2). And laborious was also the consultation process that eventually lead to this definition, as reported by M. Freedland and C. Kilpatrick, 'The United Kingdom: How Is EU Governance Transformative?', in S. Sciarra, P. Davies and M. Freedland (eds), *Employment Policy and the Regulation of Part-time Work in the European Union. A Comparative Analysis* (Cambridge, 2004).

124 *The Changing Law of the Employment Relationship*

a full-time worker.

Regulation 2(4) defines the 'comparator' as a worker who at the time when the allegedly less favourable treatment took place was also 'employed by the same employer under the same type of contract' and was 'engaged in the same or broadly similar work having regard, where relevant, to whether they have a similar level of qualification, skills and experience' and who 'works or is based at the same establishment as the part-time worker' or, where there is no full-time worker working or based at that establishment, a full-time worker who, 'works or is based [under the same or similar type of contract and under the same employer] at a different establishment'. The British definitions, in comparison with the other definitions seen above, deploy at least three special features that appear to restrict considerably the scope of application of the new regulations.

The first one has to do with the restrictive criterion of 'same type of contract' necessary to find the comparator. Regulation 2(3) provides a long list of subjects who must be regarded as being employed under different types of contract. These are, in the first place, *employees* employed under a contract that is not a contract of apprenticeship, *employees* employed under a contract of apprenticeship and *workers* who are not employees. Finally the Regulations mentions 'any other description of worker that it is reasonable for the employer to treat differently from other workers on the ground that workers of that description have a different type of contract'.[201] Given that cross-comparisons between 'different types of contract' is forbidden, the result of this framework is that of creating a gap between the spirit, if not also the letter, of the intended scope of the Directive and the one of national legislation.

Freedland and Kilpatrick's analysis of the Regulations depicts the extreme difficulties that a part-time worker looking for a comparator may face. First, they point out how these rules create some watertight and mutually exclusive categories 'considerably fragment[ing] the "worker" category and considerably restrict[ing] the comparative scope of the regulations'.

> An even more divisive provision, however, presents itself in the shape of Regulation 2(3)[d]. For this is no simple sub-category; quite unlike items (a) to [c], it forms a provision enabling the employer to cite, as a restriction upon the comparative scope of the Regulations, any description of the part-time worker which differentiates that worker from the full-time worker with whom comparison is sought, as long as the description can reasonably be said to amount to a differentiation between the types of contract which the two workers have. This means that the grounds of differentiation between full and part-time workers are not completely specified in advance; there is an open category of potentially valid differentiations. [202]

A second kind of restrictions derives from the emphasis the UK Regulations put on the method of payment of the part-time worker when they say that a 'worker is a part-time worker … if he is *paid wholly or in part by reference to the time he works*'.

---

201 Reg. 2(3)(d), as modified by the Part-time Workers (Prevention of Less Favourable Treatment) Regulations 2000 (Amendment) Regulations 2002.

202 Freedland and Kilpatrick, *The United Kingdom: How Is EU Governance Transformative?*, at 327.

Atypical Employment Relationships 125

This is likely to exclude casual or zero hours workers as well as piece-workers who are paid according to their output and not according to the number of hours they work.[203] Put in Freedland and Kilpatrick's words:

> Not only might these differentiations be numerous; it is also to be noted that they may operate cumulatively with the stated differentiation into sub-categories (a) to (e), and with each other. So, suppose that an employer can successfully argue that workers on performance-related pay have contracts of a different type from those of workers not on performance-related pay. This distinction might cut across the five sub-categories, creating ten sub-categories. A further distinction, say between workers with occupational pension schemes and without them, might turn those ten sub-categories into twenty – and so on, exponentially.[204]

These rules almost deprive of a concrete significance the fact that, on paper, the Part-time Work (Prevention of Less Favourable Treatment) Regulations 2000 apply to 'workers' rather than 'employees'. The impression is that what was given with the one hand, is taken back with the other. If the quantitative concerns reported by the ETUI study, claiming that the wording of the Regulations 'has led to the exclusion of some 93 per cent of part-time workers in the UK from protection under the Directive',[205] proved to be well founded, one can only expect future challenges of these rules before the ECJ.

Last, but not least, it seems that a further restriction in the scope can derive from the traditionally long working-hours culture pervading the UK labour market. This can further complicate the quest for a comparator given that workers working 'thirty five hours per week, plus one extra week during the year' even where 'nobody else in [a given] department work(s) longer hours' can be regarded as part-time workers and therefore will be of no use to another part-timer, working some 18 hours a week, and looking for a comparator.[206] Having said that, and keeping in mind the possible difficulties in finding a full time comparator, all national statutes on part-time work have a clear *equal treatment* and *pro-rata temporis* provision.[207] In Italy equal treatment also covers social security and state pension schemes.[208] In France this principle appears to apply but with the important caveat that 'the way in which pensions are calculated certainly penalises part-time workers'.[209] The situation is similar in Germany where the principle applies on the paper but is limited by the growth of part-time 'mini-jobs' (less than 15 hours and 400 euros per

---

203 S. Clauwaert, *Survey on the Implementation of the Part-time Work Directive/ Agreement in the EU Member States and Selected Applicant Countries – Report 73* (Brussels, 2002), p. 33.

204 Freedland and Kilpatrick, *The United Kingdom: How Is EU Governance Transformative?*, p. 299.

205 Ibid.

206 See *England* v *The Governing Body of Turnford School* [2003] WL 21047416.

207 See Italian Article 4(1) and (2) of D. Lgs. 61/2000, French Article L. 212.4 and subsequent paragraphs, the German s. 4 of TzBfG, UK Reg. 5 of Part-time Work (Prevention of Less Favourable Treatment) Regulations 2000.

208 Article 9 of D. Lgs. 61/2000.

209 Clauwaert, *Survey on the Implementation of the Part-time Work Directive*, p. 42.

week), where – in spite of the 2002 reform – 'there is some evidence of deviations from "equal treatment" with regard to pay rates and several other issues'.[210] In these three countries, pension benefits are of course determined on a pro-rata (of salary) base and are therefore considerably smaller than full-time pensions. That is not necessarily the case for other social security benefits such as *assegni di famiglia* in Italy or other 'family care' related benefits, where thresholds might apply instead of the pro-rata principle[211] or full entitlements might be provided regardless of the weekly working time. In the UK the law provides equal access on a pro-rata basis to sick and maternity pay and holidays and parental or maternity leave as well as *occupational* pension schemes with less favourable treatment requiring objective justification.

Another feature of national legislation on part-time work adopted since the second half of the 1990s has been the introduction of a number of *special rights* aiming at transforming part-time work into a more adaptable and freely chosen form of work. The idea of part-time work as an elective form of work tailored to the part-timer's needs and work/life balance probably dates back to the French notion of *temps choisi* already emerging in the 1970s and early 1980s. But it is in more recent years that workers have been given a number of rights and entitlements aimed at easing the transition from full-time work to part-time work and vice versa, enabling workers to some extent to resist to managerial pressures willing to modify their working time.[212]

For instance French full-time workers who want to work part-time have the right to be selected on a preferential basis when a part-time job requiring analogous qualifications is made available in the enterprise.[213] The same applies to a part-timer aspiring to work full time. Furthermore, French workers wishing to dedicate more time to their family life can apply for a reduction of their working time, although here the entitlement falls short of being a right, as the employer, albeit having to take into account the request, is not forced to comply with it.[214] And unless the enterprise is going through a period of financial difficulties, a worker can resist the request of the employer to modify her employment relationship.[215] In Germany, section 8 of the *Teilzeit – und Befristungsgesetz* (TzBfG) explicitly affords to full-time workers a *legal right* to part-time work, provided no agreement to the contrary was made with the employer. Though this right does not exist in enterprises employing less than 15 workers, it applies to a wide category of employees, including those in managerial positions. Article 5 of the Italian legislative decree falls short of attributing an explicit right in that sense, although a worker can now refuse a managerial request to convert his employment relationship into a part-time one, unless that had been previously

---

210 G. Bosh and T. Kalina, *Low Wage Work in Germany Overview Paper* (2nd draft, Institut Arbeit und Technik, September 2005). Available at http://www.iatge.de/projekt/2005/dynamo/papers/bosch_kalina_paper.pdf (16 January 2006).

211 For instance, in Italy, 24 hours for family cheques. But injury insurance is afforded regardless of the part-time work.

212 F. Favennec-Héry, 'Le temps vraiment choisi', *DS* (2000): 295.

213 Article L. 212.4.9 French labour code.

214 Article L. 212.4.7.

215 Article L. 212.4.9.

agreed in the initial contract[216] and approved by the local *Direzione provinciale del lavoro*. As in the case of France, part-timers in Germany and Italy have a right to be selected on a preferential basis whenever a full-time job is made available,[217] or a part-time one if the worker is a full-timer.[218]

The UK has, however taken a different approach to tackling this aspect of the regulation of part-time work which, it should be reminded, did not spring from the head of Zeus but from clause 5 of Directive 97/81. The UK government has issued a 'Best Practice Guidance' containing a number of suggestions and recommendations for employer action[219]. The 'Guidance' contains a number of suggestions not very different from the ones laid down by statutory legislation in the three countries seen above[220]. For all the merits that soft law can have in directing working practices, one can only say that this situation is not fully satisfactory and probably amounts to non-compliance with what is ultimately an EC law obligation.

Clause 5 of the Directive is certainly not drafted in an exemplary way. For instance when it says that 'Member States, following consultations with the social partners in accordance with national law or practice, *should* identify and review obstacles … which may limit the opportunities for part-time work and, where appropriate, eliminate them'[221] or that 'as far as possible, employers should give consideration to: (a) requests by workers to transfer from full-time to part-time work that becomes available in the establishment',[222] one may wonder about the obligations deriving upon Member States from such seemingly *exhortatory* language.[223] Still, if one allows

---

216 Article 5(1) of D. Lgs. 61/2000.

217 Section 9 of the TzBfG and Article 5(2) of D. Lgs. 61/2000 as modified by Article 46 of D. Lgs. 276/03, but subject to what was agreed in the worker's contract.

218 Article 5(3) of D. Lgs. 61/2000, as modified by D. Lgs. 276/03 only specifies that the employer has the duty to advertise the new positions and take into account the applications of part-timers, although collective bargaining may well provide more stringent rights.

219 DTI, *Part-time Workers. The Law And Best Practice – a Detailed Guide for Employers and Part-timers* (London, 2002), available on http://www.dti.gov.uk/employment/ employment-legislation/employment-guidance/page19479.html (15 January 2006).

220 For instance, employers shall review periodically whether advertised full-time posts could be performed by part-time workers; when approached by an applicant wishing to work part-time, employers consider whether part-time work arrangements could fulfil the requirements of the job; at all levels of the organisation, including skilled and managerial positions, employers should seek to maximise the range of posts designated as suitable for part-time working or job-sharing; employers seriously consider requests for job-sharing; larger organisations keep a database of those interested in entering job-sharing arrangements; employers look seriously at requests to change to part-time working, and where possible explore with their workers how this change could be accommodated; employers consider establishing a procedure for discussing with workers whether they wish to change from full time to part time for any reason; employers should periodically review how individuals are provided with information on the availability of part-time and full-time positions; and organisations should consider how to make it easier for workers to vary their hours.

221 Clause 5(1)(a).

222 Clause 5(3).

223 Though as Freedland and Kilpatrick say, 'this does not necessarily mean that inactivity equates to compliance'. Freedland and Kilpatrick, *The United Kingdom: How Is*

the benefit of the doubt and accepts that soft law can be used to implement principles expressed in an exhortatory way, it appears that at least the provision[224] contained in clause 5(2) should have found a place in the statutory instrument transposing the EC Directive. 'A worker's refusal to transfer from full-time to part-time or vice-versa should not in itself constitute a valid reason for termination of employment' seems precise and compulsory enough not to allow a 'soft' regulatory approach. This wording suggests the existence of nothing less than a legal right not to be dismissed for refusing to transform one's contract unless 'operational requirements of the establishment' necessitate it. In France for instance this is the case only if the company is in financial difficulties. In Italy the right seems to have been formulated in a far more absolute and unconditional way.

Fortunately it appears that so far British courts are not unduly affected by the government's omission. A decision such as that of the EAT in *Hendrickson Europe Ltd* v *Pipe*[225] clearly backs the spirit and the substance of the EC *right* spelled out in clause 5(2). In this case the employer had informed the part-time worker that he sought to have three accounting assistants instead of four, but that all three had to be full-timers. Crucially, the worker was told that if she wished to remain an employee she would have to work full time. The part-time worker arrived at the point of counter-offering to her employer 32.5 hours per week instead of her usual 28.5, but in spite of that she was dismissed. The EAT, supporting the decision taken by the Tribunal, stated that the worker had been unfairly dismissed in breach of regulation 5 of the Regulations, which provided that a 'part-time worker has the right not to be treated by his employer less favourably than the employer treats a comparable full-time worker (a) as regards the terms of his contract; or (b) by being *subjected to any other detriment* by any act, or deliberate failure to act, of his employer'.[226] The EAT expressly stated that

> Mrs Pipe was told that if she wanted to stay in employment, she would have to become a full time worker, and it is difficult to see how *one of the purposes of the Part Time Workers Regulations should not be to endeavour to protect part time workers from such pressure*, having regard to the particular circumstances[227].

Finally, another area where statutory legislation on part-time work seems to have introduced a number of ad hoc rights in order to make part-time work more palatable for workers, and for the economy in general, is the one related to equality in training opportunities and rights. French law provides that the employee 'is entitled to pay equal to the percentage of the wages he would have received had he remained at his

---

EU Governance Transformative?, at 331.

224 'A worker's refusal to transfer from full-time to part-time work or vice-versa should not in itself constitute a valid reason for termination of employment, without prejudice to termination in accordance with national law, collective agreements and practice, for other reasons such as may arise from the operational requirements of the establishment concerned.'

225 [2003] WL 1822905.

226 Emphasis added. Cf. paragraph 5.

227 Emphasis added. Cf. paragraph 16.

work'.[228] But in the fear that this might constitute a disincentive for the part-time worker it states that more favourable terms may be established by multi-industry agreements.[229] Italian Article 4(2)(a) includes training initiatives organised by the employer among the areas where the equal treatment principle applies, and so does section 10 of TzBfG. As for the UK, a similar provision is contained only in the Guidance Notes attached to the Regulations. Fortunately though, the wording of the provision seems to leave no doubt over its legal status as 'there is an obligation on employers not to exclude part-timers from training' and that '*To comply with the law:* Employers should not exclude part-time staff from training simply because they work part time. Training should be scheduled so far as possible so that staff, including part-timers, can attend'.[230] The spirit of this kind of provisions is to make sure that part-time work is no longer perceived as a low-skill section of the labour market where progressive de-skilling is the rule and labour mobility and career advancement the exception. This is in line with the new credo of the EC that suggests that a competitive economy and functioning labour market heavily depend on a highly skilled and adaptable workforce.

But in some countries recent regulation has attempted, directly or by reference to collective bargaining, to make part-time work more appealing to employers by affording them more leeway in deciding how to organise the working time of their part-time workers. While it may be too much to think that there has been an implied trade-off between equal treatment and flexible arrangements, particularly in relation to the overall quite re-regulatory (as opposed to de-regulatory) French *Aubry II* law, it is undeniable that recent legislation has reinvigorated a number of flexibility tools and arrangements. For instance in Italy the original wording of Article 3(7) of D. Lgs. 61/2000 refashioned and reintroduced the *clausole elastiche*, albeit requiring an express backing by a collective agreement and that the relationship must be one of indefinite duration. Originally, ten days' notice had been required for the employer to exercise the prerogative deriving from a *clausola elastica* and the worker under some circumstances was exceptionally entitled to revoke her prior consent. With the adoption of D. Lgs. 276/03, the ability of employers to demand extra work at short notice from part-time workers was further strengthened. Article 46 of the 2003 decree allows individual contracts to introduce both *clausole elastiche* and *clausole flessibili* (the latter allowing the employer to modify the shifts of the worker), albeit with the important proviso that national bargaining can modify *in melius* the statutory provisions. Also the ten days' notice was reduced to five. Similarly, the Italian decree of 2000 had already boosted managerial prerogatives in respect of *supplementary* work,[231] roughly replicating the framework provided for the *clausole elastiche*, and overtime work.[232] But these were further strengthened by D. Lgs.

---

228 Clauwaert, *Survey on the Implementation of the Part-time Work Directive*, 42 and Article L. 931.8.2 of the Labour Code.

229 Clauwaert, *Survey on the Implementation of the Part-time Work Directive*, 42. Cf. footnote 15, warning for changes in the area.

230 Emphasis original.

231 Article 3(2) and subsequent.

232 Article. 3(5) and subsequent.

276/03 by allowing individual contracts to regulate these time-flexibility clauses and by eliminating the pre-existing reference to a maximum threshold and to extra payments for supplementary work.[233]

France has followed an analogous, although undeniably more regulatory path to flexibility. The *lois Aubry* have on the one hand restricted the freedom that employers had enjoyed since the conservative governments' legislation of the 1990s. But on the other hand they have introduced the possibility for collective contracts to increase managerial powers in relation to the arrangement of part-time work within their enterprise. A good example of this approach is provided by the regulation of *heures complémentaires* that are now restricted, under the new wording of Article L. 212.4.3 of the French Labour Code, to a maximum of one-tenth of the normal weekly or monthly working time stated in the part-timer's contract. But Article L. 212.4.4 points out that the ratio can be increased to up to one-third of the normal working time if a clause of a sectoral collective agreement so provides. Legislation clearly stresses that *heures complémentaires* cannot produce the effect of bringing the employee's working times up to the level of the statutory or collectively agreed normal levels, and that workers' refusal to exceed the limits stated by Article L 212.4.4 can not be seen as a justification for dismissal.

Most importantly, if an employer has used, over a period of 12 consecutive weeks, a high average of weekly complementary working hours, the employment contract can be modified to take into account of this constant pattern, unless the worker objects to this modification.[234] But employers do not have to pay for the complementary hours agreed with the worker unless they use them, and in practice they can benefit from the workers' availability for extra work at zero cost. In any case payment of complementary hours is at the standard rate as opposed to *heures supplémentaires* that are paid at an extra rate. Employers, again only if collective agreements so provide,[235] can also obtain considerable freedom in distributing their part-time employees' working hours during a given month or year. Article L. 212.4.3 specifies that subsequent modifications of the initially agreed working hours plan can only be introduced if the contract of employment explicitly allows it, and seven days' notice have to be given to the worker. In addition, the French *Cour de Cassation* requires the contractual clause to specify in what circumstances these modifications can occur[236] and, since the *loi Aubry II*, the worker can refuse to accept the changes in case of its incompatibility with family commitments, training or study needs or other professional obligations.[237]

Incidentally it is worthwhile mentioning that a number of authoritative surveys indicate that part-time work has not dramatically declined in France as a consequence of the introduction of these legal arrangements,[238] and that the decline is not out

---

233 Article 3(2), 3(3) and 3(4) of D. Lgs. 61/2000 as modified by Art. 46(1)(e)–(j) of D. Lgs. 276/03.

234 Article L. 212.4.3 of the French Labour Code.

235 Article L. 212.4.6.

236 Cass. Soc. 7 juilliet 1998, Mme Rebaul, RJS 10/98, n. 1311.

237 Article L 212.4.3 al. 6.

238 European Commission, *Employment in Europe 2002* (Luxembourg, 2002), p. 179.

Atypical Employment Relationships 131

of line with the average decline in the EU as a whole.[239] Furthermore, since the reduction of the standard working time and the introduction of the new rules on part-time work, more and more French part-timers are keen to state that the type of employment relationship in which they are engaged is not a second best option but a personal choice.[240] Similarly, it does not appear that new regulation on part-time work relationships has adversely affected the number of part-time workers in the UK[241] although there are probably ongoing practices whereby less regulated forms of work are substituted for more regulated part-time employments. Advocate General Geelhoed, in *Allonby* highlighted this risk:

> By 1996, [successive one-year part-time contracts] had become financially more onerous for the employer because of legislative changes which required part-time lecturers to be accorded equal or equivalent benefits to full-time lecturers. The College employed 341 part-time lecturers. In order to reduce its overheads it decided not to renew their contracts of employment and instead to retain their services as sub-contractors.[242]

These facts emphasise the importance of understanding part-time work in conjunction with the broader issues of working time and long working hours and in the context of overall labour market regulation.

Fixed-term work

Fixed-term work, as it will be further discussed in the second section of Chapter 6, has also been the object of an EC Directive[243] which, just as in the case of part-time work, has triggered a process of re-regulation in most EU Member States and a number of elaborations of the balancing act between workers' protection and employers' aspirations, and has also secured the application of the equal treatment principle in all Member States. But in the previous paragraphs it was seen that in the case of fixed-term work, as opposed to part-time work, the goal of 'workers' protection' has often been pursued through rules restricting *recourse* to fixed-term contracts. This has been the traditional stance of Italian and French labour law, and to some extent also German jurisprudence, even if, as stressed above in the third section of this chapter, this stance was to some extent weakened in the last few years by job creation concerns. In any case in Continental Europe, and in stark contrast with part-time work, it has traditionally been perceived that legislation had to address both the

---

239 Ibid., p. 22.

240 French Ministry of Employment, 'Le temps partiel subi diminue depuis 1998' *Premières informations et Premières Synthèses 10 n 42.2* (Direction de l'animation de la recherche, des études et des statistiques du Ministère de l'emploi, Paris, 2001). Available on http://www.travail.gouv.fr/IMG/pdf/2001_-_42_-_2_-_Le_temps_partiel_subi_diminue_depuis_1998.pdf (15 January 2006).

241 European Commission, *Employment in Europe 2002*, p. 188.

242 Case C-256/01 *Debra Allonby* v *Accrington & Rossendale College*, para. 10. Opinion of AG delivered on 2 April 2003, not yet reported. Cf. also *Debra Allonby* v *Accrington & Rossendale College* [2001] IRLR 354.

243 Council Directive 1999/70/EC of 28 June 1999 concerning the framework agreement on fixed-term work concluded by ETUC, UNICE and CEEP. OJ L 175 10/7/1999 43–48.

132   *The Changing Law of the Employment Relationship*

unfairness present within the fixed-term work employment relationship, for instance by introducing rules encouraging non-discriminatory treatment, *and* the unfairness deriving from the widespread and unregulated *access* to an inherently precarious and discontinuous employment relationship, by restricting the cases in which the conclusion of fixed-term contracts was justified and lawful. On a similar line the Directive, or rather the Agreement it embodies, emphasises that 'the use of fixed-term employment contracts based on objective reasons is a way to prevent abuse' and that employment contracts of an indefinite duration are explicitly regarded as the 'general form of employment relationships'.[244] It appears that these two factors have so far been taken into due account by implementing legislation, with all Member States' statutory measures stating, as a minimum threshold, that 'fixed-term contracts cannot be concluded for a permanent task'.[245]

Nevertheless it also appears that, most evidently when comparing its contents to some national legislation of the 1970s and 1980s, the EC Directive has chosen to underline the protection of workers *within* the employment relationship, far more than the protection of workers from some inherently precarious aspects of fixed-term work. It should also be stressed that both access to and renewals of fixed-term work have been relatively eased, although within some clear statutory or collectively agreed limitations. Most notably, and in stark contrast with pre-existing French and Italian legislation, the EC Directive has a more restrictive approach to renewals of fixed-term contracts,[246] where a number of regulatory options aiming at restricting *abusive* successive contracts are presented, than to the conclusion of initial fixed-term contracts. In a way, but that is disputable, this approach may well constitute an implicit policy option of making fixed-term work a more socially acceptable and, though this might seem a contradiction in terms, a more *stable* form of work. But while the path chosen for part-time work appears, to some extent, to pursue this objective by addressing some of the inherent flaws of part-time work (such as the pressures workers may for instance suffer to modify and increase their working time) this does not seem to be the case for fixed-term work, where little or nothing is done to redress the problems deriving from the inherent precariousness of the employment relationship or the loss of seniority and career progression. In that respect it is hardly surprising that in recent years, and even months, the ECJ has revealed a rather robust approach in respect of national implementing instruments that fall short of its interpretation of Directive 99/70.[247]

In Germany the *Teilzeit – und Befristungsgesetz* (TzBfG) transposed both the Part-time and the Fixed-term Directives. The definition of fixed-term work, contained in paragraph 3(1) of the law, seems quite in line with the sprit and letter of the EC

---

244 Respectively paragraphs 7 and 6 of the General Considerations of the Preamble to the Agreement.

245 C. Clauwaert, *Legal Analysis of the Implementation of the Fixed-term Work Directive – Report 76* (ETUI, Brussels, 2003), p. 9.

246 See clause 5 of the Agreement.

247 See C-144/04, *Mangold* v *Helm* [2005] ECR I-9981; C-212/04, *Kostantinos Adeneler and others* v *Elog* [2006] ECR I-06057; C-53/04, *Marrosu and Sardino* v *Azienda Ospedaliera San Martino* (not yet reported at the time of writing).

Directive and points out that 'an employment contract of limited duration exists when the duration is determined according to a defined calendar period or results from the manner, purpose or nature of the employment'. What was clearly found not to be in line with it was paragraph 14 of the *Beschaftigungsforderungsgesetz* (Law to promote employment),[248] which effectively sought to facilitate and incentivise the conclusion of fixed-term contracts of employment with older workers. Under paragraph 14(3) of the law effectively provided that fixed-term employment contracts did not require any objective justification if, at the commencement of the contract, the employee in question was over 52 years old. The ECJ, in the *Mangold* decision, stepped into the matter and stated that this aspect of the law was incompatible, in that it was disproportionate, with the prohibiton of discrimination on grounds of age introduced by Directive 2000/78.[249]

Article 1(1) of the Italian legislative decree 368 of 6 September 2001 does not provide an explicit definition of this form of work, merely allowing 'the insertion of a limit to the duration of a contract of subordinate employment on the ground of technical, productive, organizational or substitutive reasons'. Although this wording appears to lay down a number of objective reasons for the conclusion of fixed-term contracts, commentators have stressed that the 2001 law approved by the then-newly elected centre-right majority completely abandoned the previous regulatory approach, as discussed above, where statute defined the precise cases in which the conclusion of a fixed-term contract was allowed by enumerating and narrowly defining them.[250]

The British Fixed-term Employees (Prevention of Less Favourable Treatment) Regulations 2002, taking the lead from the EC Directive, defines a fixed-term contract as the *contract of employment* that will terminate '(a) on the expiry of a specific term, (b) on the completion of a particular task, or (c) on the occurrence or non-occurrence of any other specific event other than the attainment by the employee of any normal and bona fide retiring age in the establishment for an employee holding the position held by him'.[251] At the end of the day only France maintains a regulatory framework explicitly restricting the use of fixed-term contracts to a limited and well defined list of cases, with Article L. 122.1.1 allowing such a contract only to replace a worker, to cope with a temporary increase in the activity of the undertaking, for seasonal work, with the aim of offering jobs to the unemployed and in cases where the employer undertakes to provide vocational training for the worker employed.[252] It seems no coincidence that, just as in the case of part-time work, French labour law has remained substantially unaffected by the EC Directive since the French government effectively considered it as adequately addressing the Directive's regulatory preoccupations. Therefore no specific implementing measure has so

---

248 As amended by the law of 25 September 1996 (BGBl. 1996 I, p. 1476) ('the BeschFG 1996') and by the Hartz Law of 23 December 2002 (BGBl. 2002 I, p. 14607).

249 C-144/04, *Mangold* v *Helm* [2005] ECR I-9981.

250 The so-called principle of *tassativitá nella definizione delle fattispecie giustificatrici dell'apposizione del termine.* Cf. E. Ghera, *Diritto del Lavoro* (Cacucci, Bari, 2002), p. 617.

251 Reg. 1(2).

252 Article L. 122.2.

134   *The Changing Law of the Employment Relationship*

far been taken.[253] For the sake of precision, it should be mentioned that Germany actually presents a rather more elaborate regulation of the possibility of concluding a fixed-term contract. On the one hand, paragraph 14(2) of the TzBfG lays down a non-exhaustive list of reasons or objective conditions under which it is possible to conclude fixed-term contracts with practically no limitations. On the other hand, it is also possible to conclude a contract without any objective reason or condition for a maximum of two years and three renewals, when the same hirer has not previously employed the worker.

More simply in the UK, no objective reason is needed for a fixed-term contract to be concluded and the only limit to the contractual freedom of individuals seems to be the objective existence and predictability of an event that will lead to the conclusion of the employment relationship. Italy seems to reproduce this aspect of the British regulatory approach both on this issue and in respect to the more insidious topic of renewals and succession of fixed-term contracts. Here the UK regulations, under regulation 8, merely introduce a statutory four-year limit on the use of successive fixed-term contracts, which can anyway be exceeded if this is justified on 'objective grounds'. The vagueness of this concept is not clarified by the guidance to the regulations[254] where it is stated that the 'renewal will be justified on objective grounds if it can be shown that the use of a further fixed-term contract is to achieve a legitimate objective, for example a genuine business objective, is necessary to achieve that objective (or) is an appropriate way to achieve that objective'. Furthermore regulation 8(5) introduces, in line with clause 5 of the EC Directive, the possibility of collective opt-outs from the four-year limit.

In Italy Article 4(1) of the law states that the term of the fixed-term contract 'can be extended, with the agreement of the worker, only when the initial duration of the contract was less than three years'.[255] Implicitly this means that initial fixed-term contracts for a duration of more than three years are in principle allowed. If renewed, the extension is only allowed once and only if it is justified by 'objective reasons'. In this case the maximum duration of the whole employment relationship may not be more than three years. Articles 5(3) and 5(4) regulate the contiguous issue of the succession of more fixed-term contracts with the same employer. It is stated that a worker may be rehired on a fixed-term basis if at least 10 days (if the previous contract had a duration of less than six months) or 20 days (for initial contracts lasting more than six months) have elapsed since the expiry of the previous contract. The new and more flexible sanction in case of breach of these restrictions has already been discussed in the third section of the present chapter. Exceptions are allowed for contracts lasting less than six months, in cases where the workers are over the age of 55, or for those replacing absent workers, for seasonal work and in a number of other

---

253 With the exception of the insertion of a right of fixed-term workers to receive information on vacancies in the enterprise inserted by Law 17 January 2002 under Article L. 122.3.17.1.

254 DTI, *Fixed Term Work – Guidance* for 2006 also available on the DTI website on http://www.dti.gov.uk/employment/employment-legislation/employment-guidance/page18475.html#covered (15 January 2006).

255 D. Lgs. n. 368 of 2001.

exceptional cases contained in Article 10 of the legislative decree. It has already been pointed out that the European Court will not accept unquestioningly other types of exceptions, for instance exceptions based on whether the employer is a private or private undertaking. We have already seen how France prevents the *abusive* conclusion of any fixed-term contract right from the outset by requiring a precise definition of the motives for the conclusion of the contract. Renewals are subject to the same restriction and fixed-term contracts can only be renewed once in the period of 18 months, which will anyway remain the normal maximum duration allowed[256] for a fixed-term employment relationship. The reasons justifying the creation of the fixed-term relationship must still be applicable, though now the 1982 requirement that the initial contract contain a clause allowing for the renewal has been repealed.

As far as successive fixed-term contracts are concerned, French law distinguishes between three distinct scenarios. An immediately successive contract in the same place of work is prohibited, as under Article L. 122.3.11 the employer must allow for an interval of at least one-third of the length of the expired fixed-term relationship. Of course simply moving the employee to a different task will not constitute a lawful successive contract and will trigger the re-qualification of the contract as a standard one, unless, and this is the second scenario,[257] the new job amounts to substituting for an absent worker, is a seasonal job or is in one of the '*secteurs d'activité [où] il est d'usage constant de ne pas recourir au contrat de travail à durée indéterminée*'. The third scenario was quite common before the 1982 legislation when it became evident that successive seasonal contracts had to be considered as fixed-term contracts in spite of a lengthy and continuous pattern of renewals and succession. At present the *Cour de cassation* will only re-qualify a series of seasonal contracts into a standard employment relationship if, due to the succession of fixed-term contracts, the employee effectively works continuously for the whole period during which the relationship exists.[258] Overall it appears that national regulation has not given up the idea of sanctioning abuses and substantial breaches of fixed-term work legislation by transforming the relationship into a standard one. This is still the case in France and Germany and, albeit in a less evident and committed way, in Italy and the UK.

Some attempts to normalise fixed-term work by making it compatible with career aspirations have also been made, although to a far more limited extent than in the case of part-time work. For instance all national legislations includes rules on informing fixed-term workers of vacancies in the enterprise or measures aimed at facilitating their access to and participation in training opportunities. French law provides, under the newly inserted Article L. 122.3.17.1, that the employer must provide information on vacant positions in the undertaking, a requirement that Italian Article 9(1) entrusts to collective bargaining. Under German law vacancies have to be publicised in the undertaking if the fixed-term workers are not informed directly,[259] while in the UK the employer has to inform the employee, directly or

---

256 Article L. 122.1.2.

257 Article L. 122.3.10, referring to Article L. 122.1.1, al. 3, 4 and 5.

258 Soc. 6 June 1991, RJS 7/91, n. 817.

259 Clauwaert, *Legal Analysis of the Implementation of the Fixed-term Work Directive – Report* 76, 54.

136   *The Changing Law of the Employment Relationship*

through other adequate means,[260] 'in order to ensure that (s/he) is able to exercise the right' not to be less favourably treated than employees with open-ended contracts in relation to securing a permanent position in the undertaking.[261] Regulation 3(3) provides that fixed-term employees shall not be discriminated against in the area of access to training opportunities, something that is afforded to German and French workers respectively by paragraph 19 of the German TzBfG and Article L. 931.12, also providing that workers shall be informed of their right to take leave for training purposes. Article 7(2) of D. Lgs. 368 of 2001 again entrusts this aspect of fixed-term work to collective bargaining.

Whether these measures will succeed in reducing the number of those who feel forced into fixed-term work relationships (so-called 'non-voluntary fixed-term work') is unknown, though it must be said that it appears that these instruments do not seem to address, let alone tackle, concerns such as the loss of seniority in case of successive contracts with a different or even the same employer, or the inherently precarious nature of fixed-term work. Whether the latter flaw of fixed-term work is something for labour law or for the labour market to resolve remains an unresolved dilemma. Labour law systems such as the French one are trying to address the problems deriving from a precarious working life, for instance by according to fixed-term workers an unusually high level of job-security, even higher than the one afforded to workers with open-ended contracts, only allowing for a fixed-term contract to be terminated for serious misconduct (*faute grave*), mutual agreement or *force majeure*.[262] Furthermore Article L. 122.3.4 confers upon fixed-term workers a sort of bonus (*indemnité de fin contrat*) when at the expiry of the fixed-term contract an open-ended employment contract is not offered. This bonus tops up the unemployment benefits already afforded by French law.[263] These provisions are something of a palliative for the underlying problem, but it remains to be proven that the mere dismantlement of the limits to the establishment of a fixed-term employment relationship can render the labour market dynamic enough to introduce by the back door a surrogate for the level of continuity and stability traditionally afforded by open-ended contracts.

Temporary agency work

In the last few years, and even months, agency work[264] has attracted considerable attention from national parliaments of several Continental countries and attempts have been made to introduce some EU-wide legislation on the theme.[265] In June 2003

---

260 Reg. 3(7).

261 Reg. 3(2) and 3(6).

262 Article L. 122.3.8.

263 *Indemnisation du chômage*. Article L. 351.1.

264 For a comparative overview of the regulation of temporary agency work in Europe see J. Arrowsmith, *Temporary Agency Work in an Enlarged European Union* (Office for Official Publications of the European Communities, Luxembourg, 2006).

265 Proposal for a Directive of the European Parliament and the Council on working conditions for temporary workers COM(2002) 0149 final. OJ C 203 E 27/8/2002 1–5.

the EU Council failed to reach agreement on the draft directive,[266] but interestingly enough and despite the absence of a specific EC instrument on temporary agency work, the national debate has considerably interfaced with recent EU-level discussions and proposed reforms.[267] Given this extremely fluid and incomplete background scenario, it is particularly difficult to assess to what extent legislation on temporary work is moving towards what could now be seen as the emerging third evolutionary phase in the regulation of atypical work, a phase where European law-makers are attempting to typify and normalise as far as possible the working conditions of atypical workers while, at the same time, trying to clothe atypical work with a number of special rights that should ease the social acceptance and social stability of atypical work. Still, just as in the case of fixed-term work, the suspicion remains that a sort of trade-off between equal treatment and better working conditions on the one side, and fewer constraints upon the establishment of temporary relationships on the other, is in effect taking place. The next few paragraphs will try to highlight some aspects of national regulation that appear to trace for agency work a regulatory trajectory with the analytical framework presented so far.

Of the four countries upon which this work focuses, Germany appears to be the one where a number of recent reforms seem to be introducing more rights and better working conditions for temporary workers while, at the same time, reducing the existing limitations upon the creation of temporary agency employment relationships. On the other hand, as we are about to see, collective negotiations could end up reducing some of the legal entitlements inspired by the 'equal treatment' principle.

On 15 November 2002, the German parliament passed a package of bills entitled 'Modern services in the labour market' implementing some of the proposals issued in August 2002 by the so-called Hartz Commission.[268] As far as temporary work is concerned, the new legislation stressed that temporary agency workers have to be granted full equal treatment with workers in the user company 'regarding all terms and conditions of employment',[269] with deviations from the principle being possible only through the provisions of collective agreements. The European Industrial Relations Observatory reported that 'the remuneration of workers hired out by commercial temporary work agencies in Germany is on average 30 per cent below

---

266 2512th meeting of the Council of the European Union (Employment, Social Policy, Health and Consumer Affairs), held in Luxembourg on 2 and 3 June 2003, Doc. N. 9994/03. LIMITE of 27 June 2003, p. 9. On this see Eironline, *Council Fails to Agree on Temporary Agency Work Directive*, available on http://www.eiro.eurofound.ie/2003/06/feature/ eu0306206f.html (15 January 2006). Cf. L. Zappalá, 'The Temporary Agency Workers' Directive: An Impossible Political Agreement?', *ILJ* (2003): 210.

267 As for the sceptical stance of the British Government see DTI, *Explanatory Memorandum on European Community Legislation – Amended Proposal for a Directive of the European Parliament and of the Council on Temporary Work* submitted on 10 January 2003 and available on http://www.dti.gov.uk/er/agency/em.htm (15 January 2004). But see also the terms of the 'Warwick Agreement' of 2004 in which the Labour Party committed itself to promoting the case for EU-level regulation of temporary agency work.

268 A summary of the proposals is available on http://www.eiro.eurofound.ie/2002/09/ feature/DE0209205F.html (15 January 2006).

269 'Reforms to boost labour market', *EIRR* 349 (2003): 28.

138 *The Changing Law of the Employment Relationship*

the level paid in the user company. At the end of 2001, some 341 000 people were employed at one of the country's 3645 temporary work agencies, amounting to 0.9 per cent of all employees'[270].

There are two key aspects of this legislation that directly impacted upon the regulation of temporary work in innovative ways. First and foremost, the new legislation provided for the establishment of *Personal-Service-Agenturen* (PSA) that, albeit operating as independent business units, are attached to the local Federal Employment Agencies, the *Bundesanstaltes für Arbeit*, by means of contractual agreements. These agencies employ previously unemployed people and subsequently hire them out to user companies, in the hope that 'what begins as a temporary placement ... may develop into a more permanent position'.[271] While these placements do not last for more than 12 months, the PSA and local Federal Employment Agency are responsible for ensuring that time between placements is spent in further training or retraining. The law states that for the first six weeks of the employment relationship, the pay of workers provided by the PSAs may be lower than that received by the user company's workers, although it will not be less than unemployment benefits. The Federal Employment Service pays the PSA a 'fee' that is progressively reduced as long as the unemployed is not placed into work. A further bonus is paid to the PSA in cases of successful placements, and, to create an incentive on the agency to place the unemployed as soon as possible, the value of the bonus decreases over time. PSAs are not allowed to hire out their employees to their former employer. The second key aspect relates to PSA temps as well as normal temporary workers, that is, those employed and made available to user companies through the already existing employment businesses. First and foremost the law abolished the prohibition on hiring out a temp several times to the same employer. Secondly, the so-called *Synchronisationsverbot* rule was officially repealed, and the practice of temporary agencies hiring workers only for the duration of their placement at the user company allowed. Thirdly, the 24 months maximum length for temporary contracts was eliminated and the limitations on temporary work in the construction industry were repealed.

As highlighted by some German commentators 'to compensate for the considerable relaxation of restrictions, the principles of "equal treatment" and "equal pay" were embodied in law. However, the law does also admit a way of avoiding equal pay by using a TWA collective wage agreement and this clause has in reality deprived the equal pay principle of any effect'.[272] In fact, the whole deregulatory scenario is further complicated precisely by the circumstance that the law has apparently triggered an unsuspected, and uncoordinated, enthusiasm for collective bargaining about temporary agency employment both at a federal and state level. In February 2003 DGB first reached a deal with the Federal Association

---

270 http://www.eiro.eurofound.ie/2002/12/inbrief/DE0212203N.html (15 January 2006).

271 'Reforms to Boost Labour Market', *EIRR* 349 (2003): 27.

272 C. Weinkopf, *The Role of TAW in the German Employment Model*, paper presented to the 26th Conference of the International Working Party On Labour Market Segmentation, 8–10 September 2005, Berlin/Germany, p. 13. Available at http://www.iatge.de/projekt/2005/dynamo/papers/weinkopf_paper.pdf (15 January 2006).

of Temporary Employment Agencies (BZA[273]) on a framework agreement later implemented in a series of national inter-sector collective agreements signed in May and June 2003.[274] These agreements missed the opportunity to modify *in melius* the provisions contained in the 2002 law. The equal pay principle, for instance, was *de facto* abandoned in favour of pre-set pay rates varying according to the skills required from the temporary worker during her placement in the user company. To make things worse, a second series of cross-sector collective agreements were signed by the Association of Northern Bavarian Temporary Employment Agencies (INZ[275]), a small regional employers' association, and unions affiliated to the small Christian Federation of Trade Unions (CGB[276]). The latter agreements provide for even lower pay rates, triggering both a request by the BZA to renegotiate the pay-related aspects of the collective agreements just signed with the DGB, and an unsuccessful legal challenge by the latter Confederation against the validity of the INZ-CBG agreements. Eventually this triggered a negative spiral in the negotiations in which other, more representative unions, had to take part since now employers could yield more pressure and resist the application of a strict equality principle. In the meantime, the temporary work agency Maatwerk, which operated 201 of about a total of 1000 PSA, declared bankruptcy in February 2004, triggering a crisis of confidence over the whole scheme and the costs associated with it. But a degree of relief was eventually provided by the entry into force, in August 2006, of the *allgemeines gleichbehandlungsgesetz*,[277] the German act implementing the General Equal Treatment Directive,[278] which subjected the user company to an equal treatment requirement in respect of agency workers.

Somewhat similarly, a considerable degree of confusion appears so far to surround some of the radical labour market reforms introduced by the Italian government discussed in the previous section of this chapter. As pointed out earlier, in September 2003 the Council of Ministers, presided over by Mr Berlusconi, adopted legislative decree 276/2003[279] aimed at implementing what Italian workers have come to know as the '*Riforma Biagi*', named – in a rather emotional way – after the labour law academic and government consultant murdered by an Italian terrorist group in 2002. It is worthwhile highlighting the most controversial points contained in this reform. The legislative decree abolished altogether Law 1369 of 1960, the pillar on which the Italian restrictive regulation of intermediation in the contract of employment were solidly founded.[280] Put simply, the abolition of this law introduces a new logic

---

273 *Bundesverband Zeitarbeit Personal-Dienstleistungen.*

274 So far available on http://www.eiro.eurofound.ie/2003/08/Feature/DE0308203F.html (15 January 2006).

275 *Interessengemeinschaft Nordbayerischer Zeitarbeitunternehmen.*

276 *Christlicher Gewerkschaftsbund.*

277 *Fundstelle*: BGBL I 2006, 1897.

278 Council Directive 2000/78/EC of 27 November 2000 Establishing a General Framework for Equal Treatment in Employment and Occupation [2000] OJ L303/16.

279 Decreto Legislativo 10 settembre 2003, n. 276 'Attuazione delle deleghe in material di occupazione e mercato del lavoro, di cui alla legge 14 febbraio 2003, n. 30', published in Gazzetta Ufficiale n. 235 of 9 Oct 2003 – Supplemento ordinario n. 159.

280 Article 85(1)(c).

140   *The Changing Law of the Employment Relationship*

between what is the rule and what the exception. Until the Biagi reform, trilateral relationships – in practice agency work – were the exception and their prohibition was the rule. That is no longer the case, though what is not clear is to what extent, if at all, the limitation upon intermediation in the employment contract will concretely apply.[281] The new law also introduces a number of new atypical forms of work in which multilaterality,[282] reduced working time and lack of continuity[283] in the provision of labour resources reach a climax never previously attained in Italian labour law history. Last, but not least, it modifies some aspects of existing legislation on atypical forms of work in a very controversial way.[284]

Only a handful of these changes can be discussed in this chapter, but it is clear that the *leitmotif* of all of them is a strong deregulatory and individualistic approach whose specific weight is new to Italian labour law and whose aim appears to be a controversial notion of *normalisation* of atypical work, meaning that individual parties should be free to establish whatever kind of working relationship best suits their interests. The drive behind the reform appears to be that of 'augmenting employment rates and promoting the quality and stability of work' and the law present itself as springing from 'the Community orientations in the area of employment'.[285] Article 20 of the law introduces a new form of trilateral contract of employment called *somministrazione di lavoro* (also referred to with the rather interesting English neologism 'staff-leasing') that can link the worker to the supplying agency (*somministratore*) either for a fixed term or for an *indefinite* period.[286] The latter type of contract, however, is in theory allowed 'exclusively in case of the following reasons of technical, productive or organizational character'. But, ironically, the remaining part of the article, far from specifying what these reasons are, justifying what could be a 30-year-long trilateral employment relationship, merely lays down a vast and heterogeneous number of occupations where 'staff leasing' contracts are permissible.[287] That number can be further expanded through collective bargaining.[288] In line with the law on fixed-term work, fixed-term *somministrazione* is allowed when reasons of 'technical, productive, organisational or substitutive' character so demand, with collective contracts allowed to introduce quotas upon the amount of this type of contracts (Article 20(4)). A number of formal requirements are attached

---

281 These doubts appear to torment some of the first academic comments to this new stream of legislation. See M.G. Garofalo, 'La legge delega sul mercato del lavoro: prime osservazioni', *RGL* 364 (2003). In December 2004 the *Corte di Cassazione* decided that the abrogation of Law 1369/1960 was only partial and that the workforce intermediation practices prohibited under the Law of 1960 are still to be seen as illicit unless explicitly permitted by the Biagi Law. See Sentenza n. 2583 del 26 gennaio 2004 of the Terza Sezione Penale della Corte di Cassazione.

282 Open-ended and fixed-term staff leasing contracts, Articles 20–28.

283 Intermittent and on-call work, Articles 33–40, and job-sharing, Article 41–45.

284 Article 46 on part-time work and, most crucially, Article 61 and following on quasi-subordinated workers.

285 Article 1 of the legislative decree.

286 Article 20(3).

287 Article 20(3)(a)–(n).

288 Article 20(3)(o).

to the validity of the contract, which if imperfectly concluded can always result in the transformation of the relationship into a standard one (Article 21(4)).

Article 22(3) tackles the very sensitive aspect of the *indennitá di disponiblitá* (availability compensation) to be paid to the worker employed under an open-ended *somministrazione* during the periods in which he is not assigned to a user company. This has to be decided by collective bargaining and in any case shall not be less than to what the Minister of Labour periodically decides. Interestingly, at least for a British observer, the same principle applies to on-call intermittent workers who 'oblige themselves contractually to respond to the calls of the employer'.[289] The trouble here, and this should be again immediately obvious to a British observer, is that such contractual obligations can easily be substituted by a mere *market pressure* whereby a worker feels compelled to accept the call precisely because she does not have an *indennitá di disponibilitá.*

As for part-time work, the most controversial aspect of the recent decree is certainly going to be the one concerning the extensive reform of the treatment of the *clausole elastiche* issue. In practice Article 46(1)(i) modifies Article 3(7) of D. Lgs. 61 of 2000 by providing that the 'parties to the part-time contract ... can agree flexible clauses relating to the variation of the temporal allocation' of part-time work. It should be recalled that the previous wording of this article only attributed this faculty to collective contracts and not to individual ones. Even more controversially, the modification continues by stating that individual vertical or mixed part-time contracts can also set out 'elastic clauses relating to the increase of the *duration* of the employment relationship'. In practice parties are allowed to derogate considerably from the statutory and collectively agreed rules on the *allocation* and *duration* of part-time work, something that by Italian standards is highly innovative and might clash with the previously discussed decisions of the Constitutional Court on *clausole elastiche.* This risk does not seem to be reduced by the fact that a refusal of the worker of any modifications cannot constitute a reason for dismissal[290] and seems only to be aggravated by the fact that the notice to be given to part-time workers that have agreed to *clausole elastiche* is now only two days[291] as opposed to the ten days previously required. France has also undergone a stream of liberalising reforms over the past few years. As far as the regulation of temporary work is directly concerned, the Social Cohesion Framework Act of 18 January 2005 formally sanctioned the end of the state monopoly on job placement and recognised a wider role to temporary work agencies as providers of placement services. Agencies have thus been allowed to place permanent workers as well as temporary ones.

5. Conclusions

Drawing conclusions from some thirty years of legal evolution in the regulation of atypical forms of work is not an easy task. It is suggested however that, at risk of oversimplifying the question, the observer of this evolution is left with five well-

---

289 Article 36(6).
290 Article 46(1)(k).
291 Article 46(1)(j).

142   *The Changing Law of the Employment Relationship*

defined points on what labour law has progressively achieved. These five points, also constitute five distinct, albeit at times overlapping, evolutionary phases of legal regulation and attitudes of labour law towards atypical forms of work. These five phases, or stances, of labour legislation can be described as *prohibition, conversion, encouragement/discouragement, normalisation with parity* and *normalisation without parity*. Regulation falling under these various descriptions has progressively led to a *typification, tolerance, stabilisation, promotion* and *acceptance* of some forms of atypical work. Arguably these notions have to be seen as fluid concepts whose descriptive function appears to be justified for the sake of unravelling a rather intricate sequence of regulatory experiences. Furthermore, while for many countries they can be seen as an evolutionary sequence, that is less true for other countries, such as the UK, where some phases have been skipped.

Having said that, it can be argued that these legal systems managed, by and large, to *typify* at least the most recurrent and economically relevant atypical forms of work. The needs of the new flexible firm required labour law to provide some legal certainty, if not legitimacy, for the forms through which flexible work could be acquired. While until a few decades, or even a few years ago, all deviations from the standard employment relationship resulted in considerable uncertainty over the status of the workers involved, it seems now clear that, albeit with some exceptions, part-time, fixed-term and agency workers are not excluded altogether from the protective scope of employment law solely because of the fact that one or more of the typical elements of standard work (continuity, full time, bilaterality, personality …) is missing from their working relationship. These three forms of work, at least (though the same could be seen as emerging for other forms such as teleworking) have been identified and defined by law, doctrine and jurisprudence, and have been framed within some clear contractual structures, qualifying the workers employed as dependent workers or, in the UK lexicon, employees.

Typification has the undeniable advantage of clarifying the legal status of atypical workers, to the extent that it implicitly brings them, albeit with some strings attached, within the realm of *legality*. This is something that, at least in the past, has been far from unproblematic, given the hostility that the labour movement reserved for these forms of work, seen as inherently disadvantageous and precarious and leading to the risk of a 'race to the bottom' *vis-à-vis* standard work. It is no coincidence, therefore, that Continental labour law has initially only tolerated these forms of work and only when they could be contractually typified. *Tolerance* meant that law imposed considerable restrictions upon the quantitative spread of atypical work contracts, while at the same time banning a number of working practices which, although contiguous to the 'typified atypical' forms of work, were seen as extremely detrimental to employees' standards of working life. In a way these prohibitions constituted a first layer of security in the employment relationship of atypical workers.

Progressively, employment law has attempted to introduce some degrees of *social stability* to atypical forms of work. By social stability it is meant a stage where law and, crucially, social partners aim to some extent at equalising the working conditions of those employed under atypical forms of work with those enjoyed by standard workers. A very powerful regulatory tool in this phase has undeniably been the *equal treatment* principle, usually applying both to working conditions and remuneration. Equal treatment introduced a *second* type of security *within* the employment relationship. In theory, the process of social stability should also lead to a numerical stabilisation of atypical forms of work within the productive system whereby, given a specific regulation of atypical work, businesses would decide what use to make of atypical workers and to what extent they could use them to provide labour resources previously obtained through standard work.

These phases have often intertwined with another ambition of governments and legislators, where for a number of reasons the intention has been that of *promoting* atypical work, by making it socially acceptable for a wider group of economic actors. The promotion of atypical work is a concept with two distinct limbs. The first one coincides with the idea of making atypical work appealing for workers. While in this respect the equal treatment principle undeniably played a considerable role in making atypical work socially acceptable, some labour law systems have also attempted to accord atypical workers rights and entitlements which go well beyond the regulation of the employment relationship and extend to aspects inherent in the labour market, such as easing the *voluntary* transition from one form of work to the other, or promoting training opportunities. These rights have been defined as special or atypical rights in that they try to tackle some problems that are specific to atypical workers and cannot be solved merely by transposing the same types of rights and prerogatives recognised for standard work. These special rights have afforded a *third* degree of security to the employment relationship of some atypical workers. They are also part and parcel of a new idea of economic efficiency and therefore growth and job creation, whereby it is recognised that economies and firms do not merely need numerically flexible workers but also a workforce able to enter and exit the active labour market as easily and voluntarily as possible *and* periodical training opportunities aimed at upgrading its skills. But promotion of atypical work has also meant a progressive reduction in the quantitative and qualitative limits upon its use, making it more accessible to employers as well as employees. In practice the first level of security afforded to atypical employment relationships (prohibiting some particularly problematic forms or aspects of atypical work) has progressively been eroded by this kind of promotional legislation.

Some Member States, and with respect to some forms of work, are now reaching a phase of *normalisation* in some of the most common forms of atypical work. Again the term 'normalisation' can mean different things to different people and in different countries. In Italy and Germany it seems that this notion coincides with a near-complete dismantling, through legislative, collective or individual action, of many of the limitations imposed in the past. Put simply, while in the past employment law reflected the fact that standard work was the norm and atypical work the exception (for example, by limiting it, by attempting to convert atypical work into standard work as a sanction or as a goal, by prohibiting some particularly problematic forms of atypical work), it now appears that employment law seeks to grant the contractual parties an unrestricted choice over what kind and form of employment relationship to enter. In a recent report for the European Industrial Relations Observatory, Dribbusch stigmatised the fact that German trade unionists 'estimate that perhaps only 5% of employees enjoy equal treatment' in accordance with the requirements

144 *The Changing Law of the Employment Relationship*

of German legislation.[292] As pointed out in respect of UK regulation of part-time and fixed-term work, normalisation with parity relies excessively on the identification of a suitable comparator in a 'normal job' that may not be always readily available. And in this respect some reforms introduced in France in 2005 are equally challenging to the 'normalisation with parity' model, albeit without tampering directly with the regulation of atypical work, but rather by eroding the regulatory standards of the 'norm', that is to say the regulation of standard work itself. The *ordonnance* of 2 August 2005 introduced the so called *contrat nouvelle embauche* that extended the standard three-month probation period for open-ended contracts concluded in small businesses to a longer *période de consolidation* of twenty-four months. Subsequently, in 2006, the Villepin government unsuccessfully tried to extend this rule beyond small businesses, only to confront an extremely hostile reaction from unions and French society at large.[293]

This last phase seems to bestow a new meaning upon the terms *flexibility* and *security of employment* where the former is more and more *internalised* in the employment relationship and the latter is more and more expected from a dynamic labour market and is therefore external to the employment relationship itself. This trend risks to erode, implicitly or explicitly, the second and third layer of security of the employment relationship described above. The kind of reasoning that seems to emerge in several Member States is at least at odds with the current mainstream thinking about notions of economic efficiency, continuing and sustainable growth and job creation, as supported by EC policy, as the third and fourth sections of Chapter 6 will discuss. To some extent, the impression is that recent legislation is in a way contrasting the notion of security in the labour market with the notion of security in the employment relationship. This kind of counterpoint is a misconception. Indeed if by 'labour market security' one understands the enhancement of someone's chances to move from one occupation to another while at the same time increasing her amount and quality of skills, then one can argue that this kind of security presupposes the existence of some considerable degree of security *within* the employment relationship as well.[294] It seems highly unlikely that somebody employed in a precarious and discontinuous employment relationship is going to take some time off or leave to take up a VET programme. And it is even less likely that an underpaid intermittent worker, perhaps on call, is going to refuse to take up some extra work in order to follow a higher education course. It is far more likely that these types of flexible workers are going to spend their mental and physical energies in trying to make a decent living, even if this eventually will trap them into a de-skilling process in which their human capital becomes more and more undervalued and obsolete. Of course

---

292 H. Dribbusch, *Thematic Feature on Temporary Agency Work in an Enlarged Europe – Case of Germany*, available at http://www.eiro.eurofound.eu.int/2005/06/word/de0506203t. doc (15 July 2006).

293 Ironically the reform project was included in the *Projet de loi pour l'egalité des chances*. See E. Dockès, 'Du CNE au CPE, après le jugement du Conseil de prud'hommes de Longjumeau', *DS* (2006): 356.

294 On this point see M.G. Garofalo, 'La legge delega sul mercato del lavoro: prime osservazioni', *RGL* (2003): 362.

there will be different attitudes depending on whether in a given Member State's education and vocational training are seen as public goods, and are publicly funded – and at least some aspects of the 2003 German reform of agency work seem to lean in this direction – or a sort of investment that somebody has to undertake on his own initiative and at his own expenses. But in any case, one could say, an excessive amount of *internal flexibility* seems to be at odds with the need of a modern economy to have a productive and well-trained workforce and with the sustainable growth programmes of the European Union.

In recent months the ECJ has clearly expressed that at least part of EU law is geared towards stabilising the employment relationship and limiting insecurity and extremely fragmented working patters. In the *ELOG* case it famously stated in respect of the fixed-term Directive that

> ... the benefit of stable employment is viewed as a major element in the protection of workers (see *Mangold*, paragraph 64), whereas it is only in certain circumstances that fixed-term employment contracts are liable to respond to the needs of both employers and workers (see the second paragraph of the preamble to the Framework Agreement and paragraph 8 of the General Considerations).
>
> From this angle, the Framework Agreement seeks to place limits on successive recourse to the latter category of employment relationship, a category regarded as a potential source of abuse to the disadvantage of workers, by laying down as a minimum a number of protective provisions designed to prevent the status of employees from being insecure[295]

But, as Chapter 6 will discuss, the balance between flexibility and security, both at a domestic and at an EU level, is still very much an open question.

---

295 C212/04, *Kostantinos Adeneler and Others* v *Elog* [2006] ECR I-06057, [62]–[63].

Chapter 4

The ILO Notion of the Worker and the Scope of the Employment Relationship

1. Introduction

The previous chapters explored the changes affecting the *scope* and *taxonomy* of notions of the employment relationship across different jurisdictions and legal systems. The present chapter carries out both types of analysis with respect to some ILO instruments and other recent ILO documents, attempting a more thorough conceptualisation of the scope of the employment relationship. Once more the aim is to highlight a series of conceptually distinct but deeply entrenched aspects of the changing notion of the employment relationship. The second section reconstructs the ILO's approach to defining the personal scope of application of its own instruments. For this purpose, some of the most significant ILO Conventions and Recommendations are reviewed. The following section provides an account of the ILO's legislative successes and failures in its attempt to regulate the new forms of atypical labour and employment relationships and reveals which of the many stances that legal regulation can adopt towards atypical work the ILO has decided to take. Finally, this chapter presents and discusses the latest effort made by the ILO in the area of the employment relationship, consisting of re-channelling its political resources first under the 'Decent Work' agenda and more recently under the ad hoc initiative on the scope of the employment relationship, culminating in June 2006 with the adoption of a *Recommendation Concerning the Employment Relationship*.[1]

2. The personal scope of application of ILO instruments

The ILO started its activities at a time in which mass-industrialism was progressively establishing itself as the hegemonic system of production. Its structure and composition was, at least at first, strongly dominated by 'industrially important' and predominantly European countries.[2] The main focus of its activities was clearly the regulation of the employment relationships of industrial workers'.[3] Therefore it is plausible to assume that, at least initially, the ILO legislators mainly had in the

---

1 ILO Recommendation R 198: Recommendation concerning the Employment Relationship, (95th Conference Session, Geneva, 15 June 2006).

2 A. Alcock, *History of the International Labour Organization* (Macmillan, London, 1971), pp. 40–41.

3 Ibid., p. 43.

148 *The Changing Law of the Employment Relationship*

back of their minds the imperative of addressing these types of – mainly standard subordinate – workers and their problems.

Nevertheless from a rapid overview of the most relevant ILO Conventions, it appears that most of the ILO standards refer to 'workers' rather than to, say, narrower categories such as 'subordinate employee' or 'person employed under a contract of employment' or 'dependant wage earner'. Here, we highlight this aspect of ILO instruments and focus on some of the most relevant exceptions to this general rule – exceptions that in some cases narrow down the scope of application of the relevant provisions, and in some other instances have an expansive effect. The first ILO Convention[4] to be enacted in 1919 was explicitly aimed at regulating the 'working hours of persons employed in any public or private industrial undertaking or in any branch thereof' (Article 2). Article 6 of that Convention actually provided that:

1. Regulations made by public authority shall determine for industrial undertakings –
a. the permanent exceptions that may be allowed in preparatory or complementary work which must necessarily be carried on outside the limits laid down for the general working of an establishment, or for certain *classes of workers whose work is essentially intermittent* ... [Emphasis added.]

but one might reasonably doubt that the special provision for intermittent working patterns had the same major effect on the protection of workers that it has acquired in recent times. In any case it seems plausible that, at the very least, its provisions were supposed to apply to the wide and undifferentiated category of 'all classes of *workers*'.[5] It is interesting to notice that initially the application of the Convention to China, Persia and Thailand was not contemplated, and that India was asked to adopt a sixty-hour week, and even that only in a limited number of industries.[6]

One might notice that the ILO started its legislative history by addressing with remarkable consistency the category of 'workers'. Thus, Convention 2 required that 'established systems of insurance against unemployment' should be made accessible on an equal footing both by natives and by '*workers* belonging to one Member and working in the territory of another'.[7] Convention 3, concerning the Employment of Women before and after Childbirth,[8] adopts once more an equally wide – and equally unspecified – personal scope, applying to all 'women' described as 'any female person, irrespective of age or nationality, whether married or unmarried' 'in

---

 4 ILO Convention C 1: Hours of Work (Industry) Convention (Convention Limiting the Hours of Work in Industrial Undertakings to Eight in the Day and Forty-eight in the Week), (1st Conference Session, Geneva, 28 November 1919).

 5 Ibid., Article 9(e). Emphasis added.

 6 Alcock, *History of the International Labour Organization*, p. 44.

 7 ILO Convention C 2: Unemployment Convention (Convention concerning Unemployment), (1st Conference Session, Geneva, 28 November 1919), Article 3. Emphasis added.

 8 ILO Convention C 3: Maternity Protection Convention (Convention concerning the Employment of Women before and after Childbirth), (1st Conference Session, Geneva, 28 November 1919).

The ILO Notion of the Worker 149

any public or private industrial or commercial undertaking, or in any branch thereof, other than an undertaking in which only members of the same family are employed'.[9] And a similar approach is adopted by Convention 4, concerning Employment of Women during the Night.[10]

But the initial innocence was quickly lost and the ILO drafters soon realised that a more detailed approach towards the definition of the personal scope of the Conventions produced by the Organization was needed. Thus Article 1 of the Minimum Wage Fixing Machinery Convention (C 26 of 1928) provides that:

> Each Member of the International Labour Organization which ratifies this Convention undertakes to create or maintain a machinery whereby minimum rates of wages can be fixed for workers employed in certain of the trades or parts of trades (*and in particular in home working trades*) in which no arrangements exists for the effective regulation of wages by collective agreement or otherwise and wages are exceptionally low.[11]

Similarly, in revising C 3, the ILO decided that it was necessary to highlight that maternity protection rights also had to be afforded to 'women wage earners working at home'.[12] Other than that, the drafters started specifying more and more the occupations covered and the possible exclusions that Members could lawfully introduce to the conventions when implementing and ratifying them. For instance, paragraphs 1, 2 and 3 of Article 1 of Convention 30 – concerning the Regulation of Hours of Work in Commerce and Offices[13] – provide a lengthy and detailed list of the 'persons' to whom its provisions apply and of those that could be excluded. And Convention 52 concerning annual holidays with pay contemplates an even more impressive list of occupations and sectors to which its provisions are addressed.

On the other hand, it clearly appears that the notion of 'worker' is by far the preferred option for the definition of the personal scope of application of ILO instruments. Most of the ILO Conventions produced in the first half of the previous century apply to 'workers', and among them Convention 87 and Convention 98, respectively of 1948 and 1949.[14] Article 2 of Convention 87 stresses the fact that

---

9   Articles 2 and 3.

10   ILO Convention C 4: Night Work (Women) Convention (Convention concerning Employment of Women during the Night), (1st Conference Session, Geneva, 28 November 1919), Article 3.

11   ILO Convention C 26: Minimum Wage-fixing Machinery Convention (Convention concerning the Creation of Minimum Wage-Fixing Machinery), (11th Conference Session, Geneva, 16 June 1928), Article 1. Emphasis added.

12   ILO Convention C 103: Maternity Protection Convention (Convention concerning Maternity Protection), (35th Conference Session, Geneva, 28 June 1952), Article 1.

13   ILO Convention C 30: Hours of Work (Commerce and Offices) Convention (Convention concerning the Regulation of Hours of Work in Commerce and Offices), (14th Conference Session, Geneva, 28 June 1930).

14   ILO Convention C 87: Freedom of Association and Protection of the Right to Organize Convention (Convention concerning Freedom of Association and Protection of the Right to Organize), (31st Conference Session, Geneva, 9 July 1948). ILO Convention C 98: Right to Organize and Collective Bargaining Convention (Convention concerning the Application

its provisions apply to 'Workers and employers, *without distinction whatsoever*'.[15] It is arguable though that the adoption of such an approach was not an accidental one. Although the ILO instruments of that period do not provide us with a complete taxonomy of the different employment statuses, there are some indications that the drafters must have had a clear knowledge of the differences existing between workers and, say, subordinate employees. Convention C 95 of 1949 states, in Article 2, that its provisions apply 'to all persons to whom wages are paid or payable', and it qualifies wages as 'remuneration or earnings ... which are payable in virtue of a written or unwritten *contract of employment by an employer to an employed person* for work done or to be done or for services rendered or to be rendered'.[16]

Another instrument where the ILO drafters appear to have adopted a narrow scope of application is Convention 132 of 1970.[17] Here Article 2 prescribes that 'this Convention applies to all employed persons'. But subsequently it prescribes that the competent authorities can 'exclude from the application of this Convention limited categories of employed persons in respect of whose employment special problems of a substantial nature, relating to enforcement or to legislative or constitutional matters, arise'. More significantly, Article 5 provides that:

1. A minimum period of service may be required for entitlement to any annual holiday with pay.
2. The length of any such qualifying period shall be determined by the competent authority or through the appropriate machinery in the country concerned but shall not exceed six months.

Clearly such a provision can have the effect of excluding many atypical workers and particularly those with a short-term or intermittent employment relationship. On the other hand, as subsequent paragraphs will argue, this is also an indication that, unless otherwise stated, the notion of 'worker' or 'employed person' is a considerably wide one, and possibly wider that the British 'employee' category.

Having said that, it should be noted that there are instruments such as Convention 97 of 1949 – concerning migration for employment – whose provisions apply both to migrant workers and to 'members of their families'.[18] With an equally notable expansive intention, Convention 102 provides that

> Article 9
> The persons protected shall comprise

---

of the Principles of the Right to Organize and to Bargain Collectively), (32nd Conference Session, Geneva, 1 July 1949).

15 ILO Convention C 87. Emphasis added.

16 ILO Convention C 95: Protection of Wages Convention (Convention concerning the Protection of Wages), (32nd Conference Session, Geneva, 1 July 1949). Emphasis added.

17 ILO Convention C 132: Holidays with Pay Convention (Convention concerning Annual Holidays with Pay (Revised)), (54th Conference Session, Geneva, 24 June 1970).

18 ILO Convention C 97: Migration for Employment Convention (Convention concerning Migration for Employment (Revised)), (32nd Conference Session, Geneva, 1 July 1949), Article 5(b).

a. prescribed classes of employees, constituting not less than 50 per cent of all employees, and also their wives and children; or
b. prescribed classes of economically active population, constituting not less than 20 per cent of all residents, and also their wives and children; or
c. prescribed classes of residents, constituting not less than 50 per cent of all residents; or
d. where a declaration made in virtue of Article 3 is in force, prescribed classes of employees constituting not less than 50 per cent. of all employees in industrial workplaces employing 20 persons or more, and also their wives and children.[19]

This provision, addressing the categories of 'employees', 'economically active population' and 'residents', is another clear indication that ILO legislators are, when necessary, capable of distinguishing between different categories of labourers and extending the scope of application of ILO instruments beyond the employee category.

Some ILO Conventions even manage to address, to a certain extent, self-employed people. For instance, Article 1 of Convention 153 of 1979 applies both to 'wage-earning drivers'[20] and – except as otherwise provided – 'to owners of motor vehicles engaged professionally in road transport and non-wage-earning members of their families, when they are working as drivers'.[21] As discussed in the next chapter, the EU has recently, amid many difficulties, extended its working time regulations to self-employed transport workers. Similarly, the Social Policy (Basic Aims and Standards) Convention (C 117 of 1962) provides for measures to be adopted to help both wage earners and independent producers improve their living conditions, and requires governments to take measures aimed at protecting both groups against usury. Albeit with a weaker wording, Convention 167 of 1988 'applies to all construction activities' and apart from covering 'workers' also 'applies to such self-employed persons as may be specified by national laws or regulations'.[22]

To sum up it seems evident that, most of the time, ILO instruments address the category of 'workers'. In some exceptional cases self-employed workers might also be covered by the provisions of a Convention and, at the other end of the spectrum, there are some instruments that only apply to wage earners, employed under a contract of employment. But what are the types of employment relationships included within the definition of 'worker'? Convention 158 of 1982 – concerning Termination of Employment at the Initiative of the Employer – contains some

---

19   ILO Convention C 102: Social Security (Minimum Standards) Convention (Convention concerning Minimum Standards of Social Security), (35th Conference Session, Geneva, 28 June 1952).

20   ILO Convention C 153: Hours of Work and Rest Periods (Road Transport) Convention (Convention concerning Hours of Work and Rest Periods in Road Transport), (65th Conference Session, Geneva, 27 June 1979), Article 1(1).

21   ILO Convention C 153, Article 1(2).

22   ILO Convention C 167: Safety and Health in Construction Convention (Convention on Health and Safety in the Construction Industry), (75th Conference Session, Geneva, 20 June 1988), Article 1(3).

152 *The Changing Law of the Employment Relationship*

indications of the answer to this question. In Article 2(1) it states that its provisions apply 'to all branches of activity and to all employed persons'. This definition has been increasingly used to determine the scope of ILO instruments since the early 1980s[23] and it is used alternatively to the analogous definition 'this Convention applies to all branches of economic activity and all categories of workers'[24]. But Article 2(2) of C 158 enlists a number of categories of employed persons that a state, when transposing and implementing the Convention, may lawfully exclude 'from all or some of [its] provisions':

a. workers engaged under a contract of employment for a specified period of time or a specified task;
b. workers serving a period of probation or a qualifying period of employment, determined in advance and of reasonable duration;
c. workers engaged on a casual basis for a short period.[25]

Therefore – with *a contrario* reasoning – one may legitimately conclude that, *unless otherwise stated*, Conventions referring to 'workers' or 'employed persons' cover, apart from the employee category, casual workers, fixed-term contract workers, and workers serving a period of probation or a qualifying period of employment. It is worth stressing that Convention 158 is not an exceptional case, and that other ILO instruments also adopt a similar definitional approach. For instance, Convention 172 of 1991 provides[26] that:

> For the purpose of this Convention, the term *the workers concerned* means workers employed within establishments to which the Convention applies pursuant to the provisions of Article 1, irrespective of the nature and duration of their employment relationship. However, each Member may, in the light of national law, conditions and practice and after consulting the employers" and workers' organisations concerned, exclude certain particular categories of workers from the application of all or some of the provisions of this Convention.

---

23   See Article 1(1) of ILO Convention C 154: Collective Bargaining Convention (Convention concerning the Promotion of Collective Bargaining), (67th Conference Session, Geneva, 19 June 1981); Article 1(1) of ILO Convention C 155: Occupational Safety and Health Convention (Convention concerning Occupational Safety and Health and the Working Environment), (67th Conference Session, Geneva, 22 June 1981).

24   Article 2 of ILO Convention C 156: Workers with Family Responsibilities Convention (Convention concerning Equal Opportunities and Equal Treatment for Men and Women Workers: Workers with Family Responsibilities), (67th Conference Session, Geneva, 23 June 1981).

25   ILO Convention C 158: Termination of Employment Convention (Convention concerning Termination of Employment at the Initiative of the Employer), (68 Conference Session, Geneva, 22 June, 1986).

26   ILO Convention C 172: Working Conditions (Hotels and Restaurants) Convention (Convention concerning Working Conditions in Hotels, Restaurants and Similar Establishments), (78th Conference Session, Geneva, 25 June 1991), Article 2(1). Emphasis original.

The fact that the drafters felt it necessary to stress the irrelevance of 'the nature and duration of the [worker's] employment relationship' for the purposes of the application of the Convention, is arguably due to the fact that in these two industries casual employment relationships are notably very common. And once more the drafters stress that 'certain particular categories of workers' may only be excluded, in respect of national practices, after consulting the social partners.

Having ascertained that the ILO distinguishes between the categories of *wage earners* (employed under a contract of employment), *workers* or *employed persons* (including both employees and labourers employed in atypical employment relationships) and *self-employed workers*, it is now important to try to understand what criteria are used to distinguish between the three categories. The distinction between the first and the second category is arguably of minor relevance. It is less important because most – almost all – of the ILO Conventions apply to 'workers', and this is a notion that seems to include the employee. In any case it appears that the ILO is adopting as a distinguishing element the presence of a 'written or unwritten contract of employment by an employer with an employed person for work done or to be done or for services rendered or to be rendered'.[27]

What is rather more complex is the distinction between the category of 'worker' and the category of 'self-employed'. An indication of the relevant distinctive elements can be inferred from Convention 177 of 1996 (Home Work Convention). Article 1 specifies that the term 'home work' means work carried out by a person:

1. in his or her home or in other premises of his or her choice, other than the workplace of the employer;
2. for remuneration;
3. which results in a product or service as specified by the employer, irrespective of who provides the equipment, materials or other inputs used, unless this person has the degree of autonomy and of economic independence necessary to be considered an independent worker under national laws, regulations or court decisions;

It would therefore appear that the ILO instruments make use of two different indicators for the purpose of distinguishing between workers and self-employed: *autonomy* and *economic dependence*, the first exemplifying formal dependence and the second socio-economic dependence.

In conclusion one may say that, at least on paper, the ILO scores quite high in including atypical workers within the scope of application of its instruments. Even if, as suggested in the present work, the ILO formally typifies personal work relations into three distinct categories, a striking majority of its substantial provisions apply both to typical and atypical workers. So much so as to make one think that, at the end of the day, it does not distinguish between the two and affords to all the same rights. In practice it could be argued that the ILO only distinguishes between two categories of personal work relations, that is to say *dependent* and

---

27 Cf. Article 1 of Convention 95.

154   *The Changing Law of the Employment Relationship*

independent 'workers' and that an excessive focus on the sporadic use of the notion of 'employee' is unwarranted. A recent confirmation of this view would seem to derive from the definitional approach adopted in identifying the workers to whom the 2000 Maternity Protection Convention applies, with Article 2(1) providing that this 'Convention applies to all employed women, including those in atypical forms of *dependent* work'.[28] Contrary to the accepted view that a broad personal scope may suggest a relatively light regulatory structure, it would almost appear that the ILO grants all the panoply of its rights to all – formally and economically – *dependent* workers, whether typical or not. But again, when talking about application of ILO standards, one should put everything in perspective and consider the still relatively poor level of ratification and implementation of ILO Conventions.

3. The ILO regulatory instruments on atypical work

It is clear that the ILO has adopted a unifying regulatory approach in which dependent workers are seen as the recipients of a single body of rights regardless of whether their employment relationship is typical or atypical. However this conclusion starts to become questionable when the ILO, from the mid-1990s onwards, started to produce legal instruments aimed at regulating atypical forms of work directly, rather that merely by subsuming them within the category of 'workers'. This section provides a brief description of the Conventions attempting to regulate some forms of atypical work relationships, with a specific focus on the definitional approaches adopted by them. It also places these instruments in the context of the conclusions, as discussed previously, that the ILO bestows a unitary set of rights to all dependant 'workers', and provide an explanation for the new regulatory approach adopted since the mid-1990s. Finally, it describes some more recent regulatory efforts of the ILO in this area, in particular the abortive Contract Labour Draft Convention and the successfully adopted ILO Recommendation on the Employment Relationship.

    The first ILO instrument directly addressing the regulation of atypical forms of labour was Convention 175 of 1996, concerning part-time work.[29] Article 1(a) provides that, for the purposes of the Convention, 'the term *part-time worker* means an employed person whose normal hours of work are less than those of comparable full-time workers'. Then it states[30] that the term '*comparable full-time worker* refers to a full-time worker' who:

    i.   has the same type of employment relationship;
    ii. is engaged in the same or a similar type of work or occupation; and
    iii. is employed in the same establishment or, when there is no comparable full-time worker in that establishment, in the same enterprise or, when there is no comparable full-time worker

---

    28   ILO Convention C 183: Maternity Protection Convention (Convention concerning the Revision of the Maternity Protection Convention (Revised)), (88th Conference Session, Geneva, 15 June 2000). Emphasis added.

    29   ILO Convention C 175: Part-Time Work Convention (Convention concerning Part-Time Work), (81st Conference Session, Geneva, 24 June 1994).

    30   Ibid., Article 1(c).

The ILO Notion of the Worker 155

in that enterprise, in the same branch of activity, as the part-time worker concerned ...

Finally, it is provided that 'full-time workers affected by partial unemployment, that is by a collective and temporary reduction in their normal hours of work for economic, technical or structural reasons, are not considered to be part-time workers'.[31]

There are at least two aspects of this definitional approach that are noteworthy. The first one is that the definition of part-time work is provided by reference to a comparable full-time worker. The second one is that the comparator must be engaged in the 'same type of employment relationship'. The two elements together bring us to the conclusion that the Convention arguably addresses and seeks to include in its scope two distinct types of part-time workers, *standard* part-time workers and what could be defined as *contingent* or *casual* part-time workers. The first is employed under a contract of employment, albeit one where the average working time is shorter than normal. But the fact that in the ILO terminology, the word 'worker' normally includes persons engaged in atypical employment relationships, means that the Convention covers these workers even where they are engaged in a part-time working arrangement. For instance, workers with a fixed-term contract, or workers employed under an intermittent, trilateral or casual working arrangement, cannot be *normally* excluded from the protection afforded by this instrument solely because, by reason of working for a limited amount of hours per week, they are not capable of reaching a particular qualifying threshold imposed by national legislation. Indeed, as Article 3 specifies, 'this Convention applies to *all* part-time workers', unless 'a Member [decides] after consulting the representative organizations of employers and workers concerned, [to] exclude wholly or partly from its scope particular categories of workers or of establishments when its application to them would raise particular problems of a substantial nature'.

On the other hand, Article 8 reintroduces, albeit with some restrictions, the risk that qualifying thresholds could create inopportune exclusions. This Article reads as follows:

Article 8
1. Part-time workers whose hours of work or earnings are below specified thresholds may be excluded by a Member:
a. rom the scope of any of the statutory social security schemes referred to in Article 6, except in regard to employment injury benefits;
b. from the scope of any of the measures taken in the fields covered by Article 7, except in regard to maternity protection measures other than those provided under statutory social security schemes.
2. The thresholds referred to in paragraph 1 shall be sufficiently low as not to exclude an unduly large percentage of part-time workers.

Fortunately, Article 8 does not allow national legislation to introduce a threshold aimed at excluding part-time workers in respect of the rights contained in Article 4, in particular,

---

31 Ibid., Article 1(d).

156   *The Changing Law of the Employment Relationship*

a. the right to organize, the right to bargain collectively and the right to act as workers' representatives;
b. occupational safety and health;
c. discrimination in employment and occupation.

This approach is noteworthy as it introduces a novel, *ratione materiae*, diversification of the protection afforded to atypical workers by ILO instruments. In practice part-time workers can be *de facto* deprived, through the introduction of qualifying thresholds at a national level, of important rights – listed in Article 7 – such as termination of employment protection, paid annual leave, paid public holidays and sick leave. Previous paragraphs highlighted that it was already the case that a 'Member which ratifies [a] Convention may, after consulting the representative organizations of employers and workers concerned, exclude wholly or partly from the scope of [that] Convention limited categories of workers'.[32] So, in that respect, the provision in Article 8 is not a surprise. Neither should one be surprised by the reference to Article 4 providing a limited list of rights that are inalienable and unchallengeable at the national level. Indeed, the rights contained therein were all already granted by specific Conventions[33] to all 'workers'.

On the other hand this provision also contains some novelties. The Convention was produced in the mid-1990s, a period in which the ILO was conceiving the now-famous 'ILO Declaration on Fundamental Principles and Rights at Work'. One of the aims of the Declaration, stated in clause 2, is to stress that all Members 'even if they have not ratified the Conventions in question, have an obligation arising from the very fact of membership in the Organization to respect, to promote and to realize, in good faith and in accordance with the Constitution, the principle concerning the fundamental rights which are the subject of those Conventions,' namely:

a. freedom of association and the effective recognition of the right to collective bargaining;
b. the elimination of all forms of forced or compulsory labour;
c. the effective abolition of child labour; and
d. the elimination of discrimination in respect of employment and occupation. [34]

In this context one might assume that the discourse and language of fundamental rights has slowly permeated ILO instruments, with some standards being so fundamental as to apply to every worker and without the possibility for national legislators to derogate from them.

---

32 See, for instance, Article 2(2) of C 183, Maternity Protection Convention.

33 Cf. C 87 and C 98, ILO Convention C 111: Discrimination (Employment and Occupation) Convention (Convention concerning Discrimination in Respect of Employment and Occupation), (42nd Conference Session, Geneva, 25 June 1958).

34 ILO Declaration on Fundamental Principles and Rights at Work, (86th Session, Geneva, June 1998).

It is worth noting that the ILO, in its following instrument applying to atypical workers, C 177 of 1996 concerning home workers,[35] disregarded the possibility of introducing a clause allowing a Member to derogate from any of its provisions. In the light of the subsequently adopted C 181, it is unlikely that this is going to be the trend in future instruments regulating atypical work relationships, and it seems that the absence of such a clause is probably due to the essentially exhortatory language of this specific instrument. In fact Article 4(1) provides that 'the national policy on home work shall *promote*, as far as possible, equality of treatment between home workers and other wage earners ...'[36] in the fields[37] of:

a. the home workers' right to establish or join organizations of their own choosing and to participate in the activities of such organizations;
b. protection against discrimination in employment and occupation;
c. protection in the field of occupational safety and health;
d. remuneration;
e. statutory social security protection;
f. access to training;
g. minimum age for admission to employment or work; and
h. maternity protection.

But this promotional rhetoric of the Convention is coupled with a reminder 'that many international labour Conventions and Recommendations laying down standards of general application concerning working conditions are applicable to home workers',[38] and that therefore the single aim of C 177 is 'to improve the application of those Conventions and Recommendations to home workers, and to supplement them by standards which take into account the special characteristics of home work'.[39]

Convention 181 of 1997 somewhat reproduces the regulatory pattern of the previously mentioned instruments.[40] Its ambition is to regulate employment agencies both when they act simply as an intermediary between employers and job-seekers, and also in those situations where they 'employ ... workers with a view to making them available to a third party, who may be a natural or legal person (referred to below as a "user enterprise") which assigns their tasks and supervises the execution of these tasks'.[41] The Convention applies to all categories of workers and all branches

---

35   ILO Convention C 177: Home Work Convention (Convention concerning Home Work), (83rd Conference Session, Geneva, 20 June 1996).

36   Emphasis added.

37   ILO Convention C 177, Article 4(2).

38   Ibid., preamble to the Convention.

39   Ibid.

40   ILO Convention C 181: Private Employment Agencies Convention (Convention concerning Private Employment Agencies), (85th Conference Session, Geneva, 19 June 1997).

41   Ibid., Article 1(b). It also wishes to cover situations where the agency provides 'other services relating to job-seeking, determined by the competent authority after consulting the

158   *The Changing Law of the Employment Relationship*

of economic activity (Article 2(2)) and it should be noticed that, for its purposes, the term 'workers' includes job-seekers (Article 1(2)).

Once more, the Convention allows a Member, 'after consulting the most representative organizations of employers and workers concerned',[42] to 'exclude, under specific circumstances, workers in certain branches of economic activity, or parts thereof, from the scope of the Convention or from certain of its provisions, provided that adequate protection is otherwise assured for the workers concerned' (Article 2(4)(b)).

However, Article 4 provides that:

> Measures shall be taken to ensure that the workers recruited by private employment agencies providing the services referred to in Article 1 are not denied the right to freedom of association and the right to bargain collectively.

And Article 5 that:

> In order to promote equality of opportunity and treatment in access to employment and to particular occupations, a Member shall ensure that private employment agencies treat workers without discrimination on the basis of race, colour, sex, religion, political opinion, national extraction, social origin, or any other form of discrimination covered by national law and practice, such as age or disability.

Once more, freedom of association, the right to bargain collectively and the non-discrimination principle emerge as a floor of rights that has to be afforded to all workers – whatever their employment relationship with the user enterprise – employed by the agency or to which the agency provides a placement service.

It is evident that C 181, for all its merits, has some obvious regulatory lacunae in its personal scope of application. Given that it only applies to workers who are either employees of the agency or for whom the agency provides a placement service, it does not cover all those triangular and *even more atypical* situations in which (i) despite the presence of a user enterprise, the intermediary has not the status of an agency, or (ii) if it does, it does not employ the worker directly, and (iii) all those cases – probably the majority – where there is a bilateral relationship between a worker and an employer but not one that can be easily characterised as an employment relationship. It is therefore not a surprise that the last frontier of this expansive legislative trend is constituted by the, more or less successful, attempts to ensure at least a minimal floor of rights to all these workers.

In 1996 the International Labour Organization diagnosed that the 'traditional model of the long-term employment relationship between employer and employee is currently being supplemented by a variety of "non-standard" or "atypical" forms of

---

most representative employers and workers organizations, such as the provision of information, that do not set out to match specific offers of and applications for employment'. See Article 1(c).

42   Article 2(4).

The ILO recognised in 'contract labour' one of these atypical forms of labour, stressing the risk that contract workers did 'not receive the protection intended by [traditional] labour law ... or that the employer's obligations under the law will be displaced from the enterprise in the best position to ensure their observance to an intermediary not in such position'.[44] In June 1997 the Conference, meeting in Geneva at its 85th Session, decided to trigger the ILO legislative process aimed at the production of a Convention and a Recommendation concerning contract labour.[45]

The term 'contract labour', in the ILO lexicon, was used to cover two distinct forms of work patterns. First, in Article 1(a)(i), it addressed[46] any kind of:

> direct, bilateral, relationship between an individual worker and a user enterprise, without a mutually expressed intention to establish an employment relationship.[47]

Second, in Article 1(a)(ii), it encompassed those triangular relationships in which either:

> a worker performs work for a user enterprise pursuant to a contractual arrangement between this enterprise and another enterprise which is the employer of the worker (sometimes referred to as the subcontractor); or

> a worker performs work for a user enterprise after having been referred to it by an intermediary who is not the employer of the worker.[48]

Prima facie, the scope of the proposed Convention was particularly wide. It covered both those bilateral working patterns where – in the absence of a contract of employment with the *user enterprise* (Article 2(1) – the worker appears to be a *self-employed* (albeit that the work is performed 'personally under conditions of dependency ... or subordination' (Article 1(a)) and *agency workers* (whatever their contractual relationship with the agency might be) with the exclusion of those 'employees of private employment agencies who are made available to a user enterprise to perform contract labour'(Article 1(a)). As far as the substantive protection that this draft Convention sought to afford to contract workers, Article 3 provided that Members were supposed to ensure that adequate health and safety measures were taken to prevent accidents during the course of contract labour, and that in case of related injury or disease compensation is received (Article 4). Other measures provided protection in relation to the payment of amounts due to contract

---

43   ILO, *Contract Labour – Report VI (1) to the International Labour Conference 85th Session 1997* (Geneva, 1996), p. 15.

44   ILO, *Contract Labour – Report VI (1)*, p. 6.

45   ILO, *Contract labour – Fifth item on the agenda Report V (1) to the International Labour Conference 86th Session 1998* (Geneva, 1997).

46   For the exact wording of Article 1 see ILO, *Contract Labour – Fifth Item on the Agenda*, p. 8.

47   ILO, *Contract Labour – Fifth Item on the Agenda*, p. 3, note 51.

48   ILO, *Contract Labour – Fifth Item on the Agenda*.

160 *The Changing Law of the Employment Relationship*

workers for the work performed, and any social insurance to which they might be entitled (Article 4).

At a promotional level, ratifying states were supposed to equalise the treatment between contract and standard workers (that is, with a recognised employment relationship), taking into account the conditions applicable to other workers performing similar work under similar conditions (Article 5). A more assertive wording was contained in Article 6, providing that '[m]easures shall be taken to ensure that contract [and standard] workers receive the same protection' with regard to the right to organise and to bargain collectively, freedom from discrimination in employment and minimum working age. Adequate protection was to be afforded in the fields of working time and working conditions, maternity, occupational health and safety, remuneration, statutory social security. Again it is evident that some rights were given priority over others, and it was no coincidence that these rights were once more those that are embodied in the fundamental rights discourse and displayed in the 'ILO Declaration on Fundamental Principles and Rights at Work'.

From a theoretical viewpoint, the Convention appeared to focus on a notion of *tertium genus* in which the work is provided under condition of 'dependency' and 'subordination', albeit in the absence of a formal employment contract. Genuine 'commercial arrangements' were excluded.[49] From this perspective it appears that the ILO 'contract labour' notion was much closer to the British notion of 'worker',[50] and that the stress was more on *quasi-dependency* accompanied by the element of 'personal provision' of the work or services rather than on an idea of economic dependency in a context of formal independence. But this is a secondary issue, and the draft Recommendation, in determining whether the conditions of 'dependency' or 'subordination' are met, suggested criteria focussing both on the normative aspects of the relationship (for example, 'extent to which the user enterprise determines when and how work should be performed, including working time and other condition of the contract worker'[51]) and on concepts analogous to the German notion of economic dependency (for example, 'whether the contract worker works for a single user enterprise'[52]).

It is evident that the ILO draft instrument would have substantially expanded the range of application of international labour standards. It is also evident that, if considered together with the Part-time, Home Work and Agency Work Conventions, these instruments between them would have had a wider scope of application than the European existing ones on atypical workers, even including the Proposed Directive on temporary workers. The ILO draft Convention assumed that its atypical contract workers might not be employed with a contract of employment or in an employment relationship. This assumption was true both for workers engaged in a bilateral relationship with the user company and for workers employed in a triangular relationship. Quite to the contrary, the ILO instrument explicitly excluded those who,

---

49 ILO, *Contract Labour – Fifth Item on the Agenda*, p. 3.

50 See, for instance, s. 54 of the NMWA 1998.

51 Proposed Recommendation concerning Contract Labour in ILO, *Contract Labour – Fifth Item on the Agenda*, 11, para. 2(a), note 51.

52 ILO, *Contract Labour – Fifth Item on the Agenda*, para. 2(g), note 60.

having a contract of employment with the agency,[53] are genuine employees, and only focused on genuine quasi-subordinated workers. In that respect the draft instrument had a scope of application that is very similar, in its protective aims and intentions, to the EC notion of economically dependent workers as developed in a consultation paper of June 2000 that will be discussed in the third section of Chapter 5.

On the other hand, it is evident that so far the last phase of this progress has not been able to materialise. The Draft Convention on Contract Labour received fierce opposition in some quarters,[54] and any plans to adopt it were permanently shelved. But despite this rather difficult phase, the ILO did not abandon the idea of enhancing the protection of atypical workers. The following section will explore and discuss in greater detail some recent attempts made by the ILO to subsume the protection of atypical work under a different agenda, eventually leading to the adoption of a Recommendation Concerning the Employment Relationship in June 2006. As for the Conventions on atypical workers previously adopted, it seems fair to conclude that they are inherently aiming at *normalising* atypical work by means of applying an equal treatment principle between atypical workers and workers in standard employment. But arguably this goal is in part put in jeopardy by the extreme flexibility of most of the ILO instruments on atypical forms of employment and that could easily be downgraded to a *de minimis* protection of some fundamental core rights, something potentially leading to a promotional but equally de-regulatory framework rather than to a significantly normative one.

4. The ILO initiative on the scope of the employment relationship

The 'contract labour' initiative never materialised and all the signs were that the likelihood that an ILO instrument was ever going to address the issue were, to say the least, minimal. By the late 1990s the ILO discretely started shifting the emphasis to the contiguous, albeit wider, debates about Decent Work in the informal economy and, subsequently, on the scope of the employment relationship[55] whose origins, by its own admission, 'are to be found in the resolution adopted ... following the discussion of an agenda item regarding contract labour'.[56]

In the course of its discussions in 1997 and 1998, the Committee on Contract Labour of the International Labour Conference did not complete its work, but it nevertheless succeeded in identifying the workers who should be granted protection by an international standard as persons who 'for a physical or moral person perform

---

53   And for whom some, albeit minimal protection, is afforded by ILO Convention 181(40).

54   ILO, International Labour Conference *Report V – The Scope of the Employment Relationship – Fifth Item on the Agenda* (Geneva, 2003), p. 6.

55   ILO, *Second Item on the Agenda*, Governing Body 280th Session, GB 280/2 (Geneva, March 2001).

56   Ibid., p. 10. Reference to the Resolution concerning the possible adoption of international instruments for the protection of workers in the situations identified by the Committee on Contract Labour, *Record of Proceedings*, International Labour Conference, 86 th Session, Vol. II (Geneva, 1998), pp. 33–34.

work ... personally under actual conditions of dependency on or subordination to the user enterprise and these conditions are similar to those that characterize an employment relationship under national law and practice but where the person who performs this work does not have a recognized employment relationship with the user enterprise'. The expression 'contract labour' was thus abandoned and the discussion centred upon a resolution referring provisionally to 'workers in situations needing protection'.[57]

It will be pointed out that the perspective taken by the ILO on this debate is somewhat narrower than the one adopted in the present work. An obvious reason for that is that while the ILO focused on the definitional aspects of the employment relationship, this book explores the 'notion' of the employment relationship(s). But this is also partly due to the fact that the discussion on the employment relationship evolved in the same politically tense environment which produced the abortion of the 'contract labour' initiative. Finally, it was probably also a conscious choice aimed at reducing the ambit of the discourse in order to increase its impact and therefore its chances of success. In practice the ILO framework of analysis is limited to workers who 'are not recognized as dependant workers [or who] are unable to identify their true employers'.[58] As was seen in the fourth section of Chapter 1, factors other than the watering down of the notion of dependency, and in particular the emerging element of intermittence, are also shaping the evolution of notions of the employment relationship and impacting negatively on workers' rights and entitlements. Chapter 2, for instance, pointed out that fixed-term workers, albeit considered as 'employees', might still face difficulties in qualifying for the purposes of specific labour legislation. Intermittent working patterns can deprive workers of seniority advancements. Agency employees may not benefit from an equal pay principle by not being able to identify their employer and therefore a comparator. The ILO debate appears to be taking into account only those aspects of the employment relationship that result in the worst and most evident forms of *exclusion* from the scope of labour law.

A slightly broader scope of analysis was embodied in a different, but still contiguous, ILO debate developed under the Decent Work agenda,[59]and was encapsulated in the Report on 'Decent work in the Informal Economy'.[60] Here the ILO identified, among the other categories of disadvantaged workers,

employees who have informal jobs, ... if their employment relationship is not subject to standard labour legislation, taxation, social protection or entitlement to certain employment benefits (e.g. advance notice of dismissal, severance pay, paid annual or sick leave, etc.). Reasons may include the following: the employee or the job is undeclared; the job is casual or of a short duration ....[61]

---

57 Ibid., p. 11.

58 Ibid., p. 12.

59 International Labour Conference (87th Session), *Decent Work – Report of the Director-General* (Geneva, June 1999).

60 International Labour Conference (90th Session), *Report VI – Decent Work in the Informal Economy – Sixth Item on the Agenda* (Geneva, June 2002).

61 Ibid., p. 124.

The elements of intermittence and casualisation of the employment relationship were taken on board even if only for their effects in excluding workers altogether from labour and employment legislation.

It is in the Decent Work context that the ILO has sought to specify that '*it is untrue that ILO standards are only for those in the formal economy where there is a clear employer-employee relationship*. Most ILO standards refer to "workers" rather than the narrower legal category of "employees"'.[62] This definitional approach is contrasted with some labour legislation at the national level where the ILO report highlights the existence of a number of protective loopholes. A first one may derive from the fact that national law 'has failed to keep up with the changes in the labour market and in new forms of work organization. One example is the growth of temporary work and the triangular relationships involving "temp workers", user enterprises and temporary work agencies'.[63] A second type of lacuna can derive from the fact that 'unlike international labour standards, which are intended to apply to all "workers", the labour legislation in most countries is designed to protect "employees"'.[64] These two elements, along with others highlighted by the Report (whose impact is arguably less relevant in the four countries on which this book focuses), considerably broaden the initial analytical framework of the debate as 'inherited' from the contract labour proposals.

In a subsequent report in 2003, the ILO distinctly shifted the focus of its analysis onto the scope of the employment relationship and highlighted two broad situations that could give rise to an exclusion from labour or employment legislation. The first one was the presence of 'disguised' and 'objectively ambiguous employment relationships', while the second was the existence of 'triangular employment relationships' where an employment relationship clearly exists but it is unclear who the employer is and what the worker's rights are.[65] Given the different geographical scope of the present work and the ILO study, a detailed account of the analysis carried out in the report is not provided here. Nevertheless it is important to point out that one of its findings was that while, on the one hand, the problem arising from the mismatch between 'the legal scope of the employment relationship' and 'the realities of working relationships' is a global phenomenon, on the other hand, 'the extent to which the scope of regulation of the employment relations do not accord with reality varies from country to country and, within countries, from sector to sector'.[66] This conclusion, which is in tune with the findings of the present research, has given rise to a number of divergent views over the best solutions to tackle the problem.

In that respect the ILO took, right from the outset, a cautious and gradual approach. The 2003 Report presented a number of options for international and national action. At an international level a possible course of action was the 'collection and exchange

---

62 Ibid., p. 45.

63 Ibid., p. 48.

64 Ibid.

65 International Labour Conference (91st session), *Report V – The Scope of the Employment Relationship – Fifth Item on the Agenda* (Geneva, June 2003), chapters II–III.

66 Annex II, Common statement by the experts participating in the Meeting of Experts on Workers in Situations Needing Protection (Geneva, 15–19 May 2000) in *Report V*, p. 82.

164 *The Changing Law of the Employment Relationship*

of information and promotion of good practice' and the establishment of 'technical cooperation, assistance and guidance'.[67] The report did not exclude the possibility of adopting Conventions or Recommendations to regulate the matter.[68] On the other hand it referred to the possibility of the adoption of instruments containing 'provisions establishing rights, obligations and criteria to determine whether an employment relationship exist(s)' as a rather remote one.[69] The other possibility for international regulatory action focused on the adoption of a more 'promotional' instrument where 'an important element could be to encourage member States, in consultation with employers' and workers' organizations, to establish effective mechanisms and procedures at national level to determine who is an employee'.[70] Finally the ILO envisaged the possibility of intensifying 'its dialogue with other international institutions, including financial institutions and regional entities whose actions affect national policies and regulations on employment relationships'[71].

Ultimately, on a prescriptive/normative level, the concluding document of the 2003, 91st Labour Conference provided that a

> Recommendation is considered by the Committee as an appropriate response. This Recommendation should focus on disguised employment relationships and on the need for mechanisms to ensure that persons with an employment relationship have access to the protection they are due at the national level. Such a Recommendation should provide guidance to member States without defining universally the substance of the employment relationship. The Recommendation should be flexible enough to take account of different economic, social, legal and industrial relations traditions and address the gender dimension. Such a Recommendation should not interfere with genuine commercial and independent contracting arrangements. It should promote collective bargaining and social dialogue as a means of finding solutions to the problem at national level and should take into account recent developments in employment relationships and these conclusions. The Governing Body of the ILO is therefore requested to place this item on the agenda of a future session of the International Labour Conference.[72]

The negotiations leading to the 91st Conference were successful in granting to the ILO a mandate to draft a Recommendation on the employment relationship, but they also explicitly limited the scope of that instrument. Whilst the stance of the ILO had always been to tackle both the problem of 'disguised employment relationships' and that of 'triangular employment relationships', the proceedings of the 2003 Conference clearly indicated that the 'issue of triangular employment relationships was not resolved'[73] and it was therefore unlikely be the object of future discussions aimed at producing a Recommendation. The concluding report of the ILO Conference pointed out that 'a particular form of triangular employment relationship relating to

---

67 *Report V*, pp. 75–76.

68 Ibid., p. 77.

69 Ibid.

70 Ibid.

71 Ibid., p. 78.

72 International Labour Conference (91st Session), *Provisional Record No 21* (Geneva, 18 June 2003), p. 57.

73 Ibid.

The ILO Notion of the Worker 165

the provision of work or services through temporary work agencies has already been addressed by the Private Employment Agencies Convention'.[74] But the problem with 'trilateral relationships' as discussed within the 'scope of the employment relationship' agenda, did not – and arguably still does not – lie solely in the areas regulated by Convention 181[75] but also in those situations that are not regulated by that instrument, that is to say relationships where neither the role of the agency nor the one of the user are clearly defined. As such, the issue of 'triangular relationships' was bound to re-surface, in a slightly different form, in the subsequent negotiations accompanying the drafting process of the proposed instrument.

The months and years following the 2003 Conference were fraught with painstaking consultations over the precise terms and conditions of the draft Recommendation. In March 2004 the Governing Body of the Office firmly placed its adoption on the agenda of the 2006 Conference.[76] In 2005 the Office produced a detailed report on the issue, followed by a questionnaire addressed to ILO Members and seeking to identify the essential components of the Recommendation itself.[77] The report inevitably stigmatised 'triangular' employment relationships as one of the areas of national labour relations in urgent need of clarification and, in some countries, of a deeper reconceptualisation.[78] The questionnaire therefore explicitly asked ILO Members to consider if the proposed instrument should, among other things, *'establish clear rules for situations where employees of a person ("the provider") work for another person ("the user")?'*,[79] a question that explicitly sought to reintroduce, albeit in a milder form, the issue of triangular relationships in the debate leading to the draft Recommendation.

The responses to the questionnaire led to the production of an extremely comprehensive comparative report on the scope of the employment relationship,[80] accompanied by a shorter document containing the text of the draft Recommendation itself.[81] Whilst a number of governments expressed a negative view over any type of supranational regulation of the employment relationship,[82] the majority seemed

---

74 Ibid., p. 53.

75 That is to say, where the agency is just matching labour demand and supply 'without … becoming a party to the employment relationships' and the user is the employer, or where the agency is the hirer 'employing workers with a view to making them available to a third party' that is a mere user. See third section, above.

76 ILO, *Second Item on the Agenda*, Governing Body 289th Session, GB 289/2 (Geneva, March 2004), pp. 14–17.

77 ILO, *Report V(1) – The Employment Relationship – Fifth Item on the Agenda* (Geneva, 2005), p. 57.

78 Ibid., p. 42.

79 Ibid., p. 64. See also the following questions Qu. 6(2)(c)(i), Qu. (6)(2)(c)(ii) and Qu. (6)(2)(c)(iii).

80 ILO, *Report V(2A) – The Employment Relationship – Fifth Item on the Agenda* (Geneva, 2006).

81 ILO, *Report V(2B) – The Employment Relationship – Fifth Item on the Agenda* (Geneva, 2006).

82 And namely Australia, Colombia, Czech Republic, Hungary, India, Iraq (!), and Poland, see ILO, *Report V(2A)*, (Geneva, 2006), p. 6.

166 *The Changing Law of the Employment Relationship*

to support the idea of adopting an ad hoc Recommendation. Similarly, only a small number of governments seemed to oppose any attempt to clarify situations where *'employees of a person ("the provider") work for another person ("the user")'*.[83] Accordingly the draft Recommendation sought, among other things, both to 'combat disguised employment relationships' and to 'establish standards applicable in situations in which the employed worker provides services for the benefit of a third party, with a view to determining clearly who the employer is, what rights the worker has, and who is accountable for those rights'.[84]

The scope and the content of the draft Recommendation were subject to a very close scrutiny during the 95th ILO Conference, held in Geneva in May–June 2006. Inevitably the regulation of situations in which an employed worker provides services for the benefit of a third party emerged as the most contentious issue. There is anecdotal evidence that a minority of governments – mainly from the English-speaking world – and the great majority of employers association representatives threatened to oppose any type of instrument that would even remotely address the issue of triangular employment relationships, under whatever guise. Similarly a number of governments and of union representatives threatened to boycott any instrument that failed at least to mention, if not also address, workers in triangular situations. The Office found itself in the middle of an extremely delicate, but equally important,[85] set of negotiations. The outcome of these negotiations is visible in the final wording of paragraph 4 of the Employment Relationship Recommendation 2006.[86] The recommendation reads as follows:

4.   National policy should at lest include measures to:
a.   provide guidance for the parties concerned, in particular employers and workers, on effectively establishing the existence of an employment relationship and on the distinction between employed and self-employed workers;
b.   combat disguised employment relationships in the context of, for example, other relationships that may include the use of other forms of contractual arrangements that hide the true legal status, noting that a disguised employment relationship occurs when the employer treats an individual as other than an employee in a manner that hides his or her true legal status as an employee, and that situations can arise where contractual arrangements have the effect of

---

83   Ibid., pp. 94, 99, 102, 105.

84   ILO, *Report V(2B) – The Employment Relationship – Fifth Item on the Agenda* (Geneva, 2006), p. 5.

85   At the time of the negotiations the Office considered that the adoption of the Recommendation was a vital 'make or break' decision for the future of international labour standard setting.

86   ILO Recommendation R 198: Recommendation concerning the employment relationship, (95th Conference Session, Geneva, 15 June 2006). Notice that the earlier title suggested in the preparatory works and explicitly referring to the 'scope' of the employment relationship was eventually dropped down in favour of the present title that should suggest that the instrument is more concerned with clarifying the definitions of employment relationship rather than re-elaborating its scope.

depriving workers of the protection they are due;

c. ensure standards applicable to all forms of contractual arrangements, including those involving multiple parties so that employed workers have the protection they are due;

d. ensure that standards applicable to all forms of contractual arrangements establish who is responsible for the protection contained therein;

e. provide effective access of those concerned, in particular employers and workers, to appropriate, speedy, inexpensive, fair and efficient procedures and mechanisms for settling disputes regarding the existence and terms of an employment relationship;

f. ensure compliance with, and effective application of, laws and regulations concerning the employment relationship; and

g. provide for appropriate and adequate training in relevant international labour standards, comparative and case law for the judiciary, arbitrators, mediators, labour inspectors, and other persons responsible for dealing with the resolution of disputes and enforcement of national employment laws and standards.

The Recommendation also provides a series of guidelines and indications for determining the nature of an employment relationship at a national level. According to paragraph 9, 'the determination of the existence of such a relationship should be guided primarily by the facts relating to the performance of work'. Paragraph 11 provides that to facilitate the determination of the existence of an employment relationship, Members States can consider the following three options: allowing a broad range of means and indexes for determining the employment relationship, introducing legal presumption of existence when one or more relevant indicators is present, and introducing legal presumptions that certain types of workers are always deemed to be either employees or self-employed. Paragraph 12 emphasises that the principal criteria for defining an employment relationship have to be the ones of subordination or dependence. But other indicators may equally well be the familiar 'control test', the 'integration test', the 'exclusivity' and the 'personality' tests, the 'continuity test', and the 'business risk' test. The periodicity of pay and economic dependency upon remuneration are also considered as possible indicators. The Recommendation does not discuss the relevance of these tests and indicators in the context of situations 'involving multiple parties'. Moreover the 'Final Paragraph' of the instrument states that 'This Recommendation does not revise the Private Employment Agencies Recommendation, 1997 (No. 188), nor can it revise the Private Employment Agencies Convention, 1997 (No. 181). It is unnecessary to point out that this paragraph has no practical relevance, as from a legal point of view a Recommendation could in no way revise a previously signed and ratified Convention (which is an international treaty governed by international law) and could have only revised R 181 if it *explicitly* sought to do so. But this is perhaps another testimony of how politically charged was the debate surrounding the adoption of Recommendation 198.

It is certainly too soon to say where Recommendation 198 will lead and whether this instrument will be viewed in the future as a milestone on the road to clarifying, if not also expanding, the notion of the employment relationship, or rather as a failure.

168 *The Changing Law of the Employment Relationship*

Certainly the Recommendation will be an important stepping-stone in the process, but its concrete impact will very much depend on the follow-up to its adoption and on the actions taken at a national level by governments and social partners alike. Formally 'triangular employment relationships' have been segregated outside the scope of the instrument. But in that respect there is arguably a sort of logical inevitability in approaching and addressing 'triangular employment relationships' whenever the topic of the discussion is that of clarifying the scope of the employment relationship at large. Thus, in spite of the pressures of some Members of the ILO, the issue of the triangular relationship is bound to resurface and haunt the debate of the employment relationship for the years to come, even if in the form and shape of 'measures to ... ensure that standards applicable to all forms of contractual arrangements, *including those involving multiple parties so that employed workers have the protection they are due*'.[87]

5. Conclusions

In conclusion it can be argued that the ILO claim that

> *it is untrue that ILO standards are only for those in the formal economy where there is a clear employer-employee relationship.* Most ILO standards refer to "workers" rather than the narrower legal category of "employees".[88]

is only partly valid. It is impossible to say if, right from the beginning, the use of the term 'worker' has been a conscious choice or a lucky coincidence. As seen in the second section of this chapter, a systematic analysis of the ILO instruments indicates that at least from 1950 onwards the ILO has been aware of the existence and significance of other narrower categories of persons active in the labour market. Convention 102 of 1952 – concerning Minimum Standards of Social Security – draws a line between the categories of 'employees' and 'economically active population' and 'residents'. By the mid-1980s, ILO Conventions had started using the formula 'all branches of activity and to all *employed persons*'[89] to specify their scope of application. This formula was used as equivalent to the alternative definition 'this Convention applies to all branches of economic activity and all categories of *workers*'.[90] On the other hand one could argue that the term 'worker' was chosen as a generic term that would be readily accepted in all industrialised countries and, at the same time, in countries with different levels of economic and industrial development.

But at the end of the day these are terminological speculations when confronted with the manifest problems deriving from the unsatisfactory application of employment legislation. The very fact that in recent years the ILO has been concerned with

---

87   Paragraph 4(c).

88   International Labour Conference (90th Session), *Report VI – Decent Work in the Informal Economy – Sixth Item on the Agenda* (Geneva, June 2002), p. 45. Emphasis original.

89   Article 2(1) of C 158(24).

90   Article 2 of C 156(23).

spelling out the rights and attributions of workers involved in atypical employment relationships and, more recently, the exact definition, if not notion, of the employment relationship, indicates that the Organization itself is somewhat dissatisfied with the impact that the term 'worker' has had on the scope of application of its instruments. As for the 2006 Employment Relationship Recommendation, its wording, content and context seem to suggest a preference on the part of the ILO for a binary notion of the employment relationship, albeit one with a considerably expanded definition of the 'employed worker' definition. The instrument does not seem to suggest to Members the adoption of a more elaborated notion of employment relationship encompassing intermediate categorisations of quasi-subordinate workers. The efforts made by the ILO Office to strike a compromise between those opposing and those demanding a regulation of triangular work relationships have already been discussed in detail. The current wording of the Recommendation states that national policies adopted under the auspices of the instrument should 'at least' include 'measures to ... ensure that standards applicable to all forms of contractual arrangements, *including those involving multiple parties so that employed workers have the protection they are due*'. It seems to us that this wording does not exclude, and actually advocates, a fuller and better regulation of triangular or multilateral employment relationships at a national level according to the criteria contained in the Recommendation itself.

Chapter 5

The Personal Scope of Application of EC Social Legislation

1. Introduction

Defining the personal scope of labour law has always been a difficult and solitary task for national labour law systems. It has been a difficult task because, as seen in the previous chapters, it is becoming more of a Sisyphus-like exercise, insofar as the law tries to protect those in a socially and contractually weaker position, and management and industrial innovations create newer, unforeseen and unprotected typologies of workers. It is a solitary task because, in this specific field, supranational intervention, whether from regional or international organisations, has always been minimal or non-existent. EC social law for instance, has traditionally tackled this delicate issue by means of 'subsidiarity'. Even when European legislative instruments explicitly referred to 'employees', the European Court of Justice (ECJ) has preferred to adopt a careful approach and 'decided that national courts are entitled to apply their own national definitions of employment status when applying these employment protection directives'.[1] Where it has taken a bolder stance is in the definition of the notion of 'worker' for the purposes of its freedom of movement, social security and, more recently, equal pay policies.

This chapter explores the precise state of the debate around the question of the personal scope of labour law in the relevant EC legislation. The second section highlights and analyses the different notions of employment relationship that EC law uses to define the scope of application of the various streams of legislation that affect the rights and entitlements of working persons in Europe. It points out that the EC adopts a kaleidoscopic approach with regard to the individual scope of application of its social and employment law. The third section of the chapter explores some directions of development of EC law in the intricate area of the re-conceptualisation of the scope of application of its social legislation. This analysis highlights some of the tensions and contradictions inherent to the EC discourse surrounding the notion of the employment relationship, and the influence that job-creation concerns have over its evolution. Finally, the fourth section attempts to bring together the various limbs of our analysis and presents a theoretical structure of the personal scope of EC social and employment law.

---

1   S. Deakin and G. Morris, *Labour Law*, (3rd ed., Butterworths, London, 2001), p. 148.

2. The personal scope of application of EC social and employment law

The European Community has always adopted a multifaceted approach with regard to the individual scope of application of its social and employment legislation. These paragraphs describe the numerous and distinct concepts of worker and employment relation embodied in EC legislation in the fields of social security, free movement of workers and social law.

Free movement of workers

As far as *free movement of workers* is concerned, the Community and the ECJ have shown a firm interest in making sure that a common, European notion of worker is established and accepted throughout the various Member States. Despite the absence of a specific definition in the Treaty of Rome, the ECJ has claimed that '[t] he concept of 'worker' contained in [the Treaty] Articles arises ... from Community law'[2] and must therefore be defined at an EC level.

> Otherwise, the Community rules relating to the free movement of workers would be deprived of their effect, because the meaning of these terms could be fixed and varied unilaterally, outside the control of the Community institutions, by the national legislators, who could thus at will exclude particular categories of person from the application of the Treaty'.[3]

It has also opted for a relatively wide notion of 'worker' and has structured it in a way that is arguably closer to the Continental concept of subordinated employee than to the British notion of individual employed under a contract of employment. The declared reason for such stance is that '[s]ince it defines the scope of that fundamental freedom, the Community concept of a "worker" must be interpreted broadly'.[4] The similarities with the continental doctrinal construction of the notion of subordination are clear in *Lawrie-Blum*. In that case the ECJ stated that the essential feature of an employment relationship is that 'for a certain period of time a person performs services for and under the direction of another person in return for which he receives remuneration',[5] though it subsequently stated that '[t]he existence of a relationship of subordination is a matter which it is for the national court to verify'.[6] In doing so, the national courts must consider the criteria established by the ECJ jurisprudence over the last decades. For a person to be considered a 'worker', she will have to be

---

2   Case 75/63, *Unger* v *Bestuur der Bedrijfsvereniging voor Detailhandel en Ambachten* [1964] ECR 1977.

3   Case 53/81, *Levin* v *Secretary of State for Justice* [1982] ECR 1035, [1982] 2 CMLR 467 [11].

4   Case 66/85, *Lawrie-Blum* v *Land Baden-Württemberg* [1986] ECR 2121, [1987] 3 CMLR 414 [16].

5   Ibid., [17].

6   Case C-337/97, *C.P.M. Meeusen* v *Hoofddirectie van de Informatie Beheer Groep* [2000] 2 CMLR 667 [16].

pursuing 'effective and genuine activities, to the exclusion of activities on such a small scale as to be regarded as purely marginal and ancillary'.[7]

Time is also relevant as 'the essential feature of an employment relationship is ... that for a *certain period of time* a person performs services for and under the direction of another person in return for which he receives remuneration'.[8] Nevertheless the ECJ stance has never been such as to jeopardise the position of people employed in atypical relationships. Already in *Levin*, the ECJ recognised that the rules relating to free movement of workers were also applicable to part-timers even though they earned less than the minimum required for subsistence, as defined by national – in that case Dutch – law. And in *Raulin*[9] the ECJ treated an atypical on-call employee as a worker even if '[u]nder such a contract, no guarantee is given as to the hours to be worked and, often, the person involved works only a very few days per week or hours per day' and despite the fact 'that under such an *oproepcontract* [on-call contract] the employee is not obliged to heed the employer's call for him to work'.[10] On the other hand, and even if 'the nature of the legal relationship between the employee and the employer is not decisive in regard to the application of' the relevant Treaty Articles,[11] the ECJ has admitted that the time element may be important in deciding if the activities exercised are effective and genuine. Indeed, the 'fact that the person concerned worked only a very limited number of hours in a labour relationship may be an indication that the activities exercised are purely marginal and ancillary' though this is something for the national courts to assess also taking into account, if appropriate, 'the fact that the person must remain available to work if called upon to do so by the employer'.[12]

In *Kempf* the ECJ further elaborated its notion of waged work in the context of freedom of movement. The Court interpreted the provisions of Community law relating to freedom of movement for workers in the context of a German national working in the Netherlands as a part-time employed music teacher giving 12 lessons a week at a wage of fl.984 per month and topping that up to the Dutch national minimum income by supplementary benefit under the Unemployment Benefit Act, *to the effect that*, so long as the work is 'effective and genuine' (which it was in this case) he is a 'worker' for Community purposes and is entitled to a residence permit even if he is also receiving public funds under a social security or social welfare scheme. In practice it said that atypicals are still workers even if their income is supplemented by social security benefits. Similarly, persons that have only been employed on a part-time and short fixed-term basis like *Ninni-Orasche* are also to be viewed as workers for the purposes of EU law.[13] But the limit to these interpretations

---

7   Case 53/81, *Levin*, [17]; Case C-337/97, *Meeusen*, [13].

8   Ibid., Case C-337/97.

9   Case C-357/89, *Raulin* v *Minister van Onderwijs en Wetenschappen* [1992] ECR I-1027, [1994] 1 CMLR 227.

10   Ibid., [9].

11   Ibid., [10].

12   Ibid., [14].

13   Case C-413/01, *Ninni-Orasche* [2003] ECR I-13187.

174   *The Changing Law of the Employment Relationship*

is to be found in decisions such as *Bettray*[14] where it became evident that not all working persons engaged in paid activities can qualify as workers for the purposes of EU law. In this case, the 'essential feature of an employment relationship [was] present'[15] as the person performed services under the direction of another person in return for which remuneration was received. And it was admitted that '[n]either the level of productivity nor the [public] origin of the funds from which the remuneration' derived had 'any consequence in regard to whether or not the person [was] to be regarded as a worker'.[16] Nevertheless, in that specific case, it was claimed that work under a drug rehabilitation program lacked of the elements of 'effective and genuine economic activity'.[17]

On the other hand, the Court has been clear that workers employed on a public works scheme where a considerable part of the salary is effectively paid by public funds are still to be considered 'workers' for the purposes of EU law on free movement.[18] Neither 'the origin of the funds from which remuneration is paid, nor the "sui generis" nature of the employment relationship under national law and the level of productivity of the person concerned' can have any consequence in regard to whether or not the person is to be regarded as a worker.[19] And for that matter, neither is the overall amount of pay a crucial element to assess the type of employment relationship of a working person. In fact the ECJ has established that a person working as a plumber for a religious community as part of its commercial activities, and who as a *quid pro quo* had his material needs looked after and some pocket money, had to be considered a worker for the purposes of EU legislation.[20] And so have professional athletes[21] and even job-seekers and trainees.

EU legislation and jurisprudence have accorded the principal benefits deriving from the status of worker, and in particular the right to residence, also to work-seekers, who have a right to move to another Member State to seek employment and are entitled to stay there for a 'reasonable amount of time'[22] without being deported, and even beyond that time if they can prove that they have genuine chances of being employed. Equally importantly, EU workers 'are guaranteed certain rights linked to the status of worker even when they are no longer in an employment relationship', because of involuntary unemployment, sickness or retirement.[23] Part of the ECJ

---

14   Case 344/87, *Bettray* v *Staatssecretaris van Justitie* [1989] ECR 1621, [1991] 1 CMLR.

15   Ibid., [14].

16   Ibid., [15].

17   Ibid., [17].

18   Case C-1/97, *Mehmet Birden* [1998] ECR I-7747.

19   Ibid., [28].

20   Case 196/87, *Steymann* v *Staatssecrretaris van Justitie* [1989] 1 CMLR 449.

21   Case C-415/93, *Union Royale Belge des Sociétés de Football Association (ASBL)* v *Bosman* [1996] 1 CMLR 645; Case C-176/96, *Jyri Lehtonen and Another* v *FRBSB* [2000] 3 CMLR 409.

22   In Case C-292/89, *Antonissen* [1991] ECR I-745 the ECJ considered six months to be reasonable and in Case C-344/95 *Commission* v *Belgium* [1997] ECR I-1035 it held that even three months may be enough.

23   Case 39/86, *Lair* [1988] ECR 3161.

The Personal Scope of Application of EC Social Legislation 175

jurisprudence on job-seekers has been integrated in Directive 2004/38, providing for an unconditional right of residence for everyone for up to three months (Article 6) and for the retention of such right for work-seekers who have genuine chances of finding a job (Article 14(4)(b)).[24] However, and contrary to what was held by the ECJ in *Collins*[25] just a few days before the Directive was adopted on 29 April 2004, Article 24(2) provides for the possibility of excluding job-seekers from the right to equal treatment in relation to social assistance.

In recent years European citizenship has progressively encroached upon free movement and the right to reside and has somewhat blurred part of the distinction between economically active and economically inactive persons. The latter can now enjoy some of the rights and social benefit entitlements normally afforded to workers only.[26] On the other hand economically inactive persons can still be excluded from a considerable set of welfare rights,[27] a circumstance that makes the 'EU worker' status as desirable as ever for any European citizen moving to another Member State.

Finally, it is worth recalling that self-employed workers are far from being excluded from the enjoyment of the right to free movement thanks to the attribution of the freedom to provide services and of the right to establishment, under Articles 43 and 49 of the Treaty. A complete analysis of these two freedoms is beyond the purposes of the present work; nevertheless, a summary scrutiny of their personal scope of application and of the main prerogatives they grant to the category of the self-employed is necessary.

The right of establishment entails settlement in a Member State for economic purposes, and implies permanent integration into the host State's economy, generally being exercised through a shift of a sole place of business, or by the 'setting up of agencies, branches or subsidiaries by nationals of any' Member State (Article 43(1)). It explicitly includes the 'right to take up and pursue activities as self-employed persons and to set up and manage undertakings, in particular companies and firms'. The freedom to provide services entails a person or undertaking established in one MS providing a service in another. Services 'in particular include: (a) activities of an industrial character; (b) activities of a commercial character; (c) activities of craftsmen; (d) activities of the professions' (Article 50(2)). As far as their rationales are concerned, it has been highlighted that while the right of establishment (just as free movement of workers) is concerned with eliminating discrimination on grounds of nationality, the freedom to provide services has a more distinctly 'market integration' rationale.

The notion of establishment has been granted a very generous interpretation by the ECJ. In *Gebhard* it was stated that the 'concept of establishment within the

---

24   Council Directive 2004/38/EC of 29 April 2004 on the right of citizens of the Union and their family members to move and reside freely within the territory of the Member States. [2004] OJ L158/77.

25   Case C-138/02, *Collins* [2004] ECR I-2703.

26   See cases such as Case C-85/96, *Martínez Sala* v *Freistat Bayern* [1998] ECR I-2691; Case C-184/99, *R. Grzelczyk* v *Centre public d'aide social d'Ottignies-Louvain-la-Neuve* [2001] ECR I 6193; Case C-209/03, *Bidar* [2005] ECR I-2119.

27   Case C-138/02, *Collins* [2004] ECR I 2703; Case C-406/04, *De Cuyper* v *Office national de l'emploi* [2006] ECR I-6947.

176   *The Changing Law of the Employment Relationship*

meaning of the Treaty is ... a very broad one, allowing a Community national to participate, on a stable and continuous basis, in the economic life of Member State other than his state of origin and to profit therefrom, so contributing to economic and social interpenetration within the Community in the sphere of activities as self-employed persons (see *Reyners* para. 2)'[28]. In contrast, where the provider of services moves to another Member State, the provision of the chapter on services envisage that she is to pursue her activity on a temporary basis.

Even if the ECJ has made clear that the distinguishing feature of establishment is the 'stable and continuous basis' on which the activity is carried on, it is often difficult to ascertain this distinction, for instance in cases in which the provision of services involves residence (albeit temporarily) in the host State, as in the case of a construction company which erects buildings in a neighbouring country. On the other hand it is normally easier to appreciate the distinction when the subjects involved are natural, as opposed to legal, persons.

As for secondary legislation, even before the adoption of Directive 2004/38, the now-repealed Directive 73/148, covering both the right of establishment and the freedom to provide services, had already brought the law governing the entry and residence of the self-employed into line with that applying to employees. But undeniably it was with Directive 2004/38 that EU citizens received a set of rights provided by a unified and single legal framework. Whilst all citizens, active or inactive, are granted a right to enter and reside for three months by Article 6 of the Directive, an unqualified right of residence for more than three months is only granted to citizens who 'are workers or self-employed persons in the host Member State', whereas other categories of citizens only receive qualified rights, depending on their status and economic resources.[29]

It is worthwhile pointing out that EC Directive 96/71, albeit formally adopted within the framework of EC legislation on the provision of services, has had a direct impact on the substantial rights of a specific category of 'atypical' workers, that is to say posted workers. The Directive, under Article 3, provides that the undertaking posting workers to a third country must guarantee posted workers the basic and mandatory terms and conditions of employment in force in the host state. The personal scope of application of the Directive also deserves some further discussion. Article 1(3) provides that the posting of workers covered by the Directive is the one where, 'there is an *employment relationship* between the undertaking making the posting and the worker' (emphasis added). The provision does not replicate the 'contract of employment or employment relationship' formula, typical of EC legislation on working conditions, and it is therefore arguable that it should be given a broader interpretation, coherently with its 'free movement' rationale. On the other hand it seems that Article 2(2) of the Directive, saying that for its purposes the 'definition of a worker is that which applies in the law of the Member State to whose territory the worker is posted', appears to be at odds with the traditional stance of providing a 'Community meaning' of the term 'worker' in the free movement area. Having said

---

28   Case C-55/94, *Reinhard Gebhard* v *Consiglio dell'Ordine degli Avvocati e Procuratori di Milano* [1995] ECR I-4165 [25].

29   See Article 7(1) of Directive 2004/38.

The Personal Scope of Application of EC Social Legislation   177

that, on numerous occasions the ECJ has intervened to narrow down the freedom that host Member States enjoy in defining the notion of worker, for instance when, in respect of posted workers who are third-country nationals, it held that a requirements by the host country to have been employed by the posting company for at least six months prior to the posting, and on a permanent basis, was in breach of Article 49.[30]

To sum up, it appears that EC law attributed the legal prerogatives deriving from its free movement rules to a vast array of working persons, wage earners and others. The EC has also chosen to lie down autonomously, that is to say without deriving them from the national systems, the concepts of 'worker' and 'self-employed'. The fact that it clearly dedicates, in its legislation and case law, a much greater attention to the definition of the notion of dependent workers as opposed to the self-employed is clearly another indication of the objective complexity of tackling this issue.

Social security and pensions

In the area of *social security and pensions*, Article 42 provides for the Council to

> adopt such measures ... as are necessary to provide freedom of movement for workers; to this end it shall make arrangements to secure for migrant workers and their dependants:
>
> aggregation, for the purpose of acquiring and retaining the right to benefit and of calculating the amount of benefit, of all periods taken into account under the laws of several countries;
>
> payment of benefits to persons resident in the territories of Member States.

It is interesting to notice that not only has the Council acted promptly in implementing such principles, with the adoption of Regulations 3/58[31] and 4/58,[32] but that it has been punctual and scrupulous in revising and, most importantly, expanding the scope of application of these instruments. A crucially import amendment was contained in Regulation 1390/81,[33] which extended the scope of Regulation 1408/71[34] to the self-employed. Most of Regulation 1408/71 has been repealed with the entry into force of Regulation 883/2004.[35] The substantive provisions of these Regulations are extremely complex and a full discussion of them is beyond the purposes of the present work. This section offers a description of the – wide – personal scope of Regulation 883/2004.

Article 2(1) provides that the Regulation in question applies 'to nationals of a Member State ... who are or have been subject to the [social security] legislation of one or more Member States, as well as to the members of their families and to their

---

30 See Case C-445/03, *Commission* v *Luxembourg* [2004] ECR I-10191.
31 [1958] JO 561.
32 [1958] JO 597.
33 [1981] OJ L143/1.
34 [1971] OJ L149/2.
35 [2004] OJ L200/1.

178   *The Changing Law of the Employment Relationship*

survivors'. The personal scope of application of the 2004 Regulation is therefore considerably broader that the one contained in the old 1408/71.[36] At this stage the EC instrument refrains from giving an autonomous, EC, definition of the notions of 'employed' and 'self-employed' worker, and instead opts for a definition by reference describing them as persons involved in 'any activity or equivalent situation treated as such for the purposes of the social security legislation of the Member State in which such activity or equivalent situation exists'.[37]

Prima facie, it would seem that the instruments, while having a very wide personal scope of application, adopt a definitional approach relying on the national notions of employed and self-employed workers instead of, say, introducing new and autonomous Community concepts, as in the area of free movement of workers. But this is only true up to a point, as the ECJ has – to some extent successfully – laid some solid foundations for the personal scope of application of EC social security legislation in the course of interpreting the provisions contained in the old Regulation 1408/71. Indeed, albeit formally maintaining in *de Jaeck* that EC law does not 'intend to endow the terms "employed" and "self-employed" with an autonomous Community meaning', the Court has acknowledged in *Hoekstra* that the term 'worker' must be given a 'Community meaning' to the extent that 'all those who, as such and *under whatever description*, are covered by the different national systems of social security' must be considered as 'workers' for the purposes of EC social security law.[38] In *Galinsky*, for instance, the ECJ confirmed that the Regulation applies not only to workers in employment but also to 'the worker who, having left his job, is capable of taking another' and in *Kits van Heijningen* it made clear that part-time workers were also covered *irrespective* of the number of hours worked.[39] At the end of the day, in this policy area, the EC has attempted to strike a balance between the creation of an autonomous notion of 'worker', as in the context of Article 39, and a completely parasitic one fully relying on the national legal orders for the definition of the employed and self-employed categories. The real risk with this imperfect communitarisation of the notion of 'worker' is that, in the absence of EC measures, Member States can still determine the scope of application of their national social security systems as they prefer.

---

36   Article 2(1) applied to 'employed or self-employed persons who are or have been subject to the legislation of one or more Member States and who are nationals of one of the Member States ... as well as to their families and their survivors'.

37   Article 1(a) and 1(b) of Regulation 883/2004. The old definition provided by Article 1(a)(i) of Regulation 1408/71 was 'any person who is insured, compulsorily or on an optional continued basis, for one or more of the contingencies covered by branches of a social security scheme for employed or self-employed persons'.

38   Case C-340/94, *EJM de Jaeck* v *Staatssecretaris van Financiën* [1997] ECR I-00461 [28]; Case 75/63, *Mrs M.K.H. Hoekstra (née Unger)* v *Bestuur der Bedrijfsvereniging voor Detailhandel en Ambachten* [1964] ECR 177. Emphasis added.

39   Case 99/80, *Galinsky* v *Insurance Office* [1981] ECR 941; Case C-2/89, *Bestuur van de Sociale Verzekeringsbank* v *M.G.J. Kits van Heijningen* [1990] ECR I-01755 [10]–[11].

EC social law

Where things become more complicated is in the remaining areas of *hard* law that, with some degree of approximation, can be seen as constituting the existing body of *EC social law*, that is to say, the EC legislative instruments, mainly directives, on health and safety at work, on the rights of workers in periods of industrial restructuring, on atypical workers, and on information and consultation and other collective labour law rights. By and large it is possible to say that the individual scope of application of this heterogeneous body of law leaves it to the national legal systems to define who is a worker for the purposes of its application, just like the social security and pensions legislation. Nevertheless it is arguably possible, in the light of some recent judicial decisions, to draw a distinction within this body of law, between the attitude of the ECJ towards measures on equality, health and safety, and towards the other directives on the remaining areas of social law.

Equality law   As far as EC legislation on equality is concerned, the starting point has to be Article 141 of the EC Treaty. This article provides:

1. Each Member State shall ensure that the principle of equal pay for male and female *workers* for equal work or work of equal value is applied.
2. For the purposes of this Article, 'pay' means the ordinary basic or minimum wage or salary or any other consideration, whether in cash or in kind, which the *worker* receives directly or indirectly, in respect of his employment, from his employer. ...[40]

The subject of Article 119 is therefore the 'worker'. On the other hand the Equal Pay Directive[41] provides that 'Member States shall introduce into their national legal systems such measures as are necessary to enable all *employees* who consider themselves wronged by failure to apply the principle of equal pay to pursue their claims by judicial process'.[42] Leaving aside for a moment equal pay and focusing instead on equal treatment legislation, Directive 76/207/EEC,[43] as amended by Directive 2002/73,[44] acknowledges that 'equal treatment for male and female *workers* constitutes one of the objectives of the Community'[45] but then modifies

---

40   Emphasis added.

41   Council Directive 75/117/EEC of 10 February 1975 on the approximation of the laws of the Member States relating to the application of the principle of equal pay for men and women. [1975] OJ L45/19.

42   Article 2. Emphasis added.

43   Council Directive 76/207/EC of 9 February 1976 on the implementation of the principle of equal treatment for men and women as regards access to employment, vocational training and promotion, and working conditions. [1976] OJ L39/40.

44   Directive 2002/73/EC of the European Parliament and of the Council of 23 September 2002 amending Council Directive 76/207/EEC on the implementation of the principle of equal treatment for men and women as regards access to employment, vocational training and promotion, and working conditions. [2002] OJ L269/15.

45   Preamble to the Directive. Emphasis added.

180 *The Changing Law of the Employment Relationship*

its terminology to provide that 'Member States shall ensure that judicial and/or administrative procedures ... are available to all *persons* who consider themselves wronged by failure to apply the principle of equal treatment to them, *even after the relationship* in which the discrimination is alleged to have occurred *has ended*',[46] and shall eliminate, *inter alia*, any provisions 'which are included in contracts [as well as in] rules governing the independent occupations and professions'[47] that are incompatible with the equal treatment principle. And the extension of the principle to independent and self-employed workers is rendered even more explicit by Directive 86/613/EEC[48]. So what is the meaning – or the meanings – of the terms 'worker' and 'employee' in the EC equal pay legislation context? And the significance of the terms 'worker', 'person' and 'self-employed' in the equal treatment one? In other words, who are the labourers to which these streams of legislation apply?

As far as equal pay legislation is concerned, the European Court of Justice has come up with significant help in unravelling this complex bundle and has given a comparatively wide interpretation to the terms used in the relevant EC primary and secondary legislation. As a consequence of the ECJ activity, it is widely accepted that the equal pay principles apply to both standard and atypical employees such as part-timers and job-sharers.[49] And it is also generally acknowledged that the ECJ jurisprudence on equal pay and part-timers has been the leverage used to dismantle many of the qualifying period hurdles present in some national legislation, such as that of the UK.[50] In 2000 the ECJ took an even bolder approach by applying the principle even in cases in which the same existence of an employment relationship was in doubt.[51] Finally, in a recent judgment[52], the ECJ took its jurisprudence one step further and declared that the meaning of the term 'worker' in the context of Article 141 'should include independent providers of services who are not in a relationship of subordination with the person who receives the services'[53] and implicitly argued for a correspondence of the notion of worker in the areas of equal pay and of free movement of workers.

---

46 Article 6 of Directive 76/207, as amended by Article 1(5) of Directive 2002/73. Emphasis added.

47 Article 3(2)(b) of Directive 76/207, as amended by Article 1(3) of Directive 2002/73. Emphasis added.

48 Council Directive 86/613/EEC of 11 December 1986 on the application of the principle of equal treatment between men and women engaged in an activity, including agriculture, in a self-employed capacity, and on the protection of self-employed women during pregnancy and motherhood. [1986] OJ L359/56.

49 See Case 96/80, *Jenkins* [1981] ECR 911; Case 170/84, *Bilka-Kaufhaus* [1986] ECR 1607; Case 171/88, *Rinner-Kuhn* [1989] ECR 2743; Case 33/89, *Kowalska* v *Freie und Hansestadt Hamburg* [1990] ECR I-2591.

50 Case C-167/97, *Seymour-Smith* [1999] ECR I-623.

51 Case C-78/98, *Shirley Preston and Others* v *Wolverhampton Healthcare NHS Trust and Others* [2000] ECR I-3201.

52 Case C-256/01, *Allonby* v *Accrington & Rossendale College and Others* [2004] ECR I-873.

53 Ibid., [68].

The Personal Scope of Application of EC Social Legislation 181

In *Preston*, a case dealing with Article 141 and occupational pension entitlements (which are of course a component of pay for the purposes of the application of the equal pay principle[54]), the ECJ took a great leap forward in expanding the personal scope of application of EC legislation on equal pay. The Court was asked about the legality of section 2(4) of the Equal Pay Act 1970 (EqPA), providing that a claim for membership of an occupational pension scheme (from which the right to pension benefits would flow) needed to be brought within six months after the end of any contract of employment to which the claim relates. This rule obviously had a perverse effect when the claimants were, as in the case in question, workers who 'work regularly, but periodically or intermittently, for the same employer, under successive legally separate contracts ... [and] in the absence of an umbrella contract'.[55] So, in such cases the six-month period prescribed in section 2(4) of the EqPA started to run from the end of each contract of employment and not from the end of the employment relationship between the worker and the establishment concerned. As a consequence, workers could only secure recognition of periods of part-time work, for the purpose of calculating their pension rights, if they instituted proceedings within six months after the end of *each* contract under which the work concerned was performed.

It was evident to the ECJ that this requirement was an 'excessively difficult'[56] requirement. It was also clear that the most obvious way of overcoming this hurdle was to indicate – in a way or another – that even in the absence of an explicit umbrella contract, the 'successive legally separate contracts' had to be collated so as to allow the six-month period to start flowing from

> the date on which the sequence of such contracts has been interrupted through the absence of one or more of the features that characterise a *stable employment relationship* of that kind, either because the periodicity of such contracts has been broken or because the new contract does not relate to the same employment as that to which the same pension scheme applies.[57]

Which is exactly what the Court did. The consequences of *Preston* on the British notion of employment relationship have already been examined in the second section of Chapter 2. What is clear for the purposes of the personal scope of application of EC equal pay legislation, is that Article 141 ECT applies to standard employees employed under a contract of employment, atypical workers, and also to any intermittent 'succession of short-term contracts [provide it has been] concluded at regular intervals in respect of the same employment',[58] a concept defined by the Court as a *stable employment relationship.*

The *Allonby*[59] decision is likely to have a similarly strong impact on national labour legislation in several MSs and particularly in the UK. In this case the Court

---

54 Case C-262/88 *Barber* v *Guardian Royal Exchange* [1990] ECR I-1889.
55 Case C-78/98, *Preston*, [65].
56 Ibid., [68].
57 Ibid., [70]. Emphasis added.
58 Ibid., [6].
59 Case C-256/01, *Allonby*.

182   *The Changing Law of the Employment Relationship*

was called to decide upon a number of issues concerning a claim for equal pay by an agency worker. Mrs Allonby had been employed as a part-time lecturer by Accrington, an English higher education college, until in 1996 'the College's financial obligations (became) more onerous because of legislative changes which required part-time lecturers to be accorded equal or equivalent benefits to full-time lecturers, in particular as regards retirement pensions'.[60] At that point her fixed-term position, as also those of her part-time colleagues, was not renewed and the College decided instead to retain her services as a sub-contractor hired through an agency set up for this specific purpose (called ELS). Not only did her salary and working conditions visibly deteriorate, but Mrs Allonby was also deprived from the possibility of joining the Teachers' Superannuation Scheme (TSS), whose statute limits membership to persons employed under a contract of employment.

Mrs Allonby brought a number of claims that were eventually referred to the ECJ, all pivoting around the claim that the changes in working arrangements introduced by Accrington since 1996 disproportionately affected women. The ECJ did allow the argument that Mrs Allonby's equal pay claim should be based on a male comparator who continued to be employed as a full-time lecturer at the college. This was because 'where the differences identified in the pay conditions of workers performing equal work or work of equal value cannot be attributed to a *single source*, there is no body which is responsible for the inequality and which could restore equal treatment'.[61] But the Court was more receptive to the argument directed against the exclusion of workers in Mrs Allonby's situation by the rules of the TSS solely because they were not employed under a contract of employment. The Court, suggesting that the notion of 'worker' in the context of Article 141 had to be given a meaning analogous to the one applied in the context of free movement of workers,[62] went on to assert that, admittedly, 'the term worker (does not include) independent providers of services who are not in a relationship of subordination with the person who receives the services'.[63] It thus remained to consider whether the fact that Mrs Allonby was classified as a worker employed under a contract for services would have sufficed to justify her exclusion both from the scope of Article 141(1) and from the occupational pension scheme. And in that respect the Court could have not been more explicit by stating that

> [71] The formal classification of a self-employed person under national law does not exclude the possibility that a person must be classified as a worker within the meaning of Article 141(1) EC if his independence is merely notional, thereby disguising an employment relationship within the meaning of that article.

The Court pointed out that in accordance with that reasoning, in cases such as Mrs Allonby's, where workers are excluded from the enjoyment of a right in contrast with the equality principle on the grounds of their employment relationship, the national court will in practice have to decide upon their actual employment status

---

60   Ibid., [18].
61   Ibid., [46]. Emphasis added.
62   Ibid., [67].
63   Ibid., [68].

The Personal Scope of Application of EC Social Legislation 183

taking into account 'the extent of any limitation on their freedom to choose their timetable, and their place and content of their work' and disregarding 'the fact that *no obligation is imposed on them to accept an assignment*'.[64] These last words have no doubt caused considerable apprehension to the referring judges of the UK Court of Appeal. With the *Allonby* decision, the ECJ took two big steps at once. First of all, the ECJ decision extends to the equality area a jurisprudence that had emerged in the, far less controversial context of free movement of workers.[65] At a second level it appears to be giving explicit guidance to the British court to (re)consider Mrs Allonby's status in the light of the elements of factual subordination deriving from her contractual arrangements (limitation on freedom to choose a timetable, place and content of work) while disregarding a key test used by British courts to identify a worker as somebody employed under a contract for services, that is to say, the absence of sufficient mutuality of obligation as defined in cases such as *O'Kelly*[66] and *Carmichael*.[67] Neither *O'Kelly*'s 'regular casuals' nor *Carmichael*'s 'casual and as required' workers were under any contractual obligation to accept work, and this was seen as an indication of absence of 'mutuality', ultimately depriving these workers from the 'employee' status. It would appear that the ECJ, with its reasoning, seeks precisely to anticipate this type of risk in respect of Mrs Allonby. Since current British equal treatment legislation includes all employed persons and not just 'employees' in its scope of application, it will most likely satisfy the *Allonby* test. On the other hand there is no doubt that the ECJ decision also suggest a deeper rethinking of the traditional construction of the British notion of contract of employment.

The body of EC equal treatment legislation seems to have a similarly broad, if not broader, scope of application. Indeed specific measures, as discussed above, have extended some of the applications of the principle to self-employed workers. Thus Directive 86/613/EEC therefore covers:

a. self-employed workers, i.e. all persons pursuing a gainful activity for their own account, under the conditions laid down by national law, including farmers and members of the liberal professions;
b. their spouses, not being employees or partners, where they habitually, under the conditions laid down by national law, participate in the activities of the self-employed worker and perform the same tasks or ancillary tasks.[68]

On the other hand, scholars have rightly highlighted that, in spite of this wide scope of application, the substantive provisions of the Directive 'are characterized by their generality, more akin to a Recommendation or a Resolution than a Directive',[69]

---

64   Ibid., [72]. Emphasis added.

65   Cf. Case C-357/89, *Raulin* v *Minister van Onderwijs en Wetenschappen* [1992] ECR I-1027 [9]–[10].

66   *O'Kelly* v *Trusthouse Forte plc* [1983] ICR 728.

67   *Carmichael* v *National Power plc* [1999] ICR 1226.

68   Article 2 of Directive 86/613.

69   C. Barnard, *EC Employment Law* (2nd ed., OUP, Oxford, 2000), p. 252.

184　　*The Changing Law of the Employment Relationship*

and merely outline a program of action for Member States. In the light of these considerations it becomes harder to give an overall assessment of the scope of application of this stream of anti-discrimination legislation, as there is an undeniable asymmetry between the wording and substance of the protection afforded to subordinate employees and to the self-employed.

On the other hand there is little doubt that equal opportunities legislation can 'bite' effectively, even in extremely atypical and casual employment relationship. In the *Wippel* case, for instance, the Court held that

> a worker with a contract of employment ... under which hours of work and the organisation of working time are dependent upon the quantity of available work and are determined only on a case-by-case basis by agreement between the parties, comes within the scope of Directive 76/207.[70]

Therefore, and in stark contrast with the approach of some national courts dealing with zero-hours on-call workers, the ECJ considers that casual workers employed on a part-time basis under a 'framework contract of employment' based on the principle of 'work on demand', are to be considered as workers for the purposes of equal opportunities legislation.

In the most recent tranche of anti-discrimination laws the EC has arguably adopted a slightly different approach. With Directives 2000/43/EC[71] and 2000/78/EC[72] the Community seems to be approaching discrimination in a novel way, placing greater emphasis on the 'fundamental rights' dimension of the instruments as well as on their – traditional – 'labour market regulation' aspect.[73] The scope of these Directives, as laid down in Article 3, provides that they apply 'to all persons, as regards both the public and private sectors, including public bodies, in relation to:

> conditions for access to employment, to self-employment or to occupation, including selection criteria and recruitment conditions, whatever the branch of activity and at all levels of the professional hierarchy, including promotion;
>
> access to all types and to all levels of vocational guidance, vocational training, advanced vocational training and retraining, including practical work experience;
>
> employment and working conditions, including dismissals and pay;

70　Case C-313/02, *Wippel* v *Peek & Cloppenburg GmbH & Co. KG* [2004] ECR I-9483 [40].

71　Council Directive 2000/43/EC of 29 June 2000 implementing the principle of equal treatment between persons irrespective of racial or ethnic origin. [2000] OJ L180/22.

72　Council Directive 2000/78/EC of 27 November 2000 establishing a general framework for equal treatment in employment and occupation. [2000] OJ L303/16.

73　S. Fredman, 'Discrimination in the EU: Labour Market Regulation or Fundamental Rights?' in H. Collins, P. Davies and R. Rideout (eds), *Legal Regulation of the Employment Relation* (Kluwer, The Hague, 2000), pp. 183–201.

The Personal Scope of Application of EC Social Legislation   185

membership of, and involvement in, an organisation of workers and employers, or any organisation whose members carry on a particular profession, including the benefits provided for by such organisations.'

This broad scope of application should not really be a surprise, and it is well justified in the context of fundamental rights whose language and approach is distinctly universalistic. And in the light of this consideration it is arguable that the Court, if and when the occasion arises, will also be tempted to adopt such a teleological interpretation and have recourse to the whole of its arsenal of weapons to apply the principles provided by these two Directives to as many working persons as possible, regardless of their state of economic and formal dependency.

Health and safety legislation   As far as health and safety (H&S) legislation is concerned, Directive 89/391/EEC[74] applies to 'workers' defined in its Article 3(a) as 'any person employed by an employer, including trainees and apprentices but excluding domestic servants' and, unless otherwise provided, it excludes those regarded as self-employed. This definition is slightly amplified by the somewhat fuller description of 'employer' as any natural or legal person having an 'employment relationship with the worker and having responsibility for the undertaking or establishment'.[75] But as no description is given of what an 'employment relationship' constitutes, it seems reasonable to assume that an implicit reference to national systems is made for the determination of this crucial issue. On the other hand, the scope of EC H&S legislation is specifically extended to workers on fixed-term contracts and workers in temporary employment relationships by Directive 91/383/EEC.[76] Article 2(3) of this instrument explicitly provides that Framework Directive 89/391 and the related 'daughter' directives apply equally to these atypical workers so that the definition of these workers, at least, is not completely left to the mercy of the national legal orders.[77]

At the end of the day it seems that EC H&S legislation adopts a distinctive approach to the definition of its individual scope of application. It applies, as a starting point, to 'any person employed by an employer' and focuses on the notion

---

74   The so-called framework directive. Directive 89/391/EEC of 12 June 1989 on the introduction of measures to encourage improvements in the safety and health of workers at work. [1989] OJ L183/1.

75   Ibid., Article 3(b).

76   Council Directive 91/383/EEC of 14 October 1991 on an employer's obligation to inform employees of the conditions applicable to the contract of employment relationship. [1991] OJ L206/19. See also COM(90) 228 final.

77   Article 1 of Directive 91/383 reads as follows:

'This Directive shall apply to:

1.   employment relationships governed by a fixed duration contract of employment concluded directly between the employer and the worker, where the end of the contract is established by objective conditions such as: reaching of a specific date, completing a specific task or the occurrence of a specific event;

2.   temporary employment relationships between a temporary employment business which is the employer and the worker where the latter is assigned to work for and under the control of an undertaking and/or establishment making use of his services.'

186 *The Changing Law of the Employment Relationship*

of 'employment relationship' albeit leaving that to be defined by the national legal systems. But then it claims back, almost by the back door, some of this leeway, by explicitly providing that atypical workers on fixed-term contracts and, most notably, in temporary employment relationships, have to be covered by EC H&S provisions. Such an approach has probably been taken one step further by a recent ECJ decision regarding H&S – albeit a very special aspect of H&S, that is to say, the 1993 Working Time Directive[78] (WTD). In *BECTU*[79] the issue at stake was whether the UK legal requirement of 13 weeks of continuous employment[80] to qualify for paid leave was compatible with Article 7 of the WTD. The ECJ ruled that the UK qualifying period was indeed in breach of EC law. The Court clearly stated that 'every worker'[81] is entitled to paid leave and emphasised that this was a natural consequence of the fact that workers engaged on short-term contracts 'often find themselves in a more precarious situation than those employed under longer term contracts, so that it is all the more important to ensure that their health and safety are protected in a manner consonant with the purpose of' the Directive (paragraph 63).

It should be said that the national rule was not casting doubts on the status of the workers, who were indeed considered 'employees' despite their short-term engagements. Nevertheless it is also important to stress that, in saying that the 'expression "in accordance with the conditions for entitlement to ... such leave laid down by national legislation and/or practice" must ... be construed as referring only to the arrangements for paid annual leave adopted in the various Member States' and that the delineation of any specific circumstances in which workers may exercise that right cannot be such as to 'make the existence of that right ... subject to any precondition',[82] the ECJ was substantially expanding the scope of application of that measure to a great number of workers. To revert to the vocabulary previously used in the second section of Chapter 2, it could be said that the European Court, in the *BECTU* case, has removed another *quantitative restriction* which, albeit not denying the employee status to the workers affected, *de facto* limited the individual scope of application of the WTD.

Measures concerning working conditions   The situation is, however, quite different in the remaining areas of EC social law, that is to say with regard to measures concerning working conditions. A useful example of this aspect of EC social law is Directive 91/533/EEC,[83] introducing a new, different kind of approach to the definition

---

78   Council Directive 93/104/EEC of 23 November 1993 concerning certain aspects of the organisation of working time. [1993] OJ L307/18. The Directive has been consolidated with the adoption of Directive 2003/38 of the European Parliament and of the Council of 4 November 2003 concerning certain aspects of the organisation of working time. [2003] OJ L299/9.

79   Case C-173/99, *R* v *Secretary for Trade and Industry ex parte Broadcasting, Entertainment, Cinematographic and Theatre Union (BECTU)* [2001] ECR I-4881.

80   Provided by regulation 13(7) WTR 1998.

81   Case C-173/99, *BECTU*, [46]–[47].

82   Ibid., [53].

83   Council Directive 91/533/EC of 14 October 1991 on an employer's obligation to inform employees of the conditions applicable to the contract or employment relationship.

The Personal Scope of Application of EC Social Legislation 187

of its personal scope of application. The Directive, under Article 1(1) applies to every paid employee having a *contract* or an *employment relationship* defined by the law in force in a Member State and/or governed by the law in force in a Member State. The doctrinal analysis[84] on this point rightly highlights the fact that the use of the disjunctive *or* is most probably aimed at stressing the difference existing, in many MSs' legal systems, between the notion of the employment contract and that of employment relationship. In considering the term 'employment relationship', the Commission in its Memorandum accompanying the draft Directive[85] envisaged both wholly new forms of labour and variations on traditional forms, including distance work, training schemes, work/training contracts, work outside the traditional workplace, job-sharing and on-call work. On the other hand, hard law takes away from workers what the memorandum might have sought to afford, as Article 1(2) allows MSs implementing the instrument to introduce exceptions from the application of its provisions for employees having a contract or employment relationship with a total duration not exceeding one month, and/or with a working week not exceeding eight hours, or of casual workers and/or specific nature, provided that its non-application in these cases is justified by objective considerations.

An even more cautious approach is adopted in the context of EC employment right on restructuring. This approach partly reiterates the *contract of employment or employment relationship* formula[86] but it reinforces the fact that 'employee' 'shall mean any person who, in the Member State concerned, is protected as an employee under national employment law',[87] by expressly stressing that the Directive 'shall be without prejudice to national law as regards [its] definition'.[88] Admittedly, the amendments introduced by Directive 98/50/EC to the personal scope of application now explicitly preclude the possibility that the reference to national law could turn into an exclusion of non-standard workers from the scope of some categories, but this route has not been followed in any other measure, not even by the recent Directives on atypical workers. And things are not much different in the remaining areas of EC social law relating to the regulation of working conditions, rights on restructuring of enterprises and to information and consultation, where the Community again fully adopts a 'subsidiaristic' notion of the contract of employment or employment relationship. And it seems very unlikely that the ECJ will ever be bold enough to extend its EC notion of 'stable employment relationship' to this area of legislation so as to provide a judicial extension of these protective measures to workers in atypical employment relationships.

[1991] OJ L288/32.

84 C. Barnard, *EC Employment Law*, p. 437.

85 COM(90) 563 final of 8.01.1991.

86 See for instance Article 2(2) of Council Directive 98/50 of 29 June 1998, amending Directive 77/187 EEC on the approximation of the laws of the Member States relating to the safeguard of employees' rights in the event of transfer of undertakings, businesses or parts of businesses. OJ 1998 L201/98. The two now consolidated with Council Directive 2001/23/EC of 12 March 2001. OJ 2001 L82/16.

87 Directive 98/50, Article 2(1)(d).

88 Ibid., Article 2(2).

188 *The Changing Law of the Employment Relationship*

As far as the protection of these latter categories of workers is concerned, it would seem that the path chosen by the Community is to regulate these works relationships selectively by providing *ad hoc* extensions – through the application of the non-discrimination principle – of the EC rights afforded to standard workers. The EC has therefore adopted two instruments, Directive 97/81/EC[89] and Directive 99/70/EC,[90] regulating part-time and fixed term work and embodying two Framework agreements concluded by the EC level social partners, respectively. While a fuller analysis of these two directives will be carried on in the next chapter, it is worth noting at this point that they are directed at workers having an 'employment contract or employment relationship as defined by the law, collective agreement or practice in force in each Member State'.[91]

In practice these two instruments have the major flaw of assigning to the national legal orders the prerogative of defining the individual scope of their application. This practice is supported by the ECJ jurisprudence.[92] While the Court in *Wippel* had no doubt whatsoever that Mrs Wippel was to be considered a worker for the purposes of EC anti-discrimination legislation, it was less positive when it came to assess whether her atypical, zero-hours on-call 'framework contract' qualified her as an employee for the purposes of the application of Directive 97/81. It held that 'it is for the referring court to make such determinations as may be necessary in order to verify whether that is the situation in the case before it'.[93]

In the context of atypical employment relationships this is particularly difficult since, as seen in previous chapters, national systems are certainly not a haven of clarity as far as the definition of the individual scope of labour law is concerned, and are all more or less afflicted by similar problems, albeit sometimes tackling them in different ways. To make things worse, clause 2(2) of the Framework Agreement annexed to Directive 97/81 allows Member States wholly or partly to exclude 'casual workers' from the application of the Directive. The result of this state of the affairs can easily be that what is bestowed at a supranational level is then taken away at the national one, with many atypical workers not considered as engaged in an 'employment relationship' whatsoever (for example, because their work is intermittent), and so being excluded from legislative protection.

This is a rather paradoxical situation given that, according to some authors,[94] 'it is partly because of the narrow British definition of an employment contract that employment directives use the words "contract of employment or employment

---

89 Council Directive 97/81/EC of 15 December 1997 concerning the Framework Agreement on part-time work concluded by UNICE, CEEP and the ETUC as amended by Directive 98/23/EC (OJ 1998 L131/10), consolidated [1998] OJ L131/13.

90 Council Directive 99/70/EC of 28 June 1999 Concerning the Framework Agreement on Fixed-term Work Concluded by UNICE, CEEP and the ETUC [1999] OJ L175/43, corrigendum OJ 1999 L244/64, clause 2.

91 Clause 2(1) of both Directives.

92 Case 105/84, *A/S Danmols Inventar* [1985] ECR 2639, [25]–[26].

93 Case C-313/02, *Wippel* v *Peek & Cloppenburg GmbH & Co. KG* [2004] ECR I-9483 [39].

94 R. Nielsen and E. Szyszczak, *The Social Dimension of the European Union* (Forlag, Copenhagen, 1997), p. 293

relationship"'. Chapter 1 briefly discussed the differences existing between these two notions and the exclusionary effect that the absence of a 'contract of employment' (despite the presence of an employment relationship) has traditionally had in jurisdictions such as the British one. Bercusson affirms that

> The use of the term 'relationship' requires EU law to take cognisance of a multitude of forms of work which never acquire contractual status, but are nonetheless carried out in the expectation of some form of reciprocal benefit, which may fall short of the common law concept of contractual consideration.[95]

In the light of that discussion it is safe to say that if, as is suggested by Bercusson and by Nielsen and Szyszczak, the formula used in these Directives is indeed aimed at expanding the scope of application beyond the strict British notion of the contract of employment, then these good intentions have been greatly frustrated by the reference to the 'national law' of the Member States as the appropriate jurisdictional level at which to identify the definition of the formula. As seen in the course of this chapter and book, the notion of the employment relationship has a different width in each MS, and working patterns that in some jurisdictions clearly configure a dependant employment relationship, in some others, for reasons that are specific to the national legal and jurisprudential tradition, might not. The formula therefore, by making reference to the national level, provides a rather *circular* and, ultimately, unsatisfactory definition of the personal scope of application of these Directives.

To overcome this risk there are a number of different options. The first and obvious one would be to reformulate the personal scope of EC Directives in this area. Council Directive 77/187/EC, as amended by Directive 98/50/EC, is a clear indication that this need was perceived as a pressing one in the late 1990s. The amending directive did not go as far as creating an EC notion of the contract of employment or the employment relationship, but it strengthened the traditional formula with a provision specifying that Member States shall not exclude from the scope of this Directive contracts of employment or employment relationships solely because

a. of the number of working hours performed or to be performed,
b. they are employment relationships governed by a fixed-duration contract or employment,
c. they are temporary employment relationships and the undertaking transferred is, or is part of, the temporary employment business which is the employer.[96]

Most importantly, the definitions of b) and c) are not left to 'national law', but are prescribed by reference to the definition contained in Article 1(1) and 1(2) of Directive 91/383 which, as was observed in the previous section of this chapter on

---

95 B. Bercusson, *European Labour Law* (Butterworths, London, 1996), p. 431.

96 Article 2(2) of Council Directive 2001/23/EC of 12 March 2001 on the approximation of the laws of Member States relating to the safeguard of employees' rights in the event of transfer of undertakings, businesses or parts of undertakings or businesses. [2001] OJ L82/16.

190   *The Changing Law of the Employment Relationship*

H&S, has the major benefit of providing an autonomous EC definition, detached from national law.[97] Unfortunately this legislative path is so far exceptional and no other directive on working conditions has attempted to replicate it, not even the other directives on restructuring. In fact, even Directive 2002/74, amending the old insolvency Directive 80/987, did not go as far as replicating the wording of Directive 98/50, and chose instead to provide that, whilst the definition of the term 'employee' is something for national law to define,

Member States may not exclude from the scope of this Directive:

a. part-time employees within the meaning of Directive 97/81/EC;
b. workers with a fixed-term contract within the meaning of Directive 1999/70/EC;
c. workers with a temporary employment relationship within the meaning of Article 1(2) of Directive 91/383.[98]

Article 2(3) of the Directive also provided that 'Member States may not set a minimum duration for the contract of employment or the employment relationship in order for workers to qualify for claims under this Directive'.

The second way to improve the personal scope of the working conditions Directives would be to create an EC-level definition of what a contract of employment or employment relationship is, on the lines of what the ECJ has done with the notion of 'worker' in the freedom of movement or equality areas. This possibility, though, seems to have been ruled out not only by the present state of EC directives, by the Court itself. In Case 105/84, *Danmols Inventar*,[99] the Court explicated this stance and analysed it in relation to its position in the free movement area. It first pointed out that the term 'employee' in the area of free movement 'cannot be defined by reference to the legislation of member-States [otherwise] these 'Community rules ... would be frustrated' (paragraph 24). It subsequently claimed that it was necessary to determine whether similar considerations were 'valid in defining this term in the framework of Directive 77/187'.[100] It then continued by saying that Directive 77/187 only aimed at '*partial harmonisation* of the subject in question', and that it merely sought to extend generally the protection given to employees independently by the employment laws of the different member-States in the situation where an undertaking is transferred. 'The purpose of the Directive is therefore to ensure so far as possible that the contract of employment or employment relationship continues unchanged with the transferee in order to prevent the employees involved in the transfer of the undertaking from being placed in a less favourable position solely by

---

97 As opposed to the directives on part-time and fixed-term workers, as we shall see in the next chapter.

98 Article 2(2) of Directive 2002/74/EC of the European Parliament and of the Council of 23 September 2002, amending Council Directive 80/987/EEC, on the approximation of the laws of the Member States relating to the protection of employees in the event of the insolvency of their employers. [2002] OJ L270/10.

99 Case 105/84.

100 Ibid., [25].

reason of the transfer. The Directive does not, however, aim to establish a uniform level of protection for the entire Community by reference to common criteria' (paragraph 26).

The ECJ argued that, the aim of these Directives being *partial harmonisation*, an EC notion of 'employee' for the purposes of defining the meaning of 'contract of employment or employment relationship' could not appropriately be introduced. It is quite unlikely that this stance will ever be modified, as the differentiated treatment of these areas of employment and social policy is justified, in the context of EC law, by their special rationales, which have not been invented *ad hoc* but are, on the contrary, the outcome of deeply rooted – albeit contestable – policy options and *equilibria*. It is well known that the EC has always attached particular importance to the issue of equality, particularly as far as equal pay is concerned, and it is well accepted and documented that this special concern is founded on some specific macro-economic considerations which constitute the very basis of the establishment of the European single market. Similarly, free movement of persons is a fundamental principle of EC law and one that is both a means and an end for the creation of a functioning single market. And an analogous concern is obviously accorded to social security, given the adverse effects that the imperfect transferability of acquired social security rights could have on free movement of workers. But the remaining social and employment policy areas, for reasons explored in section four, have not received the same consideration and standing, and it is unlikely that they will be able to catalyse the necessary attention to secure the same treatment as far as legislative scope and judicial interpretation are concerned.

3. The directions of development of EC law

Thus it seems evident that EC social and employment law has a two-fold approach as far as its scope of application is concerned. On the one hand it adopts a variable personal scope of application, wider or narrower depending on the policy field, even if ultimately this plurality of scopes has as a side effect the exclusion of numerous atypical workers from a great amount of legislation. On the other hand it tries to redress this state of affairs by producing *ad hoc* legislation aimed at affording specific protection – based on the principle of non-discrimination between standard workers and atypical ones – to selected categories of atypical employees, such as part-timers, fixed-term workers and, probably in the future, temporary employees. Ultimately, employees – that is to say, those workers employed under a contract of employment, whether full time, part time, fixed term or of a trilateral kind – will receive some protection from the European Union. But what about quasi-dependent workers or those workers who are not genuinely self-employed and who fall in one of the *tertium genus* categories described in the third section of Chapter 2? At present they are neglected and ignored by the European legislator. But there are indications that, in the future, things could take a different path.

In June 2000, the Commission issued a consultation document, in accordance with Article 138 of the EC Treaty, on the possible direction of Community action on

192 *The Changing Law of the Employment Relationship*

the modernisation and improvement of employment relations.[101] Amid the concerns of the Commission there was also the fate of 'economically dependent workers, who do not, or may not, correspond to the traditional notion of employee'. The Commission's apprehensions were accompanied by the persuasion that 'specific action ... in relation to ... economically dependent workers is better achieved at Community level, because of the nature, scale and effects of such action, including its impact on Community legislation and policy'.[102] To meet these needs, the Commission wished to establish 'a mechanism to review the existing legislative and contractual rules governing employment relationships'.[103] The Commission also provided a description of the problem in the following terms:

> It relates to the situation where a worker performs a task or services personally within the framework of a single organisation with a certain degree of independence as far as the time and place of performance and the final results of the work are concerned while remaining wholly or mainly economically dependent on the one user undertaking.[104]

The Commission envisaged a regulatory process aimed, *inter alia*, at 'reinforc[ing] legal certainty as regards the employment status of' these workers and at ensuring a minimal substantive protection both via statutory – and negotiated – legal intervention. Governments should:

> ensure that such economically dependent workers have an appropriate level of protection in a number of areas, e.g.:
>
> > Health and Safety at work
> > Information and consultation
> > Working time minimum requirements
> > Updating of skills
> > Equal treatment in regard to pay and terms of employment
> > Social protection[105]

It would be left to each industrial relations system, through collective negotiations at the appropriate level, to decide whether and to what extent other elements of labour law, such as dismissal legislation, should apply too.

These regulatory intentions were not solely motivated by protective concerns. Once more the *flexibility, entrepreneurship* and *changes in work-organisation* rationales are being brought forward, and the justification for Community level intervention was once again to '[e]nsure an appropriate balance between security

---

101 'The EU and the Modernisation on Labour Law. First Stage Consultation of Social Partners on modernising and improving employment relations' Bulletin EU 6-2000, Employment and social policy (9/11). See also *IJCLLIR* (2000) 429.

102 Ibid., p. 431.

103 Ibid.

104 Ibid., p. 435–436.

105 'The EU and the Modernisation on Labour Law. First Stage Consultation of Social Partners on Modernising and Improving Employment Relations' *IJCLLIR* (2000) 436.

The Personal Scope of Application of EC Social Legislation 193

and flexibility as regards economically dependent activities'.[106] In a disclaimer the Green Paper stated that it was 'not intended to support strategies to evade labour, tax and social security regulations and reduce costs in traditional employment relationships'.[107]

This initial work received some attention in some quarters of the European institutions and in April 2002 the European Parliament called on the Commission to carry out an in depth study 'on the situation of workers in new labour relations in the Member States, especially economically dependent/subordinate workers'.[108] The results of the study[109] are of considerable analytical value, and its conclusions appear to favour a reform process that, rather than introducing a third category of employment relationship, should aim at creating 'a hard core of social rights applicable to all employment relationships' and constituting a 'minimum number of guarantees for all, moving gradually towards a higher level of protection',[110] along the lines of the reforms proposed by the 1999 Supiot Report,[111] discussed in Chapter 2.

A more recent cornerstone in this process has been the 2006 Commission Green Paper *Modernising Labour Law to Meet the Challenges of the 21st Century*.[112] This consultation paper stood out for its breadth in terms of analytical scope. Its sections covered themes as important and diverse as 'Employment Transitions', undeclared work and working time. But for the purposes of the present work, the most crucial and revealing parts of the Green Paper are undoubtedly its sections 4.b and 4.c, respectively, dealing with 'Uncertainty with regard to the law' and with 'Three way relationships'. This section assesses and analyses subsection 4.b. Subsection 4.c is only cursorily addressed, since the analysis of 'Three Way Relationships' in the EC context is carried out in Chapter 6.

Subsection 4.b of the Green Paper (GP) focuses, as its heading suggests, on the 'Uncertainty with regard to the law', presumably the law defining '*the legal notion of the employment relationship*'.[113] The seven paragraphs of subsection 4.b provide a brief summary of some of the main 'inadequacies' currently affecting the definition of the 'legal nature of the employment relationship', with a particular focus on the problem of the 'disguised' employment relationships and of the 'genuinely' ambiguous employment relationships. The paper points out that 'disguised employment occurs when a person who is an employee is classified as other than an employee so as to

---

106 Ibid.

107 Ibid.

108 PE 316.330/7-12, 17 April 2002.

109 A. Perulli, *Economically Dependent/Quasi-subordinate (Parasubordinate) Employment: Legal, Social and Economic Aspects* (Brussels 2003). Also available on

http://europa.eu.int/comm/employment_social/news/2003/sep/parasubordination_report_en.pdf (15 January 2006).

110 Ibid., p. 114.

111 *Transformation of Labour and Future of Labour Law in Europe – Final Report* (June 1998). See also A. Supiot, *Beyond Employment* (OUP, Oxford, 2001).

112 EC Commission, 2006 Green Paper, *Modernising Labour Law to Meet the Challenges of the 21st Century*, Brussels 22.11.2006 COM (2006) 708 final.

113 Ibid., p. 10.

194   *The Changing Law of the Employment Relationship*

hide his or her true legal status and to avoid costs that may include taxes and social security contributions'.[114] The sub-section also discusses some of the steps taken in some national legal systems to address these inadequacies, in particular *vis-à-vis* the emerging notion of quasi-dependent and economically dependent workers, and by means of the introduction of 'mandatory legal presumptions rules', although it fails to acknowledge that the Court, as discussed in Chapter 3 of this work, has cast a very narrow role for these presumptions of status.[115]

The paragraphs composing subsection 4.b are followed by two questions, question 7 and question 8, that asking respectively whether 'greater clarity [is] needed in Member States' legal definitions of employment and self-employment to facilitate *bona fide* transitions from employment to self-employment and *vice versa*' and whether 'Is there a need for a "floor of rights" dealing with the working conditions of all workers regardless of the form of their work contract.'

Subsection 4.b raises some of the most topical and problematic issues of the debate surrounding the reform of the legal notion of the employment relationship, but it is arguably followed by two exceedingly narrow questions. Question 7, at least in its first part, appears to be asking if the current legal definitions shaping the binary model of the employment relationship are sufficiently clear or whether greater clarity is needed. As argued in the present work, this is the type of question that has been at the core of several national and, increasingly, supranational debates and the answer has been one that overwhelmingly supports further re-elaboration of the existing definitions. Indeed, few would argue that the existing notions of 'dependent employee' and 'independent self-employed', and even the emerging intermediate concept of 'quasi-subordinate worker', are adequate and/or clear. But the adequacy of the aforementioned notions can only be evaluated against a clear set of regulatory goals and rationales that these definitions seek, or are supposed to, pursue. In this respect the regulatory rationale inherent to question 7 appears to be too narrow, if not also misconceived, In fact, while the aim of facilitating 'employment transitions' between employment and self-employment is not *per se* a spurious policy goal, it overshadows other possible re-regulatory rationales that clearly transpire from the discursive part of subsection 4.b and that, arguably, should have informed question 7.

This narrowness effectively creates a worrying 'policy retargeting' by excluding from the debate what should arguably be the main policy priorities of any reform discourse addressing the legal notion of the employment relationship, namely security in employment and life, the respect of fundamental labour and social rights of workers, gender equality and the efficient and flexible use of labour resources and skills. These are all policy aims that clearly transpire from subsection 4.b and from the Green Paper as a whole, but that question 7 ignores. Secondly, the exceedingly narrow focus of the question is likely to affect the nature of the replies to the consultation paper, and therefore the scope of the suggested reform

---

114 COM(2006) 708 final, at 9. In respect of taxes see the recent decision of *Hudson Contract Services Limited* v *Her Majesty's Revenue & Customs* [2007] EWHC 73, where a similar unwillingness to imply a contract in multi-lateral employment relationships is displayed.

115 Case C-255/04, *Commission* v *France* [2006] ECR I-05251.

The Personal Scope of Application of EC Social Legislation 195

recommendations, even within the limited ambit of the labour market 'transitions' discourse. Indeed the answers are likely to focus on the reforms necessary to facilitate transitions between 'employment' and 'self-employment' (and vice-versa). Arguably a more appropriate regulatory focus should have included the reforms necessary to ease transitions between different types of 'employment statuses' (for example, between fixed term and open-ended, or between part time and full time, or between trilateral and bilateral employment relationships) and between the status of 'inactive' persons (whether because of unemployment periods, periods spent on training and retraining, or periods spent on maternity/paternity leave) and the status of 'active' persons (employed or self-employed).

Thirdly, and finally, the narrow rationale of this question is likely to affect *the substance* of the reform recommendations that the replies to the question are likely to advance. Given the present formulation of question 7, the relevant regulatory suggestions are likely to focus on reforms permitting an easier transferability of acquired social rights (for example, in the area of contributions previously made to pension funds) and on a reduction of the 'transaction costs' for employers (for example, in terms of severance pay), with only a limited emphasis on the legal notion and legal definitions of the employment relationship itself. Inevitably they would echo the rather narrow and social security oriented recommendations formulated at page 18 of the *Obstacles to the Creation of Very Small Businesses in the European Union* Report of 1998 which had little or nothing to share with the present Green Paper that, as its title suggest, focused predominantly on labour law reforms. Had a broader perspective been adopted, on the lines suggested in the present section of this work, the replies would have had to focus on clarifying and redefining the different legal notions of the employment relationship, the type of substantive rights attached to each status, as well as the legal and factual relationships existing between the different statuses.

The narrow policy rationale of question 7 also appears to be *misconceived.* Clarity over employment status is needed both *per se* (employers and workers alike need and appreciate legal certainty and legal simplicity) and as a way to protect a broader set of *policy* goals (security in employment, equity and fairness, efficient use of human resources). Question 7 underplays the importance and the need to engage into a more profound *reconceptualisation of the scope* of the employment relationship, rather than merely on *clarifying* the existing definitions. In this respect it must be noted that ILO Recommendation R-198, discussed in Chapter 4, is already pursuing the goal of clarifying (and perhaps also adapting) the employment relationship at an international level, making a similar EU-level effort partly or wholly redundant.

As for question 8, there is no doubt that 'a "floor of rights" dealing with the working conditions of all workers regardless of the form of their work contract' is indeed needed. Arguably, as discussed above and will be further clarified in the conclusions, there is evidence to suggest that such a broader 'floor of rights' is indeed already emerging partly thanks to the broad scope of application of EC equality and health and safety legislation, and that the role of national and supranational institutions and the social partners should be that of coordinating and rationalising its development. Indeed the European Community, and the ECJ, have been leading actors in the development of a broader set of rights applying to employment

196 *The Changing Law of the Employment Relationship*

relationships other than the employment relationship based on the traditional notion of contract of employment.

Clarifying the notion of the employment relationship is an extremely important task *per se*, but it should also be seen as a way of redefining the protective *scope* of employment law and social security legislation to the needs emerging from the labour markets of the 21st century. It is perhaps worthwhile recollecting the suggestion contained in paragraph 766 of the so-called 'Supiot Report', produced for the European Commission in 1998. The authors of that report suggested that the 'employment status should be *redefined*' (and not merely clarified) with the aim of guaranteeing career continuity across successive forms of work. Debatably, this is also the type of concern that originally inspired the idea of adopting a Green Paper. As reported in 2005 Social Agenda Communication,[116] the original plan was that 'in this Green Paper, the Commission will analyse current trends in new work patterns and the role of labour law in tackling these developments, by providing a *more secure environment* encouraging efficient transitions on the labour market' (emphasis added). The exceedingly narrow approach of question 7 almost suggests an aspirational use of self-employed work as a remedy to the persistently high levels of unemployment in the European Union. But there is a risk that the problem posed by 'disguised employment relationships' may well be marginalised by this emerging aspirational use of autonomous work as a new job-creation tool.

The analysis of 'three way relationships' – and questions 9 and 10 – is no less contradictory. The two questions ask:

9. Do you think the responsibilities of the various parties within multiple employment relationships should be clarified to determine who is accountable for compliance with employment rights? Would subsidiary liability be an effective and feasible way to establish that responsibility in the case of sub-contractors? If not, do you see other ways to ensure adequate protection of workers in "three-way relationships"?

10. Is there a need to clarify the employment status of temporary agency workers?

As argued in Chapters 2 and 3, there is no doubt that 'three way relationships' are far from being regulated in a satisfactorily way at a national level, and particularly in the UK. Furthermore, as shown in Chapter 6, the EC is fully aware of this state of affairs, if not else since in the recent past it proposed an ad hoc instrument for the regulation of temporary agency work,[117] that never quite made it through the EC legislative pipeline.

The Green Paper does not seem to suggest that the political deadlock that hampered the approval of the Temporary Workers Directive has been resolved or even addressed. Nor, as suggested in the previous paragraphs, is it likely that it will lead

---

116 That first envisaged the adoption of a Green Paper in this area, COM(2005) 33 final.

117 Amended proposal for a Directive of the European Parliament and the Council on working conditions for temporary workers – COM(2002) 701.

The Personal Scope of Application of EC Social Legislation   197

to any purposeful reconceptualisation of the scope and notions of the employment relationship. The following and concluding section of this chapter discusses the existing, somewhat chaotic, structure of the personal scope of EC labour law and, while discussing some of its merits and flaws, suggests ways by which it could be streamlined and rendered more coherent.

4. Conclusions: a theoretical structure for the personal scope of EC social and employment law

To sum up it can be argued that EC social and employment law has a rather kaleidoscopic approach to the definition of its scope of application. Different policy areas have produced distinct bodies of legal regulation applying to different categories of workers. *Free movement* arguably has the widest scope of all areas. The rules on free movement of workers address a broad definition of 'worker'. For a person to be considered a 'worker' she will have to be pursuing 'activities which are effective and genuine',[118] that is to say 'real and actual ..., to the exclusion of work of such small degree that it appears merely minimal and subsidiary',[119] or 'purely marginal and ancillary'.[120] The ECJ definition is wide enough to embrace situations such as the one of a person working as a plumber for a religious community as part of its commercial activities, and who as a *quid pro quo* had his material needs looked after and received some pocket money.[121] On the other hand it appears that subjects employed under drug rehabilitation programs or 'workfare' programs, where part of the remuneration is covered by public funds, may have difficulties in qualifying as 'workers' for the purposes of free movement.[122]

There would also appear to be a further requirement linked to the part of the Community definition demanding that the relationship is in place 'for a certain period of time'.[123] It is not clear if this element should be understood in the sense of a 'minimum working time' requirement or in the sense of a 'continuity' requirement. But it must be stressed that the ECJ interpretation of this 'time' element has never been such as to jeopardise the position of people employed in atypical employment relationships. Already in *Levin*, the ECJ recognised that the rules relating to free movement of workers were also applicable to part-timers even though they earned less than the minimum required for subsistence, as defined by national – in that case Dutch – law.[124] And in *Raulin*[125] the ECJ treated an atypical on-call employee as a

---

118 Case C-337/97, *Meeusen*, [13].

119 Case 53/81, *Levin*, [17].

120 Case C-337/97, *Meeusen*, [13].

121 Case 196/87, *Steymann* v *Staatssecrretaris van Justitie* [1988] ECR 6159.

122 Case 344/87, *Bettray* and C-278/94, *E.C. Commission* v *Belgium (Re Access to Special Employment Programmes)* [1996] ECR I-4307.

123 Cf. Case 66/85, *Lawrie-Blum* [1986] ECR 2121 and C-85/96, *María Martínez Sala* [1998] ECR I-2691, [32].

124 Case 53/81, *Levin* v *Secretary of State for Justice* [1982] ECR 1035, [15]–[17].

125 Case C-357/89, *Raulin* v *Minister van Onderwijs en Wetenschappen* [1992] ECR I-1027.

198   *The Changing Law of the Employment Relationship*

worker even if '[u]nder such a contract, no guarantee is given as to the hours to be worked and, often, the person involved works only a very few days per week or hours per day' and despite the fact 'that under such an *oproepcontract* the employee is not obliged to heed the employer's call for him to work'.[126]

A further element in the EC notion of 'worker' is the requirement of subordination that can be inferred from the fact that the services must be performed 'for and under the direction' of another person, but here the Court has traditionally maintained that '[t]he existence of a relationship of subordination is a matter which it is for the national court to verify'.[127] Finally, rules on freedom of establishment and provision of services also embrace self-employed workers. Most importantly, in this area we find a fully autonomous definitional approach with an independent EC notion of 'worker' completely detached from national definitions. While it is evident that this generous scope of application is backed by some strong economic concerns related to the creation of a free market, it is fair to say that in the light of Directive 2004/38[128] and some recent ECJ decisions,[129] free movement has progressively moved towards a more universalistic concept of economic and, to some extents, social citizenship going beyond the traditional domain of labour law.[130]

Social security and pensions legislation have a comparable scope; applying, as a result of the scope of application of EC Directives and Regulations in this area of law, both to dependent and independent workers. The ECJ has made it clear that atypicals and, within some limits, job-seekers must be included in the notion of 'employee' for the purposes of EC social security legislation. On the other hand, in this area, the ECJ has ultimately declined to give the term 'worker' a 'Community meaning'. In *Hoerska* the Court first advanced the proposition that 'the concept [has] a Community meaning, implying all those who, as such and under whatever description, are covered by the different national systems of social security'.[131] The problem with this formula was that, albeit formally introducing a supranational definition for the term 'worker', in practice it heavily relied on the meaning concretely given by the different national systems of social security. When it came to clarify to what extent the definitions adopted by the national systems could *de facto* deprive EU workers

---

126 Ibid., [9].

127 Case C-337/97, *C.P.M. Meeusen* v *Hoofddirectie van de Informatie Beheer Groep* [1999] ECR I-3289, [16].

128 Council Directive 2004/38/EC of 29 April 2004 on the right of citizens of the Union and their family members to move and reside freely within the territory of the Member States. [2004] OJ L158/77.

129 C-60/00, *Mary Carpenter* v *Secretary of State for the Home Department* [2002] ECR I 6279; Case C-85/96, *Martínez Sala* v *Freistat Bayern* [1998] ECR I-2691; Case C-184/99, *R. Grzelczyk* v *Centre public d'aide social d'Ottignies-Louvain-la-Neuve* [2001] ECR I 6193; Case C–209/03, *Bidar* [2005] ECR I 2119.

130 But contrary for the limits to this type of case law, see Case C-109/01, *Secretary of State for the Home Department* v *Hacene Akrich* [2003] ECR I-9607; Case C-138/02, *Collins* [2004] ECR I 2703; Case C-406/04, *De Cuyper* v *Office national de l'emploi*, decision of 18 July 2006.

131 Case 75/63, *Unger* v *Bestuur der Bedrijfsvereniging voor Detailhandel en Ambachten* [1964] ECR 1977, [1].

The Personal Scope of Application of EC Social Legislation

of their social security rights, the Court timidly admitted that the EC 'provisions are solely intended to determine the national legislation applicable and not to define the conditions creating the right or the obligation to become affiliated to a social security scheme', and that therefore

> it cannot be presumed that for the purposes of applying the provisions determining the national legislation applicable the Community legislature intended to endow the terms 'employed' and 'self-employed' with an autonomous Community meaning, based on employment law, especially since those provisions form part of a regulation whose purpose is merely to *coordinate* the social security legislation of the Member States.[132]

Equality law has also a very wide scope of application. The European legal order has traditionally invested considerable resources in promoting the equal pay principle, and this investment has traditionally been justified by the economic rationale of having a 'level playing field', a rationale already anticipated by the famous Ohlins[133] and Spaak[134] reports. For some time the ECJ supported the idea of a 'dual aim' of the equal pay principle, partly economic and partly social.[135] This was in the 1970s, a period when a 'social tint was ... added to the market colouring of the equality principle in the form of the introduction of the right to equal pay for work of equal value and the right to equal treatment for men and women in employment related areas apart from pay'.[136] But in recent times equal pay has been greatly influenced by the evolution of the EC fundamental rights discourse. In *Deutsche Post* the ECJ

> concluded that the economic aim pursued by Article 119 of the Treaty, namely the elimination of distortions of competition between undertakings established in different Member States, is secondary to the social aim pursued by the same provision, which constitutes the expression of a fundamental human right.[137]

In *Allonby*, the same reasoning was used for the first time to claim that 'the term worker used in Article 141(1) EC cannot be defined by reference to the legislation of the Member States but has a Community meaning. Moreover, it cannot be interpreted restrictively'.[138] It is too soon to define with precision what types of employment relationships and forms of work this 'non-restrictive' interpretation will be able to

---

132 Case C-340/94, *EJM de Jaeck* v *Staatssecretaris van Financiën* [1997] ECR I-00461 [27]–[28].

133 Summarised in ILO, 'Social Aspects of European Economic Cooperation' *IRL* (1956): 99.

134 Summarised in 'Political and Economic Planning' (1956) 405 *Planning*.

135 Case 149/77, *Defrenne III* [1978] ECR 1365 [26] and [27]; Joined Cases 75/82 and 117/82, *Razzouk and Beydoun* v *Commission* [1984] ECR 1509 [16]; and Case C-13/94, *P.* v *S. and Cornwall County Council* [1996] ECR I-2143 [19].

136 S. Fredman, *Discrimination Law* (Clarendon, Oxford, 2002), pp. 89–90.

137 Joined cases C-270/97 and C-271/97, *Deutsche Post AG* v *Elisabeth Sievers and Brunhilde Schrage* [2000] ECR I-929 [57].

138 Case C-256/01, [66].

200 *The Changing Law of the Employment Relationship*

embrace. But we already know that, at the very least, it should apply to any kind of 'stable employment relationship', whether typical or atypical.[139]

Equal opportunity legislation, particularly after the *Wippel* decision, has also a relatively wide scope of application even covering, to some extent, independent workers. It is likely that the principle of equal treatment could get more and more enmeshed with the EC discourse on fundamental rights, thus acquiring an even more distinctly universalistic scope of application. With the introduction by the Treaty of Amsterdam of Articles 2, 3 and 13 ECT a sounder legal basis was laid down for the EC institutions to legislate in the area of non-discrimination and equality. The opportunity, as we have seen, was quickly seized to pass two Directives: one on race discrimination[140] and the other on age, disability, sexual orientation and religion or belief.[141] It must be said that equality legislation is also receiving an impetus from the labour market concerns of the European institutions to achieve high levels of employment, if not full employment. In recent years the high rates of women's unemployment, and the correspondingly low employment rates, have been seen as causes and symptoms of economic underperformance and inefficiency, leading to the inclusion of gender equality and equal opportunities among the policies aimed at reducing unemployment in Europe under the European Employment Strategy.[142]

As far as the remaining areas of EC social law are concerned, it is probably possible to make a distinction between health and safety (H&S) legislation and the remaining areas of regulation. H&S, as opposed to free movement and to some extent social security and equality law, does not articulate an autonomous notion of 'worker', but instead it relies on the national notions. And unless otherwise specified, it also omits the self-employed. On the other hand, regulations and directives have extended selected provisions to specific categories of atypical workers and the ECJ has further improved this situation by dismantling some national qualifying periods that adversely affected non-standard workers. After all, it is undeniable that H&S legislation is backed by a rather evident economic and level playing field rationale. The first EC H&S measures sprang, in the second half of the 1970s, from the 1974 Social Action Programme and were supported by a mixture of *market integration* and *worker protection* rationales. From an economic standpoint, H&S measures were seen as considerably costly for businesses and trade, therefore Community rules on health and safety, binding on all Member States, were seen as 'allowing equal conditions for competition to prevail'.[143] Apart from that, it was feared that linguistic differences within a workplace might increase the amount of work-related injuries and hazards. The safety signs Directive 77/576 was introduced 'to reduce both the risks of accidents at work and occupational diseases due to language problems'.[144] It is therefore no coincidence that the UK, having always guaranteed to its workers relatively high levels of H&S protection, has traditionally been a strenuous supporter

---

139 Case C-78/98, *Shirley Preston*, [69].
140 Directive 2000/43/EC.
141 Directive 2000/78/EC.
142 EC, Commission *Employment Guidelines 1999*, para. 21.
143 C. Barnard, *EC Employment Law* (2nd ed., Oxford, OUP, 2000), p. 374.
144 Ibid., p. 375.

The Personal Scope of Application of EC Social Legislation 201

of EC legislation in this specific policy area. These economic concerns could well justify an expansion and rationalisation of the current patchwork scope that, in perspective might well need to be reviewed. Indeed Article 31 of the Charter of Fundamental Rights of the European Union (actually drawing on Article 3 of the Social Charter and point 19 of the Community Charter on the Rights of Workers) provides that 'every *worker* has the right to working conditions which respect his or her health, safety and dignity'.[145]

The remaining areas of social law apply, by and large, to employees having a *contract* or an *employment relationship* defined by the law in force in a Member State. In Case 105/84, *Danmols Inventar*[146] the ECJ in effect decided that, the aim of the Acquired Rights Directive being (only) *partial harmonisation*, an EC notion of 'employee' for the purposes of defining the meaning of 'contract of employment or employment relationship' could not be introduced. As stressed by Lord Slynn, the Advocate General in this case,

> there is no express definition of 'employee' or 'contract of employment' or 'employment relationship' in the Directive. This Directive does not, any more than do Council Directive 75/129 on the approximation of the laws of member-States relating to collective redundancies and Council Directive 80/987 on the approximation of the laws of the member-States relating to the protection of employees in the event of the insolvency of their employer, set out to provide a complete harmonisation of the laws of member-States in this area.[147]

Specific legislation to extend social law to atypical workers has been and is still being produced, but the situation, it has been argued, is far from being fully satisfactory.

It would appear that there are some noticeable similarities between the scope of application of EC social and employment legislation and some aspects of the reforms proposed by Alain Supiot and his colleagues in the late 1990s. This report, when discussing the options for reform of national labour law, envisaged a primary circle of universal social rights that would be guaranteed to all regardless of the type of work performed; a second circle of rights based on unpaid work; a third circle of rights applicable to 'the common law of occupational activity', some of which are already enshrined in Community law (for example, health and safety); and finally, a fourth circle of rights for subordinate employees.[148] EC social and employment legislation displays a similarly organised, albeit probably more fragmented and not as coherent, structure of its scope of application and we believe that, for all its merits, this type of discourse presents a number of difficulties that hopefully the discussion carried out in the last section should have made more evident. Here, we first discuss some points that are peculiar to the scope of application of EC law in this area, and then draw a more general set of conclusions.

---

145 Emphasis added.
146 Case 105/84 .
147 Ibid.
148 A. Supiot, *Beyond Employment* (OUP, Oxford, 2001), p. 55.

First, EC social policy and labour law measures only seem to apply to *any* kind of employment relationship when their existence is directly functional to the creation of the single market. Legislative instruments that do not have this strong and direct economic justification are unlikely to address a great variety of employment relationships. In the next chapter we shall explore EC directives which directly address the regulation of atypical employment relationships to ascertain whether this stream of legislation succeeds in covering the areas left unprotected by the more generalist EC social policy and labour law.

On the other hand, and this is the second point one can make, there are some incoherencies. Some measures that are manifestly aimed at redressing some market failures are not given an adequate standing and their personal scope of application is visibly inappropriate. We are referring here to instruments such as Directive 91/533/ EC. In this case it can be said that the economic rationale, for all its rhetoric, has been unable to defeat some political resistances.

Thirdly, it seems to us that it should be possible to combine the EC *economic rationale* and the *personal scope* of EC social instruments in a more effective and coherent way. The broad notion of 'worker' is certainly appropriate to be associated with freedom of movement given its strong market creation rationale. The concept of 'continuous employment relationship' certainly accords with the initial attention given to the market disruptive effects of gendered pay inequalities. But one can argue that EC H&S legislation, given its economic and social relevance, might merit something more that its present patchwork personal scope, whereby specific Directives and Regulations are progressively extending H&S provisions to particular types of employment relationships, and that it ought to be closely associated to the 'continuous employment relationship' notion, if not also with the 'worker' notion as provided by Article 31 of the EU Charter of Fundamental Rights. On the same line of reasoning it can be argued that EC 'working conditions' legislation needs to be rationalised, with measures aimed at redressing market failures (by correcting information failure or by diffusing the costs of negative externalities), receiving a broader scope of application focusing on the *continuity* and *personality* of the provision of labour, as emphasised by the notion of the 'continuous employment relationship'.

Fourthly, it seems plausible that the progressively emerging human rights rationale could expand the scope of application of some specific areas of EC labour legislation such as equal pay, equal opportunity and probably, in the long run, health and safety at work.

Last, it is arguable that the Directives which deal with restructuring of enterprises should keep at pace with industrial changes and include in their scope at least some atypical employment relationships on the line of the extended scope of the Acquired Rights Directive as modified with Directive 98/50/EC.

In the light of these five distinct points it is possible to draw some conclusions regarding the possibility of reforming the social law EC in a meaningful way for the national labour law systems. The EC system is a good example of the fact that a strong, apparently uncontroversial, economic rationale can guarantee a certain level of universality for some limited types of legal rights and freedoms, but that a number of controversies arise when the economic rationale has to give way to other consideration of a different nature. Arguably the Community institutions, and the social partners, should use this mix of economic and, increasingly, human rights rationales to establish a 'floor of rights' based on an EC notion of 'employment relationship' similar to the one established in the context of EC equality law. This notion, which should become an EC notion just as the concept of 'worker' is for the purposes of free movement, should be applied both to EC H&S and equal treatment legislation as well as to EC legislation on 'working conditions'. In the following chapter we analyse those measures that, at least on paper, directly address the taxonomy of the employment relationship by directly regulating non-typical employment relationships. We also explore the impact that some other types of pressures, inherent to EC policies such as the Employment Strategy, can have – directly or indirectly – upon the subject matter of the present work.

Chapter 6

EC Regulation of Atypical Forms of Work – Between Employment Law and Employment Policy

1. Introduction

This chapter discusses and analyses the efforts made by the European Community to regulate forms of work other than typical open-ended employment relationships. In the vocabulary of this work we have referred to this type of ad hoc regulation as one addressing the *taxonomy* of the employment relationship rather than the *scope* of what is, or could be seen, as typical subordinate work. This chapter is linked to Chapter 3, which provides a similar analysis in respect of legislation affecting and addressing changes in the taxonomy of the employment relationship at a national level. There is a considerable degree of intersection between the fourth part of that chapter, where some national measures implementing or inspired by the EC Directives on atypical work were discussed, and some parts of the present chapter where a number of aspects of those Directives are further clarified. The fourth part of Chapter 3 pointed out that national rules attempting to strike a balance between flexibility and security and between more and better jobs in the area of part-time and fixed-term work, have been partly inspired by the two EC Directives on atypical work.[1] To avoid duplication, this chapter will not analyse the ways in which EC law on atypical workers has manifested its effects at a national level.

This chapter analyses the scope of application and regulatory approach adopted by the EC Directives on atypical workers and assesses their function and relationship with other EC law and policy areas that also have an impact on atypical and flexible employment. This objective is pursued by exploring four main themes, all of them pertaining to the EC-level regulation of atypical work. The second section examines the regulatory rationale and scope of application of the legislative instruments already adopted, or proposed, at the EC level to regulate atypical work. It reviews the two Directives on atypical work,[2] highlighting their similarities and – crucially

---

1 Council Directive 97/81/EC of 15 December 1997 concerning the Framework Agreement on Part-time Work concluded by UNICE, CEEP and the ETUC as amended by Directive 98/23/EC ([1998] OJ L131/10), consolidated [1998] OJ L131/13. Council Directive 99/70/EC of 28 June 1999 concerning the Framework Agreement on Fixed-term Work concluded by UNICE, CEEP and the ETUC [1999] OJ L175/43, corrigendum [1999] OJ L244/64.

2 Council Directive 97/81/EC and Council Directive 99/70/EC.

206   *The Changing Law of the Employment Relationship*

– their differences, and briefly discusses the so-far unsuccessful project of adopting a Directive on temporary work.[3] The two existing Directives display some differences in their scope of application, with Directive 99/70 providing more generous leeway for Member States (MSs) seeking to narrow down the impact of the equal treatment principle when implementing that measure.

The third section partly shifts the analytical focus of the work outside the legislative framework of European law, and assesses the extent to which the *policy* framework of the European Employment Strategy (EES) has a direct, or indirect, impact on the regulation of atypical forms of work. The final parts of the third section again place under scrutiny the two Directives on atypical work with the aim of understanding what their relationship with the EES is. To be more precise, this third section of the chapter seeks to explore the semantics of some key words and concepts such as 'flexibility', 'security' and 'more and better jobs' as developed in the EES context. This part of the chapter will advance two main claims. First of all that the EES notions of 'flexibility' and 'security' support the promotion of atypical work, and that at least initially this encouragement was within a framework establishing equality of treatment between atypical and typical work, a regulatory dynamic that in Chapter 3 was defined as *normalisation with parity*. Secondly, it is argued that the publication of the Employment Taskforce Report *Jobs, Jobs, Jobs* in 2003 constitutes a watershed moment for the EC concepts of flexibility and security and, eventually for the emerging notion of 'flexicurity'. While this more recent phase of the EC notion of 'flexicurity' does not directly call into question the normalisation with parity model, it challenges the regulatory framework sustaining the standard contract of employment by advocating its deregulation. The third section of this chapter discusses the meaning of 'flexicurity' in the context of the two Directives on atypical work. A tension is progressively emerging between EC employment law on atypical workers, as interpreted by the ECJ,[4] and some of the job creation preoccupations inspiring the EES and the 'flexicurity' approach. This tension is emerging in spite of the fact that some job-creation concerns had already permeated Directive 99/70 on fixed-term work, far more than, for instance, Directive 97/81 on Part-time Work.

The fourth section considers whether, in the evolution of the EES and in the context of the dialogue between MSs and European institutions established under the EES auspices, these European institutions have managed to superimpose a clear and coherent notion of flexicurity on the national systems, at least by supporting normalisation with parity as the dominant regulatory model in Europe. It is suggested that this does not seem to be the case and in the fifth section it is pointed out that the initial flexicurity concept appears to have undergone such a number of

---

3   Commission Proposal for a Directive of the European Parliament and the Council on Working Conditions for Temporary Workers COM(2002) 149 final [2002] OJ C203 and Amended Proposal for a Directive of the European Parliament and the Council on Working Conditions for Temporary Workers COM(2002) 701 final.

4   In cases such as C-144/04, *Mangold* v *Helm* [2005] ECR I-9981; C-212/04, *Kostantinos Adeneler and Others* v *Elog* [2006] ECR I-06057; C-53/04, *Marrosu and Sardino* v *Azienda Ospedaliera San Martino* (not yet reported at the time of writing).

transformations that it may end up by legitimising, or producing, national regulatory frameworks which opt for a 'flexicurity' notion inspired by a *normalisation without parity* regulatory model, while at the same time bringing about a deregulation of the standard contract of employment.

2. EC legislative measures on atypical work

The European Community only really started regulating atypical employment in the late 1990s. In that respect, one may well say that EC legislation on atypical workers has a relatively recent history, at least when compared with the national experiences in this area. But EC attempts to regulate atypical work date back to the 1970s and 1980s and they are a clear indication of the awareness of European institutions of the emerging complexity and increasing fragmentation of the employment relationship. The *Council Resolution of 21 January 1974 concerning a social action programme*[5] already stressed the need 'to protect workers hired through temporary employment agencies and to regulate the activities of such firms with a view to eliminating abuses therein'.[6] In the 1980s the Commission took a proactive stance and presented a 'first … proposal for a directive concerning voluntary part-time work [modified by the Commission in 1983] and [a] second proposal for a directive relating to temporary work and fixed term contracts. Neither of these proposals [was] adopted'.[7] In 1989 the Community Social Charter identified a need for action to ensure an improvement in the conditions of those engaged in 'forms of employment other than open-ended contracts, such as fixed-term contracts, part-time working, temporary work and seasonal work'.[8] This apparent social policy rationale was coupled with the economic rationale of preventing that 'the development of terms of [atypical] employment such as to cause problems of social dumping, or even distortion of competition, at Community level'.[9] It seems, arguably, that the EC was tempted for some time to adopt a stance aimed at discouraging the unregulated spread of these forms of work.

Following the Charter, the Commission proposed three Directives concerning atypical work: one on health and safety,[10] a second applying the principle of

---

5   Council Resolution of 21 January 1974 Concerning a Social Action Programme [1974] OJ C13/1.

6   [1974] OJ C13/3.

7   Communication from the Commission Concerning its Action Programme Relating to the Implementation of the Community Charter of Basic Social Rights for Workers COM(89) 568 final.

8   [1989] OJ C323/44.

9   Communication from the Commission Concerning its Action Programme Relating to the Implementation of the Community Charter of Basic Social Rights for Workers COM(89) 568 final.

10   Which eventually was modified and adopted as Council Directive 91/383/EC [1991] OJ L206/19.

non-discrimination to atypical workers[11] and a third one overtly aiming at the 'Approximation of Laws of the Member States Relating to Certain Employment Relationships with Regard to Distortion of Competition'[12] and attempting to introduce a 'level playing field' in the regulation of atypical work. The latter two Directives provided a general and comprehensive definition of atypical work, including:

    i. part-time employment involving shorter working hours than statutory, collectively agreed, or usual working hours;

    ii. temporary employment relationships in the form of:

    a. fixed-term contracts, including seasonal work, concluded directly between the employer and the employee, where the end of the contract is established by objective conditions such as reaching a specific date, completing a specific task or the occurrence of a specific event; and

    b. temporary employment which covers any relationship between the temporary employment business (a temp agency), which is the employer, and its employees (the temps), where the employees have no contract with the user undertaking where they perform their activities. In other words, the employees have a contract with the temp agency which sends them to work as a temp for a user company needing additional staff.[13]

This definition had the obvious advantage of not relying on national notions of employment relationship or contract of employment. In that respect, one may say that the EC was taking a strong stance in the regulation of atypical work. There is scarcely any vestige of this approach in the definition adopted by Directive 91/383/EC which, as opposed to the other two draft Directives, was finally approved by the Council.

It is worth pointing out that the European institutions never questioned the very existence or legitimacy of these atypical forms of work. 'Even if what are termed "atypical" forms of employment are contested in some quarters, they nonetheless constitute an important component in the organization of the labour market'.[14] Given this pragmatic approach and given the economic concerns about 'social dumping', it is hardly surprising that, ultimately, EC regulation converged upon the 'equal treatment' formula and the combating of discrimination against atypical workers. Not only was this formula able to strike a compromise between social and economic concerns but it also managed to uphold a different type of concern aiming at 'normalising' atypical work in general and part-time work in particular.

---

11 Proposal for a Council Directive on Certain Employment Relationships with Regard to Working Conditions COM(90) 228 final [1990] OJ C224/4.

12 Proposal for a Council Directive on the Approximation of Laws of the Member States Relating to Certain Employment Relationships with Regard to Distortions of Competition COM(90) 228 final OJ C224/6.

13 Proposal for a Council Directive on the Approximation of Laws of the Member States Relating to Certain Employment Relationships with Regard to Distortions of Competition COM(90) 228 final OJ C224/6.

14 Communication from the Commission Concerning its Action Programme relating to the Implementation of the Community Charter of Basic Social Rights for Workers COM(89) 568 final.

Indeed, the social and economic concerns which provided the initial impetus for the regulation of atypical work were quickly coupled with some labour market management concerns aimed at increasing employment rates, particularly by means of expanding part-time and fixed-term employment. This clearly transpires from a reading of the EU consultations and negotiations that eventually led to the adoption of the two Directives. In these negotiations, the social partners, the Member States and the European institutions quickly reached agreement on the 'need to ensure that part-time work is attractive and that part-time workers are properly treated'.[15] It appeared that the 'equal treatment' formula was ideally suited to broker a Social Dialogue agreement that satisfied opposite and in principle conflicting needs. Employers would be able to foster and strengthen change in working time practices, trade unions would have improved working conditions for atypical workers while reducing any temptation to a race to the bottom and the EC institutions were laying down a 'floor of rights' in this area while promoting their job creation agenda.

This approach was adopted in Directive 97/81/EC[16] and Directive 99/70/EC.[17] The Part-time Work Directive applies to the 'employment contract or employment relationship as defined by the law, collective agreement or practice in force in each Member State'.[18] But fortunately this paragraph was qualified by clause 3, providing that the 'term "part-time worker" refers to an employee whose normal hours of work, calculated on a weekly basis or on average over a period of employment of up to one year, are less than the normal hours of work of a comparable full-time worker'. This appears to restrict the MSs' discretion to reduce the scope of application of the Directive in the course of implementing it. On the other hand the scope of this definition is narrowed down by clause 2(2), allowing MSs to 'exclude wholly or partly from the terms of this Agreement part-time workers who work on a casual basis'.

The same pattern is reproduced by Directive 99/70/EC on fixed-term work. It applies to 'fixed term workers who have an employment contract or employment relationship as defined in law, collective agreements or practice in each Member State'.[19] But it then defines 'fixed-term worker' as 'a person having an employment contract or relationship entered into directly between an employer and a worker where the end of the employment contract or relationship is determined by objective conditions such as reaching a specific date, completing a specific task, or the occurrence of a specific event'.[20] Moreover, Member States, under clause 2.2(b), may *consult* the social partners and provide that the implementation of the Directive shall not apply to initial vocational training relationships and apprenticeship schemes, and to employment contracts and relationships concluded within the framework of

---

15 *Flexibilité du temps de travail et sécurité des travailleurs – première phase de consultation avec les partenaires sociaux conformément a l'article 3 de l'accord social annexe au traite* SEC(95) 1540/3, 1.

16 Directive 97/81/EC.

17 Directive 99/70/EC.

18 Clause 2(1) of both Directives.

19 Directive 99/70/EC, clause 2.

20 Ibid., clause 3(1).

specific public or publicly supported training, integration, and vocational retraining program. No similar provision is made in the Part-time Work Directive. Indeed, clause 2.2 of Directive 97/81 only allows MSs to exclude from the scope of the Directive 'part-time workers who work on a casual basis' and this only for 'objective reasons' and after 'consultation with the social partners *in accordance with national law*' (emphasis added).[21]

But most importantly the Fixed-term Work Directive does not apply to those temporary workers 'placed by a temporary work agency at the disposition of a user enterprise'.[22] One would hope that this lacuna would be effectively filled by the adoption of the EC Draft Directive on Temporary Workers.[23] Article 1 in the amended draft provides that the 'directive applies to workers with a contract of employment or employment relationship with a temporary agency, who are posted to user undertakings to work temporarily under their supervision'. Article 3, in defining the notion of 'worker', once more provides that such is 'any person who, in the Member State concerned, is protected as worker under national employment law'. But the new draft, as opposed to the original one, now adds in Article 3(b) that a temporary worker shall be defined as a 'person with a contract of employment or an employment relationship with a temporary agency with a view to being posted to a user undertaking to work temporarily under its supervision'. What is particularly unsatisfactory is the fact that Article 1(3) reiterates the wording of Clause 2.2(b) of the Fixed-term Work Directive and provides that, after consulting the social partners, the equal treatment requirement can be excluded where temporary agency work is 'concluded under a specific public or publicly supported training, integration or vocational retraining programme'. If there is added to this the fact that Article 5(4) provides for an exemption form the application of the equal treatment principle in the area of pay where the relationship lasts less than six weeks, the scope of the draft Directive appears to be disappointingly narrow. In any case it has already been pointed that this legislative proposal is facing some very strong resistance[24] and, particularly after the stalemate reached in the EU social policy and employment Council meeting of 4 October 2004,[25] it is unlikely that any progress on this front will take place in the near future.

21　It is worthwhile noticing that the 2003 Implementation Report compiled by the Commission suggest that none of the four countries this book focuses on chose to trigger this exclusion. See EC Commission, *Report by the Commission's Services on the Implementation of Council Directive 97/81/EC of 17 December 1997 Concerning the Framework Agreement in Part-time Work Concluded by UNICE, CEEP and the ETUC* (Brussels, 2003).

22　Ibid., preamble to the Directive.

23　Commission Proposal for a Directive of the European Parliament and the Council on Working Conditions for Temporary Workers COM(2002) 149 final [2002] OJ C203 and Amended Proposal for a Directive of the European Parliament and the Council on Working Conditions for Temporary Workers COM(2002) 701 final.

24　Cf. L. Zappalà, 'The Temporary Agency Workers' Directive: An Impossible Political Agreement?', *ILJ* (2003): 310–317.

25　Council of the EU, *Press Release – 2606th Council Meeting – Employment, Social Policy, Health and Consumer Affairs* (12400/04, Presse 264, Luxembourg, 4 October 2004), p. 14.

3. The EU notions of 'flexibility', 'security' and 'flexicurity'

Labour lawyers in Europe are only too aware of the interactions between employment policy and employment law and of the relevance of soft law measures in the sphere of labour law and employment policy, particularly at the EC level. Already by 1996, well before the establishment of a structured framework for the EES, there was a feeling that 'Community policies might be effectuated, not so much by means of assumption of regulatory powers, but rather by being translated into adopted principles, which would authorize and require a critique of national action and practices'.[26]

This section considers how some of these 'principles', such as flexibility and security,[27] enshrined in the framework of the EES, have progressively evolved as a consequence of the continuous engagement between national and Community institutions typical of the EES process. The present section seeks to clarify their meanings in the context of the EES and, subsequently, of the two Directives on atypical work. For reasons pertaining to the scope and structure of this book, this chapter will not be able to focus on other contiguous issues such as the origins of the term 'flexicurity' at a national level,[28] or the structure, functioning and nature of the EES[29] outside the ambit of the EU notions of flexibility and security. Another important preliminary consideration to be made at this stage is clarifying the use of the term 'flexicurity'. The Community notion of 'flexicurity' is as complex and elusive as it is appealing and suggestive and, until recently, the EU itself was very cautious in the use of this term. In fact, in its official documents, it preferred instead to refer to 'flexibility' and 'security' as separate, albeit notionally interdependent, concepts. None of the EU Directives use the term 'flexicurity', while three of them explicitly refer to 'flexibility' and/or 'security'.[30] As far as EC soft law instruments and

---

26 M. Freedland, 'Employment Policy' in P. Davies, A. Lyon-Caen, S. Sciarra and S. Simitis (eds), *European Community Labour Law. Principles and Perspectives on European Labour Law: Liber Amicorum Lord Wedderburn of Charlton* (Clarendon Press, Oxford, 1996), p. 308.

27 It is worthwhile pointing out that the EU rarely uses the term 'flexicurity' in its official documents. For instance, the term as such has never been used in the Employment Guidelines adopted under the EES between 1998 and 2005 and only appears in the 'Explanatory Memorandum' accompanying the 2006 'Proposal for a Council Decision Guidelines for the Employment Policies in the Member States', COM(2006) 32 final, 25.01.2006.

28 Anecdotal evidence suggest that the term itself was coined by the Social-democratic Danish Prime Minister Poul Nyrup Rasmussen after his election in 1993 in a period where Denmark was facing high unemployment levels and radical reforms of the labour market were about to be undertaken. But the basic concept composing the notion of 'flexicurity', and in particular the concept of 'active labour market policy', in many respects predate the creation of the term itself. See the historical analysis of M. Freedland e N. Countouris, 'Diritti e doveri nel rapporto tra disoccupati e servizi per l'impiego in Europa', *GDLRI* (2005): 557.

29 For a comprehensive legal analysis of the EES see the excellent D. Ashiagbor, *The European Employment Strategy – Labour Market Regulation and New Governance* (OUP, Oxford, 2005).

30 Council Directive 97/81/EC of 15 December 1997 Concerning the Framework Agreement on Part-time Work concluded by UNICE, CEEP and the ETUC as amended by Dir 98/23/EC (OJ 1998 L131/10), consolidated [1998] OJ L131/13. Council Directive 99/70/EC

212   *The Changing Law of the Employment Relationship*

employment policy documents are concerned, the word 'flexicurity' never appeared in the Employment Guidelines adopted under the EES between 1998 and 2005 and only first materialised in the 'explanatory memorandum' accompanying the 2006 Joint Employment Report[31] and in the 'proposal for a Council decision guidelines for the employment policies in the Member States'.[32] Even the famous Wim Kok report on job creation[33] did not explicitly mention the neologism 'flexicurity'. The Employment Committee and the Social Security Committee only started elaborating on the notion of 'flexicurity' in 2006.[34] Conversely, the terms 'security' and 'flexibility' have a longer history and they already appeared in the 1989 'Communication from the Commission concerning its Action Programme relating to the implementation of the Community charter of basic social rights for workers', the document that effectively put on the agenda the adoption of an EC instrument for the regulation of part-time and fixed-term work, after the first failed attempts of the early 1980s.[35] But the first EC policy paper that systematically and profusely referred to these two concepts was the *Green Paper – Partnership for a New Organisation of Work* of 1997.[36] Employment guidelines adopted in the context of the European Employment Strategy have also regularly referred to these two concepts.[37] While a systematic analysis of all the different national concepts of 'flexibility' and 'security' is clearly beyond the scope of the present chapter,[38] the present section will discuss the notions of 'flexibility', 'security', and 'flexicurity' as developed at a Community level.

In this quest it is perhaps appropriate to start from the precursors of the EES, that is to say, from those policy papers drafted in early and mid-1990s that constituted the ideological and political backbone of the Luxembourg Job summit and, subsequently, the EES. For a number of practical reasons the main focus will be on what was probably the last paper drafted before the whole EES machinery was set up, the *Green Paper – Partnership for a New Organisation of Work*.[39] It is noteworthy that

---

of 28 June 1999 Concerning the Framework Agreement on Fixed-term Work concluded by UNICE, CEEP and the ETUC [1999] OJ L175/43 corrigendum OJ 1999 L244/64.

31   Joint Employment Report 2005/2006 'More and Better Jobs: Delivering the Priorities of the European Employment Strategy' (2006).

32   COM(2006) 32 final.

33   European Employment Taskforce, *Jobs, Jobs, Jobs – Creating More Employment In Europe* (2003).

34   The Employment Committee, the Social Protection Committee, 'Flexicurity – Joint Contribution of the Employment Committee and the Social Protection Committee', 12 May 2006 (final).

35   In this document the term 'job security' appeared in the context of the promotion of 'equal opportunities between women and men' and discrimination on grounds of pregnancy, and 'flexibility' was developed in the context of collective redundancies and working time. See COM(89) 568 final, at 17–18, 37.

36   COM(97) 128, in particular at paras 30–32.

37   See for instance the 1998 Employment Guidelines Council Resolution of 15 December 1997 [1998] OJ C 30/1.

38   For a discussion on the various notions of flexibility and security see Chapter 2 of *Employment in Europe 2006*.

39   EC Commission, *Green Paper – Partnership for a New Organisation of Work* COM(97) 128 final 16.4.1997.

EC Regulation of Atypical Forms of Work

from the official records of the European Commission this Green Paper appears to have directly influenced one of the most crucial and controversial 'pillars' of the EES, the Adaptability pillar, directly dealing with *flexibility* and *security*.

The special European Council in Luxembourg in November 1997 gave political support to the ideas presented in the Green Paper. The third pillar of the Employment Guidelines, adaptability, emphasised the importance of the organisation of work and invites the social partners to play a leading role in this respect.[40] The 1997 Green Paper, for its part, placed a strong emphasis on the fact that in a modern economy subject to cyclical restructuring and reorganisation, flexibility and security must necessarily go hand in hand.

> The reorganisation of work often causes uncertainty. Workers need above all to be reassured that after the changes are made they will still have a job and that this job will last for a reasonable time. At the same time, once the changes are made, the new organisation of work can offer workers increased security through greater involvement in their work, more job satisfaction and the possibility of developing skills and long-term employability.[41]

A 'more stable, versatile and contented labour force' was perceived as a beneficial factor for businesses that, according to the Green Paper, are 'looking for interchangeable skills and adaptable working patterns, including working time arrangements'. Here the emphasis is upon finding a balance between flexibility and security both *within* the employment relationship and *within* the labour market. As for the former, more working time flexibility and more workers' participation are advocated, and reassurances are given that the new organisation of work can 'offer ... long term employability'. This does not exclude a recognition that restructuring can bring about an obsolescence of some skills, but active *labour market* policies based on training initiatives are seen as capable of providing an answer to that by 'upgrading the existing workforce in order to achieve better quality, higher productivity and new forms of work organisation' while at the same time helping businesses 'to recruit substitutes, while the workers are being trained'[42] introducing a sort of 'job-rotation' between training and productive work.

The impression is that the 1997 document introduced a 'flexibility and security' framework where workers are encouraged to scale down and otherwise modify their working patterns, and take up training and educational courses or other types of voluntary career breaks, from the perspective of a stable employment relationship and the prospect of a 'long employability' in future working life. The idea seems to be that while workers go through these skills-maintenance and skills-upgrading periods, other workers ('young and unemployed people',[43] presumably employed under atypical contracts), whose skills are deemed to be sufficient to perform the tasks they will be undertaking, would temporarily replace them. A strong clue supporting

---

40   EC Commission, Communication *Modernising the Organisation of Work – A Positive Approach to Change* COM(98) 592 final 12.10.1998.

41   Ibid., para. 31.

42   Ibid., para. 70.

43   Ibid.

214   *The Changing Law of the Employment Relationship*

this interpretation is the use of the expression 'job-rotation', a Danish company-based active labour market policy concept whereby 'the skills of the employees are up-graded and at the same time the work is carried out in the enterprises while the employees are away on training courses'.[44]

Only a few months later, on 15 December 1997, the Council produced its first Resolution introducing the 1998 Employment Guidelines. All the policy strings developed up to that point were pulled together in what became known as the 'four-pillar based EES approach'. It is in the third pillar, 'Encouraging Adaptability in Business and their Employees' that the Strategy spells out its tactics with respect to 'flexibility' and 'security' in employment.[45] These tactics follow three different paths. The first path is left in the hands of the social partners who are invited to negotiate, 'in particular at sectoral and enterprise levels', agreements defined as 'flexible working arrangements'[46] aimed at modernising the organisation of work. A second encouragement is addressed to Member States' legislators who should 'examine the possibility of incorporating in [their] law more adaptable types of contract, taking into account the fact that forms of employment are increasingly diverse'. In line with the 'equal treatment' principle that the EC was at that time endeavouring to foster in its Directives on atypical work, the Guidelines state that 'those working under contracts of this kind should at the same time enjoy adequate security and higher occupational status'.[47] Thirdly, under the adaptability pillar, the Guidelines ask MSs to re-examine obstacles to training and human resources development and 'also examine any new regulations to make sure they will contribute to reducing barriers to employment and helping the labour market adapt to structural change in the economy'.

It seems that the Adaptability pillar, at least from the outset, pursues a flexicurity equation not significantly different from the one already elaborated in the 1997 *Modernising the Organisation of Work* document. The elements of this equation appear to be that flexicurity consists of a combination of three elements directly affecting labour market regulation: *flexible working arrangements*, *equal treatment* and training in the sense of *life-long learning*.

For the next three years the structure, content and, to a great extent, the actual wording of the Adaptability pillar remained substantially unaltered. Some minor changes were introduced in 2001[48] with a new emphasis placed on health and safety in the workplace and an explicit invitation to the social partners to conclude agreements to facilitate training programmes and report on the steps taken in the area

---

44   EC Commission, *Commission Draft for the Joint Employment Report 1997* (Brussels, 30 September 1997, p. 34). Also reported in the 1998 Joint Employment Report EC Commission DGV *Employment Policies in the EU and in the Member States – Joint Report 1998* (Office for Official Publications of the European Communities, Luxembourg, 1999), pp. 35, 62, 64.

45   Though undeniably other pillars do influence the issue.

46   The 1998 Employment Guidelines Council Resolution of 15 December 1997 [1998] OJ C30/1, 4.

47   Ibid., 30/5.

48   Council Decision of 19 January 2001 on Guidelines for Member States' Employment Policies for the Year 2001 [2001] OJ L22/24.

of flexible work and modernisation of the workplace. The same emphasis on making 'sure that those working under new flexible contracts enjoy adequate security and higher occupational status' was maintained in 2001 and in the overall similar 2002 Guidelines.[49] The 2003 Guidelines, adopted after the much awaited five-year review of the EES, radically modified the four-pillar approach and their contents were subdivided into ten distinct but overlapping 'policy priorities'. Tracing through the issues previously addressed under the adaptability pillar is not particularly straightforward, but the term 'flexibility' is always used in association with the word 'security'.

Most importantly, the 2003 guidelines offered a clearer definition of the concept of 'quality' of work, a term seen as a 'multi-dimensional concept addressing both job characteristics and the wider labour market'. It appears that the strong link with the notions of flexibility and security introduced by the 1997 Green Paper has been maintained, with flexibility and security for the workforce being derived both from the employment relationship and the labour market. Thus the 2003 Guidelines are at pains to stress that 'quality ... encompasses intrinsic quality at work, skills, lifelong learning and career development, gender equality, health and safety at work, flexibility and security, inclusion and access to the labour market, work organisation and work-life balance, social dialogue and worker involvement, diversity and non-discrimination, and overall work performance'.[50] Undeniably the EES in 2003 appeared to have a clear *promotional* intention coupled with the idea of *normalisation with parity*. It promoted 'diversity of contractual and working arrangements' but always in an optic of 'favouring career progression, a better balance between work and private life and between flexibility and security'.[51] The emphasis placed on 'making work pay' and promoting 'development of human capital' certainly did not allude to a precarious and discontinuous *working life*.

But 2003 was a year of radical and deep soul-searching for the EC and in particular for the EES. A Report by the Employment Taskforce chaired by Wim Kok of November 2003 signalled the fact that

> The European Union is at risk of failing in its ambitious goal, set at Lisbon in 2000, of becoming by 2010 the most competitive and dynamic knowledge-based economy in the world capable of sustainable economic growth with more and better jobs and greater social cohesion.[52]

Effectively the Report pointed out that the Lisbon goals would be missed in the absence of a radical shake up in the EES. The report made a series of general and country-specific suggestions. A crucially important set of suggestions was contained

---

49 Council Decision of 18 February 2002 on Guidelines for Member States' Employment Policies for the Year 2002 [2002] OJ L60/67.

50 Council Decision of 22 July 2003 on Guidelines for the Employment Policies of the Member States [2003] OJ L197/17.

51 Ibid., 197/18.

52 Wim Kok, *Jobs, Jobs, Jobs – Creating More Employment in Europe* (Brussels, 2003).

216 *The Changing Law of the Employment Relationship*

in the part of the document dealing with 'Promoting flexibility with security on the labour market'. Here the report suggested, among the other things, that

> Employers must be able to adapt the size of their workforces by interrupting contracts without excessive delays or costs when other measures, such as working time flexibility or re-training of workers, have reached their limits. Overly protective terms and conditions under standard employment contracts can deter employers from hiring in economic upturns ...
>
> ... Member States should assess and where necessary alter the level of flexibility provided in standard contracts in areas such as periods of notice, costs and procedures for individual or collective dismissal, or the definition of unfair dismissal.[53]

Although the report did not fail to mention the importance of 'security for workers', and the need to 'prevent the emergence of a two-tier labour market', the emphasis was clearly placed on a rather aggressive notion of flexibility. The Commission and the Council integrated the findings of the report into their Joint Employment Report for the Spring Council of 2004, which confirmed the need for decisive action by Member States along the lines suggested by the Taskforce and paved the way for the EES reform of 2005.[54]

Thus the 2005 Integrated Guidelines, extended – as expected – for the following year, first suggested a departure from their earlier cautious approach and envisaged the need for national policies to offer 'support for transitions in occupational status'.[55] The title of Guideline 21, 'Promote flexibility combined with employment security and reduce labour market segmentation, having due regard to the role of the social partners', seems to suggest the usual search for a compromise between the liberal goal of promoting different contractual and working time arrangements and employment security. But crucially this compromise seems to be characterised by an *equalisation with parity model* (exemplified by the goal of reducing labour market segmentation) where the norm, the standard contract of employment, is rendered more flexible and de-regulated.

As Simon Deakin and Hanna Reed have put it, the Employment Guidelines

> are a curious mix of neo-liberal policy objectives, which stress deregulation and individual responsibility for training and labour market mobility, and neo-corporatist strategies, which envisage collective solutions to the reconciliation of flexibility and security.[56]

It seems clear that the notion of 'flexibility and security' incorporated in the EES has a more neo-liberal meaning after 2004 than it had before, whereby the standard

---

53 Ibid., p. 28.

54 EC Commission, 'Working Together for Growth and Jobs – A New Start for the Lisbon Strategy' COM(2005) 24.

55 Council Decision of 12 July 2005 on Guidelines for the Employment Policies of the Member States [2005] OJ L205/21, 205/26.

56 S. Deakin and H. Reed, 'The Contested Meaning of Labour Market Flexibility: Economic Theory and the Discourse of European Integration', in J. Shaw (ed.), *Social Law and Policy in an Evolving European Union* (Hart, Oxford, 2000), p. 95.

contract of employment becomes the target of de-regulatory practices. Neither of the two meanings challenges the 'normalisation with parity' model discussed in Chapter 3 of this book. But it is clearly the neo-liberal notion of 'flexicurity' that is increasingly reflected in the new Integrated Guidelines introduced in 2005. This mutation is even clearer if one looks at the recent EU level elaborations on the notion of 'flexicurity'.

The EU notion of 'flexicurity': from content to method?

A very powerful vector in this progressive mutation of the notions of 'flexibility and security' and, ultimately, 'flexicurity' has been the EES and the open method of coordination, which also provided the context in which the notion of 'flexicurity' first emerged. In fact, the first official document using this term was the 'explanatory memorandum' accompanying the 2006 'Proposal for a Council Decision Guidelines for the Employment Policies in the Member States'.[57] But the document only made an *ob iter* reference to 'flexicurity' and neither its theoretical meaning nor its practical implications were fully explored. In that respect, the commission *Green Paper – Modernising Labour Law to Meet the Challenges of the 21st Century*[58] of 2006 constitutes a turning point, and one that will be further consolidated with the publication, in Summer 2007, of a 'commission communication on flexicurity … which will set out to develop the arguments in favour of the 'flexicurity' approach and to outline a set of common principles by the end of 2007 to help Member States steer the reform efforts'.[59]

There is hardly any doubt that 'flexicurity', as last highlighted by the February 2007 employment and social policy council,[60] is about to become another 'Euro-buzz-word'. Its meaning, though, remains elusive. Unsurprisingly, the drafting of the 2006 Green Paper and of the 2007 Communication have been and are being marred by disagreements over a possible 'community' definition of the term. The main reason for these definitional difficulties is that since, logically, the meaning of 'flexicurity' depends of the relative meaning of its two components, flexibility and security, a substantive EC definition of the former is impossible unless the latter two concepts are also defined at a Community level. But as pointed out in the previous paragraphs, while it may be possible to appraise a series of common trends in the national developments of the national notions of flexibility and security, differences between MSs labour market regulations are still both visible and extremely relevant, and so is the balance that each one of the strikes between the various conceptions of flexibility and security.

Nevertheless, an attentive analysis of the most recent EC documents on 'flexicurity' would appear to suggest that a possible exit from this deadlock may be

---

57 COM(2006) 32 final.

58 COM(2006) 708 final.

59 Ibid., at p. 4.

60 Council of the European Union, 2786th Council Meeting, Employment, Social Policy, Health and Consumer Affairs (Brussels, 22 February 2007). See 6226/07 (Presse 23) at http://www.consilium.europa.eu/ueDocs/cms_Data/docs/pressData/en/lsa/92911.pdf.

218   *The Changing Law of the Employment Relationship*

emerging. The key to break this deadlock, according to the authors of the present work, is the progressive shift of the focus of the EC debate from the substance and the *contents* of the notion of 'flexicurity' to 'flexicurity as a *method*'. This shift is fairly perceptible in the 2006 Green Paper and in the December 2006 Commission Annual Progress Report,[61] and more clearly discernible in the conclusions of the February 2007 employment and social affairs council meeting.

'Flexicurity' has a central role in the 2006 Green Paper. As the documents states,

> this Green Paper looks at the role labour law might play in advancing a "flexicurity" agenda in support of a labour market which is fairer, more responsive and more inclusive, and which contributes to making Europe more competitive.[62]

On the other hand, the Paper never clarifies the exact contents of the term. In its first section, after a swift reference to the notion of flexibility endorsed by the Wim Kok report, the Green Paper suggests that:

> Other policy components of the 'flexicurity' approach include life-long learning enabling people to keep pace with the new skill needs; active labour market policies encouraging unemployed or inactive people to have a new chance in the labour market; and more flexible social security rules catering for the needs of those switching between jobs or temporarily leaving the labour market.[63]

The preference for a notion of 'flexicurity' that supports numerical and functional flexibility and security outside the employment relationship, to the detriment of security within it, is particularly visible in the December 2006 Progress Report:

> Member States are showing considerable interest in 'flexicurity' but most are still implementing only some of its elements, such as measures to reduce the tax burden on labour to 'make work pay' and to boost labour demand. There has been limited progress on the other elements: modernising social protection and benefit systems and putting in place coherent life long learning strategies. And not enough Member States are modernizing employment protection legislation – except at the margins (providing greater opportunities to new entrants or marginal workers). In order to overcome labour market dualism (insiders/outsiders) in a number of Member States, greater security and employability for those at the margins will need to *go hand in hand with greater flexibility for those on permanent contracts.*[64]

What the Green Paper described as an 'approach' in the 2006 Green Paper, became a fully fledged 'method' in the recent employment and social affairs council meeting. The Council concluded that:

---

61   Communication from the Commission to the Spring European Council Implementing the Renewed Lisbon Strategy for Growth and Jobs 'A year of delivery'. COM(2006) 816 final.

62   COM(2006) 708 final, at 4.

63   Ibid.

64   COM(2006) 816 final, at 9.

To proceed with the structural improvement of employment performance, Member States should enhance flexicurity as a method ....

Flexicurity should ease the transitions between different stages of working life. The internal and external components of flexicurity should mutually reinforce one another, so that at the same time the modernisation of labour law, investment in training and active labour markets, and the provision of adequate social protection and income security can take place in a context of modern work organisation. Flexicurity should also be conducive to addressing precariousness, reducing segmentation on the labour market, and combating undeclared work. The social partners have an important role to play here. The commission communication on flexicurity should be instrumental in preparing a range of flexicurity pathways to find the right mix of policies tailored to labour market needs. [65]

What is evident is that 'flexicurity' as a method is something for Member States to develop, albeit within the framework of EC coordinating activities provided by the EES and OMC. MSs are asked to enhance 'flexicurity as a method', while the Commission is asked to 'prepar[e] a range of flexicurity *pathways* to find the right mix of policies tailored to labour market needs'. Clearly, the real issue at stake is the extent to which the flexicurity 'method' and the national 'pathways' are also going to influence the contents of the 'flexicurity' reform approach. The recent emphasis placed on flexibility and security outside the employment relationship, to the detriment of security within the employment relationship, would suggest that method and content are going to be more closely related than the mantra of 'flexicurity as a method' would *prima facie* suggest, but a final assessment of this dynamic will have to await the publication of the 2007 Communication on 'flexicurity'. [66]

EC employment law on atypical forms of work

EC legislative measures on atypical work might have followed a different procedural conception and development, but there is a clear temporal, and arguably political, coincidence between the making of the Directive on fixed-term work and some of the conceptualisation produced in the early stages of the EES. While the Framework Agreement incorporated in the Part-time Work Directive[67] introduces itself by stating that it 'is a contribution to the overall European strategy on employment',[68] the Fixed-term Work Directive[69] establishes a direct link with the EES when it declares that it springs, *inter alia*, from the invitation addressed by the 1999 Guidelines to 'the social partners at all appropriate levels to negotiate agreements to modernise the organisation of work, including flexible working arrangements, with the aim of making undertakings productive and competitive and achieving the required

---

65 See 6226/07 (Presse 23), above, at 8, para. 3.

66 In this respect, a recent update of the europa.eu website presenting 'the four components' of 'flexicurity' (Flexible contractual arrangements, ALMPS, Lifelong learning, Modern social security systems) seems to pre-empt in part the current efforts by EMCO and the social partners trying to produce an ad hoc Communication on 'flexicurity'.

67 [1998] OJ L14/9.

68 [1998] OJ L14/12, preamble.

69 [1999] OJ L175/43.

balance between flexibility and security'.[70] The Fixed-term Framework Agreement also establishes a link with the EES in seeking to constitute a 'contribution towards achieving a better balance between "flexibility in working time and security for workers"'.[71]

Chapter 3 highlighted the fact that in national experiences, and in some quarters, fixed-term work has been regarded with greater suspicion and distrust than part-time work. Directive 99/70 does reflect some of these concerns. In the preamble to the Agreement, the social partners had already stressed that 'contracts of an indefinite duration are, and will continue to be, the general form of employment relationship'. Subsequently, clause 5 introduces a number of alternative limitations to 'abusive' renewals of successive fixed-term contracts. But if one considers clause 2.2(b) after exploring the EES context, it is arguable that the EES-backed notion of 'flexibility and security', at least as originally enshrined in the 'pre-Kok era', may be deprived of the essential equal-treatment element whenever some publicly supported job creation programs are involved. Given the fact that in the national experiences of the MSs, as highlighted in Chapter 3, the regulation of temporary work has been even more contentious than the regulation of fixed-term work, it is hardly surprising that some tensions emerged in the drafting process of the currently stalled proposal for a Temporary Agency Work Directive. The Economic and Social Committee (Ecosoc), attempted to modify the wording of the 'publicly supported' job creation exception. It proposed 'amending the wording of this point, replacing "after consulting the social partners" with "when there are agreements with the social partners"'.[72] But the proposed amendment did not appear in the final version of the draft.

4. Looking at the national employment policies through the distorting mirror of National Action Plans and Employment Recommendations

The previous section pointed out that the EES notion of flexicurity has consistently supported a *normalisation with parity* model, whereby atypical and flexible work is indeed encouraged at a national level, but on an 'equal treatment basis' with standard work. It was also pointed out that after the publication of the Wim Kok Report a new notion of 'flexibility and security' has arguably emerged. While maintaining the 'normalisation with parity' feature,[73] this new notion seems to promote a progressive deregulation of some aspects of the standard contract of employment, the norm against which the equalisation with parity model is supposed to work. Also, it was highlighted that the notions of flexibility and security as initially developed by the EES appear to be at odds with some clauses of the Fixed-term Work Directive and of the Temporary Agency Work Draft Directive providing for the 'equal-treatment'

---

70 Ibid., para. 6 of the preamble.

71 [1999] OJ L175/45. Cf. also [1999] OJ L175/46, para. 5.

72 Opinion of the Economic and Social Committee on the Proposal for a Directive of the European Parliament and the Council on Working Conditions for Temporary Workers [2003] OJ C61/124, 126.

73 As indicated by the 2005 Integrated Guidelines seeking, among the other things, to reduce labour market segmentation.

principle to be excluded when publicly supported job creation initiatives so require. It was also stressed how, in that respect, there seems to be somewhat of a chasm between the Part-time Work Directive and the Fixed-term Work Directive.

This section explores if, and to what extent, the EC has been able to strike a better and more coherent and consistent balance in its notion of flexicurity when engaging with Member States through the EES. One would assume that the EC would have attempted to superimpose the ESS notion of flexicurity on the MSs through the intricate web of soft-law tools such as Joint Employment Reports (JERs) and Recommendations that constitute the elements of the *direct dialogue* between Community institutions and individual[74] MSs within the Employment Strategy known as the Open Method of Coordination (OMC).[75] The next paragraphs argue that, on the contrary, the outcome of this dialogue appears to be that the initial meaning of 'flexicurity' has been placed under serious strain and its – somewhat limited – initial balance and coherence appear to be irremediably upset, as already paradigmatically reflected by the Wim Kok Report and by the wording of the 2005 Integrated Guidelines discussed earlier.

There are some indications that the EC is even less capable of maintaining a coherent approach to its notions of flexicurity and quality of work in the context of these more country-specific means of dialogue, particularly when commenting upon existing or proposed national legislation presented in the National Action Plans (NAPs), or National Reform Programmes, as they have come to be known after the 2005 reform of the EES. The result, and this is probably the most worrying note, is that the whole EES structure ends up by bestowing a considerably degree of legitimacy upon a number of very different national measures incorporating very different mixtures of security and flexibility.

The EES and flexicurity in Italy and France between 2000 and 2003

Here, some concrete examples of the alleged incoherencies produced by the EES framework are given. They will seek to do that by focusing on Italy and France and analysing some Recommendations, JERs and NAPs adopted between 2000 and 2003. The choice of Italy and France as our examples is due to the fact that, in the period of reference, these two countries adopted important reforms under different government majorities, as already highlighted in Chapter 3. They are therefore ideally placed to offer some clues on how, if at all, effective a framework the ESS is, when it comes to shaping national regulatory processes. More precisely, our review will try to find an answer to one main question: Has the 'normalisation with parity model' enshrined in the EES notions of flexibility and security at least been able to shape the regulatory path of national reforms on atypical workers?

---

74 As opposed to the Guidelines that address the generality of the MSs.

75 On the EES and the OMC, D. Ashiagbor, *The European Employment Strategy – Labour Market Regulation and New Governance* (OUP, Oxford, 2005).

222   *The Changing Law of the Employment Relationship*

With its 2000 NAP, presented in April of that same year, Italy announced to the EC the implementation of[76] Directive 97/81. It appears that the drafters of the NAP were particularly scrupulous in spelling out the new rules on supplementary work and the balance between flexibility and security achieved in what they defined as the 'elasticity pact with respect to work shifts that recognises a worker's "right to a change of mind" in the face of subjective motivations and entitles such a worker to go back to previously established working hours, which may not be unilaterally changed by the employer'. The fourth section of Chapter 3 pointed out how much controversy the initial formulation of these '*clausole elastiche*' had caused before the Italian Constitutional Court, convinced as it was that a working schedule which accorded too much flexibility to management could impair the workers' fundamental rights to a decent pay and family life. The French[77] National Action Plan (PNA) stressed that for 'part-time workers some new guarantees have been defined, notably in the area of complementary hours, breaks, minimal contractual duration, so that in the end the agreements mark a step forward towards a practice of part-time work closer to [the notion of] *temps choisi*'. As a proposition for future action, the French NAP announced that 'a better framing of precarious work must be defined so as to prevent an abusive use of fixed-term contracts and temporary work to cover some permanent posts in enterprises that would normally be occupied by employees hired under contracts of indefinite duration', clearly favouring a 'professional mobility of such workers towards permanent jobs'.[78]

The 2000 JER acknowledges the information received from the Italian Government by stating that in Italy a 'non-discrimination principle and [a requirement of] worker's consent were included in the part-time regulation particularly to prevent an unfavourable impact on women'.[79] On the other hand, it showed no signs of appreciation to the progress of active labour market reforms in Italy, stating that 'full implementation of the preventative approach is proceeding slowly' and that 'action is required, especially in the fields of active policies aimed at preventing and/or reducing youth and long term unemployment and gender gaps'.[80] As for France, the JER praised the fact that 'negotiations on the reduction of working time have often led to agreements between the social partners, making it possible to speed up the modernisation of work organisation',[81] but it stressed that 'strengthening the preventive measures offered to young people/adults who have been unemployed for 6/12 months' had to be a priority for the next years.[82]

The 2001 Recommendations[83] did not suggest any further action in the area of part-time work in Italy and merely encouraged France to 'pursue efforts to modernise

---

76   The Government of Italy, *National Action Plan for Employment Implementation Report, Year 2000 – Italy* (April 2000), p. 25.

77   PNA 2000, p. 15.

78   Ibid., p. 39.

79   Joint Employment Report (JER) 2000, p. 175.

80   Ibid., p. 172.

81   Ibid., p. 157.

82   Ibid.

83   Council Recommendation of 19 January 2001 on the Implementation of Member States' Employment Policies [2001] OJ L22/33.

EC Regulation of Atypical Forms of Work 223

work organisation and monitor closely the net effects of the implementation of the 35-hour week legislation'.[84] On the other hand Italy was particularly encouraged 'in the context of employability policies', to 'take further action to prevent the inflow of young and adult unemployed people into long-term unemployment'.[85] The 2001 Italian NAP,[86] drafted nearly a year after the election of a new centre-right parliamentary majority, expressed satisfaction with the part-time work reform approved by the previous centre-left Government.

> Insofar as it concerns the flexible types of contract that – in line with European guidelines – although flexible have to guarantee a suitable protection and a satisfactory employment of workers, it should be noted that in the past year two legislative decrees have dealt with part-time work. The measures introduced by these decrees aimed at increasing its flexibility of use through significant innovations, such as the possibility of changing the work shift schedule and of making supplementary work.[87]

The 2001 NAP could not yet announce the implementation of the Fixed-term Work Directive, whose legislative process was stalling due to a number of disagreements between the social partners; that was finally achieved by legislative decree in September 2001. On the other hand the NAP could point to the progress made in the implementation of the reform of the Public Employment Services and to a number of actions adopted to transform some temporary public work activities, the *lavori socialmente utili*, into permanent jobs.[88] The concomitant French NAP[89] detailed the latest evolutions of the 35-hour working week legislation and the introduction of the right for part-time civil servants to take up a second job. It also announced the 'agreement to minimise temporary employment in the three civil services'[90] concluded in July 2000 and stated that the Government continued 'to implement early individual intervention programmes for the unemployed and to increase their use for preventive purposes'.[91]

The 2001 JER did highlight the fact that Italian 'difficulties in the social dialogue were slowing up the on-going modernisation of work organisation',[92] also pointing out the persisting problems in the PES reform, while the 2002 Recommendations stated that 'work organization needs to be further modernised' and encouraged the Government to 'continue to increase labour market flexibility with a view to better combining security with greater adaptability to facilitate access to employment' and to 'improve the effectiveness of active labour market policies'.[93] None of the

---

84   Ibid., [2001] OJ L22/32.

85   Ibid., [2001] OJ L22/33.

86   Italy, *2001 National Action Plan for Employment* (May 2001).

87   Ibid., p. 26.

88   Ibid., pp. 11–12.

89   *National Action Plan for Employment 2001 and Overview of 2000 – France* (May 2001).

90   Ibid., p. 39.

91   Ibid., p. 3.

92   JER 2001, p. 60.

93   Council Recommendation of 18 February 2002 on the Implementation of Member States' Employment Policies (Recommendations 2002) [2002] OJ L60/76.

224 *The Changing Law of the Employment Relationship*

documents, though, pointed out any problem in respect of part-time work. As for France, the 2001 JER highlighted that the 'focus is now on quality in work: more stable, better paid jobs which are more knowledge-intensive and which have the best organisational conditions and job security'. However as far as security in the labour market was concerned, it also stressed that the 'results in 2001 with regard to increasing individualised and preventive measures for unemployed people fall short of expectations'.[94] Both points were taken up by the 2002 Recommendations n. 4 and n. 3 respectively.[95]

The French 2002 NAP[96] explicitly addressed these issues, presenting a number of initiatives to combat the high inactivity rates among young people and long-term unemployment[97] and recording the introduction of new legislation 'to modernise work organisation and to reconcile the flexibility requirements of employers and the job security needs of employees'.[98] It pointed out that working time reduction had led to '410,000 commitments to job creation and job preservation'[99] and announced the launch of a think tank to conduct research on 'making careers secure'.[100]

The Italian 2002 NAP[101] was the occasion for the Italian government to announce to the EC the labour market reforms debated in that period. The NAP specifically addressed the Recommendations of the previous year encouraging an increase of 'labour market flexibility'. The implementations of the fixed-term work Directive was mentioned but in the subsequent paragraph the NAP already announced the planned reforms of this kind of contract, aiming at making it 'even more accessible, coherently with what is provided by European legislation'.[102] The NAP went on to describe what it purported to be a reform aimed at implementing the suggestions put forward in the Barcelona European Council of March 2002, the *disegno di legge delega in materia di mercato del lavoro*, also known as the *rifoma Biagi* ('Biagi reform').

> The [reform], which is still the object of an ongoing debate between the social partners, intervenes in a structural manner on the existing regulatory framework. [The reform] aims at removing the regulatory obstacles that still hamper the use of flexible contractual typologies. In that respect, fixed-term contracts are rendered more accessible, in line with the requirements of the European regulatory framework; interim contracts, along with temporary work contracts, are reformed as to facilitate the encounter between labour demand and supply; new contractual types, which take into account the changing needs of economic production and business organisation, are introduced ('intermittent work', *lavoro a progetto*) with the aim of 'sanitising' the labour market from the improper use

---

94 JER 2001, p. 54.

95 Recommendations 2002, OJ L60/75.

96 *National Action Plan for Employment 2002 – France* (June 2002).

97 Ibid., p. 9.

98 Ibid., p. 10.

99 Ibid., p. 55.

100 Ibid., p. 56.

101 Italia, *Piano Nazionale per l'Occupazione* (Giugno 2002).

102 Ibid., p. 29.

of some work relationships existing at present. The proposed reforms concerning the termination of the employment relationship are also part of this context.[103]

Chapter 3 analysed the impact of the *rifoma Biagi* on Italian employment legislation. It was argued that this reform represented a sort of de-regulatory and neo-liberal climax in the recent production of labour legislation in Italy. In particular it was claimed that, perhaps for the first time, these reforms introduced some elements of what can be defined as 'normalisation without parity' in the regulation of atypical employment relationship. The attempts to reform unfair dismissal legislation and the new rules applying to temporary agency work and to the new *parasubordinati* workers (the so-called *collaboratori a progetto*) indicated a regulatory approach that clearly emphasised the *flexibility* aspects and underplayed the *security* elements of the Italian *flexicurity* concept. Although the government managed to secure the consensus of a number of unions on these reforms, the larger Italian trade union refused any compromise on the reform of unfair dismissal contained in Article 18 of the *Statuto dei Lavoratori*, and the reforms pertaining to the regulation of atypical work contracts were adopted amidst a climate of social and political tension. It is also worth noticing that in the 2002 NAP the Italian government was implicitly claiming that these reforms were inspired by – if not also a direct consequence of – EC-level developments.

At the same time, France appeared to have taken a markedly different path in striking a balance between flexibility and security, also perceived as dictated from the requirements enunciated by the EES measures. Put simply, French and Italian employment law were taking two different paths and adopting two distinct notions of 'flexicurity'. Was the EES going to be able to steer these noticeable regulatory deviations and produce a convergence towards its own notion of 'flexicurity'? The JER of 2002 provides a further evidence that although, at a theoretical and general level, the EC does have a vision of what the balance between security and flexibility should be, it is extremely reluctant to take a firm stance towards national solutions that deviate from that EC notion, allowing MS considerable leeway in deciding their own employment policies. When reading the 2002 Joint Employment Report, one almost has the impression that the Community institutions are unquestioningly accepting all the claims advanced by national governments. In respect of the announced Italian reforms, the 2002 JER stated:

> *This policy mix, centred on employability and adaptability, is expected to influence equal opportunities through an easier recourse to part-time work, and to increase quality in work through reducing undeclared work and the reducing the disparity between protected and flexible work, while security in work and other quality aspects are not analysed.*[104]

The JER of 2002 erroneously assumed that the reform proposals on unfair dismissal had received a positive appraisal from both sides of industry; in fact, CGIL refused to sign the agreement and, as seen in Chapter 3, these reforms were never implemented.

---

103 Ibid.
104 JER 2002, p. 79.

226   *The Changing Law of the Employment Relationship*

> *The government proposal to revise Art 18 of the Workers Statute ended with a tripartite agreement on labour policies with the majority of trade unions and the employers.*[105]

Finally they issued a very limited warning, hardly highlighting the tensions inherent to the Italian reforms:

> Once the proposed measures for flexibility are implemented, particular attention seems necessary for the security and quality aspects in order to avoid the risk of marginalisation for the long-term unemployed and women, especially in the South.[106]

The EES appears to be quite successful at enunciating a vision of the reforms that are needed at a European and national level but it appears to be unable to shape these reforms according to its vision. The 2002 JER in its general part provides a clear definition of flexibility and security. *Flexibility*, seen as the capacity for firms to adjust to market demand, can be notionally subdivided into two 'complementary' categories, *external flexibility* and *internal flexibility*. The former is defined in terms of the capacity to 'hire and fire' and includes 'the use of temporary or fixed term contracts ... to adapt to unforeseen circumstances and changing trends such as changing demands or skill requirements and allows firms to adjust their production quickly'. *Internal flexibility* is linked to the 're-organisation of the existing workforce (working time, working methods, training, mobility) [and] constitutes a longer term approach to managing change and to the development of skills and competencies, with clear advantages in terms of productivity and capacity to adjust'.[107] *Security* is also a two-faceted concept, meaning, from a *static* point of view 'stability of the working relationship and the availability of a safety net in case of job loss', and from a *dynamic* one 'non-discrimination between forms of working contracts and arrangements, and the acquisition and preservation of employability, so as to facilitate adaptation to change and mobility within and between jobs'. From this latter perspective, 'access to training and career development are essential aspects of job security'.[108]

This definition gives some support to the idea, developed in this chapter and in Chapter 3, that the EC employment policy notions of 'flexibility and security' arguably advocate a combination of flexibility and security in both the *labour market* (by granting 'external flexibility' and 'dynamic security') *and* the *employment relationship* (through the recognition to workers of some 'internal flexibility' and 'static security'). Certainly, measures concentrating solely on flexibility in the employment relationship and security in the labour market, or vice versa, do not meet the requirements and policy goals of the earlier elaborations of the ec on flexibility and security. In this optic it is not surprising to see that the JER of 2002 praised 'certain restrictions on the renewal of fixed-term contracts ... introduced in France and Germany to prevent the abuse of such contracts',[109] or that some scepticism

---

105 Ibid.
106 Ibid., p. 80.
107 JER 2002, p. 45
108 Ibid.
109 Ibid., p. 47.

EC Regulation of Atypical Forms of Work   227

is shown towards the aforementioned Italian plans to 'increase ... labour market flexibility (flexible contracts – part time and interim – and relaxation of some rules on individual dismissal) [since] the ways to combine flexibility and security are not detailed and the policy mix could lead to the marginalisation of "disadvantaged" groups and generally in the South'.[110] But again it seems that the following 2003 Recommendations miss once more the point when they generally praise the Italian 'initiatives aiming at labour market flexibility and security, *inter alia* the introduction of new labour contracts and the liberalisation of employment services, ... taken by the Government at the beginning of 2003'[111] and exhort the latter to 'implement, where appropriate in consultation with the social partners, measures to increase labour market flexibility and modernise work organisation'.[112]

But arguably the new EC 'flexibility' approach discussed in the previous section of this chapter is definitely 'flexible' enough to accommodate the various national 'paths to flexicurity', without questioning the policy approaches of national governments in respect of atypical work. What is also evident though, is that in recent years the ECJ has shown itself unwilling to conform to this evolutionary trend. As discussed in Chapter 3, a number of recent court decisions have reprimanded several Member States for enthusiastically embracing the promotion of fixed-term work in the context of national employment policies aimed at satisfying some of the job-promotion preoccupations underpinned, directly or indirectly, by the EES.[113] This has clearly brought to light the problems deriving from the lack of coordination between EC employment law and EC employment policy.

5. Divergences between EES and EC employment law on atypical work and the European Court of Justice

Political scientists have for some time provided us with a plausible explanation for this extremely incoherent state of affairs. In their 1999 analysis, Knill and Lehmkuhl[114] draw a distinction between three different types of European policy-making: *positive integration, negative integration*, and what they call '*framing integration*', each reflecting different paths to European regulatory integration. In the latter type of policy making, the EU institutions wish 'to change the political climate at the domestic level in order to increase support for domestic reforms that may facilitate future steps towards integration'[115] and might well adopt measures

---

110 Ibid., p. 79.

111 Council Recommendation of 22 July 2003 on the Implementation of Member States' Employment Policies [2003] OJ L197/26.

112 Ibid., p. 27.

113 See C-144/04, *Mangold* v *Helm* [2005] ECR I-9981; C-212/04, *Kostantinos Adeneler and Others* v *Elog* [2006] ECR I-06057; C-53/04, *Marrosu and Sardino* v *Azienda Ospedaliera San Martino* (not yet reported at the time of writing).

114 C. Knill and D. Lehmkuhl, 'How Europe Matters: Different Mechanisms of Europeanization', *European Integration Online Papers* (1999). Available at http://eiop.or.at/eiop/pdf/1999-007.pdf (15 January 2006).

115 Ibid., p. 9.

228 *The Changing Law of the Employment Relationship*

that are 'non-compulsory and provide for far-reaching discretion regarding the process of implementation at the domestic level'.[116] In practice under this kind of approach, EU institutions are not so much concerned about reaching a specifically defined regulatory aim but rather seek to provide a policy 'frame' for national level reforms. The hope and political intentions of the 'framers' is to initiate a *process*, which should 'provide additional legitimisation for domestic leaders to justify the content and implementation of national reform policies'[117] and which should embody 'the concept of reform to resolve specific problems',[118] while at the same time ruling out a number of policy options, supported by 'reform opponents',[119] falling outside the frame which has been set up. While 'framing policy' strategies have a number of success stories to tell us about, the authors also remind us of a number of examples where the reform impact was minimal or non-existent. But to these risks it is probably possible to add a new one that is specific to the EES. It appears here that the European institutions are extremely preoccupied with the success of the *process*, rather than with reaching a specific aim or set of aims. Therefore, given the controversial and highly ideological nature of employment policy, they have adopted, or are presenting to their national interlocutors, a very wide 'frame' that can legitimise a variety of different reforms at the domestic level.

The core of these concerns is implicit in the excellent work of Diamond Ashiagbor. The author approaches the EES through the analytical lens of 'reflexive theory' and highlights the voluntary as well as the more coercive aspects of soft law in the context of the Employment Strategy. But Ashiagbor also takes this analysis a step further, by suggesting that the weaknesses implicit in the EES and soft regulation are somewhat increased, and in a distinctly neo-liberal and de-regulatory way, by the context provided by the Stability and Growth Pact. To use the author's words,

> It is questionable whether 'soft' coordination, on its own, is able to provide a sufficiently robust normative framework to balance the economic policy discourse which continue to dominate the Employment Strategy and the Lisbon Strategy. The policy 'experimentation' which is the hallmark of the open method in fact permits diversity only within a framework firmly wedded to sound public finances, comprehensive economic reform and restructuring of labour markets, thus limiting the extent to which Member States can depart from the Employment Strategy without also breaching the BEPGs and the Stability and growth Pact.[120]

But with respect to the EES it must be borne in mind that this 'framing policy' or 'new form of governance' is deeply interconnected with a 'positive integration' policy area, that of EC employment *law*, whose delicate equilibrium risks being compromised by the EES policy manoeuvres. Indeed the EES gap between abstract theoretical conceptualisation, typical of any framing or soft regulatory policy, and

---

116 Ibid., p. 10.

117 Ibid., p. 12.

118 Ibid., p. 13.

119 Ibid., p. 13.

120 D. Ashiagbor, *The European Employment Strategy – Labour Market Regulation and New Governance* (OUP, Oxford, 2005), p. 241.

country-specific guidance can lead to some considerable tensions between national employment policies and the EC and the national 'hard' employment law framework where, arguably, the room for political manoeuvring of the national and EC institutions is more limited. As a concrete example of this risk it is arguably possible to suggest that the reforms undertaken in Germany, with the support of collective bargaining, in 2003 and in 2004, where agency workers appear to be deprived of a right to equal-treatment *vis-à-vis* standard workers in respect of pay, is an early warning of this risk that the equal treatment principle may be excluded where temporary agency work is used as a labour market and job creation mechanism. Similar rationales could soon back national reforms aimed at using fixed-term contracts as job-creation tools under publicly supported programmes.

It is known that this kind of preoccupation was shared in some European quarters in Europe during the negotiations in the early years of this decade concerning the draft Directive on Temporary Agency Work. The provision contained in Article 1(3) of the draft instrument was at the centre of the heated debate that took place in the 2004 meeting of the Council of Social Affairs that eventually led to the rejection of the Commission proposal. While earlier EES and EC Employment Law instruments attempted to introduce a regulatory framework inspired by the 'normalisation with parity' principle, recent EES developments might be unconsciously supporting and justifying a 'normalisation without parity' approach.

As discussed above, and in Chapter 3 of this work, the ECJ is clearly unwilling to endorse such a trend. In *Mangold* the court conceded that Member States 'unarguably enjoy broad discretion' in their employment policies. However it swiftly pointed out that whenever the application of National Employment Policy legislation leads to a situation in which workers may be offered fixed-term contracts of employment, which may be renewed an indefinite number of times, this 'significant body of workers [is] in danger, during a substantial part of its members' working life, of being excluded from the benefit of stable employment which, however, as the framework agreement makes clear, constitutes a major element in the protection of workers'.[121]

In subsequent decisions the Court took a similarly vigilant stance in respect of National Employment Policies, effectively providing that national paths to 'flexicurity' will have to comply with the fundamental principle of non-discrimination and, ultimately, with a community concept of flexibility and security that stems from EC employment law and affords a privileged status to standard employment.

In spite of the Court's clear position, it goes without saying that tensions between EC employment law and EC employment policy are bound to emerge again in the years to come. Arguably this is not an acceptable risk and some steering mechanism should be devised to avoid these kind of tensions that are bound to occur whenever the subject matter of a 'framing policy' is also the focus of a policy of positive integration as in the case of European employment policy and European employment law. The idea of approaching soft harmonisation through hard law, as proposed by Ashiagbor, is of very great interest in this respect. 'In other words, social rights and labour standards need to be built into economic policies such as the Employment

---

121 C-144/04, *Mangold* v *Helm* [2005] ECR I-9981, at para. [64].

Strategy, but so as to preserve a space for national diversity'[122] but also, one could add, so as to make sure that EC employment law and EC employment policy are increasingly reconciled with each other.

In conclusion, it appears that while the legal theory has traditionally been concerned with the effects that EC employment law could have on the national regimes of labour protection, the EES developments could have some far-reaching, though not necessarily intended, effects that extend well beyond its stated scope. In a sense, the risk is that the EES could become a 'captive' of national dominant political preferences and legitimise some profoundly different regulatory frameworks, some of them even in contrast with other harmonisation policies of the EC.

---

122 Ibid.

Conclusions

Adapting the Employment Relationship and Adopting Employment Contracts

The Introduction to this book set out the task of providing an analysis of the changes of the *scope* and *taxonomy* of employment relationships in four European Union (EU) Member States (MSs): the United Kingdom, Germany, France and Italy. The book's analysis began by exposing that the nature of these changes is at least as much a legal one as it is a factual one, but argued that economic determinism should not be prevalent in the evaluation of the changing notion of the employment relationship. This is not to say that the changing legal notion of the employment relationship is not linked to some deeper economic dynamics. It is merely to point out that the object of analysis may be an increasingly extensive and varied set of work arrangements, to use a neutral word, but it is still a set of *legal* problems that legislators and judiciaries should seek to address and regulate. This is arguably an important consideration and one that emerges quite clearly from the comparative analysis carried out in the previous chapters.

In those chapters, comparative analysis was first of all used to discuss and evaluate the role of legislation in modelling and fostering the binary notion of employment relationships in contracts. Chapter 1 discussed the ways in which law contributed to the shaping of a unitary notion of the contract of employment based on the elements of personal subordination in the performance of work, continuity, full and fully defined working time and bilaterality. The 'unitary' aspects of this analysis were clearly portrayed, highlighting both its descriptive limitations and what eventually became its prescriptive effects on labour legislation and legal thinking across European systems. The contract of employment, and its legal construction, soon emerged as the central organising idea of labour law all over Europe, although its scope varied across national systems and in some countries, such as Italy,Germany and France, it coexisted with some elements of a wider notion of the employment relationship.

It was then observed that progressively employers started modifying the terms on which they would purchase the labour resources necessary for the needs of their businesses and the stance that legislators and governments adopted in the face of these changes was discussed. Some of these arrangements – though by no means the majority – have been such that the traditional legal elements that were and still are used to construct the typical notion of subordinate employment relationships have been watered down or have disappeared altogether. An increasing number of employment relationships now display enhanced autonomy in the organisation and provision of work, greater intermittence and discontinuity and, often, the presence of more than two parties for the purposes of organising, supplying and providing labour resources to a business. It was argued that these elements, and a sometimes-misconceived understanding of their meaning and function, have often been seen as depriving workers from some or all of the apparatus of protection provided by labour legislation.

The text then provided a coherent matrix for understanding the several attempts made at a national and supranational level to address the problems emerging from the changing legal notion of the employment relationship. It argued that the majority of these attempts can be understood as falling into two major types of re-regulatory response. Firstly, they can fall into the type of actions aimed at reshaping and expanding the scope of the employment relationship and, simultaneously, the personal scope of application of labour law. Secondly, they can be seen as attempts to provide ad hoc regulation for some recurrent patterns of atypical work. Chapter 2 discussed in some detail the efforts made by national legal orders to re-define the traditional notion of the employment relationship, often with the adoption of new ad hoc tests, in attempting to expand its boundaries and to attribute (at least in part) legal protections to workers previously excluded. Further, it was shown that in several European countries, since the mid 1970s, employment law had started to articulate a third category of workers, broadly located between the dependent employee and the self-employed. Thirdly, the analysis presented some more recent debates suggesting a progressive regulatory shift towards broader organising concepts such as the worker's labour market status over her working-life cycle, or new notions and categorisations of work relationships such the 'personal work contact' and the 'personal work nexus'. Some of these discourses are currently being echoed, to some extent, in the supranational – ILO and EC – arena, as Chapters 4 and 5 emphasised.

Chapters 3, 6 and some parts of Chapter 4 discussed what the present work has termed as the 'typificatory' treatment of atypical forms of work, whereby legislative and judicial intervention have isolated a number of new employment relationships and forms of work (for example, part-time, fixed-term work, agency work, on call work and so on) and have created ad hoc legal and contractual structures aimed at affording to the workers concerned some of the protections traditionally granted to 'typical' employees. Chapter 4 stressed that this kind of activity has evolved through a number of different stages and amid some tensions and disagreements at a national level, where often 'regulation' of atypical forms of work has been regarded with suspicion of constituting an encouragement to 'precarious flexible' work or even dismissed as a sort of Trojan horse introduced in the 'citadel of labour law'. In other modes of regulatory interaction with the theme of the present work, legislators have either tried to *prohibit* some atypical employment relationships or, have sought to *transform* them into typical and standard contracts of employment. Traces of the latter strategy are still evident in most national and supranational legislation regulating fixed-term work.

On the other hand it would appear that the current tendency in regulating atypical work is that of promoting their social acceptance while fostering an element of equal treatment between those employed in atypical works and those in typical employment. This is a regulatory approach described in this book as 'normalisation with parity'. It was argued that this approach has inspired national and supranational legislation on part-time and fixed-term work and, although less consistently, legislation and legislative proposals on temporary agency work. 'Normalisation with parity' appears

Conclusions

to have established itself as the favoured regulatory framework, seen as capable of reconciling both social and economic aspirations in the area of labour regulation. Recent statutes and supranational regulatory instruments have cautiously started introducing some *special rights* going beyond those granted to standard workers and aimed at increasing the degree of social acceptance of some forms of atypical work. These special rights are aimed at tackling some problems and contingencies peculiar to atypical forms of work and at recognising that 'normalisation with parity' can be frustrated by the absence of a suitable 'comparator'. As a consequence of this type of regulation, some of these new forms of work, such as part-time work for instance, have been so much 'assimilated' within the scope of labour law as to appear atypical only by reference to the old, progressively declining, notion of the standard employment relationship.

However it was also highlighted that the 'normalization with parity' approach is increasingly challenged by a 'normalization without parity' one. 'Normalization without parity' has three main facets. It is in one sense a *default* position whenever, in the absence of any *jus cogens* prohibitions applying to a particular employment relationship, workers are forced by high unemployment rates – and by the 'workfare' state regulatory framework – to accept under-regulated and under-protected employment relationships. This seems to be the case with very lightly regulated agency work in the UK. Secondly, it is progressively emerging as the regulatory model for dealing with some atypical employment relationships that are progressively being subjected to a systematic typificatory activity but without any serious intention of according equal-treatment with standard work. Clear examples of this last tendency are the emergence of the so-called *lavoro a progetto* in Italy, discussed in the third section of Chapter 2, and also some recent legislation adopted in Italy and Germany in respect of atypical and agency workers, discussed in the fourth section of Chapter 3. Moreover, the fifth section of Chapter 6 pointed out that this regulatory strategy might also be emerging at the EC level as a consequence of some unresolved tensions and lack of coordination between European employment law and the European Employment Strategy.

It appears that we are currently witnessing a transitional phase, in which the legal and social framework is still trying to adjust to some radical transformations of the legal terms under which labour is provided in the labour market and the economy. The first chapters of the present work showed that this 'time-lag' is not a new phenomenon and that there are good reasons to believe, at least from an analytical point of view, that there has been some considerable progress in understanding the needs deriving from these changes and the possible strategies by which they can be addressed. The problem of defining the personal scope of application of *labour legislation* is by no means a secondary one. But first of all it is important to understand what changes are affecting the legal notion(s) of the employment relationship. The central argument of this book is precisely that these changes and their effects on the personal scope of application of labour legislation *need to be tackled through a number of different and mutually supportive approaches*. The process leading to an expansion of the *scope* of the subordinate employment relationship, on the form in which it has been discussed in Chapter 2, can be seen as a first response as it provides good and immediate results in terms of the number and types of working patterns covered. Countries like France are a relatively successful example of the results that legal presumptions and jurisprudential tests can achieve. This strategy could be successfully refocused along the lines of some national and supranational experiences. Recent British and EC legislation attempt to regulate and define specific rights – for instance anti-discrimination, pay, health and safety – and subsequently define which are the work relationships and activities to which these rights and prerogatives should be attributed. Clearly, in this respect, fundamental freedoms or human rights should be accorded to the broadest possible constituency.[1] Though this was not the central focus of discussion in this work, there seems to be a general consensus – and an evident one when looking at the past and recent ILO experiences – that some core collective labour rights should also be treated as fundamental rights.

In that respect recent ECJ decisions such as *Allonby*[2] show the inadequacy of the traditional British notion of contract of employment as the central and overarching organising idea for the labour law systems. This type of reasoning in many respects overlaps with the analysis of those authors who support a distinctly new, broader[3] and perhaps more relational approach in reforming the centre of gravity of labour law.[4] As discussed in Chapter 1, one of the most recent and thought-provoking proposals suggests a reconceptualisation of work relations along two novel notions, the *Personal Work Contract* and the *Personal Work Nexus*.[5] Undeniably, national and supranational reform discourses on the employment relationship will have to re-focus their attention on the 'personal provisions of work' element. In the meantime though, a readily available expanded notion of the employment relationship could be found in the concept of 'employment relationship' developed by the European Community and the European Court of Justice for the purposes of EC equality legislation, as argued in Chapter 5.

But it is also important to address directly and specifically some of the emerging forms of atypical work. Past experience indicates that at a first level this entails a definitional effort aimed at articulating the legal elements which characterise and delineate each atypical or marginal work relationship. Subsequently it is important to translate these elements into appropriate contractual types and discuss what rights these contractual types should enjoy. This is an exercise that can only be carried through legislative reform; this book has explored a number of reform proposals, while new ones are constantly emerging. At the end of the day it would appear that legal systems are currently facing a fundamental choice between persisting with the *normalisation with parity* strategy and embarking upon a *normalisation without*

---

1   On a similar line see A. Perulli, *Economically Dependent/Quasi-subordinate (Parasubordinate) Employment: Legal, Social and Economic Aspects* (Brussels, 2003), pp. 116–117.

2   C-256/01, *Allonby* v *Accrington and Rossendale Community College* [2004] ECR I-873.

3   M.R. Freedland, *The Personal Employment Contract* (OUP, Oxford, 2003).

4   B. Hepple, 'Restructuring Employment Rights', *ILJ* (1986): 69; H. Collins, P.L. Davies and R.W. Rideout, *Legal Regulation of the Employment Relation* (Kluwer, London, 2000).

5   M. Freedland, 'From the Contract of Employment to the Personal Work Nexus', *ILJ* (2006): 1.

parity route. The latter option is often supported in the conviction that less security in the employment relationship can lead to better economic performance and thus more security in the labour market. Normalisation with parity, on the contrary, sees job-security and economic performance as elements integral to personal employment relationships. It seems reasonable to believe, for example, that a worker employed in a precarious employment relationship is less likely to take leave for training and skill-upgrading purposes than one in a well protected and remunerated one. In any case we have argued that even normalisation with parity is not a 'one size fits all' solution. This strategy would probably prove to be ineffective at addressing some aspects of precariousness and insecurity that are inherently and structurally linked to some particularly capricious forms of atypical work, particularly whenever a suitable comparator is not readily available. Paraphrasing the European Court of Justice, legislation should engage with some categories of atypical work relationship that could otherwise become a potential source of abuse to the disadvantage of workers by laying down a minimum 'number of protective provisions designed to prevent the status of employees from being insecure'.[6] According to the present work a mix of prohibition, conversion and normalisation with parity, coupled with the provision of some ad hoc tailored rights, should be the preferred way to look at future reforms concerning atypical work.

The combined use of these two regulatory strategies (expansion of scope and regulation of specific atypical forms of work) may well generate a new equilibrium situation similar to that achieved for numerous decades through the binary model of employment relationship. It would be a *dynamic equilibrium*, but, according to the findings of the present work, it is possible to say that this was the case even during the 'golden era' of the binary model of the employment relationship. But while this historical perspective may give some reasons to be optimistic for the future, this optimism has yet to be translated into a successful quest for the understanding of the continuously changing labour market environment, of the needs and aspirations that it produces in human beings, and the ways by which law and society can and should address these aspirations. It is hoped that this book has provided some degree of systematisation of some of the different discourses that are moving in that direction, as well as making a small original contribution in the reform steps to take.

---

6   C-212/04, *Kostantinos Adeneler and Others* v *Elog* [2006] ECR I-06057, [62]–[63].

Bibliography

Books and monographs

A. Alcock, *History of the International Labour Organization* (Macmillan, London, 1971)

G. Altieri and C. Oteri, *Terzo rapporto sul lavoro atipico in Italia: verso la stabilizzazione del precariato?* (IRES-CGIL 2003)

A. Amin, *Post-Fordism: a Reader* (Blackwell, Oxford, 1994)

A. Arnull, A.A. Dashwood, M. G. Gross and D. A. Wyatt, *European Union Law* (4th edn Sweet & Maxwell, London 2000)

J. Arrowsmith, *Temporary Agency Work in an Enlarged European Union* (Office for Official Publications of the European Communities, Luxembourg, 2006)

D. Ashiagbor, *The European Employment Strategy – Labour Market Regulation and New Governance* (OUP, Oxford, 2005)

L. Barassi, *Il contratto di lavoro nel diritto positivo Italiano* (Societa' editrice libraria, Milano, 1901)

B. Bercusson, *European Labour Law* (London, Butterworths, 1996)

D. Brodie, *A History of British Labour Law* (Hart, Oxford, 2003)

C. Barnard, *EC Employment Law* (2nd ed OUP, Oxford, 2000)

G. H. Camerlynck and G. Lyon-Caen, *Droit du travail* (Dalloz, Paris, 1976)

G. H. Camerlynck, *Le Contrat de Travail* (2nd edn, Dalloz, Paris, 1982)

U. Carabelli and B. Veneziani (eds.), *Du travail salarié au travail indépendant: permanences et mutations* (Cacucci, Bari, 2003)

S. Clauwaert, *Legal Analysis of the Implementation of the Fixed-term Work Directive-Report 76* (ETUI, Brussels, 2003)

S. Clauwaert, *Survey on the implementation of the Part-time Work Directive/ Agreement in the EU member states and selected applicant countries - Report 73* (ETUI, Brussels, 2002)

H. Collins and K. Ewing and A. McColgan, *Labour Law* (Hart, Oxford, 2001)

H. Collins, P.L. Davies and R.W. Rideout, *Legal Regulation of the Employment Relation* (Kluwer, London, 2000)

J.A.-M. Coyle Shapiro, L.M. Shore, M.S. Taylor, and L.E. Tetrick (eds), *The Employment Relationship – Examining Psychological and Contextual Perspectives* (OUP, Oxford, 2004)

P. Craig and G. De Burca, *EU Law - Text, Cases and Materials* (2nd edn, OUP, Oxford, 1998)

P.L. Davies, 'The Relationship Between the European Court of Justice and the British Courts over the interpretation of Directive 77/187/EC' (Working Paper No 2 European University Institute, 1997)

P. Davies and M. Freedland, *Labour Legislation and Public policy: a Contemporary*

238 *The Changing Law of the Employment Relationship*

History (Clarendon, Oxford, 1993)

R. De Luca Tamajo, 'Dal lavoro parasubordinato al lavoro "a progetto"' (Working paper No 25 CSDLE 'Massimo d'Antona', 2003)

S. Deakin, 'The Contract of Employment: a Study in Legal Evolution' (working paper No 203 ESRC Centre for Business Research University of Cambridge, June 2001)

S. Deakin, 'The many futures of the Contract of Employment' (Working Paper No 191 ESRC Centre for Business Research University of Cambridge, December 2000)

S. Deakin and G. Morris *Labour Law* (3rd ed Butterworths London 2001)

S. Deakin and G. Morris *Labour Law* (Hart, Oxford, 2005)

S. Deakin, *The Contract of Employment: a Study in Legal Evolution* (ESCR Working paper No 203, June 2001)

S. Deakin, *The many futures of the contract of employment* (CBR Working Paper No 191, December 2001)

S. Deakin, *The Comparative Evolution of the Employment Relationship* (Working Paper No 317 ESRC Centre for Business Research University of Cambridge December 2005)

S. Deakin and F. Wilkinson, *The Law of the Labour Market – Industrialization, Employment and Legal Evolution* (OUP, Oxford, 2005).

DTI, *Discussion Document on Employment Status in Relation to Statutory Employment Rights* July 2002, mainly page 26 and following. Available on http://www.dti.gov.uk/er/individual/statusdiscuss.pdf (15 January 2004)

DTI, *Explanatory memorandum on European Community Legislation - Amended proposal for a directive of the European Parliament and of the Council on temporary work* submitted on 10 January 2003 and available on http://www.dti.gov.uk/er/agency/em.htm (15 January 2004)

DTI, *Fixed-term work: a guidance to the regulations* (DTI, London, 2001)

DTI, *Revision of the Regulations covering the private recruitment industry – Regulatory impact assesment* (June 2002)

K. Ewing, *Working Life –A New Perspective on Labour Law* (Lawrence & Wishart, London, 1996)

A. Fox, *Beyond Contract: work, power and trust relations* (Faber, London, 1974)

S. Fredman, *Discrimination Law* (Clarendon, Oxford, 2002)

M. Freedland, *The Contract of Employment* (Clarendon, Oxford, 1976)

M. Freedland, *The Personal Employment Contract* (OUP, Oxford, 2003)

French Ministry of Employment, 'Le temps partiel subi diminue depuis 1998' *Premières informations et Premières Synthèses 10 n 42.2* (Direction de l'animation de la recherche, des études et des statistiques du Ministère de l'emploi, Paris, 2001)

G. Gembillo (ed), *W Heisenberg - Indeterminazione e realtà* (Guida, Napoli, 1991)

E. Ghera, *Diritto del Lavoro* (Cacucci, Bari, 1998)

E. Ghera, *Diritto del Lavoro* (Cacucci, Bari, 2000)

E. Ghera, *Diritto del Lavoro* (Cacucci, Bari, 2002)

E. Ghera, *Diritto del Lavoro* (Cacucci, Bari, 2006)

P. A. Hall and D. Soskice, *Varieties of Capitalism – The Institutional Foundations of*

Comparative Advantage (OUP, Oxford, 2001).

U. Hotopp, *Recruitment agencies in the UK* (DTI, 2001)

P. Ichino, *Il tempo della prestazione nel rapporto di lavoro* (Giuffrè Milano 1985), Vol. II *Estensione temporale della prestazione lavorativa subordinata e relative forme speciali di organizzazione*

C. Knill and D. Lehmkuhl, 'How Europe Matter: Different Mechanisms of Europeanization' (1999) 3 European Integration online Papers (EIoP) No 7

Y. Kravaritou-Manitakis (ed), *New Forms of Work – Labour Law and Social Security aspects in the European Community* (Dublin, European Foundation for the Improvement of Living and Working Conditions, 1988)

R. Lewis and J. Clark, *Labour Law and Politics in the Weimar Republic- Otto Kahn-Freund* (Blackwell, Oxford, 1981)

D. Mardsen, *A Theory of Employment Systems* (OUP, Oxford, 1999)

K. Marx, *Capital – A Critical Analysis of Capitalist Production Volume 1* (Lawrence & Wishart, London, 1974)

A. Mazeaud, *Droit du travail* (LGDJ Montchrestien, Paris, 2002)

R. Nielsen and E. Szyszczak, *The Social Dimension of the European Union* (Handelshøjskolens Forlag, Copenhagen, 1997)

L. Nogler, 'La certificazione dei contratti di lavoro' (Working paper No 23 CSDLE 'Massimo d'Antona', 2003)'

J. Pélissier, A. Supiot and A. Jeammaud, *Droit du Travail* (Dalloz, Paris, 2000)

J. Pélissier, A. Supiot and A. Jeammaud, *Droit du Travail* (Dalloz, Paris, 2006)

A. Perulli, *Economically dependent / quasi-subordinate (parasubordinate) employment: legal, social and economic aspects* (Brussels, 2003)

M. Piore and C. Sabel, *The Second Industrial Divide: Possibilities for Prosperity* (Basic Books, New York, 1984)

M. Rodriguez-Pinero y Bravo Ferrer, *Individual dismissal in the Member States of the European Community: The Advantages and Difficulty of Community Action* Report for the Commission of the EC, DGV V/5767/93 EN

R. Rowthorn and R. Ramaswamy, *Deindustrialization – Its Causes and Implications* (IMF Publication Services, Washington, 1997)

A. Supiot (ed), *Au delà de l'emploi. Transformations du travail et devenir du droit du travail en Europe* (Flammarion, Paris, 1999)

A. Supiot, *Beyond Employment. Changes in Work and the Future of Labour Law in Europe* (OUP, Oxford. 2001)

A. Supiot, *Critique du Droit du Travail* (PUF, Paris, 2002)

TUC, *The Hidden One-in-Five – Winning a Fair Deal for Britain's Vulnerable Workers* (2006)

S. Walby to the House of Commons Select Committee on Education and Employment in *Part-Time Working* (volume 2, 2nd report 1998-99)

M. Weiss, *European Employment and Industrial Relations Glossary: Germany* (Sweet & Maxwell, London, 1992)

M. Weiss and M. Schmidt, *Labour Law and Industrial Relations in Germany* (3rd edn Kluwer, The Hague, 2000)

K. Zweigert and H. Kötz *An Introduction to Comparative Law* (2nd edn Clarendon

240 *The Changing Law of the Employment Relationship*

Oxford 1987) 41.

Contributions to books

P. Alleva, 'Ridefinizione della fattispecie di contratto dellavoro. Prima proposta di legge' in G. Ghezzi (ed), *La disciplina del mercato del lavoro, proposte per un testo unico* (Ediesse, Roma, 1996), 195

U. Carabelli, 'Flessibilizzazione o Destrutturazione del Mercato del Lavoro? Il Lavoro Interninale in Italia ed in Europa' in *Scritti in Onore di Giugni* (Cacucci, Bari, 1999), 185

B. Coriat, 'Technical flexibility and mass production' in G. Benk and M. Dunford (eds.), *Industrial Change and Regional Development* (Belhaven, London, 1991), 150

M. D'Antona, 'Ridefinizione della fattispecie di contratto di lavoro. Seconda proposta di legge' in G. Ghezzi (ed), *La disciplina del mercato del lavoro, proposte per un testo unico* (Ediesse, Roma,, 1996) 95

P. Davies, 'Transfer of Undertakings' in S. Sciarra, *Labour Law in the Courts: National Judges and the European Court of Justice* (Hart, Oxford, 2001), 130

P. Davies and M. Freedland, 'Employees, workers, and the autonomy of labour law' in H. Collins, P. Davies and R. Rideout (eds), *The Legal Regulation of the Employment Relation* (Kluwer, London, 2000), 275

P. Davies and M. Freedland, 'Changing Perspectives Upon the Employment Relationship in British Labour Law', in C. Barnard, S. Deakin and G. Morris, *The Future of Labour Law – Liber Amicorum Sir Bob Hepple* (Oxford, 2004), 129

R. De Luca Tamajo and R. Flammia and M. Persiani 'La crisi della nozione di subordinazione e della sua idoneità selettiva dei trattamenti garantistici. Prime proposte per un nuovo approccio sistematico in una prospettiva di valorizzazione di un tertium genus: il lavoro coordinato' in AA.VV. *Nuove forme di lavoro tra subordinazione, coordinazione, autonomia*b (Cacucci, Bari 1997)

S. Deakin, 'The Evolution of the Contract of Employment, 1900-1950' in N. Whiteside and R. Salais, *Governance, Industry and Labour Markets is Britain and France – The Modernising State in the mid-twentieth Century* (Routledge, London, 1998), 213

S. Deakin and H. Reed, 'The Contested Meaning of Labour Market Flexibility: Economic Theory and the Discourse of European Integration' in J. Shaw (ed), *Social Law and Policy in an Evolving European Union* (Oxford, Hart, 2000)

S. Fredman, 'Discrimination in the EU: Labour market regulation or fundamental rights?' in H. Collins, P. Davies and R. Rideout (eds), *Legal Regulation of the Employment Relation* (Kluwer, The Hague, 2000), 183

M. Freedland, 'Employment Policy' in P. Davies, A. Lyon-Caen, S. Sciarra and S. Simitis (eds), *European Community Labour Law. Principles and Perspectives on European Labour Law: Liber Amicorum Lord Wedderburn of Charlton* (Clarendon, Oxford, 1996), 308

M. Freedland, 'The role of the contract of employment in modern labour law' in L. Betten (ed), *The Employment Contract in Transforming Labour Relations*

(Kluwer, Deventer, 1995), 17

M. Freedland and C. Kilpatrick, 'The United Kingdom: how is EU governance transformative? in S. Sciarra, P. Davies and M Freedland (eds), *Employment Policy and the Regulation of Part-time Work in the European Union A Comparative Analysis* (CUP, Cambridge, 2004)

E. Ghera, 'Subordinazione, statuto protettivo e qualificazione del rapporto di lavoro', in D. Garofalo and M. Ricci (eds), *Percorsi di Diritto del Lavoro* (Cacucci, Bari, 2006), 332

G. Giugni, 'Aspects Juridiques de l'Économie Informelle' in *Les transformations du droit du travail – Études offertes à Gérard Lyon-Caen* (Dalloz, Paris, 1989), 259

A. C. Neal, 'Comparative Labour Law and Industrial Relations: 'Major Discipline?' – Who Cares?' in C. Engels and M. Weiss (eds), *Labour Law and Industrial Relations at the Turn of the Century – Liber Amicorum in Honour of Prof. Dr. Roger Blanpain* (Kluwer Law International, The Hague, 1998), 55

V. Pinto, ' La categoria giuridica delle collaborazioni coordinate e continuative e il lavoro a progetto', in P. Curzio (ed), *Lavoro e diritti a tre anni dalla legge 30/2003* (Cacucci, Bari, 2006), 431

M.V. Roheling ,'Legal Theory: Contemporary Contract Law Perspectives and Insights for Employment Relationship Theory' in J.A.-M. Coyle Shapiro, L.M. Shore, M.S. Taylor and L.E. Tetrick (eds), *The Employment Relationship – Examining Psychological and Contextual Perspectives* (Oxford, 2004), 76

C. Smith, 'From Automation to Flexible Specialization' in A. Pollert, *Farewell to Flexibility?* (Blackwell, Oxford, 1991), 155

J. Tomaney, 'New Work Organization and Technology' in A. Amin (ed), *Post-Fordism: a Reader* (Blackwell, Oxford, 1994), 164

B. Veneziani, 'The Evolution of the Contract of Employment' in B Hepple (ed) *The Making of Labour Law in Europe: A Comparative Study of Nine Countries up to 1945* (Mansell, London, 1986), 35

T. Walsh, 'Flexible Employment in the Retail and Hotel Trades' in A. Pollert, *Farewell to Flexibility?* (Blackwell, Oxford, 1991), 104

M. Weber, 'The Origins of Industrial Capitalism in Europe' in W.G. Runciman (ed), *Weber Selections in Translations* (CUP, Cambridge, 1978), 335

K. W. W. Wedderburn, 'The Right to Strike: Is There a European Standard?' in K.W. W. Wedderburn, *Employment Rights in Britain and Europe: selected papers* (Lawrence & Wishart, London, 1991), 289

Articles

'Political and Economic Planning' (1956) *Planning,* 405

'Reforms to boost labour market' (2003) 349 *EIRR,* 27

'Social Aspects of European Economic Cooperation' (1956) *ILR,* 99

'The EU and the Modernisation on Labour Law. First Stage Consultation of Social Partners on modernising and improving employment relations' (2000) 16

242 *The Changing Law of the Employment Relationship*

IJCLLIR, 436

B. Alibert, 'Le contrat de travail temporaire' (1974) *DS*, 10

J. Atkinson, 'Flexibility or Fragmentation? The UK Labour Market in the Eighties' (1987) *Labour and Society*, 87

V. Ballestrero, 'L'ambigua nozione di lavoro parasubordinato' (1987) *Lavoro e Diritto*, 41

M. Biagi, 'Italy', (1999) *BCLR*, 274

R. Castel, 'Droit du travail: redéploiement ou refondation?' (1999) *DS*, 441

R. H. Coase, 'The Nature of the Firm' (1937) *Economica*, 386

H. Collins, 'Employment Rights of Casual Workers' (2000) *ILJ*, 73

H. Collins, 'Flexibility and Stability of Expectations in the Contract of Employment' (2006) *Socio-Economic Review*, 139

W. Däubler, 'Working people in Germany' (1999) Comp *Labor Law & Pol'y Journal*, 78

W. Däubler and M. Le Friant, 'Un récent exemple de flexibilisation législative: la loi allemande pour la promotion de l'emploi du 26 avril 1985' (1985) *DS*, 715

G. Davidov, 'Who is a Worker?' (2005) *ILJ*, 57

A. Davies, 'Casual Workers and Continuity of Employment' (2006) *ILJ*, 196

S. Deakin, 'The Changing Concept of 'Employer' in Labour Law' (2001) *ILJ*, 75

E. Dockès, 'Du CNE au CPE, après le jugement du Conseil de prud'hommes de Longjumeau' (2006) *DS*, 356

F. Favennec-Héry, 'Le travail á temps partiel: changement de cap' (1999) *DS*, 1005

F. Favennec-Héry, 'Le travail á temps partiel' (1994) *DS*, 165

F. Favennec-Héry, 'Le temps vraiment choisi' (2000) *DS*, 295

G. Ferraro, 'Dal lavoro subordinato al lavoro autonomo' (1998) *GDLRI*, 461

F. A. Flammand and M.-L. Morin, 'L'activité professionnelle indépendante: quelle protection juridique ?' (2001) 346 *Le Notes du Lirhe*, 6

S. Fredman, 'Women at Work: The Broken Promise of Flexicurity', (2004) *ILJ*, 305

M. Freedland, 'Equal Treatment, Judicial Review and Delegated Legislation' (1994) *ILJ*, 255

M. Freedland, 'From the Contract of Employment to the Personal Work Nexus' (2005) *ILJ*, 1

M. Freedland e N. Countouris, 'Diritti e doveri nel rapporto tra disoccupati e servizi per l'impiego in Europa' (2005) *GDLRI*, 557

M. Fuchs, 'Germania' (2000) *GDLRI*, 593

L. Gaeta, 'Lodovico Barassi, Philipp Lotmar e la cultura giuridica tedesca' (2001) *GDLRI*, 176

A. Garilli, 'Il contratto di lavoro e il rapporto di impiego privato nella teoria di Lodovico Barassi' (2001) *RGL*, 375

M. G. Garofalo, 'La legge delaga sul mercato del lavoro: prime osservazioni' (2003) *RGL*, 359.

M. G. Garofalo, 'Un Profilo Ideologico del Diritto del Lavoro' (1999) *GDLRI*, 9

G. Giugni, 'Giuridificazione e deregolazione nel diritto del lavoro italiano' (1986)

GDLRI, 331

B. Hepple, 'European Rules on Dismissal Law' (1997) *CLLJ*, 204

B. Hepple, 'Restructuring Employment Rights' (1986) *ILJ*, 69

B. Hepple, 'United Kingdom' (1999) *BCLR*, 380

A. Hoeland, 'A Comparative Study of the Impact of Electronic Technology on Workplace Disputes: National Report on Germany' (2005) *Comp. Labor Law & Pol'y Journal*, 152

A. Jeammaud, 'L'assimilation des franchisés aux salariés' (2002) *DS*, 158

A. Jeammaud, 'L'avenir sauvegardé de la qualification de contrat de travail. À propos de l' *arrêt Labanne*' (2001) *DS*, 227

O. Kahn-Freund, 'Servants and Independent Contractors' (1951) *MLR*, 505

O. Kahn-Freund, 'Blackstone's neglected child: the contract of Employment' (1977) *LQR*, 508

O. Kahn-Freund, 'Status and Contract in Labour Law' (1967) *MLR*, 642

O. Kahn-Freund, 'Uses and Misuses of Comparative Law' (1974) 37 *MLR*, 1

O. Kahn-Freund, 'A note on status and contract in modern labour law' (1967) *MLR*, 635

S. Laulom, 'Francia' (2000) *GDLRI*, 559

S. Leonardi, 'Il lavoro coordinato e continuativo: profili giuridici e aspetti normativi' (1999) *RGL*, 3

S. Leonardi, 'Parasubordinazione e Contrattazione Collettiva. Una Lettura Trasversale degli Accordi Siglati' (2001) *Quaderni di Rassegna Sindacale*, 1

A. Lyon-Caen, 'Actualité du contrat de travail, brefs propos' (1988) *DS*, 541

A. Lyon-Caen, 'Le recours au travail à durée limitée' (1983) *DS*, 18

A. Lyon-Caen, 'Plasticité du capital et nouvelles formes d'emploi' (1983) Special issue Sept-Oct *DS*, 10

U. Müchenberger, R. Wank and H. Buchner, 'Ridefinire la nozione di subordinazione? Il dibattito in Germania' (2000) *GDLRI*, 329

L. Nogler, 'Sulla inutilità delle presunzioni legali relative in tema di qualificazione dei rapporti di lavoro' (1997) *RIDL*, 311

J. Pelissier, 'Travail á durée limitée et droits des salariés' (1983) *DS*, 18

G. Pera, 'Sulle prospettive di estensione delle tutele al lavoro parasubordinato' (1998) *RIDL*, 371

P. Pigassou, 'L' évolution du lien de subordination en droit du travail et de la Sécurité sociale' (1982) *DS*, 578

G. Poulain, 'La loi du 3 janvier 1979 relative au contrat de travail à durée déterminée' (1979) *DS*, 68

P. Saint-Jevin, 'Existe-t-il un droit commun du contrat de travail?' (1981) *DS*, 517

M. Schneider, 'A juridical Approach to the Notion of Independent Labour. A Critical Study of the French and German Systems' (2000) *IJCLLIR*, 337

J. Schregle, 'Comparative Industrial Relations' (1981) *ILR*,15

A. Supiot, 'Les nouveaux visages de la subordination' (2000) *DS*, 139

B. Teyssié, 'La loi du 28 janvier 1981 sur le travail à temps partiel' (1981) *DS*, 520

B. Veneziani, 'Contratto di lavoro, potere di controllo e subordinazione nell'opera di

244 *The Changing Law of the Employment Relationship*

Ludovico Barassi' (2002) *GDLRI*, 39

R. Wank, 'Germany'(2005) *BCLR*, 19

M. Weiss, 'Germany'(1999) *BCLR*, 255

L. Zappalà, 'The Temporary Agency Workers' Directive: An Impossible Political Agreement?' (2003) *ILJ*, 310

ILO and EC materials (selected)

International Labour Organisation:

ILO, *Contract Labour- Report VI (1) to the International Labour Conference 85th Session 1997* (Geneva, 1996)

ILO, *Contract labour- Fifth item on the agenda Report V (1) to the International Labour Conference 86th Session 1998* (Geneva, 1997)

Committee on Contract Labour, *Record of Proceedings*, International Labour Conference 86th Session Vol. II (Geneva, 1998)

International Labour Conference (87th Session), *Decent work - Report of the Director-General* (Geneva, June 1999)

ILO, *Second Item on the Agenda* Governing Body 280th Session GB 280/2 (Geneva, March 2001)

International Labour Conference (90th Session), *Report VI Decent Work in the informal economy – Sixth item on the agenda* (Geneva, June 2002)

ILO, International Labour Conference *Report V- The scope of the employment relationship – fifth item on the agenda* (Geneva, 2003)

International Labour Conference (91st session), *Report V- The scope of the employment relationship – fifth item on the agenda* (Geneva, June 2003)

International Labour Conference (91st Session), *Provisional Record No 21* (Geneva, June 2003)

ILO International Labour Conference, *Report V(1) – The Employment Relationship – Fifth Item on the Agenda* (Geneva, June 2005)

ILO International Labour Conference, *Report V(2A) – The Employment Relationship – Fifth Item on the Agenda* (Geneva, June 2006).

European Community:

Communication from the Commission Concerning its Action Programme relating to the Implementation of the Community Charter of Basic Social Rights for Workers COM(89) 568 final.

EC Commission, *Green paper – Partnership for a new organisation of work* COM (97) 128 final 16.4.1997.

EC Commission, Communication *Modernising the Organisation of work – A positive approach to change* COM(98) 592 final 12.10.1998.

EC Commission DGV, *Commission Draft for the Joint Employment Report 1997* Brussels, 30 September 1997

EC Commission DGV, *Joint Employment Report Employment Policies in the EU and in the Member States – Joint Report 1998* (1999)

EC Commission, *Joint Employment Report 2000*

EC Commission, *Joint Employment Report 2001*

EC Commission, *Joint Employment Report 2002*

EC Commission, *Report by the Commission's Services on the Implementation of Council Directive 97/81/EC of 17 December 1997 Concerning the Framework Agreement in Part-time Work Concluded by UNICE, CEEP and the ETUC* (Brussels, 2003)

EC Commission, *Joint Employment Report 2005/2006 'More and Better Jobs: Delivering the Priorities of the European Employment Strategy'* (2006)

EC Commission, *Green Paper 'Modernising Labour Law to Meet the Challenges of the 21st Century'* COM(2006) 708 final

European Employment Taskforce, *Jobs, Jobs, Jobs – Creating More Employment In Europe* (2003)

Flexibilité du temps de travail et sécurité des travailleurs – première phase de consultation avec les partenaires sociaux conformément a l'article 3 de l'accord social annexe au traite SEC(95) 1540/3.

The Government of France, *Plan National pour l'Emploi 2000*

The Government of France, *National Action Plan for Employment 2001 and Overview of 2000 – France* (May 2001)

The Government of France, *National Action Plan for Employment 2002 - France* (June 2002)

The Government of Italy, *National Action Plan for Employment Implementation Report, Year 2000 – Italy* (April 2000)

The Government of Italy, *2001 National Action Plan for Employment* (May 2001)

The Government of Italy, *Italia - Piano Nazionale per l' Occupazione* (Giugno 2002)

Index

accidents, work-related 23–4
agency workers 38–9, 159–60
  see also temporary agency work
angestellter 35
apprentices 18
arbeitnehmerahnliche
atypical employment relationship 87–9
  see also fixed-term work; part-time
    work; temporary agency work
  definition 208
  European Community (EC) 207–10,
    219–20
  International Labour Organization (ILO)
    154–61
availability compensation 141

Biagi Law 8, 139–40, 225
bilaterality 38–9, 52
Britain
  see United Kingdom

capitalism 17
casual workers 27, 41, 48–9, 155, 183, 184,
  188
  see also decasualisation
Collaborazioni Coordinate e Continuative
  (co.co.co) 8, 72–3, 76–7
collective bargaining 27, 28–9
commodity exchange 19
compagnons 18
comparative legal analysis 9–12
continuity of employment 34–9, 48–50, 69
contract labour 159–62
contracts of employment 153
  see also employment relationship
  common law 19
  continuity 48–50
  contract of service 28
  European Community (EC) 189–91
  France 21–2
  Germany 22–3
  industrial revolution 16–25

intermediation 38–9
Italy 22, 32
legal presumptions 63–4
manual workers 27
personal 82
reform of 52–4
Roman Law 19
unitary notion of 25–39, 40
United Kingdom 19–21, 30
contracts of service 20, 28
contrat première embauche (CPE) 6
contratto a progetto 76–7
control test 26–7, 31, 45–6

decasualisation 37 *see also* casual workers
Decent Work 162–3
Diensvertrag 23

EC
  see European Community
  economic dependency 33, 64–6, 192–3
  economic determinism 7
  economic reality 33
EES
  see European Employment
  Strategy
  employee status
  intermittent work 68–71
  judicial intervention 60–63
  qualifying period 68–9
  qualitative exclusions 59–68
  quantitative exclusions 68–71
  statutory intervention 63–8
employees 58–71, 153–4
  see also workers
  definition 36, 66
employment agencies 38–9, 50–52, 97,
  157–61, 207
employment businesses 97–8
employment contracts
  see contracts of employment
employment law 29

comparative study 10–11
European Community (EC) 193–7,
219–20, 228–9
human resource management 4
reform 81–3, 193–7
scope of 5, 59–68
employment policy 229
employment relationship
see also contract of employment
atypical 87–9 *see also* fixed-term work;
part-time work; temporary agency work
bilaterality 38–9, 52
binary 3, 29
breakdown 39–52
contractual framework 52–4
deregulation 42–5
discontinuity 47–8
disguised 163–4
European Community (EC) 187,
189–91
intermediation 50–52
intermittence 47–8
International Labour Organization (ILO)
161–8
legal dimension 2–3
long-term 34–9
multilaterality 50–52
origins 16–17
regulation 4–7, 42–5
scope of 161–8
substitution 47
triangular 163–6 *see also* temporary
agency work
trilaterality 50–52
enhanced autonomy 45–7
equal pay 180–82
equal treatment 6–7, 208–9, 214, 220–21
temporary agency work 229
equality 18–19
equality law in the European Community
179–85
European Community (EC)
atypical work 207–10, 219–20
contracts of employment 189–91
discrimination law 184–5
economic dependency 192–3
employment agencies 207
Employment Guidelines 216
employment law 228–9

atypical work 219–20
reform 193–7
employment relationship 187, 189–91
equal pay 180–82
European Employment Strategy (EES)
211–30
fixed-term work directive 131–2, 188,
209–10
flexicurity 211–12, 217–19
framing policy 227–8
free movement of workers 172–7
health and safety law 185–6
job-seekers 174–5
*Modernising Labour Law to Meet the
Challenges of the 21st Century*
(Green Paper) 193–7
part-time work 173
Directive 122–3, 127–8, 188, 209
*Partnership for a New Organisation of
Work* (Green Paper) 212–13
pensions 177–8, 181
posted workers 176–7
provision of services 175–6
regulatory integration 227–8
restructuring 187
right of establishment 175–6
self-employed workers 175–6, 182
Social Charter 207
social security 177–8
temporary agency work 210
transfer of undertakings 187
working conditions 186–91
European Employment Strategy (EES)
211–30
2003 Guidelines 215
adaptability pillar 213–15
flexible working 214–16
flexicurity 214, 220–27
framing policy 228
job security 214–15
policy priorities 215
quality of work 215
exclusive service 20–21

fixed-term work 89–92, 131–6, 229
contracts 6, 29
European Community Directive 131–2,
188, 209–10
regulation 110–16

Index   249

flexibility 226
flexibility and security *see* flexicurity
flexible working 214–16
flexicurity 211–12, 214, 217–19, 220–27
framework contracts 70
France
    contract of employment 21–2
        legal presumptions 63–4
    fixed-term work 90–91, 133–4, 135
        regulation 111–12
    flexicurity 222, 223, 224, 225, 226
    judicial intervention in employment
        law 60
    part-time work 92–3
        flexibility 130
        Part-time Work Directive 122
        regulation 105–7
        special rights 126
    subordination 60
    temporary agency work 96
        regulation 116–18
freedom 18–19
freedom of contract 19

Germany
    contract of employment 22–3
    decasualisation 37
    economic dependency 65–6
    fixed-term work 90, 132–3, 134
        regulation 114–15
    Kapovaz 107–8
    part-time work 93–4
        regulation 107–8
        special rights 126
    Personal-Service-Agenturen (PSA) 138
    quasi-subordination 72, 78
    self-employed workers 66
    social security legislation 65–6, 78
    subordination 60
    temporary agency work 95–6, 229
        equal pay 139–9
        regulation 118–19, 137–9
guild system 17–18

health and safety law in the European Com-
    munity 185–6
homeworking 47, 153, 157
human resource management 4

impiegato 35–6
industrial revolution 16–25
injuries, work-related 23–4
integration test 33, 47
intermediation 38–9, 50–52
intermittent work 68–71, 148
International Labour Organization (ILO)
    agency workers 159–60
    atypical work 154–61
    contract labour 159–62
    contract of employment 153
    Decent Work 162–3
    employees 153–4
    employment agencies 157–61
    employment relationship 161–8
    fundamental rights at work 156, 158
    home work 153, 157
    instruments, personal scope of 147–54
    part-time work 154–6
    quasi-subordination 160–61
    self-employed workers 151, 153–4,
        159–60
    temporary agency work 157–61, 163–6
    workers 148, 149–50, 151–4
Italy
    availability compensation 141
    collective agreements 74
    continuity of employment 69
    contract of employment 22, 32
        preventive certification 66–7
    contratto a progetto 76–7
    fixed-term work 90, 133, 134
        regulation 112–14
    flexicurity 222, 223, 224–5, 227
    part-time work 94, 105
        regulation 108–9
        special rights 126–7
    quasi-subordination 72–8
    Smuraglia proposal 75
    staff-leasing 140–41
    subordination 60–61, 64–5
    temporary agency work 96–7
        flexibility 141
        regulation 119–20, 139–41

job rotation 214
job security 29–30, 214–15
    see also flexicurity
job-seekers 174–5

job-sharing 108
judicial intervention in employment law
    60–63

Kapovaz 107–8

labour legislation *see* employment law
livret ouvrier 22
locatio conductio 19, 22
locatio d'ouvrage 22
louage de service 21–2, 23

manual workers 27
maternity 148–9
methodology of research 9–12
minimum wage 149
*Modernising Labour Law to Meet the
    Challenges of the 21st Century* (EC
    Green Paper) 193–7
multilaterality in employment relationship
    50–52
mutuality of obligation test 49, 70

National Employment Policies 229
normalisation
    with parity *see* equal treatment
    without parity 6, 8, 229
notice periods 21

outsourcing 45–7

parasubordinati
part-time work 92–4
    contracts 6
    definition 123–4
    European Community (EC) 173
        Directive 122–3, 127–8, 188, 209
    flexibility 129–30
    pensions 125–6
    regulation 105–10, 121–6
    special rights 121–31, 126–31
    training 128–9
Partnership for a New Organisation of Work
    (EC Green Paper) 212–13
pensions 177–8
    European Community 181
    part-time work 125–6
personal contract of employment 82
personal performance of work 33–4

Personal-Service-Agenturen (PSA) 138
personality test 47
posted workers 176–7
production, modes of 18
project-workers 8
PSA *(Personal-Service-Agenturen)* 138

qualitative exclusions from employee status
    59–68
quality of work 215
quantitative exclusions from employee
    status 68–71
quasi-subordination 71–81, 160–61
    United Kingdom 78–80

security 226
    see also job security
self-employed workers 66, 151, 153–4,
    159–60
    European Community 175–6, 182
servant, definition 31
Smuraglia proposal 75
social security 177–8
staff-leasing 140–41
statutory intervention in employment law
    63–8
sub-contracting 47
subordination 27–8, 29–30, 60–63
    see also quasi-subordination
    attenuated 63
    France 60
    functional 30–34
    Germany 60
    Italy 60–61
    personal 30–34
    presumption of 37
substitution in employment relationship 47

teleworking 47
temporary agency work 94–105, 210
    equal treatment 229
    International Labour Organization (ILO)
        157–61, 163–6
    regulation 116–21, 136–41
training for part-time workers 128–9
transfer of undertakings 187
trilaterality in employment relationship
    50–52
typification of employment 5

Index

umbrella contracts 70
unemployment 42, 148
United Kingdom
    contract of employment 19–21, 30, 183
        unitary 26–7
    dependency test 61–2
    fixed-term work 91–2, 133, 134
        regulation 115–16
    freedom of contract 19
    intermediation in employment contracts
        38–9
    mutuality of obligation test 49, 70, 183
    part-time work 92
        best practice 127
        comparators 124–5
        definition 123–4
        payments 124–5

        regulation 109–10
        special rights 127–8
    quasi-subordination 78–80
    temporary agency work 97–104
    workers 79–80

welfare states 28
work, definition 81
workbooks 22
workers 79–80, 148, 149–50, 151–4
    see also agency workers; casual
    workers; employees; posted workers;
    self-employed workers
    European Community 172–5
    free movement of 172–7
working conditions 186–91
workmen, definition 27

CPSIA information can be obtained
at www.ICGtesting.com
Printed in the USA
BVHW01*0049100318
510073BV00004B/22/P